The Best
Science Books &
A-V Materials
for Children

Other AAAS Reference Sources

AAAS Science Book List, 1978–1986. Compiled and edited by Kathryn
   Wolff, Susan M. O'Connell, and Valerie J. Montenegro
The Best Science Books for Children. Compiled and edited by Kathryn
   Wolff, Joellen M. Fritsche, Elina N. Gross, and Gary T. Todd
The Best Science Films, Filmstrips, and Videocassettes for Children.
   Compiled and edited by Kathryn Wolff, Joellen M. Fritsche, and Gary T.
   Todd
Science Books & Films (a review journal published five times per year).
   Kathleen Johnston, Editor.

The Best
Science Books &
A-V Materials
for Children

An annotated list of science and mathematics books,
films, filmstrips, and videocassettes
for children ages five through twelve
selected from the pages of *Science Books & Films* magazine

Compiled and edited by
Susan M. O'Connell
Valerie J. Montenegro
Kathryn Wolff

AMERICAN ASSOCIATION FOR THE ADVANCEMENT OF SCIENCE

Library of Congress Cataloging-in-Publication Data

O'Connell, Susan M.
  The best science books and A-V materials for children.

  Includes index.
  1. Science—Juvenile literature—Bibliography. 2. Science—Study and
teaching—Audio-visual aids—Bibliography. 3. Children's
literature—Bibliography. 4. Bibliography—Best books—Science. I.
Montenegro, Valerie J. II. Wolff, Kathryn, 1926–   III. Title.
Z7401.027   1988   [Q163]   016.5   88-10575
ISBN 0-87168-316-4

Special thanks are due to Richard O'Connell for the indexing software.

AAAS Publication 87-11

Full reviews of the books and audio-visual materials listed in this volume were
published in the magazine *Science Books & Films*.

© Copyright 1988
American Association for the Advancement of Science
1333 H Street, NW, Washington, DC 20005

Printed in the United States of America

Table of Contents

Expanded Table of Contents

Subjects are listed according to Dewey Decimal classification

Books

A-V Materials

Preface

The Best Science Books & A-V Materials for Children continues the American Association for the Advancement of Science (AAAS) series of references for librarians, teachers, and parents concerned about science information and education. This volume is not intended to be a catalog or comprehensive listing of science books and audio-visual materials that have entered the kindergarten-through-junior-high market between 1982 and 1987. The superlative in the title means that the more than 800 books and 400-plus films, filmstrips, and videocassettes included here have been reviewed by experts in the relevant sciences and have emerged from the examination with "recommended" or "highly recommended" test results.

The books and films we have annotated here not only have passed the test of accuracy. Their creators have gone beyond mere dry recitations of facts to successfully portray for young readers and viewers the excitement of science as a discovery process. So,these annotations—based on longer, signed reviews by scientist volunteers and first published in the AAAS review journal *Science Books & Films (SB&F)*—have a critical value for teachers, librarians, media specialists, and others faced with selecting the best and most useful print and nonprint science materials from among the thousands of titles released each year.

The reviewers recruited by *SB&F* not only are experts in some field of science, but they also have a keen interest in elementary science education. (In fact, *SB&F* is the only science book review journal that insists that all its reviewers be specialists with scientific background in the appropriate fields.) Books and A-V materials that earn *SB&F*'s recommended or highly recommended ratings are, first, free of serious errors or deficiencies in explanations of science content or processes. But beyond that, their authors and producers have employed above-average-to-excellent ways of presenting those facts to attract and hold the attention of their youthful audiences. Completeness, clarity, organization, illustration quality, and instruction value are among the specific criteria considered by *SB&F* reviewers, who also judge the suitability of the materials for certain grade levels.

In keeping with the Association's position as the largest general science organization in the United States, the scope of materials included here goes beyond the life and physical sciences to encompass mathematics, engineering and technology, medicine, and the social and behavioral sciences. The best efforts of 75 film distributors and nearly 120 book publishers are represented. The original reviews and the selective annotations published here were undertaken as part of AAAS's constitutional mandate to "increase public understanding and appreciation of the importance and promise of the methods of science in human progress," in the expectation that focusing on the youngest members of that public represents the most effective strategy for raising science literacy among future workers and voters.

We dedicate this volume to all those school and public librarians, teachers, and parents who, though short on funds and shelf space, are determined to select superlative science books and A-V materials for their students, patrons, and offspring. We sincerely hope that our work will make yours a little easier.

Susan McDowell O'Connell
June 1988

Books

Book Annotations

The books annotated in this volume are arranged alphabetically within Dewey Decimal categories. Each book is indexed by author[s], by title, and by publisher's series (where applicable). Significant words in each Dewey category head are also included in a title and subject index, along with other words identifying specific topic areas covered.

The citations for individual books contain the bibliographic information supplied by the publisher at the date of publication. The various parts of the citation and the abbreviations used are as follows:

[1] Wentworth, Lisa [2] (Ed.). [3] *Things to Know About.* [4] (Illus.; trans.; from the Look Before You Leap Series.) [5] Morristown, NJ: Silver Burdett, [6] (distr.: James, Inc.), [7] 1985. [8] (c. 1984). [9] 48pp. [10] $8.96; $4.95 (paper). [11] 84-50439. [12] ISBN 0-382-06781-9; 0-382-06961-7. [13] Index; glossary; C.I.P. [14] ▶ EP

[15] Annotation

1. Author[s] or editor[s] name[s]
2. Editor
3. Title, edition
4. Illustrated; translated; series name
5. Publisher's name
6. Distributor's name (if any)
7. Date of publication
8. Copyright date (if different from year of publication)
9. Number of pages
10. Price. The first price is for the casebound edition; the second is for the paperpack edition (if any); price[s] are those listed at the date of publication
11. Library of Congress number
12. International Standard Book Number. The first number is for the casebound edition; the second is for the paperback edition (if any)
13. Indicates that the book contains an index, a glossary, and Library of Congress Cataloging in Publication data

14. Reading/interest level[s] as assigned by the subject-matter specialist who reviewed the book:

K	Kindergarten	EA	Grades 5 and 6
EP	Grades 1 and 2	JH	Grades 7–9
EI	Grades 3 and 4		

15. Annotations are based on much longer reviews prepared by subject-matter specialists and published in *Science Books & Films*, the book and film review journal of the American Association for the Advancement of Science. Back issues of *SB&F* are available either from AAAS or from University Microfilms, Ann Arbor, MI 48106.

Books should be ordered directly from the publisher or distributor listed. Current addresses can be found in the *Literary Market Place: The Directory of American Book Publishing*, which is published yearly by R. R. Bowker Co., 1180 Avenue of the Americas, New York, NY 10036.

General Knowledge

001.64 Electronic data processing

See also 621.38 Electronic engineering and computers.

Berger, Melvin. *Computers: A Question and Answer Book.* NY: Crowell, 1985. viii + 102pp. $11.50. 85-47530. ISBN 0-690-04479-8. Index; C.I.P. ▶ EI,EA,JH

Berger provides a competent introduction to what computers do, how they work, how they are used, where they came from, and what we can expect of them in the future. He uses a series of questions and answers organized by topic and occasionally elaborates on his answers in later discussions. Includes a detailed index.

Burke, Anna Mae Walsh. *Microcomputers Can Be Kidstuff: A Friendly Guide to Using a Micro in Your Home and School.* (Illus.) Rochelle Park, NJ: Hayden, 1983. 173pp. $8.95 (paper). 83-181. ISBN 0-8104-5202-2 (paper). Glossary; index; C.I.P. ▶ EA,JH

A useful introductory manual that could be used in a middle-school computer literacy class. Historical background does not overwhelm with details. Basic information is relayed via Burke's well-organized, friendly approach: what a computer is, what its components are, what a computer may be asked to do, how you would instruct it using flowcharts, languages (BASIC and Pilot), and programs. Unusual sample programs and a special section of questions and answers guide students on the use of their own particular machines.

Clark, James I. *Video Games.* (Illus; a Look Inside Bk.) Milwaukee: Raintree, 1985. 47pp. $11.64. 84-9790. ISBN 0-8172-1410-0. Glossary; index; C.I.P. ▶ EA,JH

This beautifully illustrated book presents a history of arcade games, from pinball to Odyssey, Pong, and other, more modern video games. There is a brief overview of the technology that produces the chips for the games. Programming techniques are also covered, including examples of simple BASIC programs. Graphics, the programming of motion, and how pixels are used to produce interesting visuals are described. The book ends with a thought-pro-

3

voking discussion of artificial intelligence in future games. Clear, accurate, and well organized; includes a pronunciation guide.

Cohen, Daniel. *Computers.* (Illus.; a Question & Answer Bk.) NY: Simon & Schuster, 1983. 127pp. $8.50. 83-10355. ISBN 0-671-49340-X. Index; C.I.P. ▶ JH

Through a series of questions and answers, readers will learn a lot of terminology, become aware of important issues—such as personal privacy—gain some understanding of the limits of the computer, and learn some current uses of computers in word processing, data banks, video games, and various types of prediction. The book does not instruct about computer programming or operating. Enjoyable, accurate, and interesting, *Computers* is great for browsing and leisure reading, and a short list of suggested readings is included. A welcome addition to middle-school libraries.

Cooper, Carolyn E. *Electronic Bulletin Boards.* (Illus.; a Computer-Awareness First Bk.) NY: Watts, 1985. 66pp. $9.40. 84-21579. ISBN 0-531-04907-8. Glossary; index; C.I.P. ▶ EA,JH

This excellent introduction to electronic bulletin boards is for those unaware of their existence or who want to get started using one. The book describes many types of bulletin boards, such as The Source and CompuServe, and illustrates how individuals can set up their own bulletin board. An excellent source list for further information is included.

D'Ignazio, Fred. *The Star Wars Question & Answer Book About Computers.* (Illus. by Ken Barr.) NY: Random House, 1983. 61pp. $7.99; $4.95 (paper). 82-19030. ISBN 0-394-95686-9; 0-394-85686-4 (paper). Glossary; C.I.P. ▶ JH

This excellent beginner's guide to the hows and whys of computers and their application in business, science, health, education, and the home provides answers to questions such as, Are computers smart? What is the difference between a calculator and a computer? and, What was the first arcade game? Unfortunately, the book has no index or table of contents, so specifics are hard to locate. Even so, it is a useful introductory volume for junior high school students.

Graham, Ian. *Computer and Video Games.* (Illus.; from the Usborne Computer Bks. Series.) Tulsa, OK: Educational Development Corp., 1982. 48pp. $6.95; $3.95 (paper). ISBN 0-86020-6823; 0-86020-6815 (paper). Glossary; index. ▶ EA,JH

Chock full of vital information presented in a sparkling, unique format with a rainbow of colorful cartoons and humorous illustrations, this book is so inviting that it will attract the most hardened computer phobes. There are chapters on how a computer works, how a computer plays games, and how computers make sound effects and synthesize speech. Outstanding!

Green, Laura. *Computer Pioneers.* (Illus.; a Computer-Awareness First Bk.) NY: Watts, 1985. 86pp. $9.40. 84-20864. ISBN 0-531-04906-X. Glossary; index; C.I.P. ▶ EI,EA,JH

Green discusses pre-20th-century computers and mathematics and scientists as well as some business and programming pioneers. A good starting point for anyone interested in the history of computer science, the book could be used by teachers and students in computer literacy courses.

Holland, Penny. *Looking at Computer Sounds and Music.* (Illus.; an Easy-Read Computer Activity Bk.) NY: Watts, 1986. 32pp. $9.40. 85-22508. ISBN 0-531-10097-9. Glossary; index; C.I.P. ▶ **EA,JH**

This sturdy book will be a useful reference in elementary- and middle-school classrooms and libraries. It provides a good introduction to music synthesis, speech recognition and synthesis, and how such capabilities can help computer users. Rather than explain too much, the author has included a variety of activities. Except for a BASIC program, these activities don't require a computer but do demonstrate concepts.

Hyde, Margaret O. *Artificial Intelligence.* (Illus.; a revision of *Computers That Think?*) Hillside, NJ: Enslow, 1986. 128pp. $12.95. 85-20573. ISBN 0-89490-124-9. Index; C.I.P. ▶ **EA,JH**

Artificial intelligence, a half-breed offspring of computer science and psychology, has found applications in a host of fields—economic decision theory, chess, medical and automotive diagnosis, business planning, industrial process and quality control (robots), language translation and conversion, and even direct psychotherapy. This book surveys many of these applications and familiarizes the reader with some basic concepts and issues. The bibliography of 21 readily available books is a springboard for anyone interested in the science underlying the examples.

Naiman, Arthur. *What Every Kid and Adult Should Know About Computers.* (Illus. by Rick Hackney.) Hasbrouck Hghts., NJ: Hayden, 1985. viii + 183pp. $6.95 (paper). 84-29762. ISBN 0-8104-6336-9 (paper). Index; C.I.P. ▶ **EA,JH**

This little book provides brief sketches on why one should learn about computers, how they work, graphics techniques and software, using computer bulletin boards and networks, and simulations. A chapter introduces software to help write programs, and the book describes popular small computers on the market. Nicely indexed; suitable for anyone naive about computers.

Simon, Seymour. *How to Talk to Your Computer.* (Illus. by Barbara and Ed Emberley; a Let's-Read-and-Find-Out Science Bk.) NY: Crowell, 1985. 32pp. $11.50; $3.95 (paper). 84-45337. ISBN 0-690-04449-6; 0-06-445010-4 (paper). ▶ **EI,EA**

Meet the Computer. 84-45338. ISBN 0-690-04447-X; 0-06-445011-2 (paper).

How to Talk to Your Computer illustrates the different levels necessary for communication by comparing what happens when you ask a friend, then a computerized robot, to throw a ball. The robot's computer requires detailed directions, but when the robot's computer is given the definition and instructions, it too can throw the ball. This good introduction also gives sample programs in BASIC and Logo. Any youngster who has begun to read and wants to know what computers are will find *Meet the Computer* engaging. Each page gives a complete presentation of one fundamental architectural aspect of computers: the power switch, keyboard, screen, CPU, RAM, ROM, input, output. Readers are led through the normal sequence of operations: starting a computer, loading a program file, running the program, and viewing the results. The color illustrations are very good and well integrated with the text. On completing *Meet the Computer*, young readers will understand, in general, what a computer is and how it works.

Stevens, Lawrence. *Computer Graphics Basics.* (Illus. by Art Seiden.) Englewood Cliffs, NJ: Prentice-Hall, 1984. 48pp. $9.95. 84-6826. ISBN 0-13-164054-2. Glossary; index; C.I.P. ▶ **EA,JH**

This interesting introduction to computer graphics provides a brief description of the subject in a number of ways. Hardware includes drawing pads, pens, joysticks, and mice. Software includes both graphing and drawing programs that work with specific hardware. Logo is the primary language, although some pictures are created using instructions in BASIC. The illustrations are outstanding. Upper-elementary and junior-high students interested in learning about some of the things a computer does should enjoy this book.

Stockley, Corinne, and Lisa Watts. *Usborne Guide to Computer Jargon.* (Illus.; from the Usborne Computer Bks. Series.) Tulsa, OK: Educational Development Corp., 1983. 48pp. $8.95; $5.95 (paper). ISBN 0-86020-738-2; 0-86020-737-4 (paper). Index. ▶ **JH**

This slim paperback simply and briefly explains a wide range of specialized words that refer to computer equipment, tools, parts, and supplies. Some concepts are explained, and every page is illustrated. The organization is by subject, such as keyboard, screen, inside the computer, and software, and there is a wonderful index in the back.

White, Jack R. *How Computers Really Work.* (Illus.) NY: Dodd, Mead, 1986. 112pp. $11.95. 86-6318. ISBN 0-396-08768-X. Index; C.I.P. ▶ **EA,JH**

White clearly and concisely introduces readers to the internal workings of computers, dealing briefly with such key concepts as binary numbers, machine and batch cycles, DOS, programming languages, and artificial intelligence. Also included is an example of the many steps required for a computer to complete a simple task. The text is supplemented with a few well-placed photographs, diagrams, and charts. One of the few books presently available for this age group that describes the internal operations of a computer.

Wicks, Keith. *Working with Computers.* (Illus.; from The World of Science Series.) NY: Facts On File, 1986. 64pp. $9.95. 84-1654. ISBN 0-8160-1071-4. Glossary; index; C.I.P. ▶ **EA,JH**

This book is designed to introduce the novice to the world of computers by combining text and illustrations. Not an in-depth presentation, it is intended to answer questions that many students have when first introduced to computers. Outstanding color illustrations together with text take the reader through the nature of computers and the uses of computers. Topics include gaming, word processing, music production, and industrial applications, including robotics.

Wold, Allen L. *Computer Science: Projects for Young Scientists.* (Illus.) NY: Watts, 1984. 128pp. $10.40. 83-23572. ISBN 0-531-04764-4. Index; C.I.P. ▶ **EA,JH**

This book is about how microcomputers can be used in the preparation and presentation of science projects for science fairs and other purposes. There is a wealth of good advice on computer presentations as a facet of showmanship, with an emphasis on general concepts and broad topics. Packs an impressive collection of tips and sugestions into 119 pages but offers little to readers who want computerized science projects spelled out in detail.

001.642   Computer software

Holland, Penny. *Looking at Word Processing.* (Illus.; an Easy-Read Computer Activity Bk.) NY: Watts, 1986. 32pp. $9.40. 85-22494. ISBN 0-531-10098-7. Glossary; index; C.I.P. ▶ **EI,EA**

This attractive children's book on word processing gently introduces many of the basic concepts through written narrative and suggested activities that require access to a computer with appropriate software. The book is a good companion to the usual user manual and its mundane examples. The reading level is about fourth grade, but many children above and below that level will be more than casually interested. The activities are enticing and the illustrations provide the color and gaiety necessary to keep a child's interest.

Naiman, Arthur. *MacBook: The Indispensable Guide to Macintosh Software and Hardware.* (Illus.) Hasbrouck Heights, NJ: Hayden, 1985. xviii+318pp. $15.95 (paper). 85-16834. ISBN 0-8104-6560-4 (paper). Index; C.I.P. ▶ **EA,JH**

This informative, readable, entertaining introduction and reference to the Apple Macintosh personal computer explains how the Macintosh is different from (nearly) all other computers, then takes the reader logically and completely through what is built in and what can easily be bought, such as peripheral devices and programs. One of the few computer books that is not boring.

Schatt, Stanley, and Jane Abrams Schatt. *Bank Street Writing with Your Apple.* (Illus.) Berkeley, CA: Sybex, 1984. x+182pp. $9.95 (paper). 84-512-41. ISBN 0-89588-189-6 (paper). Index. ▶ **EA,JH**

This book offers guidance to parents who have invested in a computer for their children's educational development. It offers well-organized and concise instructions for using the *Bank Street Writer* software package for creative writing, developing files, creating recipes, doing homework, and managing a home business.

Watts, Lisa, and Mike Wharton. *Machine Code for Beginners.* (Illus. by Naomi Reed and Graham Round.) Tulsa, OK: Educational Development Corp., 1984. 48pp. $8.95; $5.95 (paper). ISBN 0-86020-736-6; 0-86020-735-8 (paper). Index. ▶ **EI, EA,JH**

This comic book approach to microcomputer machine code is a definite improvement over vendors' manuals. Both 6502 and 8080 code are presented. The user is instructed to translate everything into hexadecimal and is given a BASIC program to read the hex and load the appropriate binary. The book is satisfactory for the schoolchild with a microcomputer that has the right kind of microchip.

BASIC

Carlson, Edward H. *Kids and the IBM-PC/PCjr.* (Illus. by Paul D. Trap.) Chatsworth, CA: DATAMOST (8943 Fullbright Ave., 91311-2750), 1983. 238pp. $19.95 (paper). ISBN 0-88190-265-9 (paper). Glossary; indices; C.I.P. ▶ **JH**

Approaches programming in BASIC with a straightforward and clear instructional style while avoiding "kid" language; includes sophisticated subjects, such as debugging long programs, structured programming, and user-friendly programs; contains many excellent analogies, clever illustrations, useful references appendices, and frequent opportunities for practice. Most topics are presented as techniques to be used in creating computer games, which is sure to hold the interest of the 10-to-14-year-olds at whom the book is aimed. All in all, an excellent tool for learning BASIC on the IBM-PC.

Grauer, Robert T., Judy Gordon, and Marsha Schemel. *More BASIC Is Child's Play: IBM Edition.* (Illus. by Dianne Thompson Brin and Thomas Vahey.) Englewood Cliffs, NJ: Prentice-Hall, 1985. xiv + 251pp. $21.95 (paper). 85-528. ISBN 0-13-601097-0 (paper). Glossary; index; C.I.P. ▶ **EA,JH**

Here is a useful and simple introduction to the IBM PC and PCjr and to IBM BASIC. Written for youngsters but equally useful to parents and other adults encountering IBM microcomputers for the first time, the easy-to-read text is enhanced by cartoon figures of children named Peter and Patty and their dog Byte. Short quizzes, puzzles, and programs are provided. Carefully conceived and attractively produced, *More BASIC* will serve its users well.

Holland, Penny. *Looking at BASIC.* (Illus. by Patti Boyd; an Easy-Read Computer Activity Bk.) NY: Watts, 1985. 32pp. $9.40. 84-13834. ISBN 0-531-04893-4. Glossary; index; C.I.P. ▶ **EA,JH**

Using pig Latin as an example of code language, the book presents BASIC as "some English words, some symbols, and some rules." Short programs in BASIC are developed in the text as examples; readers are guided through some computer operations and program entry through the keyboard, and computer organization and operation are presented. Includes suggestions for further experimentation and references to other books on BASIC.

Larsen, Sally Greenwood. *Computers for Kids: Commodore 64 Edition.* (Illus.) Morris Plains, NJ: Creative Computing Press, 1984. 89pp. $5.95 (paper). 83-23165. ISBN 0-916688-63-1 (paper). Glossary; C.I.P. ▶ **EA**

A large-print manual intended for fifth- and sixth-grade children, this book will help those using the Commodore C-64. Of particular significance is the explanation of the Commodore disc operating system and the listing of a useful BASIC disc controller program. The book also covers most simple BASIC language operators and functions, with the notable exception of string-handling functions. There are many short, illustrative programs, a useful glossary of computer terminology, and a section of notes for teachers and parents.

Lipson, Shelley. *More BASIC: A Guide to Intermediate-Level Computer Programming.* (Illus. by Janice Stapleton.) NY: Holt, Rinehart and Winston, 1984. xiii + 64pp. $9.95. 83-26533. ISBN 0-03-070722-6. Glossary; index; C.I.P. ▶ **EA**

This appealing book for fifth and sixth graders is surprisingly clear. Some knowledge of BASIC is expected, but the first chapter presents a brief, thorough review that could possibly suffice for the novice programmer. Young readers could certainly use this as a first programming book, if assisted by parents or knowledgeable peers. Machine-independent BASIC is presented through string arrays and random numbers. From this book, interested readers could "graduate" to vendor manuals and the idiosyncrasies of a particular machine.

Markle, Sandra. *Kids' Computer Capers: Investigations for Beginners.* (Illus. by Stella Ormai.) NY: Lothrop, Lee & Shepard, 1983. 128pp. $6.95 (paper). 83-807. ISBN 0-688-02429-7 (paper). Glossary; index; C.I.P. ▶ **EA,JH**

This highly informative and fun book introduces programming concepts along with computer history. Peppered throughout are quizzes and answers. BASIC is introduced through simple programs that demonstrate commands up to the complexity of conditionals and loops.

Simon, Seymour. *The BASIC Book.* (Illus. by Barbara and Ed Emberley; a Let's-Read-and-Find-Out Bk.) NY: Harper & Row, 1985. 32pp. $11.50; $3.95 (paper). 85-42736. ISBN 0-690-04472-0; 0-06-445015-5 (paper). C.I.P. ▶ **EA**

The BASIC Book encourages and instructs the reader on entering BASIC programs on a microcomputer. Animation, color, and graphics are used to capture interest and to make instructions explicit. In following the instructions, the reader uses the microcomputer and gains experience with statements, line numbers, and command words. The BASIC programs are approached sequentially, and lists of the programs and sample outputs are displayed. A dictionary and explanations of commands provide a basis for learning BASIC and trying out various uses of it.

LOGO

Allen, John R., Ruth E. Davis, and John F. Johnson. *Thinking About [TLC] Logo.* (Illus.) NY: Holt, Rinehart and Winston, 1984. iv + 236pp. $16.95 (paper). 83-10771. ISBN 0-03-064116-0 (paper). C.I.P. ▶ **JH**

This book about Logo programming, problem solving, and artificial intelligence contains beautiful illustrations and is written in a zany, humorous style. It provides complete coverage: the fundamentals of Logo, turtle graphics, deductive logic, using a database with Logo, Logo functions, and a form of list processing plus some advanced concepts in mathematics, logic, and computer science. Earthy, quaint, clever, and cute, this book also introduces teens to some very advanced logico-mathematical concepts.

Ruane, Pat, and Jane Hyman. *A Beginner's Guide: Logo Activities for the Computer.* (Illus. by Leslie Morrill.) NY: Messner, 1984. 125pp. $9.79; $8.95 (paper). 84-5090. ISBN 0-671-50634-X; 0-671-49923-8 (paper). Glossary; index; C.I.P. ▶ **EP,EI,EA,JH**

This beginner's guide must rank as one of the most easily understood and thought-provoking introductions to the graphics commands in Logo. Written for novice programmers, the book guides readers from the basic commands through to the more complex ones, such as for color and animation. The attention of first-time readers will be captured by the intriguing examples; those with more experience will be fascinated by the suggestions for enhancements. The book's clear definitions, examples, and debugging hints help make it readable and usable for self-teaching and reference.

Simon, Seymour. *Turtle Talk: A Beginner's Book of Logo.* (Illus. by Barbara and Ed Emberley; a Let's-Read-and-Find-Out Science Bk.) NY: Crowell (Harper & Row), 1986. 32pp. $11.50. 85-47890. ISBN 0-690-04521-2. Glossary; C.I.P. ▶ **EP,EI,EA,JH**

Turtle Talk explains the simplest (but most important) Logo commands in an enjoyable manner. Each command is introduced on its own page or half page, along with suitable drawings and cartoons to aid understanding. Includes a useful glossary of terms—nearly complete with only 18 words in it, showing that even a potentially confusing computer language can be explained clearly with a minimum number of terms. The book covers such terms as clearscreen (CS), left (LT), right (RT), and all the necessary commands to move the "turtle" around on the screen. The book ends by explaining how to write a procedure, the key to designing beautiful shapes and writing simple programs.

Watt, Daniel. *Learning with Apple Logo.* (Illus. by Paul D. Trap; a Byte Bk.) NY: McGraw-Hill, 1984. 322pp. $19.95 (paper). 83-26828. ISBN 0-07-068571-1 (paper). Index; C.I.P. ▶ **K,EP,EI,EA,JH**

Here is a book designed to help adults and children learn Apple Logo together. Instruction progresses from materials for the youngest student through more complex concepts for teen-agers and adults. Instructions show Logo being used for geometry, drawing, and interactive games, activities with numbers as well as words and lists, questions and answers, and even writing poetry. Graphics indicating pitfalls, explorations, and helpful hints are interspersed throughout the encouraging text. Watt's book is extremely versatile and can be used at home or at school with youngsters who range from preschool age to teen-age.

Watt, Daniel. *Learning with Logo.* (Illus. by Paul D. Trap.) NY: McGraw-Hill, 1983. ix + 365pp. $19.95 (paper). 83-2619. ISBN 0-07-068570-3 (paper). Index; C.I.P. ▶ **EA**

Learning with Logo is written for children and adults learning together. Watt begins by defining Logo and describing the environment in which it is best learned. In clear, concise prose, Logo commands are introduced and used. A collection of clever turtle emblems highlights problems, suggestions, and "powerful ideas." Suggestions for further exploration encourage experimentation. The book is successful documentation, and accomplishes the difficult task of teaching the adult while teaching the adult to teach the child.

001.94   Mysteries

See also 130–133 Paranormal phenomena and parapsychology.

Branley, Franklyn M. *Is There Life in Outer Space?* (Illus. by Don Madden; a Let's-Read-and-Find-Out Science Bk.) NY: Crowell, 1984. 32pp. $11.50. 83-45057. ISBN 0-690-04374-0. C.I.P. ▶ **EI**

Branley discusses the possibilities of life in outer space, reviews past speculations about life on the moon and on Mars, and explains that no evidence of life has been found (or is likely to be found) there or elsewhere in the solar system. He clearly favors the view that there must be life somewhere out there, but he leaves room for dissent by concluding, "What do you think?" This book is illustrated with brightly colored drawings and black-and-white photographs. Young people will especially enjoy the fanciful drawings of various hypothetical space beings.

O'Neill, Catherine. *Amazing Mysteries of the World.* (Illus.) Washington, DC: National Geographic Society, 1983. 103pp. $6.95. 83-13444. ISBN 0-87044-497-2. Index; C.I.P. ▶ **EA**

O'Neill examines some of the mysteries of the world and tries to explain how scientists continually search for explanations. Some of the mysteries that she explains include those that are associated with the earth, such as lightning, swamp lights, undersea life, and ancient cultures, and those that are associated with the universe. A final section deals with such unusual phenomena as UFOs, unicorns, mermaids, and monsters. Excellent illustrations, including photographs and artistic diagrams, as well as such classroom activities as crossword puzzles, games, and problem sets.

030 General encyclopedic works
See also 503 Science: dictionaries and encyclopedias.

Ardley, Bridget, and Neil Ardley. *The Arco Book of 1,001 Questions and Answers.* (Illus.) NY: Arco, 1984. 156pp. $8.95. 83-26614. ISBN 0-668-06161-8. Index; C.I.P. ▶ **EA,JH**

This collection of diverse and interesting facts is useful for learning a little bit about a lot of different things. Topics include the universe, earth, animals, plants, the human body, and general knowledge. A complete table of contents and index make topics easy to find; excellent color photographs and illustrations accompany each subject.

Ardley, Neil, et al. *Why Things Are: The Simon & Schuster Color Illustrated Question and Answer Book.* (Illus.) NY: Julian Messner, 1984. 127pp. $8.95. ISBN 0-671-49897-5. Index. ▶ **EA,JH**

Enhanced by many color photographs and illustrations of good quality, this book is a compendium of questions and answers on a number of topics, including plants and animals, science, transportation, space, the earth, the past, and how people live. Each question has a short answer in bold type followed by a more detailed answer. Each question-answer combination takes up only one-third of a page. Although accurate and well organized, this "browsing book" should not be used for more than quick reference.

Blumberg, Rhode, and Leda Blumberg. *The Simon and Schuster Book of Facts and Fallacies.* (Illus. by Paul Frame.) NY: Simon and Schuster, 1983. 159pp. $9.59. 83-6697. ISBN 0-671-47612-2. Index; C.I.P. ▶ **EA,JH**

Well-defined leading questions or statements are followed by answers and background information. The book covers diverse topics: mammals, insects, plants, health, sports, weather, history, and more in biology, zoology, and earth sicence. Whether you are an elementary student or a full-fledged scientist, the book has facts that you can learn and apply every day, or incorporate into formal lessons in general science. The answers are scientifically sound and easy to understand. A valuable resource to stimulate interest in science and a pragmatic source of information for students of general science or beginning biology.

Jollands, David (Ed.). *Language and Communication.* (Illus.; Vol. 2 of the Science Universe Series.) NY: Arco, 1984. 64pp. ea. $79.60 (set); $9.95 ea. 83-26651. ISBN 0-668-06176-6. Glossary; index; C.I.P. ▶ **EA,JH**

Sight, Light, and Color (Vol. 3.) 83-26645. ISBN 0-668-06177-4.

Energy, Forces, and Resources (Vol. 4.) 83-26619. ISBN 0-668-06178-2.

Machines, Power, and Transportation (Vol. 5.) 84-6449. ISBN 0-668-06179-0.

Measuring and Computing (Vol. 6.) 84-6307. ISBN 0-668-06180-4.

Earth, Sea, and Sky (Vol. 7.) 84-6312. ISBN 0-668-06181-2.

Patterns of Life on Earth (Vol. 8.) 84-6318. ISBN 0-668-06182-0.

Each page in this beautifully illustrated series provides an array of bright photographs and clear explanatory diagrams. Unfortunately, the written text is not uniformly superior. Many sections are excellent; others are pedestrian— a few to the point of being misleading or even wrong. Throughout, metric terms are used without English conversions in parentheses. Volume 2 gives an especially good historical review of carefully selected topics. Volume 3 is a jewel of clarity, accuracy, beauty, and charm, with some well-put information that is simplified but not distorted. Volume 4 is another winner, with a good summary that recaps its consistently excellent treatment of technology topics. Even high-school students and adults who are not specialists will enjoy it. Volume 5 also deals competently with modern technology, and readers will finish it considerably wiser about their daily technological environment. Volume 6 gives a useful presentation of measurement topics, from small to large, but some information on computers is dated. Volume 7 glows with brilliant illustrations but suffers from a pedestrian text. The numerous meteorological diagrams are clear and helpful. The astronomy in this volume overlaps in large measure the astronomy in Volume 1, but the presentation is considerably better. Volume 8 provides a straightforward presentation of evolution, wisely stating the scientific case for evolution clearly at the elementary level. The overall selection of topics relating to evolution is excellent, and the book manages to crunch a broad view of all living things into only 61 pages.

[*Editors' note:* Volume 1, *Exploring Space and Atoms*, was adjudged by its reviewer to be only acceptable rather than recommended because it makes numerous statements that allow for misrepresentation.]

Paton, John (Ed.). *Knowledge Encyclopedia.* (Illus.) NY: Arco, 1984. 415pp. $16.95. 83-73345. ISBN 0-668-06137-5. Index. ▶ **EA,JH**

Here is a work designed for use at home by the whole family and in school for students just learning general subjects. The entries are short, simple, accurate, and on topics likely to be of interest. Information is easily found. The subjects cover history, science, biography, nature, geography, games, peoples, arts, warfare, and geology. The pictures and drawings are excellent, as are the schematic presentations of difficult concepts.

Raintree Publishers. *Cold-Blooded Animals.* (Illus.; from the Let's Discover Series.) Milwaukee: Raintree, 1986. 78–80pp. ea. $313.33 (set); $12.44 ea. (paper); $199.60 (set, paper). 86-584. ISBN 0-8172-2603-6; 0-8172-2484-6 (paper). Glossary; index; C.I.P. ▶ **EP,EI**

The Earth. 86-578. ISBN 0-8172-2604-4; 0-8172-2585-4 (paper).

Flying. 86-567. ISBN 0-8172-2613-3; 0-8172-2594-3 (paper).

Land Travel. 86-641. ISBN 0-8172-2611-7; 0-8172-2592-7 (paper).

Outer Space. 86-565. ISBN 0-8172-2614-1; 0-8172-2595-1 (paper).

People and Customs. 86-583. ISBN 0-8172-2603-8; 0-8172-2483-8 (paper).

People of Long Ago. 86-562. ISBN 0-8172-2606-0; 0-8172-2587-0 (paper).

The Prehistoric World. 86-585. ISBN 0-8172-2601-X; 0-8172-2582-X (paper).

The Sea. 86-579. ISBN 0-8172-2605-2; 0-8172-2586-2 (paper).

Ships and Boats. 86-564. ISBN 0-8172-2612-5; 0-8172-2593-5 (paper).

Sport and Entertainment. 86-651. ISBN 0-8172-2609-5; 0-8172-2590-0 (paper).

Warm-Blooded Animals. 86-649. ISBN 0-8172-2600-1; 0-8172-2581-1 (paper).

What People Do. 86-563. ISBN 0-8172-2607-9; 0-8172-2588-9 (paper).

The World of Machines. 86-568. ISBN 0-8172-2610-9; 0-8172-2591-9 (paper).

You and Your Body. 86-642. ISBN 0-8172-2608-7; 0-8172-2589-7 (paper).

Index. 86-646. ISBN 0-8172-2615-X; 0-8172-2596-X (paper).

These science, technology, and social studies reference books are useful supplementary reading, interest builders for younger students, and a simplified research source for older students with low reading skills. The format is consistent throughout: contents (four to eight sections listed), brief text with colorful illustrations, glossary with pronunciation aids, further reading (sources from the 1960s to early 1980s), questions to test recall and suggest research, simple projects, and an index. Information is basically accurate, occasionally oversimplified, and sometimes covers trivial details apparently related to available pictures. The general index for the set is comprehensive, with helpful cross references. Some volumes provide more detailed discussion and opportunity for research than others. These are on warm-blooded and cold-blooded animals, the prehistoric world, the sea, and three of the books on transportation—on ships and boats, flying, and outer space. At least one important current topic has no mention—acid rain. The focus in *Land Travel* and *People and Customs* is primarily on the United States. *Outer Space* gives nonexistent treatment of U.S. and U.S.S.R. female astronauts; *What People Do* shows some pictures of women in nontraditional jobs; *Machines* shows very traditional and sexist roles in the section on home machines. *You and Your Body* is the least successful volume in terms of subject selection, organization, international perspective, and illustrations. The anatomical drawings are less realistic and appealing than drawings in other volumes. There is a mention of pregnancy in the glossary but not in the index, yet a pregnant woman is shown and described. No father is pictured on the pages on pregnancy and childbirth. As a whole, however, the set is recommended for its broad coverage of subjects, many international examples, exquisite photographs, funny cartoons, colorful drawings, and activities for school and at home. Regrettably, the bindings and covers will not withstand heavy use.

World Book. *The World Book Encylopedia.* (Illus.) Chicago: World Book, 1985. 1400pp. $599 (set). 84-50815. ISBN 0-7166-0085-4. Index. ▶ **EA,JH**

This 22-volume encyclopedia is designed for elementary and secondary students and their families. It provides good coverage of a wide range of names and topics, many of them in science. Included are an index; student guides to writing, speaking, and research skills; and over 200 brief study guides comprising references, topics for study, and questions to enhance and focus the study of selected topics. The reading level varies with the sophistication of the topic: simple concepts and reading levels are presented at the beginning of long articles and for topics generally consulted by young readers; sophisticated concepts and reading levels are provided at the end of articles and for topics usually consulted by older children. Major articles include additional reference sources; many have study questions. Pertinent up-to-date entries appear, such as one for AIDS, as well as entries of special interest to minorities (such as one on the black dancer Arthur Mitchell) and women (such as the one on the nineteenth century astronomer Maria Mitchell). This encyclopedia is well illustrated and printed; useful to students for preparing school reports or for general browsing. An annual update in the form of a yearbook is available.

069.9 Science museums

Alexander, Liza. *A Visit to the Sesame Street Museum.* (Illus. by Joe Mathieu; a Pictureback Bk.) NY: Random House, 1987. 29pp. $1.95. 87-1685. ISBN 0-394-88715-8. ▶ **K,EP**

In this book, the idea is conveyed correctly that museums now have special programs for children and, increasingly, interactive exhibits (as opposed to the passive ones of years ago). There is no mention, however, of the fact that most museums charge admission and that special programs for children can be expensive. The illustrations are cute.

Brown, Vinson. *Building Your Own Nature Museum for Study and Pleasure, 2nd edition.* (Illus. by Don Greame Kelley.) NY: Arco, 1984. xii + 161pp. $12.95; $7.95 (paper). 84-12393. ISBN 0-668-06057-3; 0-668-06061-1 (paper). Index; C.I.P. ▶ **EI,EA,JH**

This second edition benefits from Brown's additional experience of a book written 30 years ago and insight. Topics covered include obtaining and classifying specimens, trading specimens, mounting and labeling, arranging displays, exhibiting, and drawings and paintings. The appendices ("Topics to Investigate," "Books to Read," and "Where to Get Supplies") are informative and useful; however, the book does not mention herbariums or how to preserve plants in a dried state.

Cutchins, Judy, and Ginny Johnston. *Are Those Animals Real? How Museums Prepare Wildlife Exhibits.* (Illus.) NY: Morrow, 1984. xx + 75pp. $11.75. 84-1049. ISBN 0-688-03879-4. Glossary; index; C.I.P. ▶ **EA**

All the standard museum techniques (including taxidermy, modeling, freeze drying, dioramas, and imaginative reconstruction of extinct animals) are clearly and simply described and illustrated with informative black-and-white photographs. Most appropriate for 10- to 11-year-olds, although much of the information will also interest older children. The large type and chatty style, however, may tend to discourage teen-age readers. This book should be on the biology shelves of elementary school libraries, and would be an excellent gift for any child interested in natural history.

Philosophy and Related Disciplines

130–133 Paranormal phenomena and parapsychology
See also 001.94 Mysteries.

Cohen, Daniel. *ESP: The New Technology.* (Illus.) NY: Messner, 1986. xii + 116pp. $9.59. 85-29857. ISBN 0-671-61151-8. C.I.P. ▶ JH

Cohen gives an overview of the field of parapsychology, presenting the material in a balanced way by providing both the pros and cons of various research approaches. A chronology of developments in parapsychology, from early Greece to modern computer labs, provides a very readable framework. All technical terms are well defined. This book is a good starting point for young readers interested in this area. Its broad scope and balanced presentation avoid the sensationalism typical of the many popular media reports on ESP.

Weiss, Ann E. *Seers and Scientists: Can the Future Be Predicted?* (Illus. by Paul Plumer). NY: Harcourt Brace Jovanovich, 1986. 80pp. $13.95. 86-11964. ISBN 0-15-272850-3. Index; C.I.P. ▶ EA,JH

Weiss examines the origins and present-day applications of the mystical art of prophecy and the rational science of prediction. The author begins her historical review of prophecy 1,000 years before the birth of Mesopotamia with hepatoscopists who studied the liver of sacrificed animals to predict the future. The book progresses on to astrology, dream interpretation to predict the future, and seers with "visions" or "ESP." The science of prediction is traced from the laws of probability first introduced by Pascal in 1653 and amplified by Galileo, whose four theoretical, fundamental laws of probability were soon put to practical use. Weiss also shows how machines were invented and used for weather forecasting and predicting natural disasters. She presents her information in a logical and well-organized manner and provides examples of both prophecy and prediction and an examination of their strengths and weaknesses.

150 Psychology

155.4 Child psychology
See also 362.5–.8 Services for various demographic groups; 649.65 Sex education.

Aylesworth, Jim. *The Bad Dream.* (Illus. by Judith Friedman.) Niles, IL: Whitman, 1985. 32pp. $9.25. 85-685. ISBN 0-8075-0506-4. C.I.P. ▶ K,EP

Friedman's sepia-and-white illustrations give this book a magical, dreamy quality that is enhanced by the simple language of the story. A child's frightening dream is presented in archetypal fashion, and the comforting response of the parents provides a soothing resolution. The portrayal of the parents as calm and helpful is well designed to help children deal with the distinction between reality and fantasy.

Bates, Betty. *Herbert and Hortense.* (Illus. by John C. Wallner.) Niles, IL: Whitman, 1984. 40pp. $9.25. 84-2387. ISBN 0-8075-322-3. C.I.P. ▶ K,EP

This book contains a delightful trio of stories about a boy and a girl who happen to be rhinos. All three stories present real-life situations that children are likely to encounter. The first story describes what it is like to be the new child in class, with the lesson not to judge someone solely on the basis of appearance. The second story is about jealousy, the third about the importance of cleanliness and neatness. Delightfully illustrated with black-and-white drawings, *Herbert and Hortense* will teach children valuable lessons.

Chevalier, Christa. *Spence and the Sleepytime Monster.* (Illus. by the author.) Niles, IL: Whitman, 1984. 29pp. $9.25. 83-25988. ISBN 0-8075-7574-7. C.I.P. ▶ K,EP,EI

Spence believes that he has seen a monster in his bedroom and is sure that it will return. When the monster does reappear, it turns out to be Spence's cat. Spence's mother shows how the shadows of the cat could look like a monster. Parents will find the book very useful in helping their youngsters to overcome superstitions and irrational fears. The story shows how evidence can have different interpretations depending on a person's viewpoint. The approach of Spence and his gently sympathetic mother to a frightening problem is nicely done. An especially good book to read aloud to preschoolers.

Hines, Ana Grossnickle. *All by Myself.* (Illus.) NY: Clarion, 1985. 32pp. $10.95. 84-19882. ISBN 0-89919-293-9. C.I.P. ▶ K

This beautifully illustrated, easy-to-read book about night toilet training would be appropriate for parents to read to children or for reading in nurseries or daycare centers. The author presents the development task of staying dry at night in the correct context of being one more thing a child accomplishes on the road to independence. Maternal participation in the child's growth and development is stressed. However, the author's hypothesis that children wet their beds simply because they are afraid of the dark is somewhat naive.

Horner, Althea J. *Little Big Girl.* (Illus. by Patricia Rosamilia.) NY: Human Sciences, 1986. 32pp. $13.95; $5.95 (paper). 81-20164. ISBN 0-89885-098-3; 0-89885-287-0 (paper). C.I.P. ▶ K

This story is about a child who sees herself as a baby because she is addressed in that fashion by her family. The adults become aware of her desire to grow up and wisely change their attitude toward her. The story is simple but makes its point clearly. The illustrations are appropriate and do not overpower the narrative. Because the vocabulary is carefully chosen, the book can be read by a child or it can be read to children as young as four years old.

Kline, Suzy. *SHHHH!* (Illus. by Dora Leder.) Niles, IL: Whitman, 1984. 28pp. $9.25. 83-26032. ISBN 0-8075-7321-3. ▶ **K**

Kline presents situations in which a little girl tries to get attention from various people, only to be told to be quiet. You feel sorry for her and realize as a parent (if you are one) how often you have told your child or children to be quiet or have put them off when they wanted to do something with you. The point is made in simple one-line sentences and excellent, life-like illustrations, which are done in black and white with touches of color. This book should heighten parents' awareness of their children's feelings and show how often children are ignored because of an adult's problem or involvement in some activity.

Sharmat, Marjorie Weinman. *My Mother Never Listens to Me.* (Illus. by Lynn Munsinger.) Niles, IL: Whitman, 1984. 26pp. $9.25. 84-17201. ISBN 0-8075-5347-6. ▶ **K,EP,EI**

In this humorous book, we meet a five-year-old boy who does his best to manipulate and gain his mother's attention, to distract her in any way from a book she's reading. He describes wild and shocking things, but nothing works. Finally defeated, the boy simply asks for a kiss, and his mother responds. This book briefly dramatizes one aspect of a parent-child relationship: the youngster's demand for control and, through losing the battle, his gaining affection simply by asking for it.

Swenson, Judy Harris, and Roxane Brown Kunz. *No One Like Me.* (Illus.; photographs by Robert C. Sorgatz.) Minneapolis: Dillon, 1985. 40pp. $8.95. 85-7027. ISBN 0-87518-307-7. Glossary; C.I.P. ▶ **EP,EI**

This book will help children reinforce their sense of individuality and understand the worth and dignity of each person. Eric, a fourth grader, narrates and introduces us to his friends and classmates, telling us of their special talents and disabilities. Although Eric is dyslexic and failed first grade, he amply demonstrates that limits in one area do not limit a person in other ways. This book offers each child reassurance of self while laying the foundation for sensitivity to others. The focus is on the individual and the shared commonalities that ought to unite us rather than the superficial differences that often divide us.

155.937 Death and dying

Clardy, Andrea Fleck. *Dusty Was My Friend: Coming to Terms with Loss.* (Illus. by Eleanor Alexander.) NY: Human Sciences, 1984. 32pp. $12.95. 83-6203. ISBN 0-89885-141-6. C.I.P. ▶ **EI,EA**

Eight-year-old Benjamin learns that his best friend, Dusty, has been killed in an automobile accident. Over the next several months, Benjamin must come to grips with the personal loss of his friend and find some meaning in Dusty's death. Through her sensitive portrayal of one child's reaction to the loss of a friend, Clardy does provide a format for allowing a young reader to learn about and come to terms with the reality of death. The story and illustrations are well done, but the scope is limited. Children may view death as desertion; they may also find an outlet for their feelings through play and drawing. These matters are not dealt with.

Hickman, Martha Whitmore. *Last Week My Brother Anthony Died.* (Illus. by Randie Julien.) Nashville, TN: Abingdon, 1984. 26pp. $10.95. 84-2891. ISBN 0-687-21128-X. C.I.P. ▶ **EP,EI**

Using full-page illustrations, this book presents a complicated and personal subject—the death of a loved one. The story involves a young girl's grief over the death of her baby brother and her reflections on happier times. She is comforted by a man who has had a similar experience and who helps her develop hope for the future. The book is a useful tool for encouraging discussion of this scary and confusing issue. Parents, teachers, and counselors may find it helpful as a guide to reaching children on their own level of understanding.

Simon, Norma. *The Saddest Time.* (Illus. by Jacqueline Rogers; a Concept Bk.) Niles, IL: Whitman, 1986. 40pp. $10.25. 85-15785. ISBN 0-8075-7203-9. C.I.P. ▶ **EP,EI**

The Saddest Time describes three separate situations in which young children react to death. Those dying represent different age groups in different settings. The only attempt to weave the stories together is a series of poems that present death as part of life. The book's merit is in its educational approach to sensitizing children to death in both acute and chronic situations and to its occurrence at any age in a variety of settings.

Stiles, Norman. *I'll Miss You, Mr. Hooper.* (Illus. by Joe Mathieu.) NY: Random House and Children's Television Workshop, 1984. 16pp. $4.99. 83-27013. ISBN 0-394-86600-2. ▶ **K,EP**

This relatively brief but conceptually superb and extremely well-written book discusses death and the loss of a loved one. The preface provides an excellent guide for parents on how to use the book to help their children understand this fact of life. One of the many insightful features of the book is how well it explains that when a child loses a loved one, it is important for parents to emphasize that other family and friends will remain to ensure that the child is safe and will not be abandoned. The text also teaches the child about memories and how good it is to have known someone who made the child feel happy.

172 Political ethics

Gallaz, Christophe, and Roberto Innocenti. *Rose Blanche.* (Illus. by Roberto Innocenti.) Mankato, MN: Creative Education, 1985. 32pp. $14.95. 85-70219. ISBN 0-87191-994-X. ▶ **JH**

This work by two European authors breaks new ground by taking children into the realm of politics and moral conduct. Rose Blanche is the child who relates the events in a spare text that complements the powerful illustrations by Innocenti. The story itself, as improbable as it may be, is a vehicle that can enable parents and teachers to convey to children the horror and devastation associated with the Nazi era in Germany.

Social Sciences

306 Cultural anthropology

Barrett, Ian. *Tundra and People.* (Illus.; from the Nature's Landscape Series.) Morristown, NJ: Silver Burdett, 1982. 91pp. $15.96. 82-50395. ISBN 0-382-06670-7. Glossary; index. ▶ JH

Well written and well illustrated with good sketches and photographs, this book provides an excellent geological perspective. Both flora and fauna are equally described as integral participants in tundra life. The Viking explorations and fur trading by the Russians and the British are presented well. The key chapter focuses on the ice ages.

Bell, Neill. *Only Human: Why We Are the Way We Are.* (Illus. by Sandy Clifford; from the Brown Paper School Bk. Series.) Boston: Little, Brown, 1983. 125pp. $12.45; $7.70 (paper). 83-9826. ISBN 0-316-08816-1; 0-316-08818-8 (paper). C.I.P. ▶ EA,JH

By comparing different kinds of cars with various classifications in the animal kingdom, the book helps the reader see where a number of creatures fall in the scheme of things and how man fits in. Cartoon drawings highlight the text. Many areas are covered, incuding instructions for doing a family tree and an explanation of the concept of evolution. Families, marriage traditions, culture, life stages, and belief in the supernatural are also discussed. Tests, games, and diagrams help get points across. This book could be used in social studies or science classes, but also makes for interesting and fun reading for personal pleasure alone.

Carson, James. *Deserts and People.* (Illus.; from the Nature's Landscapes Series.) Morristown, NJ: Silver Burdett, 1982. 88pp. $15.96. 82-50396. ISBN 0-382-06669-3. Glossary; index. ▶ JH

Examines the climatology of deserts and explains why they occur in certain areas of the world. The book focuses on four different groups of people who have adapted to desert living and also covers the history of their art and religion. The Sahara Desert is described in depth. High-quality, full-color photographs are used. Junior-high students may need help with the vocabulary in the early chapters.

Hertz, Ole, and trans. by Tobi Tobias. *Tobias Catches Trout.* (Illus. by the author.) Minneapolis: Carolrhoda, 1984. 30pp. ea. $7.95 ea. 83-27224. ISBN 0-87614-263-3. ▶ **K,EP,EI**

Tobias Goes Ice Fishing. 83-26356. ISBN 0-87614-260-9.

Tobias Goes Seal Hunting. 83-26357. ISBN 0-87614-262-5.

Tobias Has a Birthday. 83-27287. ISBN 0-87614-261-7.

These books describe life in modern Greenland, where hunting and fishing are the major means of subsistence for a population derived from ancient migrations of Danes and Eskimos. The illustrations are colorful yet simple, and the translation from the Danish is generally accurate. The books are remarkably successful in providing accuracy without burdensome detail. All four share an excellent symmetry in the level of detail of the illustrations and the text, and each book is organized around an event. Taken together, these books give a nice view of life in the settlements of Greenland.

Lye, Keith. *The World Today.* (Illus.; from The World of Science Series.) NY: Facts On File, 1986. 64pp. $9.95. 84-1654. ISBN 0-8160-1072-2. Glossary; index; C.I.P. ▶ **EI**

This book describes the inhabitants of North America, South America, Europe, the Soviet Union, Asia, Africa, Oceania, and the Polar regions. It begins with a short history of the human race and ends with a discussion of our changing world. Because each chapter is brief, the book is suitable for a simple overview of the world and its cultures for young children who know how to read, but it is insufficient for anyone seeking detailed information. Nicely illustrated with maps and photographs of people in natural settings; as a means of showing how different, yet similar, people are all over the world, this book is effective.

Sutter, Frederic Koehler. *Amerika Sāmoa: An Anthropological Photo Essay.* (Illus.) Honolulu: University of Hawaii Press, 1984. viii + 128pp. $24.95. 84-51832. ISBN 0-8248-0990-4. Glossary; index. ▶ **EP,EI,EA,JH**

Sutter has captured a fleeting moment in modern Samoan history. Concentrating on transitional as well as traditional life styles, he has produced a handsome volume of slick photographs that capture the "best" flavors of the islands. Each technically excellent photograph is captioned with either an original Samoan proverb or a quoted passage from early ethnographies. Contains far more photography than anthropology.

Sutton, George Miksch. *Eskimo Year.* (Illus. by the author.) Norman: University of Oklahoma Press, 1985. xviii + 321pp. $14.95. 84-28086. ISBN 0-8061-1933-0. C.I.P. ▶ **EA,JH**

Sutton arrived on Southampton Island, or Shugliak, on August 17, 1929, and left two days short of a year later. His diary of that year is a genuine classic. He writes about the island's plants and animals, but the aspect of the book that will have enduring significance is Sutton's observations of and stories about an Eskimo culture that has now disappeared. Good supplemental reading for junior-high students; elementary-school teachers will find interesting stories here to read to their classes.

306.7–.8   Relations of the sexes; marriage and family

See also 362.5–.8 Services for various demographic groups; 649.65 Sex education.

Brown, Laurene Krasny, and Marc Brown. *Dinosaurs Divorce: A Guide for Changing Families.* (Illus.) Boston: Atlantic Monthly Press, 1986. 32pp. $13.95. 86-1079. ISBN 0-87113-089-0. Glossary.   ▶ **K,EP,EI**

The Browns use their lovable, personified dinosaurs skillfully to drive home their points. Eleven divorce topics are presented in comic-strip format with individual frames giving specific thoughts on situations created by divorce. The information is not original, but it is presented in understandable terms, emphasizing love and understanding. The text suggests specific actions in various situations. An informative, charming, appealing presentation of a topic often dealt with only in clinical terms with little appeal for the child reader.

Kempler, Susan, Doreen Rappaport, and Michele Spirn. *A Man Can Be . . .* (Illus.; photographs by Russell Dian.) NY: Human Sciences, 1985. 32pp. $13.95; $5.95 (paper). 80-25356. ISBN 0-89885-046-0; 0-89885-208-0 (paper). C.I.P.   ▶ **K,EP**

This illustrated book shows many of the qualities, emotions, and behaviors of men. The excellent black-and-white photographs with accompanying brief captions effectively portray men interacting with their sons to show a boy what he can expect of a man and what he can look forward to becoming in adulthood. However, girls and women have been excluded in the depiction of several "masculine" qualities. Nevertheless, a good addition to an elementary school or personal library.

Leiner, Katherine. *Both My Parents Work.* (Illus.; photographs by Steve Sax; from the My World Series.) NY: Watts, 1986. 48pp. $8.90. 85-26362. ISBN 0-531-10101-0. C.I.P.   ▶ **K,EP**

Text, photographs, and stories from ten real families show what kinds of jobs mothers and fathers typically have, how parents' work schedules affect their children's daily lives, and the special responsibilities of children when their parents work. The stories are told by children of varying ages, from a five-year-old girl to a thirteen-year-old boy. A child who reads this book can come away with a more realistic sense of how the modern family operates and can learn that children of working families are not alone.

Perry, Patricia, and Marietta Lynch. *Mommy and Daddy Are Divorced.* (Illus.; a Pied Piper Bk.) NY: Dial, 1985. 32pp. $6.95; $3.95 (paper). 77-86268. ISBN 0-8037-577-0; 0-8037-0233-7 (paper).   ▶ **K,EP,EI**

This excellent little book, in which the black-and-white photographs on every page are fully as important to the story as the brief words of five-year-old Ned, is a masterpiece. It is about a divorced family, in which the parents are both clearly involved with the two boys (Ned and Joey, three). Dad's twice-weekly visits punctuate interactions that are set against the comfort of home life with mother and the leisurely chance for the boys to play with each other, to feel excited about dad's visit, to feel angry and sad about his leaving, and to "work through" distress with each parent, as well as to ask questions about why their parents divorce.

Stanek, Muriel. *All Alone After School.* (Illus. by Ruth Rosner.) Niles, IL: Whitman, 1985. 30pp. $9.25. 84-17243. ISBN 0-8075-0278-2. ▶ **K,EP,EI**

Children of single-parent families and families in which both parents work outside the home will be interested in Josh, a young boy who learns that he will be coming home to an empty house after school because his mother has just taken a full-time job. Josh's emotional reactions to the change, from initial apprehension to confidence, are endearingly portrayed. Challenges such as a stranger at the door are faced and successfully met. The author weaves some needed precautionary information into the text, but the emphasis is clearly on feelings, which are clearly communicated in words that capture the emotions of a child alone at home.

Vigna, Judith. *Grandma Without Me.* (Illus. by the author.) Niles, IL: Albert Whitman, 1984. 29pp. $9.75. 83-26031. ISBN 0-8075-3030-1. C.I.P. ▶ **K,EP,EI,EA**

This wonderful little book tells the story of a three-year-old boy (in his words) who, after the divorce of his parents, is cut off from the grandmother he dearly loves. Accompanied by colorful illustrations, the boy tells what he and grandma mean to each other and how they plan to keep in touch. This book beautifully shows the broader threat that is posed by divorce and the patience and acceptance needed before valued, cross-familial relationships can be restored.

327 Nuclear war; arms control

Lampton, Christopher. *Star Wars.* (Illus.; a First Bk.) NY: Watts, 1987. 70pp. $9.90. 86-26688. ISBN 0-531-10314-5. Glossary; index; C.I.P. ▶ **EA**

Star Wars is a reasonably good treatment of the science and politics that surround the Strategic Defense Initiative (SDI). Lampton explains the pros and cons of SDI to a young audience. This is a formidable task since most adults do not comprehend the complexities of SDI (in fact, many adults could benefit from this quick primer). The science is presented clearly and is well illustrated. The combined presentation of the scientific and political nature of SDI makes the book thought-provoking.

Seuss, Dr. *The Butter Battle Book.* (Illus. by the author.) NY: Random House, 1984. 42pp. $7.99. 83-21286. ISBN 0-394-86580-4. ▶ **K,EP,EI,EA**

This book covers the major social issue of the escalating arms race. It has two opposing cultures, the Yooks and Zooks. The Yooks butter their bread butter side up, and the Zooks butter their bread butter side down. The antagonism starts with a wall between the two sides and escalates through a series of fanciful weapons until each side has a soldier standing on top of the wall holding an egg-sized ultimate weapon that could blow up the other side. The book ends with the question of "Who's going to drop it first?" This abrupt ending unnerved the younger children to whom I read this book, but it emphasizes the real problem of the world's arms race and leads into a discussion of "What will the real or final outcome be?"

Vigna, Judith. *Nobody Wants a Nuclear War.* (Illus. by the author.) Niles, IL: Whitman, 1986. 40pp. $10.75. 86-1654. ISBN 0-8075-5739-0. C.I.P. ▶ **K,EP,EI**

A sweetly illustrated, well-written story of the fears young children may have from hearing and seeing televised scenes describing nuclear war. Vigna avoids propaganda and tells the story of a brother and sister who construct a "safe" hiding place after seeing such a program. Their mother reassures them by describing how adults work to prevent war. The text is supplemented by the author's excellent sketches that reassure children that "nobody wants a nuclear war." The reading level is simple enough for grades one through three, but younger children might receive the most psychological benefit. The book might give parents ideas for attacking other fears children are exposed to by the media. An upbeat but not unrealistic book.

330 Economics

Mitgutsch, Ali. *From Gold to Money.* (Illus. by the author; a Start to Finish Bk.) Minneapolis: Carolrhoda, 1985. 24pp. $5.95. 84-17488. ISBN 0-87614-230-7. C.I.P. ▶ **K,EP,EI**

Unfamiliar words—such as counterfeiting, pillory, bartering, and minting—are used and defined in context; the book can be useful in social science classes and as a basis for experimentation with bartering. The evolution of bartering is clearly explained and cheerfully illustrated. A unique and interesting addition to elementary school libraries.

333.79 Energy and energy resources
See also 371.42 Careers; 507 Science: study and teaching; 621 Applied physics.

Ardley, Neil. *Understanding Energy.* (Illus.; from the Understanding Science Series.) Morristown, NJ: Silver Burdett, 1986. 65pp. $13.95. 85-27784. ISBN 0-382-09184-1. Index; C.I.P. ▶ **EI,EA**

The author begins with a broad introduction to many kinds of energy, each illustrated by a high-quality photograph, then describes each kind in detail. Readers learn how energy is obtained, measured, used, saved, stored, changed from one form to another, and lost or wasted. Fascinating sections trace the history of man's use of energy and predict some future sources. The descriptions are clear and completely accurate, and examples are great for building intuition about the abstract concepts. Everything possible is done to connect energy ideas to the readers' experience. The illustrations are exceptional, and the book even includes some home projects.

Asimov, Isaac. *How Did We Find Out About Solar Power?* (Illus. by David Wool; How Did We Find Out Series.) NY: Walker, 1981. 62pp. $7.95. 81-2469. ISBN 0-8027-6422-3. Index; C.I.P. ▶ **JH**

Asimov describes the development of solar power and gives appropriate emphasis to the various discoveries involved, but does not emphasize the *process* of discovery. He clearly shows the solar origins of almost all energy we have, then looks at the future, leaving the reader with the impression that the only significant use of solar energy will be from space solar power stations that transmit energy to the earth's surface. Small-scale uses are not even mentioned. Overall, however, a readable and accurate book.

Carey, Helen H. *Producing Energy.* (Illus.; a First Bk.) NY: Watts, 1984. 64pp. $8.90. 84-7400. ISBN 0-531-04830-6. Glossary; index; C.I.P. ▶ **EA**

Encapsulating energy production in 64 pages for a presumably naive audience is a truly formidable task. This may explain some of this book's shortcomings, such as the limited emphasis on renewable sources and the fact that some of the book's statements may lead to misunderstandings. ("Special batteries," for example, do not "soak up large amounts of electricity.") Some 30 new terms are presented in boldface in context and then elaborated a bit in the glossary. There are fewer black-and-white illustrations and photographs than in most books for children, but they do successfully enhance the text.

Cross, Mike. *Wind Power.* (Illus. by Ron Hayward Assocs.; from the Energy Today Series.) NY: Gloucester, 1985. 32pp. ea. $9.90 ea. 85-70600. ISBN 0531-170071. Glossary; index ▶ **EA,JH**

Hawkes, Nigel. *Oil.* 85-70598. ISBN 0531-170055.

McKie, Robin. *Solar Power.* 85-70599. ISBN 0531-170063.

Strachan, James. *Future Sources.* 85-70597. ISBN 0531-170047.

Part of an eight-book series on energy, these books are consistent in writing quality and have excellent illustrations. The reading level is upper elementary and lower junior high, but the illustrations are detailed enough to be used by high school and college students for a basic understanding of energy. Each book can be read in about 15 minutes and can be considered a chapter in the world's energy story, providing just enough information to pique the interest of young students. Supplemented with further reading and lectures from an instructor, students will learn quite a bit about our energy sources.

Kraft, Betsy Harvey. *Oil and Natural Gas.* (Illus.; a First Bk.) NY: Watts, 1982. 64pp. $7.90. 82-6975. ISBN 0-531-01411-8. Glossary; index; C.I.P. ▶ **JH**

A well-written, comprehensive presentation about the nonrenewable resources of oil and natural gas. Kraft explains how deposits were formed and discovered, cleaned, refined, and transported. The world-wide distribution of oil and natural gas is reviewed. Illustrated with many good quality black-and-white photographs.

Langley, Andrew. *Energy.* (Illus.; from the Topics Series.) NY: Bookwright, 1986. 32pp. $10.40. 86-70182. ISBN 0-531-18085-9. Glossary; index. ▶ **K,EP,EI**

A good attempt to tell young readers what energy is and does. The book starts with a description of the power of the sun and concludes with what to expect in the future. On balance, it treats the generation and conservation of energy as well as such a brief book can, using vivid illustrations to tell its story along with the text. However, the concept of renewable and nonrenewable energy is never introduced, leaving young readers with no real concept of why conservation becomes a practical tool for the present. A good classroom text or supplemental reader.

Mitgutsch, Ali. *From Swamp to Coal.* (Illus. by the author; a Start to Finish Bk.) Minneapolis: Carolrhoda, 1985. 24pp. $5.95. 84-17465. ISBN 0-87614-233-1. C.I.P. ▶ **K,EP,EI**

Presents concepts in such an abstract way that young children will have more difficulty than they should understanding what happens to turn trees and vegetation into coal and then to change coal into the power to run the electric lights in the house. Still, *From Swamp to Coal* could be used by early elementary children for basic information, but for a deeper understanding, adult intervention will be necessary. The color and charm of the illustrations add a great deal to the book's overall value.

333.91   Waterbodies and water supply

> *See also* 551.46 Oceanography and underwater exploration; 551.48 Hydrology; 574.5263 Ecology of aquatic environments; 574.92 Marine biology and ecology.

Gunston, Bill. *Water.* (Illus.; from the Visual Science Series.) Morristown, NJ: Silver Burdett, 1982. 48pp. $13.00. 82-50389. ISBN 0-382-06659-6. Glossary; index. ▶ JH

A compendium of factual information, such as how water was originally formed, what it is, where it is found, and water in the human body, in the home, and in industry. This book covers much more than "the water cycle," but one information item does not build on another. *Water* is like an encyclopedia, and readers can dip in at any point. The book includes a helpful glossary and reference. Illustrations, most in full color, and diagrams are essential and constitute about half of the text. Highly recommended as a resource book for junior-high students.

Seixas, Judith S. *Water: What It Is, What It Does.* (Illus. by Tom Huffman; from the Read-alone Series.) NY: Greenwillow, 1987. 56pp. $10.25. 86-14926. ISBN 0-688-06607-0. C.I.P. ▶ EI,EA

This book explores the water cycle and how to preserve our tiny percentage of usable water. Wonderful illustrations help to clarify the concepts. Seixas gives a thorough presentation of what water is, where it is found, and how it is recycled. The power of water is discussed in terms of erosion and the use of water as a power source for generating electricity. An excellent classroom resource for a unit on water or ecology and also an enjoyable book for leisure reading at home or for preparing an independent project.

Social Problems and Services

362.2 Mental illness; nursing homes

Delton, Judy, and Dorothy Tucker. *My Grandma's in a Nursing Home.* (Illus. by Charles Robinson.) Niles, IL: Whitman, 1986. 32pp. $10.25. 86-1640. ISBN 0-8075-5333-6. C.I.P. ▶ **EP,EI**

In this book, a young boy must accommodate himself to the reality of Grandma's new home and her strange behavior. (Grandma has Alzheimer's disease.) The book traces Jason's evolution from confusion to a tacit understanding of the limitations and beauty of the aged. From a somewhat frightening experience to the realization that he can participate in the life of the elderly, Jason provides an instructive example for all readers, showing that age generates changes but that changes can and must be lived with. Through text and illustrations, young readers are given assistance in understanding what can be a troubling stage of life.

Guthrie, Donna. *Grandpa Doesn't Know It's Me.* (Illus. by Katy Keck Arn-steen.) NY: Human Sciences/Alzheimer's Disease and Related Disorders Association, 1986. 32pp. $13.95; $5.95 (paper). 85-30550. ISBN 0-89885-302-8; 0-89885-308-7 (paper). C.I.P. ▶ **EP,EI**

Guthrie demonstrates that when young children are given accurate, honest information in understandable terms, they can cope as well as participate in the care of the afflicted relative. The author takes a positive, nonthreatening stance throughout to motivate youngsters to voice their natural feelings and concerns. Parents and teachers will find that this approach promotes open discussion for instructional purposes and provides a story for youngsters to compare their own experiences with. A fine effort to facilitate family communication about Alzheimer's disease.

Litchfield, Ada B. *Making Room for Uncle Joe.* (Illus. by Gail Owens.) Niles, IL: Albert Whitman, 1984. 26pp. $9.25. 83-17036. ISBN 0-8075-4952-5. C.I.P. ▶ **EP,EI,EA,JH**

This brief book is about Uncle Joe, an adult with Down's syndrome, who must leave the institution where he has been living to move in with his sister's family. The story is told through the eyes of the 10-year-old nephew, and it is largely about how the children overcome their prejudices about retarded people, how the children and Uncle Joe accommodate each other, and how they come to like each other. The beautiful drawings help bring the story alive and are needed because the story is somewhat abstract.

Rappaport, Doreen. *"But She's Still My Grandma!"* (Illus. by Bernadette Simmons.) NY: Human Sciences, 1982. 32pp. $12.95. 81-20236. ISBN 0-89885-072-X. C.I.P. ▶ EI,EA

In this warm and interesting story, a young girl named Jessica wants to visit her paternal grandmother, who resides in a nursing home. The story enables readers to gain insight into some of the common difficulties of the aged: loss of memory, separation from loved ones, and institutionalization. The interplay between Grandma Pearl and Jessica is realistic and made more vivid by the excellent illustrations.

362.292–.293 Alcoholism and drug addiction

Garner, Alan. *It's O.K. to Say No to Drugs! A Parent/Child Manual for the Protection of Children.* (Illus. by Rick Detorie; from the It's O.K. Series.) NY: TOR, 1987. 117pp. $3.95 (paper). 86-50963. ISBN 0-812-59456-8 (paper). ▶ EP,EI,EA,JH

This excellent, practical book, if used extensively by parents and in schools, could give children the necessary information and experience to say "no" to drugs. The book strongly points out that drugs include tobacco and alcohol and that these are often a child's introduction to other drugs. The most helpful feature is the use of extensive stories to help parents and their children discuss situations that may arise and learn how to say "no" to them. Overall, an excellent book to use in a discussion group.

Seixas, Judith S. *Drugs: What They Are, What They Do.* (Illus. by Tom Huffman; from the Read-alone Series.) NY: Greenwillow, 1987. 47pp. $10.25. 86-33624. ISBN 0-688-07399-9. C.I.P. ▶ EI,EA

This book presents an easy-to-read exploration of psychoactive drugs and their impact on the human body. Seixas uses appealing analogies to help children relate to the negative impact drugs have on the body and the ability to function in daily routines. The book describes gateway drugs, stimulants, sedatives, hallucinogens, and narcotics, using their common street names. It combines readable text and clever illustrations about the different kinds of psychoactive drugs, how they are used, how they make one feel, and what their effects are. Includes an important chapter on "How to Say No," giving the reader many appropriate responses if asked to try drugs.

Stepney, Rob. *Alcohol.* (Illus.; from the Understanding Drugs Series.) NY: Watts, 1987. 64pp. $11.90. 87-50597. ISBN 0-531-10433-8. Index. ▶ EA,JH

This book deals with what alcohol is, what it takes to get drunk, and the physical and psychological problems associated with alcohol. The topics tend to be covered briefly, but the reader should be able to get an introductory overview. Stepney successfully uses interesting statistics and anecdotes to draw the reader in and to make the subject personally relevant. The appendices, which include a list of sources of help, are interesting and could prove useful.

362.4 Physical handicaps

Blue, Rose. *Me and Einstein: Breaking Through the Reading Barrier.* (Illus. by Peggy Luks.) NY: Human Sciences, 1985. 64pp. $13.95; $5.95 (paper). 79-11387. ISBN 0-87705-388-X; 0-89885-185-8 (paper). C.I.P. ▶ EI,EA,JH

This is a story about Bobby, a nine-year-old boy who suffers from dyslexia. It is a sensitive account of a bright child who has managed to hide his inability to read through ingenious strategies but who is finally "caught" when he enters third grade and encounters more difficult assignments and a teacher insensitive to the nature of his problem. The story line provides an accurate account of the world of the dyslexic child, but unfortunately deals only briefly with how Bobby's condition is finally identified and treated.

Kuklin, Susan. *Thinking Big: The Story of a Young Dwarf.* (Illus.; photographs by the author.) NY: Lothrop, Lee & Shepard, 1986. 48pp. $10.25. 85-10425. ISBN 0-688-05826-4. C.I.P. ▶ EP,EI

A thoughtful and informative look at the life of an eight-year-old girl who is a dwarf. The text stresses the ways in which Jamie is like all children but also shows how she must cope with living in environments that are not designed for "little people." Kuklin's numerous excellent photographs show Jamie going about her daily activities. The problems of discrimination and teasing are not slighted. This book can be used by a parent or health-care professional with a physically challenged child, with children in a mainstreamed class, or with children who have questions about how it feels to be physically different. There is an epilogue that provides accurate facts about this medical condition and its treatment.

Levine, Edna S. *Lisa and Her Soundless World.* (Illus. by Gloria Kamen.) NY: Human Sciences, 1984. 32pp. $14.95 (paper). 73-14819. ISBN 0-89885-204-8 (paper). C.I.P. ▶ EI,EA,JH

Levine has successfully translated her professional expertise into an effective educational book for children on the subject of deafness. She introduces Lisa, an eight-year-old hearing-impaired child, and describes the ways Lisa was taught to communicate. Unlike many similar books, this one combines sensitive and accurate information with a writing style both entertaining and educationally appropriate for children, beginning at age eight.

Rosenberg, Maxine B. *My Friend Leslie: The Story of a Handicapped Child.* (Photographs by George Ancona.) NY: Lothrop, Lee & Shepard, 1983. 43pp. $9.50. 82-12734. ISBN 0-688-01690-1. C.I.P. ▶ K,EP

My Friend Leslie sensitizes children to the problem encountered by a handicapped child mainstreamed into a regular classroom. The story is about the friendship between Leslie, a kindergartner, and her friend Karin, and it explains Leslie's various handicaps in a realistic and sensitive manner. Although the prose seems both idealistic and stilted, the photography is excellent, capturing both the joy and trust of friendship and the frustrations of being nearly blind and hearing impaired. The book should be of great help to parents, teachers, and children who come in contact with the mainstreamed handicapped, particularly because the term "mainstream" is never used.

362.5–.8   Services for various demographic groups

See also 155.4 Child psychology; 306.7–.8 Relations of the sexes; marriage and family; 649.65 Sex education.

Anderson, Deborah, and Martha Finne. *Jason's Story: Going to a Foster Home.* (Illus. by Jeanette Swofford; a Child Abuse Bk.) Minneapolis: Dillon, 1986. 48pp. ea. $9.95 ea. 85-25414. ISBN 0-87518-324-7. Glossary; C.I.P. ▶ **EP,EI**

Neglect and the Police. 85-25379. ISBN 0-87518-323-9.

Margaret's Story: Sexual Abuse and Going to Court. 85-25417. ISBN 0-87518-320-4.

Michael's Story: Emotional Abuse and Working with a Counselor. 85-25400. ISBN 0-87518-322-0.

Robin's Story: Physical Abuse and Seeing the Doctor. 85-25383. ISBN 0-87518-321-2.

This series of five illustrated children's books is targeted toward and responsive to children caught in the family life problems of physical abuse, sexual abuse and court testimony, neglect, emotional abuse, and foster home placement. Each story begins with the main character presenting the crisis from his or her perspective and concludes with a successful resolution through outside intervention. The message throughout is, "It's not your fault." These books should allay many fears that children have regarding a worsening of their situation. Children's rights issues are explicated in an enlightening manner. A list is provided of the people who may be safely approached to intervene.

Girard, Linda Walvoord. *Adoption Is for Always.* (Illus. by Judith Friedman.) Niles, IL: Albert Whitman, 1986. 29pp. $10.25. 86-15843. ISBN 0-8075-0185-9. ▶ **K,EP,EI,EA,JH**

This excellent book with its beautiful drawings addresses the problems adopted children experience in coming to terms with their adoptive status. The author presents the story of Celia, now approximately age 6, who was adopted as a newborn through an agency. Celia's fears are shown in the story, as is her search for information and reassurances that adoption is permanent. Highly recommended for adoptive families, professionals, and the general public. This sensitive reference could be used in elementary through graduate classrooms.

Girard, Linda Walvoord. *Who Is a Stranger and What Should I Do?* (Illus. by Helen Cogancherry.) Niles, IL: Whitman, 1985. 32pp. $9.25. 84-17313. ISBN 0-8075-9014-2. C.I.P. ▶ **K,EP,EI**

In a didactic manner, this book presents to children the concept of strangers. Various settings and situations are presented with simple, straightforward suggestions of how to deal with them. Clear and potentially valuable rules are established. Girard offers ten speculative questions that allow children to apply the principles she advances. These ten items and the notes to parents are particularly useful and well done. Many useful illustrations.

Hickman, Martha Whitmore. *When Can Daddy Come Home?* (Illus. by Francis Livingston.) Nashville, TN: Abingdon, 1983. 40pp. $9.50. 82-22652. ISBN 0-687-44964-3. C.I.P. ▶ **EP,EI**

With large, bold type and attractive illustrations, this interesting, provocative book tells the story of a young boy whose father is imprisoned and the boy's reaction to this, as well as his friends' reactions. His plight is contrasted to that of a peer whose father is seriously ill. This is a warm story with a positive outcome that will provide a reassuring experience for a family in similar circumstances. Useful for parents, teachers, and counselors to help evoke feelings and prompt discussion.

Lindsay, Jeanne Warren. *Do I Have a Daddy? A Story About a Single-Parent Child.* (Illus. by DeeDee Upton Warr.) Buena Park, CA: Morning Glory Press, 1982. 44pp. $7.95. 82-81645. ISBN 0-930934-10-5. C.I.P. ▶ **K,EP**

The story of Erik, who has no father at home and never did have, provides a viable model for parents who must deal with a difficult and often embarrassing situation. The author's solution seems simple: tell the truth to your child in a nonjudgmental manner, leave the avenues of communications open, and provide appropriate substitute father figures. The illustrations leave room for parents who read the book to children to add words or to change the story to fit the circumstances of each family. The book emphasizes the value of discussing topics that are not easily talked about between parent and child and offers a pleasant, nonthreatening manner for doing so.

Meyer, Linda D. *Safety Zone: A Book Teaching Children Abduction Prevention Skills.* (Illus. by Marina Megale; foreword by John and Revé Walsh.) Edmonds, WA: Franklin Press, 1984. 30pp. $3.00 (paper). 84-080039. ISBN 0-9603516-8-X. ▶ **K,EP,EI,EA**

Safety Zone is designed to be used by parents and children together. Its central message is that informed children are safer children. The book's core pages delineate hypothetical situations that are intended to be read to 3- to 11-year-old children. After each situation is described, questions are asked to encourage discussion by children. Other sections present guidelines for parents to follow if their child is missing, ways to minimize the likelihood of a child being abducted, guidelines for community involvement, and a list of support organizations and books.

Stanek, Muriel. *My Mom Can't Read.* (Illus. by Jacqueline Rogers.) Niles, IL: Whitman, 1986. 32pp. $10.25. 86-1637. ISBN 0-8075-5343-3. C.I.P. ▶ **EP,EI**

An engaging and informative work of fiction that would help children in the primary grades recognize and deal with a situation where one or both of their parents cannot read. The story realistically portrays a little girl's confusion over her mother's avoidance of situations that require reading, then the joy they experience together as they both try to meet the challenge of learning to read. The black-and-white illustrations are detailed and beautifully drawn.

Vogel, Carole G., and Kathryn A. Goldner. *The Dangers of Strangers.* (Illus. by Lynette Schmidt.) Minneapolis: Dillon, 1983. 31pp. $10.95. 83-7174. ISBN 0-87518-253-4. C.I.P. ▶ **K,EP,EI**

This pioneering book seeks to prevent injury to naive youth, and it stresses the "No!" response to strangers. In addition, it reinforces children's trust in family and friends—a trust that is properly challenged by materials for older children who are subjected to abuse by parents and family friends. Recommended for use with young children, but other materials may be needed for balance between Erikson's life principle of trust and the realities of personal abuse by strangers and, indeed, by friends and family.

Watcher, Oralee. *Close to Home.* (Illus. by Jane Aaron.) NY: Scholastic, 1986. 48pp. $12.95; $5.95 (paper). 86-6671. ISBN 0-590-40330-3; 0-590-40331-1 (paper). Index; C.I.P. ▶ **EI,EA,JH**

This book, addressed directly to children, alerts them that sometimes they can be caught in a precarious situation and must decide quickly how to protect themselves. Four stories with colorful illustrations decribe children in difficult situations involving strangers or a divorced parent taking or inviting children to leave with them. Regrettably, all the abductors portrayed are male. Recommended for school-age children and caring adults concerned with helping children learn self-protection skills.

363.7 Environmental problems and protection

See also 333.79 Energy and energy resources; 551.46 Oceanography and underwater exploration; 574.5 Ecology of organisms.

Lafavore, Michael. *Radon: The Invisible Threat.* (Illus.) Emmaus, PA: Rodale, 1987. 256pp. $16.95; $12.95 (paper). 87-4829. ISBN 0-87857-697-5; 0-87857-712-2 (paper). Glossary; index; C.I.P. ▶ **EA,JH**

This very informative and well-written book on radon deals with its hazards, sources, dispersement, and corrective measures. It is well organized and clearly presents the technical issues without distortion. The description of radon and its hazardous aspects is well done, and balanced comparison of the risks from radon exposure with other experiences, such as smoking and chest x-rays, is given. The author also offers remedial actions to be followed should radon be detected. Appendices list especially helpful sources of governmental assistance and radon testing services. The book's only shortcoming is its redundancy in chapters seven and eight—most readers will become bored.

Pettigrew, Mark. *Radiation.* (Illus.; from the Science Today Series.) NY: Gloucester, 1986. 32pp. $10.40. 86-80075. ISBN 0-531-17023-3. Glossary; index. ▶ **EA,JH**

Half the pages of this short, attractive book on radiation are devoted to photographs and drawings, allowing fewer than 16 pages of text on the topic. The author emphasizes that radiation is everywhere and deals with the many types of radiation that can and can't be seen. Common effects of radiation on the human body are explored. The book briefly discusses many types of radiation, including heat, ultraviolet, and nuclear, and emphasizes their biological effects and uses, such as for carbon dating and treating cancer. The text is carefully written and accurate. The book even describes how to build a display model that shows how some types of radiation are absorbed.

Woods, Geraldine, and Harold Woods. *Pollution.* (Illus.) NY: Watts, 1985. 64pp. $9.40. 84-20982. ISBN 0-531-04916-7. Glossary; index; C.I.P. ▶ **EI,EA,JH**

Readers will be inspired by this well-written, well-illustrated volume that treats most instances of pollution, with examples ranging from the Cuyahoga River and Love Canal to Three Mile Island and Los Angeles smog. The conservation ethic is discussed with sufficient balance so that the frailty of "spaceship earth" is understood. However, the book does not cover noise, indoor air, or visual pollution, nor is the role of politics and citizen involvement in the issues addressed.

Science
Education

See also 507 Science: study and teaching; 510 Mathematics; 520.7 Astronomy: study and teaching; 530 Physics; 540 Chemistry; 550 Earth sciences; **Life Sciences** section; 580 Botanical sciences; 591 Zoology; **Technology** section; **Medicine** section.

Daughtry, Duanne. *What's Inside?* (Illus.) NY: Knopf, 1984. 26pp. $8.99. 83-19565. ISBN 0-394-86249-X. C.I.P. ▶ **K,EP**

Eleven pairs of photographs invite preschool and early-elementary grade readers and their parents or teachers to guess, discuss, then find out what is inside the object presented in the first photograph of each pair. Concepts of size, shape, and quantity could be easily developed through use of this well-illustrated, black-and-white picture book. Beyond that, understanding the concepts of inside and outside is vital to a child's ability to discriminate between what is self and what is not self.

Gillham, Bill, and Susan Hulme. *Let's Look for Opposites.* (Illus.; photographs by Jan Siegieda; from the Let's Look For Series.) NY: Coward-McCann, 1984. 22pp. $4.95. 83-24065. ISBN 0-698-20614-2. C.I.P. ▶ **K**

A pictorial description of opposites, such as full/empty, top/bottom, wet/dry, dirty/clean, and big/little, this book is a good tool to help youngsters acquire a visual understanding of the concept. The pictures are excellent, both in their clarity of illustrating the concept and within their paired sets. The paired pictures consistently maintain common elements and do not distract the learner from focusing on the critical distinguishing feature.

Kuntz, Margy. *Adventures in Earth Science: Process-Oriented Activities for Grades 4–6.* (Illus. by Bradley Dutsch; from the Doing Science: Adventures Series.) Belmont, CA: David S. Lake Publishers, 1987. 48pp. ea. $5.95 ea. ISBN 0-8224-2318-9. ▶ **EP,EI,EA**

Adventures in Life Science: Process-Oriented Activities for Grades 4–6. ISBN 0-8224-2317-0.

Adventures in Physical Science: Process-Oriented Activities for Grades 4–6. ISBN 0-8224-2319-7.

Lowery, Lawrence, and Carol Verbeeck. *Explorations in Earth Science: Process-Oriented Activities for Grades 1–3.* (From the Doing Science: Explorations Series.) ISBN 0-8224-2315-4.

Explorations in Life Science: Process-Oriented Activities for Grades 1–3. ISBN 0-8224-2314-6.

Explorations in Physical Science: Process-Oriented Activities for Grades 1–3. ISBN 0-8224-2316-2.

These workbooks for "doing science" consist of tear-out pages with permission for teachers to photocopy them for classroom distribution. A teacher's plan and discussion questions are provided for each lesson. Generally accurate and fairly complete, the workbooks cover many topics in earth science, life science, and physical science and come in two series, "Explorations" for grades one through three, and "Adventures" for grades four through six. The well-thought-out activities include taking measurements, making graphs, and contemplating Venn diagrams. Unfortunately, biological adaptation and geological time are discussed without mention of evolution. The series does a good job of exposing students to physical things and concepts without involving hazardous experiments.

Seguin-Fontes, Marthe. *If the Sea Were Sweet.* (Illus.; a Thinking Cap Bk.) NY: Larousse, 1984. 32pp. $6.95. ISBN 0-88332-436-9. ▶ **K,EP,EI**

This book shows young readers what imagination can do while it entertains through the poetic rhythm of the text and the creative illustrations. The idea of a sea made of sugar leads to such creative possibilities as gumdrop pebbles, raspberry fish, and iceberg birthday cakes. The author allows young minds to wander, then starts to pull them back to the realities of the sea as it is. One of the more creative and mind-expanding books written for children, *If the Sea Were Sweet* will stimulate children to stretch their minds while thoroughly enjoying themselves.

Seymour, Peter. *Colors.* (Illus.; a Turn & Learn Bk.) NY: Macmillan, 1984. 7pp. ea. $5.95 ea. ISBN 0-02-782080-7. ▶ **K,EP**

Numbers. ISBN 0-02-782090-4.

Opposites. ISBN 0-02-782130-7.

Playtime, Worktime. ISBN 0-02-782140-4.

Colors, Numbers, Opposites, and *Playtime, Worktime* are well constructed with colorful drawings and moving parts that appear reasonably durable. The movement mechanism is unique in that motion on one page places the tab in the start position on the next page. The books will aid in concept development, object identification, and pattern recognition. Could be used independently by first graders; preschool and kindergarten children will require assistance with the reading.

Spizman, Robyn Freedman. *Lollipop Grapes and Clothespin Critters: Quick, On-the-Spot Remedies for Restless Children, 2–10.* (Illus.) Reading, MA: Addison-Wesley, 1985. viii + 168pp. $5.95 (paper). 84-24548. ISBN 0-201-06497-9. Index; C.I.P. ▶ **K,EP,EI**

This outstanding book presents almost 400 activities for children and their parents. The activities—clearly labeled as to the age group to which they may appeal—are fun and will encourage meaningful interaction between children and their parents; many of them will also help children develop skills that will be reflected in positive school performance. For example, some encourage memory development, the ability to categorize, improvement of one's knowledge of the world, and small and large motor development. The bulk of materials required can be found in most households. Another interesting idea employed is division of activities according to where they might best be done— within the home or community, park, doctor's office, and so on.

Toney, Sara D., with Sherryl K. Kohr and Deborah Corsi. *Smithsonian Surprises: An Educational Activity Book.* (Illus.) Washington, DC: Smithsonian Institution, 1985. 96pp. $7.95 (paper). 85-600046. ISBN 0-87474-909-3 (paper). C.I.P. ▶ **EP,EI,EA,JH**

This "toy chest" contains projects that can easily be done by a six-year-old, as well as sprinkles of exotic information for the 18- to 80-year-old to discover. The fun-filled activities include word games, construction with paper, preparation of ice cream, and making a kite. The text is clear, concise, and not condescending. The photographs, drawings, and directions are excellent. The recipe format allows easy organization, and the more difficult activities are identified by a star.

Williams, Robert A., Robert E. Rockwell, and Elizabeth A. Sherwood. *Mudpies to Magnets: A Preschool Science Curriculum.* (Illus.) Mt. Rainier, MD: Gryphon House, 1987. 157pp. $12.95. 87-80528. ISBN 0-876-5911-28. ▶ **K**

The familiar science activities in this book are grouped into three curious categories: science center activities, building with science, and science for a crowd. All of the activities can be used for independent study, teacher demonstrations, or small-group study. The activities in the book are fun explorations to expand children's innate curiosity about the world.

371.42   Careers

Carter, Adam. *A Day in the Life of a Medical Detective.* (Illus.; photographs by Bob Duncan.) Mahwah, NJ: Troll, 1985. 32pp. ea. $9.75 ea.; $2.50 ea. (paper). 84-8851. ISBN 0-8167-0097-4; 0-8167-0098-2 (paper). ▶ **EP,EI,EA**

Paige, David. *A Day in the Life of a Librarian.* (Illus.; photographs by Michael Mauney.) 84-8552. ISBN 0-8167-0101-6; 0-8167-0102-4 (paper).

A Day in the Life of a Sports Therapist. (Illus.; photographs by Roger Ruhlin.) 84-2433. ISBN 0-8167-0099-0; 0-8167-0100-8 (paper).

A Day in the Life of a Zoo Veterinarian. (Illus.; photographs by Michael Mauney.) 84-6538. ISBN 0-8167-0095-8; 0-8167-0096-6 (paper).

The "Day in the Life" series provides an in-depth look at unusual and exciting occupations. Each of the four books realistically describes the long hours and demands usually associated with creative careers. The volume on the zoo veterinarian is informative, nonsexist, and sensitive to the issue of animal welfare. The other volumes are less satisfactory in choice of setting or focus. Photographs, although abundant, are often stilted by their posed nature. Given teacher guidance, however, the series could serve as good support material for career education units.

Kessel, Joyce K. *Careers in Dental Care.* (Illus.; photographs by Milton J. Blumenfeld; an Early Career Bk.) Minneapolis: Lerner, 1984. 36pp. $5.95. 83-25551. ISBN 0-8225-0345-X. C.I.P. ▶ **K,EP,EI,EA**

Careers in Dental Care contains simple descriptions of various dental specialties, as well as general dentistry, the dental auxiliary field, and the service industry. Oral pathology, dental research and education, and dental public health are not covered. Each page consists of a career description and accompanying photograph. Although the photographs are of good quality, they are not always well selected, falling short of truly indicating the nature of the specialty. However, this attractive little book would be useful as a focus for group discussion.

Millard, Reed, and the Editors of Science Book Associates. *Energy: New Shapes/New Careers.* (Illus.) NY: Messner, 1982. 192pp. $9.29. 82-12433. ISBN 0-671-42478-5. Glossary; index; C.I.P. ▶ **EA,JH**

This interesting, concisely written book provides students with an excellent source of background information and employment opportunities in the energy industry. The author examines careers that range from ceramic engineer to power plant operator—what type of work the job entails, the salary, and education or training necessary for employment. This career information is provided after a 100-page overview of the challenges that face the energy industry. Highly recommended for students, guidance counselors, and school and public libraries.

Sipiera, Paul P. *I Can Be a Geologist.* (Illus.; an I Can Be Bk.) Chicago: Childrens Press, 1986. 32pp. $10.60. 86-9598. ISBN 0-516-01897-3. Glossary; index; C.I.P. ▶ **EP,EI**

Here are two important messages about geologists: they are as varied as the different tools they use and as diverse as the products they produce, and they don't do their best work without some self-sacrifice and an ability to adapt to a technology-rich workplace. Using 37 up-to-date photographs and an economical narrative, Sipiera broadens stereotypical ideas about the profession. Many photographs have a strong sense of action. Covers earthquakes, volcanic, glacial, and planetary studies, petroleum and mineral prospecting, and satellite imagery analysis.

Mathematics and Physical Sciences

Erlanger, Ellen. *Isaac Asimov: Scientist and Storyteller.* (Illus.; from The Achievers series.) Minneapolis: Lerner, 1986. 56pp. $7.95. 86-10675. ISBN 0-8225-0482-0. Index; C.I.P. ▶ **EA,JH**

This brief biography of author-scientist Isaac Asimov lacks depth, but it is enlivened with a generous selection of interesting photographs of Asimov and numerous anecdotal accounts of his early life and career. Asimov's many writing achievements are explored. The book puts different stages of Asimov's career into historical perspective, detailing the world events that inevitably influenced or involved Asimov. The annotated bibliography includes those books by Asimov that are most suitable for a young audience.

Kruszelnicki, Karl. *Even Greater Movements in Science.* (Illus. by David Wales and Judy Calman.) Chicago: Chicago Review (distributor), 1986 (U.S. distribution). 95pp. $5.95 (paper). ISBN 0-908121-16-4 (paper). ▶ **EA,JH**

This attractive little paperback contains 28 radio scripts on scientific subjects. In 350 to 700 words, the scripts give intriguing snapshots of recent research. Because these scripts were written for radio, they are highly informal and sometimes humorous, providing a marked contrast to the usual short newspaper and magazine articles on scientific subjects. The striking illustrations by talented pen-and-ink artists dramatically illuminate this compilation. A gem for any student's or teacher's library.

Rahn, Joan Elma. *Holes.* (Illus. by the author.) Boston: Houghton Mifflin, 1984. 32pp. $9.95. ISBN 0-395-35389-0. ▶ **K,EP**

This brief lesson on holes is a good introduction to the larger issue of man and the environment. Eleven chapters describe holes—natural and man-made—as they serve various functions as diverse as passageways and information carriers (stencils). Written in a simple style, the book is appropriate for teachers who want to read a lesson to their kindergarten or primary grade students. Because of the vocabulary, only students who have well-developed reading abilities at the intermediate level could read the book for themselves.

500.1 Natural history

See also 574.5 Ecology of organisms.

Berenstain, Stan, and Jan Berenstain. *The Berenstain Bears' Nature Guide.* (Illus.) NY: Random House, 1984. 64pp. $3.95 (paper). 75-8070. ISBN 0-394-86602-9 (paper). C.I.P. ▶ **EI,EA**

The Berenstain bears describe "nature" along with other topics, such as animals, mammals, birds, reptiles, amphibians, fishes, insects, plants, and earth science. The illustrations are engaging and well done, and focus attention on the many interesting and accurate facts presented. This book should be on the shelf of every child's library. The facts in it could certainly be understood by most young children, and third and fourth graders should be able to read it easily.

Comstock, Anna Botsford. *Handbook of Nature Study.* (Illus.) Ithaca: Cornell University Press, 1986 (c. 1911, 1939, 1967; reprint). xxii + 887pp. $49.50; $19.50 (paper). 85-29144. ISBN 0-8014-1913-1; 0-8014-9384-6 (paper). Index; C.I.P. ▶ **EA,JH**

Where else but in this 3-lb., 900-page paperback can students find so many answers to their endless questions—about animals, plants, rocks and minerals, climate and weather, and about the skies at night—that is, about one's environment? First appearing in 1911, this popular natural history handbook has been republished dozens of times, for the most part with little change other than updating. Part one explains various ways to teach nature study at all levels, part two gives detailed information about our common animals, part three covers plants, and the final section discusses the earth and sky. The illustrations, many of them by talented nature photographers, are excellent.

Criswell, Susie Gwen. *Nature with Art: Classroom and Outdoor Art Activities with Natural History.* (Illus.; a Spectrum Bk.) Englewood Cliffs, NJ: Prentice-Hall, 1986. xiv + 146pp. $9.95 (paper). 85-31702. ISBN 0-13-610304-9 (paper), Index; C.I.P. ▶ **K,EP,EI,EA,JH**

Adults will find this book a delightful aid in helping children to explore and observe natural phenomena. For each topic, accurate and interesting facts and a related art or craft activity are presented. The simple activities require few materials and can be completed in a short time. Since the book is meant to be read by the adult, not the child, it can be geared to a wide range of ages. There are no experiments for children to carry out, and they are not asked to make scientific inquiries, but to look closely at nature. A treat for any adult who wants to encourage children to observe nature and its history through the use of arts and crafts.

501–502 Science: theory and techniques

Fredericks, Anthony D., Brad K. Cressman, and Robert D. Hassler. *The Science Discovery Book.* (Illus.) Glenview, IL: Scott, Foresman, 1987. xx + 59pp. $9.95. ISBN 0-673-18344-0. ▶ **EI,EA**

Designed for the teacher of grades four through six, *The Science Discovery Book* is a set of 42 activities or experiments to be conducted by students in small groups or pairs; the materials required are all readily available in the home and school. The activities are grouped into the areas of the life, physical, and earth sciences, and all use the basic methodology of science—measuring, observing, classifying, experimenting, and so on. The questions in the activities are meant to stimulate the students' curiosity and provide an opportunity for them to interact with the investigation and discovery processes.

Kramer, Stephen P. *How to Think Like a Scientist: Answering Questions by the Scientific Method.* (Illus. by Felicia Bond.) NY: Crowell, 1987. 44pp. $11.50. 85-43604. ISBN 0-690-04563-8. Index; C.I.P. ▶ **EA**

According to the author, to think like a scientist you must ask a question, gather information, form a hypothesis, test the hypothesis, and tell others what you have found. A strength of this book is its clarity. Good examples of how to design and conduct experiments based on daily experiences are presented. Fourth through sixth graders would probably benefit from the book's structured approach. The scope of the book is narrow, but in the absence of a better treatment of the topic, instructors could use the book as a reference. However, other examples and opinions on what constitutes scientific thinking should be offered to students.

Kumin, Maxine. *The Microscope.* (Illus. by Arnold Lobel.) NY: Harper & Row, 1984. 30pp. $9.95. 82-47728. ISBN 0-06-023523-3. C.I.P. ▶ **K,EP**

"That's how we got the microscope" is the last line of this children's poem about Anton von Leeuwenhoek, which originally appeared in 1809. This volume contains a historical note that points out that although Leeuwenhoek did not invent the microscope, he made 247 microscopes in his lifetime and saw many things that no one else had seen. Adults as well as children will enjoy this poem and its extraordinary illustrations.

Pringle, Laurence. *"The Earth Is Flat"—and Other Great Mistakes.* (Illus. by Steve Miller.) NY: Morrow, 1983. 72pp. $8.50. 83-7966. ISBN 0-688-02466-1. Index; C.I.P. ▶ **EI,EA**

This fun book contains the basic message, "to err is human." The first section is about ancient, mistaken notions, such as "the earth is flat." The second section highlights projects that went astray, including the leaning in the tower of Pisa. The third part is about misjudgments, such as the Edsel, and the fourth addresses such monumental errors as the sinking of the *Titanic*. The final section, "Taking a Chance," discusses the courage of Galileo and others who stood firm in their decidedly unpopular beliefs. Well illustrated and well written, this book is ideal supplemental classroom reading in many subjects, including science, history, and English.

Stangl, Jean. *The Tools of Science: Ideas and Activities for Guiding Young Scientists.* (Illus.) NY: Dodd, Mead, 1987. xii + 147pp. $16.95; $8.95 (paper). 86-29197. ISBN 0-396-08965-8; 0-396-08966-6 (paper). Index; C.I.P. ▶ **EI,EA,JH**

The activities are grouped under a different scientific principle in each chapter and demonstrate magnification, weight, time, light, temperature, electricity, and chemistry. The last section includes puzzles. All the activities use the basic methodology of science: observe, experiment, classify, and discover. In each chapter, Stangl lists the materials needed, explains the activity, and offers further ideas. A resource of ideas and activities for teaching scientific principles for teachers of grades three through eight to supplement the school's science curriculum.

Stwertka, Eve, and Albert Stwertka. *Make It Graphic! Drawing Graphs for Science and Social Studies Projects.* (Illus. by Carol Hillman; a Study Skills Bk.) NY: Messner, 1985. 64pp. $9.29. 84-22651. ISBN 0-671-54287-7. Index; C.I.P. ▶ **EA,JH**

Well written, with interesting and varied examples accompanied by clear illustrations. Well-chosen examples are followed by clear instruction on how to construct the type of graph being discussed. The types of graphs discussed are line graphs, bar graphs, pie charts, and pictographs. Chapters conclude with suggested problems that students would find interesting. An excellent addition to a classroom set of reference books or a school library for grades five to nine.

503 Science: dictionaries and encyclopedias

See also 030 General encyclopedic works; 507 Science: study and teaching.

Ackerman, Jerome J., et al. (Eds.). *The Raintree Illustrated Science Encyclopedia, Vols. 1–20.* (Illus.) Milwaukee: Raintree, 1984. viii + 96pp. (per vol.). $332.67 (set). 83-11030. ISBN 0-8172-2325-8 (set). Index; C.I.P. ▶ **EA,JH**

This impressive encyclopedia set is beautifully illustrated with many photographs, paintings, and charts. Some of the vocabulary may be daunting for younger students, but the relatively short length of the articles provides a comforting counterbalance. Schools with science projects will be interested in the suggested projects connected with a select number of entries. This detailed, comprehensive set will be helpful to patrons of small-to-medium-sized public libraries—not only students but adults who feel intimidated by what their children are learning in school and by the "explosion" of scientific knowledge.

Bishop, Cynthia, and Deborah Crowe (Eds.) *Science Fair Project Index, 1981– 1984.* Metuchen, NJ: Scarecrow, 1986. vi + 686pp. $47.50. 86-6571. ISBN 0-8108-1892-2. C.I.P. ▶ **EA,JH**

This second supplement to *Science Fair Project Index, 1960–1972* lists hundreds of science projects and experiments selected from more than 140 books, pamphlets, and science magazines published from 1981 through 1984. It is a welcome addition to any science collection and a must for those libraries serving science-fair enthusiasts. The emphasis is on actual projects, experiments, and techniques for displaying projects. The addition of more experiments on ribonucleic acid, comets, rockets, space biology, and computers makes this volume especially interesting and useful to students.

Brown, Peter Lancaster. *Astronomy.* (Illus.; from the World of Science Series.) NY: Facts On File, 1984. 64pp. ea. $9.95 ea. 84-1654. ISBN 0-87196-985-8. Glossary; index; C.I.P. ▶ **EA,JH**

Burton, Maurice. *Insects and Their Relatives.* ISBN 0-87196-986-6.

Cooper, Chris, and Jane Insley. *How Does It Work?* ISBN 0-8160-1066-8.

Cooper, Chris, and Tony Osman. *How Everyday Things Work.* ISBN 0-87196-988-2.

Fekete, Irene, and Jasmine Denyer. *Mathematics.* ISBN 0-87196-990-4.

Fekete, Irene, and Peter Dorrington Ward. *Your Body.* ISBN 0-87196-989-0.

Lambert, David, and Ralph Hardy. *Weather and Its Work.* ISBN 0-87196-987-4.

Lambert, David, and Jane Insley. *Great Discoveries and Inventions.* ISBN 0-8160-1062-5.

The books cited above are from a 25-volume encyclopedia set. Each of these volumes covers one major theme that is presented by topic and subtopic and deals mainly with highlights of the various themes. On each pair of pages, a brief but generally accurate essay deals with some aspect of the topic. Each book contains a two-page glossary and more that 120 illustrations, most of which are full color and quite well done. If users sought information on a specific theme, it is possible that the indices in these volumes could be sufficient to direct them to the appropriate pages. Overall, this series is attractive, and the materials do not seem to contain the potential to cause major misconceptions. The books should intrigue 8-to-12-year-olds with their colorful formats and interesting current topics, even though some of the anecdotes may be difficult. Children are likely to enjoy using the set in conjunction with school projects.

Hollyer, Belinda, Jennifer Justice, and John Paton. *How, Why, When, Where.* (Illus. by Collin and Moira Maclean.) NY: Arco, 1984. 224pp. $11.95. 84-2837. ISBN 0-668-06159-6. Index; C.I.P. ▶ **EA,JH**

This question-and-answer book is divided into four main sections: "How It Happened Long Ago," "Plants and Animals," "How Things Happen," and "People and Places." Although there is an extensive index, there is no table of contents. Each main section is divided into subsections that address two or three questions. It is not obvious just why these particular topics were selected, and there is little continuity from section to section, although the illustrations are attractive and supplement the written information nicely. Should not be used as a substitute for a more complete reference, but will be interesting reading for those looking for a compact source of facts about a wide variety of topics.

McCorry, Vivian (Ed.). *New Encyclopedia of Science,* 16 vols. (Illus.) Milwaukee: Raintree, 1985. 2,257pp. (total). $349.50 (set). ISBN 0-8172-5000-X. Index. ▶ **EA,JH**

Topics are current (to 1985) and are discussed in a familiar yet challenging vocabulary. Many of the discussions are several pages long and conclude with suggestions for experiments. The authors include such topics as quantum theory, metabolism, archeology, and short biographies of outstanding people in science. The index is adequate, and the cross references within the subject areas are sufficient. The photography, diagrams, and other art work are assets. Missing, but not critical for the intended readers, is a list of the contributing authors and a bibliography. On the whole, the *New Encyclopedia of Science* is a well-prepared resource for young readers, especially when compared with the other available encyclopedias of science.

Olney, Ross, and Patricia Olney. *How Long? To Go, to Grow, to Know.* (Illus. by R. W. Alley.) NY: Morrow, 1984. 40pp. $9.50. 83-13392. ISBN 0-688-02773-3. C.I.P. ▶ **EA,JH**

How Long provides the curious reader with a number of facts, many trivial. The illustrations are neither exciting nor boring, although some are cluttered. Very young readers will not understand many of the abstract concepts used;

despite its somewhat juvenile appearance, the book is really not suitable for students younger than 10 or 11. Older students will enjoy the facts, and the book is suitable for the fifth- to seventh-grade classroom as a reference for both students and teachers.

Owl Magazine, The Editors of. *Owl's Question & Answer Book #1: Answers to Questions Kids Ask About Birds, Cats, Bats, UFOs, and More.* (Illus.) Racine, WI: Western, 1983. 45pp. ea. $6.95 ea. 83-80459. ISBN 0-307-12450-9. Index. ▶ EI,EA

Owl's Question & Answer Book #2: Answers to Questions Kids Ask About Dinosaurs, Horses, Snakes, Space, and More. 83-80459. ISBN 0-307-12451-7.

Here is quality educational material that is also interesting. All questions that deal with the same topic are answered on the same page. Colorful illustrations and photographs supplement the questions and often help to explain the answers, which are usually clear, concise, and easily read by children. Occasionally, answers are simplified to the point of being misleading, and some questions are trivial. Overall, however, the books achieve their goal of educating while entertaining.

507 Science: study and teaching

See also 371.3 Methods of instruction.

Allison, Linda, and David Katz. *Gee, Wiz! How to Mix Art and Science; or, the Art of Thinking Scientifically.* (Illus. by Linda Allison; from the Brown Paper School Bk. Series.) Boston: Little, Brown, 1983. 128pp. $12.95; $7.70 (paper). 83-9834. ISBN 0-316-03444-4; 0-316-03445-2 (paper). C.I.P ▶ EA

Young people with inquisitive minds will find lots to think about in this new member of the Brown Paper School series. Cartoons, drawings, diagrams, and the text guide the reader through many kinds of experiments on subjects such as chromatography, bubbles, capillary action, properties of water, immiscible liquids, optical illusions, magnification, symmetry, balance, and kinetics. Most of the directions and explanations are clear, but a few of the diagrams are cramped and confusing. Could be used for fun at home or school science projects.

Arnold, Caroline. *Natural Resources: Fun, Facts, and Activities.* (Illus. by Penny Carter.) NY: Watts, 1985. 32pp. $9.40. 84-19598. ISBN 0-531-04898-5. Glossary; index; C.I.P. ▶ EI,EA

The simple projects for observing grass, wind, rocks, and so on should help upper-elementary children start thinking about their surroundings as resources. Only advanced students—in terms of intelligence and motivation—will be likely to do the projects alone. Understanding of such words as "water," "wood," and "land" will be broadened by the book's glossary, which contains resource-oriented definitions; however, the nontechnical vocabulary is sometimes a bit abstract and difficult. The poster art illustrations are sprightly.

Bank Street College Media Group. *Let's Explore the Seasons!: Science Activities for Grades 1 and 2.* (Illus. by Kyle Baker and Juan Suárez Botas; from the Barron's Bunny Book Series.) Woodbury, NY: Barron's, 1986. 64pp. $2.95. ISBN 0-8120-3625-5. ▶ EP,EI

Seasons! is a good attempt to fill the need for useful science materials for early elementary students. It is well written, and the colorful illustrations are useful in explaining and describing the different seasons. Although not a substitute for doing science experiments, the activities presented, which include games, punchouts, mazes, rhymes, puzzles, and stories, go a long way toward helping young children learn about the seasons. Children will love doing the activities, and teachers will welcome the ideas.

Berenstain, Stan, and Jan Berenstain. *The Berenstain Bears' Science Fair.* (Illus.) NY: Random House, 1984. 64pp. $3.95 (paper). 76-8121. ISBN 0-394-86603-7 (paper). C.I.P. ▶ **EI,EA**

The authors have done an excellent job with a difficult topic seldom covered in children's books: science fairs and experiments that children can build and enter in their school's science fair competition. The authors explain various science concepts that the children could use—for example, simple machines, states of matter, and energy. Excellent illustrations and ideas abound. This book should be in the room of every science teacher or in every school library as an important resource for educators, teachers, and students alike.

Brown, Robert J. *200 Illustrated Science Experiments for Children.* (Illus.) Blue Ridge Summit, PA: Tab, 1987. vi + 186pp. $7.95 (paper). 86-23196. ISBN 0-8306-2825-8 (paper). Index; C.I.P. ▶ **EP,EI,EA**

These experiments are very simple and contain pictures to explain the scientific processes going on. Most use common household materials, and the author explains the experimental process and the reasoning behind each experiment. Some of the experiments might be considered tricks, while others are projects to build. The scientific principles covered concern air, sound, water, light, heat, vibration, mechanics, biology, chemistry, electricity, and magnetism. Parents, youth clubs, and teachers looking for fun activities to pique student interest will find them here.

Children's Television Workshop. *3-2-1 Contact Activity Book, No. 1.* (Illus.) Morristown, NJ: Silver Burdett, 1984. 64pp. 3.00 (paper). ISBN 0-382-06802-5 (paper). ▶ **EI,EA**

This colorful activity book focuses on many different areas of science. The activities include crossword puzzles and word hunts; mazes; pictures and descriptions of animals and inventions; true-false quizzes; directions for folding and flying paper airplanes and boomerangs and for making color wheels and star wheels; finding butterflies and shapes that match; illusions and writing with invisible ink; descriptions of real and imaginary animals with a challenge to discover which is which; and matching animals with the foods they eat. The activities will keep even 12-year-old children occupied for many hours, providing them and those younger with opportunities to develop and use thinking skills and to learn science concepts while having fun.

Cobb, Vicki. *The Secret Life of Hardware: A Science Experiment Book.* (Illus. by Bill Morrison.) NY: Lippincott, 1982. 90pp. $9.50. 81-48607. ISBN 0-397-31999-1. Index; C.I.P. ▶ **EA,JH**

The basic chemistry and physics of hardware-store items are described, and instructions are given for home investigations to find out more about them. The investigations range from simple observations to fairly complicated examinations of cleaners, polishers, paints, glues, hand tools, and electricity. More explicit safety precautions are desirable concerning toxic chemicals, and readers should have been warned never to experiment with 110-volt line current. Nevertheless, the writing is clear, and welcome touches of humor are introduced by the author and the illustrator.

DeCloux, Tina, and Rosanne Werges. *Tina's Science Notebook.* (Illus. by Tara Sullivan.) Mill Valley, CA: Symbiosis, 1985. 50pp. $10.95. ▶ **K,EP**

DeCloux and Werges introduce young children to their first experiences in science through many hands-on activities. Ten chapters cover such diverse topics as seasons, seeds, predators and prey, Christmas pine cones, gravity, whales, eggs, and birds. Some concepts are briefly explored while others are covered in more depth. Most needed materials are provided as tear sheets at the end of each lesson; other equipment is available in most schools. Useful as a supplemental teaching tool with its valid hands-on activities and clear, accurate information.

Gardner, Robert. *Energy Projects for Young Scientists.* (Illus.; from the Projects for Young Scientists Series.) NY: Watts, 1987. 127pp. $11.90. 86-32433. ISBN 0-531-10338-2. Index; C.I.P ▶ **JH**

This is an excellent resource for junior and senior high school students preparing energy projects for science fairs. In addition to emphasizing safety, the author provides an accurate definition of the scientific method of research, including observation, hypotheses, theories, and experimental checks. Important references and data are presented.

Gardner, Robert. *Ideas for Science Projects.* (Illus.; from the Experimental Science Series.) NY: Watts, 1986. 143pp. $10.90. 87-9238. ISBN 0-531-10246-7. Index; C.I.P. ▶ **EA,JH**

This book is a real treasure. It is designed to help the student find a science project idea that is a scientific investigation. Gardner does not give cookbook directions and does not tell results. He briefly introduces a subject and then proposes questions that leave the student *wondering*. More than 100 topics are touched on from all areas of science, and most could be investigated using items a student could get without much difficulty. A good resource for teachers looking for ideas for designing unique, probing labs and a great gift for young students who are interested in science and who like trying things themselves.

Gardner, Robert. *Science Around the House.* (Illus. by Frank Cecala.) NY: Messner, 1985. 123pp. $9.29. 85-8873. ISBN 0-671-54663-5. Index; C.I.P. ▶ **EI,EA,JH**

This book demonstrates that, through simple experiments using items found in every household, young people can do fascinating experiments involving the elementary laws of physics and some basic principles of chemistry. It challenges youngsters to see for themselves how the laws of Newton, Galileo, and others were discovered. The black-and-white illustrations are adequate guides to effective laboratory work. No conclusions are given for the experiments—a strong plus in motivating the experimenter to complete them. Teachers can use the book effectively to motivate their students.

Goodwin, Peter H. *Engineering Projects for Young Scientists.* (Illus.; from the Projects for Young Scientists Series.) NY: Watts, 1987. 126pp. $11.90. 86-32528. ISBN 0-531-10339-0. Index; C.I.P. ▶ **JH**

An excellent, accurate introduction to many basic physics concepts, engineering design methods, and the scientific research procedure. The author is a physics teacher with the outstanding ability to present some difficult physical concepts in an interesting, "fun" style. Practical problems and science fair projects based on engineering and physics concepts are described. Subject areas include force, friction, motion, sound waves, light waves, and mechanics.

Hillerman, Anne. *Done in the Sun: Solar Projects for Children.* (Illus. by Mina Yamashita.) Santa Fe, NM: Suntone Press, 1983. 31pp. $6.95 (paper). 83-638. ISBN 0-86534-018-8 (paper). C.I.P. ▶ **EP,EI**

The text of this quality book consists of experiments and activities through which children can learn about the effects of our sun and have a good time in the process. The text is clear, well organized, and easy to read. The experiments should hold young readers' interest, and the illustrations supplement the text well. However, the experiments do not always explain the practical applications of the sun's effects, and cover only a limited area of the vast importance of the sun. Despite minor weaknesses, the book is still a good learning tool and a prime example of how much fun learning can be.

Kerrod, Robin. *All Around.* (Illus.; from the Science Alive Series.) Morristown, NJ: Silver Burdett, 1987. 56pp. ea. $12.96 ea. 86-31428. ISBN 0-382-09424-7. Glossary; index; C.I.P. ▶ **EI,EA**

Changing Things. 86-29627. ISBN 0-382-09421-2.

Living Things. 86-29785. ISBN 0-382-09423-9.

Moving Things. 86-29651. ISBN 0-382-09422-0.

Topics from the life, earth, and physical sciences include plants and animals, earth, air, weather, stars, planets, energy, light and color, forces, electricity, and solids, liquids, and gases. The content is accurate and the illustrations and photographs are excellent, but the processes of science are generally neglected in the text. The importance of science in our society is given adequate treatment, and the activities section of each volume should aid the reader in developing an understanding of the inquiring nature of science. The activities illustrate the major concepts covered in the text and can be completed by students with common materials.

Lai, Elizabeth, and Monica Schwalbe (Eds.). *Explorations 1: Science Activities for Young People.* (Illus.) Toronto: Canadian Stage & Arts Publications, 1983. 74pp. $9.95 (paper). ISBN 0-919952-19-4 (paper). Index. ▶ **JH**

This activity book contains a good variety and sampling of interesting experiments for young people. The instructional format for each of the activities begins with exploration and procedures followed by development of the particular topic more fully. The material is accurate, clear, organized, and complete, with black-and-white illustrations. Well adapted for junior-high students, it could be used alone or to supplement a textbook and other exploration activities.

Levenson, Elaine. *Teaching Children About Science: Ideas and Activities Every Teacher and Parent Can Use.* (Illus. by Deborah A. Coulombe; a Spectrum Bk.) Englewood Cliffs, NJ: Prentice-Hall, 1985. x + 214pp. $14.95 (paper). 85-9583. ISBN 0-13-891730-2 (paper). Index; C.I.P. ▶ **EP,EI,EA**

This generously sized science book of activities for youngsters is directed to parents and teachers with suggestions on how they should use it. The activities are organized around several topics, including magnetism, static electricity, sound, light, air and water, weather, and earth science, and are arranged sequentially from the concrete to the abstract. The book's major objective is to develop skills and intellectual thought; each topic is thoroughly explored. A very good resource book for all elementary science programs, and to extend learning in the home.

Mitgutsch, Ali. *From Sea to Salt.* (Illus, by the author; a Start to Finish Bk.) Minneapolis: Carolrhoda, 1985. 24pp. $5.95. 84-17466. ISBN 0-87614-232-3. C.I.P. ▶ **K,EP,EI**

Although its vocabulary is not on the kindergarten level, this book can be read to kindergarten children and be used to start discussions about how one obtains salt through various desalinization processes. The concepts of evaporation and brine are clearly explained, and the charming, colorful drawings add interest. Using the book's information, a class could experiment with obtaining salt from brine through evaporation, both by drying salt water and by boiling it, so that the concepts would be even clearer.

National Science Teachers Association. *Science Fairs and Projects.* (Illus.) Washington, DC: National Science Teachers Assn., 1984. 40pp. $6.00 (paper). ISBN 0-87355-030-7 (paper). ▶ **K,EP,EI,EA,JH**

A compilation of articles from *Science and Children* and *Science Teacher* magazines (1966–1984) written by teachers to assist teachers, students, and parents through the science project season. All of the articles are relevant and well written, and 16 of them are designed to facilitate planning, development, completion, exhibition, and reporting of projects. They encourage students to use experimental designs, generate hypotheses, record observations, and draw inferences.

Ontario Science Centre Staff. *Scienceworks: An Ontario Science Centre Book of Experiments.* (Illus. by Tina Holdcroft.) Reading, MA: Addison-Wesley, 1986. 86pp. $7.95 (paper). ISBN 0-201-16780-8 (paper). ▶ **EA,JH**

A fascinating collection of do-it-yourself science demonstrations for young beginners. Each demonstration has detailed instructions and an explanation of the phenomenon being explored. Only inexpensive and readily available materials are used. Instructive and amusing black-and-white drawings accompany the discussion of each activity. More than 60 activities span the gamut of science, from simple tricks involving physical principles to explorations of human physiological reactions. Although many of the effects studied are familiar, they are treated in a provocative and engaging way that should attract and hold a child's interest.

Simon, Seymour. *Soap Bubble Magic.* (Illus. by Stella Ormai.) NY: Lothrop, Lee & Shepard, 1985. 48pp. $10.25. 84-4432. ISBN 0-688-02684-2. C.I.P. ▶ **K,EP**

Interracial, nonsexist illustrations accompany a text designed to encourage children to think for themselves and experiment to find the answers to their questions. The experiments use simple, inexpensive home or schoolroom materials, some of them made by the child. The instructions include appropriate safety warnings and ways to avoid making a mess. The systematic approach will help a child to develop an organized approach to satisfying curiosity.

Smith, Norman F. *How Fast Do Your Oysters Grow? Investigate and Discover*

Through Science Projects. (Illus.) NY: Messner, 1982. 95pp. $8.79. 82-60649. ISBN 0-671-42629-X. Index; C.I.P. ▶ **EA,JH**

Smith introduces students to the scientific method by describing the stages of a well-planned scientific investigation. He explains how to select the topic, plan the investigation, choose the equipment and test procedures, record and graph data, draw conclusions, and report results. The book's brevity and excellent figures, which show items such as data collection and graphs, should appeal to students. Any student who is contemplating a science project should read this book.

Smithsonian Family Learning Project. *Science Activity Book.* (Illus.) NY: GMG, 1987. 96pp. $8.95 (paper). ISBN 0-939456-51-6 (paper). ▶ **K,EP,EI,EA,JH**

This book for parents to use with their children begins by introducing a brief rationale and question-asking strategy. Then 20 easy-to-complete science activities focus on "doing science." Each is relatively nondirective, allowing for innovation and experimentation. Ranging from fingerprinting to making cheese, these activities invite participation, can be done easily and inexpensively at home, and should lead to success. Though designed for home use, they would also work at school. Highly recommended.

Taylor, Ron. *Projects.* (Illus.; from The World of Science Series.) NY: Facts On File, 1986. 64pp. $9.95. 84-1654. ISBN 0-8160-1076-5. Glossary; index; C.I.P. ▶ **EA,JH**

Projects presents science as an exciting hands-on activity. Activities abound in astronomy, earth science, fossil and mineral collections, chemistry, physics, magnetism, electricity, botany, zoology, and ecology. There is a section on science puzzles, optical illusions, and building a computer. Excellent illustrations assist in understanding of science concepts introduced. This volume presents science as a vivid and stimulating experience.

510 Mathematics

Dadas, John E. *Simple Math Programs in BASIC for Your Personal Computer.* (Illus.) NY: Arco, 1985. x + 118pp. $7.95 (paper). 85-20153. ISBN 0-668-05992-3 (paper). C.I.P. ▶ **EA,JH**

Dadas designed this book to help personal computer users learn and practice simple mathematical and typing skills. The book contains complete listings of BASIC programs that can be used on the TRS-80 or IBM PC. (Minor changes are required to run the programs on the Apple II series, Commodore, IBM PCjr, Atari, TI-99/4A, and Timex 1000/Sinclair ZX 81.) Programs include addition, subtraction, multiplication, and division operations, ratios and proportions, and geometry.

Hague, Kathleen. *Numbears: A Counting Book.* (Illus. by Michael Hague.) NY: Henry Holt, 1986. 32pp. $10.45. 85-27006. ISBN 0-03-007194-1. C.I.P. ▶ **K,EP**

This well-illustrated book shows an aspect of early number counting, one to twelve, in a reader about cuddly bears. The technical quality of the illustrations is superb, and there is basic instructional value in the counting concept. Parents will enjoy showing the pretty pictures to their young children while reinforcing counting at the same time.

Haney, Jan P. *Calculators.* (Illus.; a Look Inside Bk.) Milwaukee: Raintree, 1985. 47pp. $11.64. 84-9791. ISBN 0-8172-1407-0. Glossary; index; C.I.P. ▶ EA,JH

Covers the history of calculators, integrated circuits, chip technology, programming, adding/subtracting, and binary code descriptions. The last section describes interesting and entertaining games that can be played with calculators. This book is well done and should be quite informative and useful to readers of any age.

Keedy, M.L., and Marvin L. Bittinger. *Introductory Algebra, 4th edition.* (Illus.) Reading, MA: Addison-Wesley, 1983. xv + 582pp. $20.95 (paper). 82-13771. ISBN 0-201-14785-8 (paper). Index; C.I.P. ▶ JH

This fourth edition of a well-established workbook is supplemented by a computerized test bank that can be run on TRS-80 or Apple II microcomputers. Videotapes and audio cassettes, as well as an instructor's guide, answer booklet, student's guide, and placement test, are available. Covers linear and quadratic expressions, their manipulation, and the solution of equations and inequalities. The illustrations are good, and there is a wealth of exercises, both routine and challenging. Beyond the attraction of microcomputer support, this is a substantial textbook.

Mori, Tuyosi. *Socrates and the Three Little Pigs.* (Illus. by Mitsumasa Anno.) NY: Philomel (Putnam), 1986. 44pp. $13.95. 85-21564. ISBN 0-399-21310-4. C.I.P. ▶ EI,EA

In this entertaining book that combines learning with fun, Socrates is the name of the wolf in the story of the three little pigs. He is trying to determine in which of five houses he is most likely to find one or more of the pigs. The outstanding illustrations show all the possibilities, and the reader discovers the basic ideas that underlie combinations, permutations, probabilities, odds, and making choices.

Schwartz, David M. *How Much Is a Million?* (Illus. by Steven Kellogg.) NY: Lothrop, Lee & Shepard, 1985. 40pp. $15.00. 84-5736. ISBN 0-688-04049-7. C.I.P. ▶ K,EP

Beautifully detailed, full-page illustrations and a brief text explain the concepts of million, billion, and trillion to young readers. A skeptical adult reader may examine the author's calculations supporting each statement, which are at the end of the book. Young children will enjoy looking at the wonderful pictures first and pondering the large numbers next. An alert teacher will help them to explore other ways of thinking about bigness.

Slocum, Jerry, and Jack Botermans. *Puzzles Old & New: How to Make and Solve Them.* (Illus.) The Netherlands: Plenary and ADM International (dist. by Univ. of Washington Press), 1986. 160pp. $19.95. ISBN 0-295-96350-6. ▶ EI,EA,JH

A tantalizing encyclopedia of puzzles of every degree of difficulty and form: one-piece puzzles, exquisitely elegant Japanese puzzle boxes, intricate silver rings from Turkey, ancient puzzles of unknown origin, and some of disputed origin, such as the recent Rubik/Nichols's cube. Puzzle experts will find new puzzles, excellent photographs of long forgotten but highly prized ones, and superb construction details. But do not expect a complete exposé of all the secrets!

Stenmark, Jean Kerr, Virginia Thompson, and Ruth Cossey. *Family Math.* (Illus.) Berkeley: Lawrence Hall of Science, University of California, 1986. 319pp. $15.00. Index. ▶ **EP,EI,EA,JH**

Let's put the fun back into mathematics, involve parents in children's math work, and focus on children and parents learning math together—that's the implicit message of this very good activity book. Much of the book is gleaned from earlier math education publications, many of which are classics. The emphasis on problem solving and strategies, as well as on hints about how to use hands-on material, adds up to an extremely helpful learning process for both student and parent. The activities that accompany each major topic— recreations, puzzles, games, real-life applications, discoveries—are meant to be fun and to make student and parent more aware, confident, and encouraged.

Weiss, Sol. *Helping Your Child with Math.* (Illus.) NY: Prentice-Hall, 1986. vii + 280pp. $19.95. 85-11151. ISBN 0-13-386343-3. Index; C.I.P. ▶ **EI,EA,JH**

Weiss's book is addressed specifically to parents. The basic skills, from addition and fractions to decimals and geometry, are all covered. In each chapter, Weiss explains the concept and offers specific and commonsense strategies, exercises, and applicable games. He also covers problem solving and addresses the use of computers and calculators. Although there are not enough exercises in each chapter for full mastery of each concept, this is an excellent supplement to classroom texts.

520　Astronomy

Anno, Mitsumasa. *Anno's Sundial.* (Illus.) NY: Philomel, 1985 (released in the U.S., 1987). 30pp. $16.95. 86-91447. ISBN 0-399-21374-0. C.I.P. ▶ **EA,JH**

Anno has tackled a difficult subject in a stunningly attractive manner. Pop-up models emerging from colorful backgrounds engage the reader and allow scientific concepts to come alive. Students cannot help but try to construct their own sundials using the many accurate and helpful suggestions. While the book is expensive for its size, the purchaser is more than repaid by hours of fun and instruction in the art, both scientific and otherwise, of sundial construction. All middle-school libraries should possess this book because teachers of earth and space science can engage their students' attention by using the many models in its pages.

Couper, Heather, and Nigel Henbest. *Astronomy.* (Illus.) NY: Watts, 1983. 38pp. $9.90. 83-50112. ISBN 0-531-04651-6. Glossary; index. ▶ **EI,EA**

If an elementary school library or a town library needed one book to introduce children to astronomy, this would be a good choice. It is short but filled with basic facts presented in a reasonably easy-to-read format. There are many colorful illustrations, mostly reproduced from original watercolors. The emphasis is on the earth and this solar system, with only passing attention given to stars, galaxies, nebulae, and so forth.

Lampton, Christopher. *Astronomy: From Copernicus to the Space Telescope.* (Illus.; a First Bk.) NY: Watts, 1987. 96pp. $9.90. 86-23436. ISBN 0-531-10300-5. Glossary; index; C.I.P. ▶ **EA,JH**

Contributors to the science of astronomy are covered clearly and in enough detail for the reader to understand why a particular person or theory is historically noteworthy. Scientific discoveries are carefully placed within their historical and social context so the reader can understand the relationship of ideas to each other and to the environment from which they came. Diagrams elucidate the text, and historical photographs and drawings of the astronomers add an extra dimension of reality to the discussion. This is an exciting introduction, for it weds the theoretical astronomer to the observational astronomer in all of us.

Moché, Dinah L. *Astronomy Today.* (Illus. by Harry McNaught; from the Library of Knowledge Series.) NY: Random House, 1982. 96pp. $6.95 (paper). 82-5211. ISBN 0-394-84423-8 (paper). Index; C.I.P. ▶ **EA**

A well-organized and abundantly illustrated introduction to current astronomical topics. The book guides the reader through the elementary concepts of night and day to the tools used by astronomers. Descriptions of the planets include fascinating historical stories and legends that detail the planets' physical relationships with the sun and the earth. In addition to color illustrations of the planets' topographical features, the book contains drawings of the "robot explorers" that have collected scientific data gathered by the Mariner, Pioneer, and Voyager space probes.

520.7   Astronomy: study and teaching

See also 371.3 Methods of instruction.

Berger, Melvin. *Star Gazing, Comet Tracking, and Sky Mapping.* (Illus. by William Negron.) NY: Putnam's, 1985. 80pp. $7.99. 84-8302. ISBN 0-399-61211-4. Index; C.I.P. ▶ **EI,EA,JH**

This elegant and useful book about naked-eye astronomy features star charts for each month, which highlight the 30 constellations visible from the United States. The myths and stories about the constellations and their stars are told along with excellent instructions for best viewing. Careful directions are also included for making an astrolabe and for many other interesting naked-eye projects, including looking for comets and observing meteors, reporting sightings to appropriate scientific organizations, and making latitude-specific star charts. Recommended as a source of activities for elementary and junior-high teachers and for anyone who wants to learn to see the skies with a minimum of equipment and a maximum of pleasure.

Branley, Franklyn M. *What Makes Day and Night, revised edition.* (Illus. by Arthur Corros; a Let's-Read-and-Find-Out Science Bk.) NY: Crowell (Harper & Row), 1986. 32pp. $11.95; $3.95 (paper). 85-47903. ISBN 0-690-04523-9. C.I.P. ▶ **K,EP**

This small book is amply illustrated with large drawings in color, making it appealing to beginning readers and to younger children who like to have someone read to them. The vocabulary is simple enough for a primary grade child to understand, with little adult assistance, that the earth spins and that this spinning results in day and night. Young readers should find the book and activities interesting, and nonreaders will enjoy the colorful illustrations.

Couper, Heather, and Nigel Henbest. *Telescopes and Observatories.* (Illus.; a Space Scientist Bk.) NY: Watts, 1987. 32pp. $10.90. 86-51415. ISBN 0-531-10361-7. Glossary; index. ▶ **EA**

Telescopes and Observatories jumps all over the electromagnetic spectrum, creating some confusion as the reader moves from chapter to chapter. The authors deserve commendation for limiting their book to the subjects of what observatories are and how they work; it would have been very easy for them to get sidetracked into discussions of discoveries and to only partially cover the main topic. This book also contains a very good discussion of the Hubble Space Telescope and charge-coupled devices (CCDs).

Dickinson, Terence. *Exploring the Night Sky: The Equinox Astronomy Guide for Beginners.* (Illus. by John Bianchi.) Scarborough, Ontario: Camden House, 1987. 72pp. $15.95; $9.95 (paper). ISBN 0-920656-64-1; 0-920656-66-8 (paper). Glossary; index. ▶ **EA,JH**

A good introduction to astronomy for young readers. The first section takes one on a voyage from earth to the far realm of superclusters of galaxies. The author wisely offers only a little unsupported speculation about the unknowns of our universe, and he makes a significant effort to point out our inability to understand the physical nature of many of these celestial objects due to our lack of firsthand observation and the incomprehensible vastness of the subject. The final section guides the reader in personally viewing the night sky and locating constellations as well as selected stars, clusters, and planets from the Northern Hemisphere.

Hamer, Martyn. *The Night Sky.* (Illus.; An Easy-Read Fact Bk.) NY: Watts, 1983. 32pp. $8.90. ISBN 0-531-04619-2. Glossary; index. ▶ **EA,JH**

Accurate, informative, well written, and well illustrated, this book can be used for various purposes that range from a resource for a bright ten-year-old to a quick read for an adult who wishes to obtain a rudimentary but accurate understanding of observational astronomy. The excellent illustrations enhance the book's value immensely.

Lampton, Christopher. *The Space Telescope.* (Illus.; a First Bk.) NY: Watts, 1987. 70pp. $9.90. 86-23351. ISBN 0-531-10221-1. Index; C.I.P. ▶ **EA**

An excellent treatment of the theory, design, background of, and future plans for the Hubble space telescope. The text manages to be fairly complete in its scope and is well illustrated. It begins with a brief treatment of astronomical history, moves to present-day telescopes, then spells out the requirements for a space-based telescope. Lampton handles the presentation of the contruction and operation of the Hubble telescope well and describes in some detail the plans for research involving it.

Raymo, Chet. *365 Starry Nights: An Introduction to Astronomy for Every Night of the Year.* (Illus. by the author.) Englewood Cliffs, NJ: Prentice-Hall, 1982. xi + 225pp. $21.95; $12.95 (paper). 82-7511. ISBN 0-13-920520-9; 0-13-920512-8 (paper). Glossary; C.I.P. ▶ **EA,JH**

A novel presentation of elementary descriptive astronomy offered in a year-round sequence of daily readings. The readings feature the celestial phenomena that are visible in the early evening in the mid-latitudes of the northern hemisphere at the times of the year appropriate to the months given for each of the readings. Raymo develops students' familiarity with the naked-eye appearance of the constellations. However, no mathematics is included, the solar system is neglected, and little of the underlying science behind what we see is presented. The pages are brimming with diagrams and constellation sketches along with excellent supporting descriptions.

Simon, Seymour. *Look to the Night Sky: An Introduction to Star Watching.* (Illus.; a Puffin Bk.) NY: Penguin, 1983. 87pp. $3.95 (paper). 79-1329. ISBN 0-14-049185-6 (paper). Index. ▶ **EA,JH**

This introduction to the joys of stargazing is an observational primer rather than an elementary astronomy textbook. The excellent overview of the night sky as a naked-eye observatory covers the hourly drift of the stars, the seasonal progression of the constellations, and the perils of light pollution. Succeeding chapters describe the major constellations, the moon, planets, comets, and meteors. Clear and concise throughout; especially handy simple sky maps illustrate the use of pointer stars as celestial signposts.

Snowden, Sheila. *The Young Astronomer.* (Illus. by Martin Newton.) Tulsa, OK: Educational Development Corp., 1983. 32pp. $7.95; $4.95 (paper). ISBN 0-86020-652-1; 0-86020-651-3 (paper). Index. ▶ **EA,JH**

The reader gets an excellent overview of the universe and learns practical steps for observations with the unaided eye, binoculars, and small telescopes. The colorful illustrations are appealing, scientifically accurate, and instructive. Subjects covered include choosing equipment, motions in the night sky, constellations, the life stories of stars, gaseous nebulae, the planets, the sun and eclipses, and comets and meteors. (Scant coverage of the "new" astronomy, which is concerned with the wavelength ranges outside the visual.) A fine first reference book and guide.

523.1 Universe

Adler, David A. *Hyperspace! Facts and Fun from All over the Universe.* (Illus. by Fred Winkowski.) NY: Viking, 1982. 72pp. $10.95; $4.95 (paper). 81-70404. ISBN 0-670-38908-0; 0-670-05117-9 (paper). C.I.P. ▶ **EA,JH**

Adler introduces young readers to our solar system and outer space. He describes each planet and provides its temperature, composition, atmosphere, speed of revolution, and number of moons. The historical background of space exploration is traced from Yuri Gagarin's initial flight in 1961. The word puzzles, space codes, mathematical problems, riddles, and space games will whet readers' appetites. The text is accurate and clearly written and will appeal to young readers.

Couper, Heather, and Nigel Henbest. *Galaxies and Quasars.* (Illus: from the Space Scientist Series.) NY: Watts, 1986. 32pp. $10.90. 86-50351. ISBN 0-531-10265-3. Glossary; index. ▶ **EA,JH**

This volume explores the universe, beginning with our "star city," the Milky Way. The types and distances of other galaxies, the "scale of space," and modern astronomical tools/techniques are then explained, allowing readers to go on to discover mysterious quasars and the expanding universe. A clever "spotter's guide," resembling a spiral-bound logbook, explains how and where to observe some of these objects. Projects range from simple (naked-eye viewing) to ambitious (needing a telescope). The writing is lively, although the vocabulary is often sophisticated, and more actual photographs, rather than paintings, should have been used. Recommended for all students beginning the study of astronomy.

Darling, David J. *The Galaxies: Cities of Stars.* (Illus. by Jeannette Swofford; from the Discovering Our Universe Series.) Minneapolis: Dillon, 1985. 64pp. $9.95 ea. 84-23092. ISBN 0-87518-285-2. Index; C.I.P. ▶ **EA,JH**

The New Astronomy: An Ever-Changing Universe. 72pp. 84-23083. ISBN 0-87518-288-7.

Other Worlds: Is There Life Out There? 63pp. 84-23069. ISBN 0-87518-287-9.

The Stars: From Birth to Black Hole. 64pp. 84-23067. ISBN 0-87518-284-4.

The Universe: Past, Present, and Future. 55pp. 84-23068. ISBN 0-87518-286-0.

The typeface and general design of the five books in this series are appropriate for upper-elementary students, but the concepts and vocabulary will challenge even junior-high students. Each volume contains roughly 20 pages of text with 50 new vocabulary words, 20 pages of pictures—mostly high-quality photographs—a glossary, appendices of activities and amateur astronomical groups, and an index. Of special interest to young readers, each volume begins with a list of short facts and questions and answers about astronomy. Overall, the volumes are well organized and fill a gap in what has previously been available in astronomy books for young readers. However, by trying to be comprehensive, the author has introduced virtually all of modern astronomy at a rate of about one new idea per sentence. Thus, no depth of explanation is possible.

Jaspersohn, William. *How the Universe Began.* (Illus. by Anthony Accardo.) NY: Watts, 1985. 48pp. $9.90. 85-10545. ISBN 0-531-10032-4. C.I.P. ▶ **EI,EA**

This first book of a series about the universe and early life on earth is clearly written, using simple terms to discuss the big-bang model of how the universe began. Brief descriptions of the formation of stars, the nine planets, and the solar system are included. This well-written book presents the text in verse-like form for easy, quick reading. Black-and-white illustrations complement the written material.

Ridpath, Ian. *Space.* (Illus.; from the Silver Burdett Color Library Series.) Morristown, NJ: Silver Burdett, 1983. 49pp. $14.00. 83-50389. ISBN 0-382-06726-6. ▶ **EA,JH**

A fascinating book in its use of color, wonderful photographs and sketches, and layout. Each topic is laid out on facing pages, with little text on each page; most of the pages are devoted to illustrations and descriptions of the topic. This book covers the gamut of what you might want to know about space: the sun and stars, the moon and planets, archaeoastronomy, galaxies, rockets, the search for extraterrestrials, and uses of space.

523.2–.4 Solar system

Barrett, N.S. *Night Sky.* (Illus.; from the Picture Library Series.) NY: Watts, 1985. 32pp. ea. $9.40 ea. 85-50158. ISBN 0-531-10004-9. Glossary; index; C.I.P. ▶ **EP,EI**

Planets. 85-50159. ISBN 0-531-10005-7.

Sun & Stars. 85-50161. ISBN 0-531-10007-3.

These little books provide an attractive, visual way to capture the interest of primary grade children and to introduce them to the world of astronomy. The large-print text provides accurate information supporting the illustrations (about 60 percent of the text area), and a surprisingly large number of ideas are mentioned. Browsing will give children a taste of the topic and, one hopes, motivation to seek further information. *Planets* presents vignettes of each of the planets and mentions asteroids but ignores comets and meteorites, the other solar-system objects. *Night Sky* covers telescopes, the moon, planets, comets, meteorites, stars, and galaxies. The descriptions are very short, however, and the two constellation charts, which show the sky as seen from the north and south poles, are useless for children trying to find any of them in the night sky. *Sun & Stars*, a useful book, contains a nice diagram of the life cycle of stars, and color photographs of star clusters and galaxies. The big bang, the birth and death of stars, and black holes are all mentioned. Unfortunately, the book does not warn children never to look directly at the sun.

Boase, Wendy. *Space Voyager.* (Illus.) NY: Little Simon (Simon & Schuster), 1984. 31pp. $5.95. ISBN 0-671-50765-6. ▶ **EI,EA**

This book uses an imaginary spacecraft trip to explore the planets in our solar system. Chock full of interesting facts, it points out the similarities and differences among the planets. The book's main weakness is that it concentrates on facts about each individual planet while ignoring the all-important sun and its relationship to the planets, as well as the relationship of the planets to each other. Despite its simplistic approach, it's a fun book that should appeal to young readers and serve as an excellent classroom supplement for an elementary science curriculum.

Branley, Franklyn M. *Mysteries of the Satellites.* (Illus.; diagrams by Sally J. Bensusen; from the Mysteries of the Universe Series.) NY: Lodestar (Dutton), 1986. viii + 72pp. $11.95. 85-20770. ISBN 0-525-67176-5. Index; C.I.P. ▶ **EI,EA**

Mysteries of the Satellites deals with the natural satellites of the planets. The information is as up to date as possible, and presented on a level that young readers can understand. The book should be included in all libraries for young people as a scientifically current reference for information about the satellites.

Branley, Franklyn M. *Saturn: The Spectacular Planet.* (Illus. by Leonard Kessler.) NY: Crowell, 1983. 57pp. $11.95. 81-43890. ISBN 0-690-04213-2. Index; C.I.P. ▶ **EI,EA,JH**

This brief discussion of Saturn, its ring system, and its moons begins with naked-eye and telescope observations and culminates with information from the Pioneer and Voyager missions. The black-and-white illustrations include both sketches and photographs, and are effectively incorporated into the text. The author is careful to avoid leading the reader to accept certain explanations of Saturnian structures—such as the rings—when alternative theories abound. The message is that science doesn't always know—a good lesson for elementary school children to learn.

Branley, Franklyn M. *What the Moon Is Like.* (Illus. by True Kelley; a Let's-Read-and-Find-Out Science Bk.) NY: Crowell, 1986. 32pp. $11.50. 85-47904. ISBN 0-690-04511-5. (Also available from Harper & Row as a Harper Trophy paperback. $3.95. ISBN 0-06-445-052-X). C.I.P. ▶ **EI,EA**

The text, drawings, and photographs of this interesting book are designed to stimulate questions and discussion about the moon and the Apollo lunar landings. The book is primarily intended for third to fifth graders, but even kindergarteners will enjoy having it read to them.

Couper, Heather, and Nigel Henbest. *The Moon.* (Illus; from the Space Scientist Series.) NY: Watts, 1986. 32pp. $10.90. 86-50350. ISBN 0-531-10266-1. Glossary; index. ▶ **EA**

This book may help young readers learn not only the basics about the moon, but a bit about ongoing debates as well. After contrasting the earth and moon in a variety of ways, the authors provide a fairly standard treatment of the moon's phases, tides, and eclipses (even librations). Results from both Soviet and U.S. moon probes are covered well, though briefly. Probably the best example illustrating the processes of science is discussion of the three leading theories of the moon's origin (still unsettled). While more care and accuracy should have gone into this book's production, it still contains a good summary of current knowledge about earth's nearest neighbor in space.

Kerrod, Robin. *Stars and Planets.* (Illus. by Ron Jobson.) NY: Arco, 1984. 125pp. $6.95 (paper). 84-70796. ISBN 0-668-06263-0 (paper). Glossary; index. ▶ **EA,JH**

This attractive paperback is both an informative guide and a colorful and authoritative introduction to astronomy. It is loaded with color photographs, drawings, diagrams, and charts, including 18 pages of star maps and eight pages of lunar charts. The discussions of each subject within the 30 "chapters" are necessarily brief; however, this book should stimulate anyone curious about the nature and wonders of the universe.

Simon, Seymour. *Jupiter.* (Illus.) NY: Morrow, 1985. 32pp. ea. $11.75 ea. 85-2922. ISBN 0-688-05796-9. C.I.P. ▶ **EI**

Saturn. 85-2995. ISBN 0-688-05798-5.

More than a dozen of the incredibly beautiful and exciting pictures taken by Voyagers 1 and 2 of the planets Jupiter and Saturn and their satellites are reproduced. The accompanying text is clearly written and accurate but fairly routine; information similarly presented can be found in other children's books but without the extraordinary photographs. Unfortunately, the type is too large; older children may assume the book is for younger children when, in fact, the text is just right for them and too advanced for younger children.

Simon, Seymour. *The Moon.* (Illus.) NY: Four Winds Press, 1984. 32pp. $10.95. 83-11707. ISBN 0-590-07883-6. C.I.P. ▶ **K,EP,EI**

A nice summary of some basic facts about the moon and the Apollo missions. The book accurately describes, in simple, declarative sentences, the surface of the moon and some of the investigations there by the astronauts. Striking black-and-white photographs often cover a full page.

Williams, Geoffrey T., and Dennis F. Regan. *Adventures in the Solar System: Planetron and Me.* (Illus. by Borje Svensson.) Los Angeles: Price/Stern/Sloan, 1986. 64pp. $7.95 (includes cassette). ISBN 0-8431-1552-1. ▶ **EI,EA**

This book combines an interesting adventure story with recent data concerning the solar system. Willy, a little boy, is whisked away by his new-found toy and friend, Planetron, to get a first-hand view of the solar system. Planetary information, such as temperature, composition, length of day, and surface gravity, is provided in inset boxes. The data and the visual depictions of the sun and the planets are accurate and reflect the most recent findings. Also, the story line lends itself well to integrating scientific information about the solar system into the dialogue.

523.6   Comets

Branley, Franklyn M. *Halley: Comet 1986.* (Diagrams by Sally J. Bensusen.) NY: Lodestar Books (dist. by Dutton), 1983. 83pp. $10.95. 82-9919. ISBN 0-525-66780-6. Index; C.I.P.   ▶ **EA,JH**

This good, concise, and accurate account of comets in general and Halley's in particular begins with a historical review of the sightings of Halley's comet and the earthly events attributed to these sightings, then gives a brief description of the theory of how comets work, discusses their possible origins, and describes famous comets from the past. The final two chapters deal with Halley's return in 1986, and describe the activities of the International Halley Watch. Short, well written, nontechnical, and interesting. The illustrations are clear and simple, and a short bibliography of nontechnical information sources is provided.

Hamer, Martyn. *Comets.* (Illus., an Easy-Read Fact Bk.) NY: Watts. 1984. 32pp. $9.40. 83-51585. ISBN 0-531-03779-7. Glossary; index.   ▶ **EA**

The vocabulary in this thorough presentation of comets is fairly sophisticated. Many words may be quite difficult for the young reader to pronounce; unfortunately, no phonetic spellings are included. Each page of text has a corresponding page containing an illustration or photograph, and there are clarifying, written explanations of the illustrations and photographs. Because of its technical nature and sophisticated vocabulary, it could be a useful classroom tool for the study of outer space.

Krupp, E.C. *The Comet and You.* (Illus. by Robin Rector Krupp.) NY: Macmillan, 1985. 48pp. $12.95. 84-20152. ISBN 0-02-751250-9.   ▶ **EI,EA**

Despite its somewhat misleading title, *The Comet and You* contains more information about our scientific knowledge of comets than conjectures about the influence of comets on our health and general well being. It is well endowed with analogies to help young readers. The composition of the nucleus, the gases that form the tail, and the effects of the solar wind on the nucleus of comets are explained very simply. The black-and-white illustrations are quite well done and convey much more of the excitement of comet studies than the text, which is sometimes dry. Will not go out of date even after Halley's Comet has left.

Petty, Kate. *Comets.* (Illus. by Mike Saunders; from the First Library Series.) NY: Watts, 1985. 32pp. $9.40. 85-50511. ISBN 0-531-10024-3. Index.   ▶ **K,EP**

The format of *Comets* is like that of most young children's nonfiction books—pictures on each page accompanied by a simple text. Here, the illustrations create a feeling for an outer space of black sky and twinkling stars. The text asks several questions and answers them, as well as briefly introducing what a comet is and its place in outer space. Should appeal to beginning readers as well as preschoolers, since it provides an exciting glimpse of one of the fascinations of outer space.

523.7–.8 Sun and stars

Brandt, Keith. *Sun.* (Illus. by Lynn Sweat; from the Venture into Reading Series.) Mahwah, NJ: Troll, 1985. 32pp. $7.59; $1.95 (paper). 84-2715. ISBN 0-8167-0190-3; 0-8167-0191-1 (paper). C.I.P. ▶ **EI,EA**

Large, sometimes whimsical, full-color cartoons or paintings illustrate the subject matter at each turn of the page. The type is large enough for third-grade readers and detailed enough to interest slower readers in grades six and seven. Compressed here are virtually all the basic concepts about the sun that can be taught to elementary students. The short, explicit sentences describe food chains, the solar system, galaxies, events on and in the sun itself, the sun's rays, effect of the sun on the earth's atmosphere, eclipses, and domestic uses for solar energy. Accurate, clear, and well organized.

Couper, Heather, and Nigel Henbest. *The Sun.* (Illus.; from the Space Scientist Series.) NY: Watts, 1986. 32pp. $10.40. 85-51135. ISBN 0-531-10055-3. Glossary; index. ▶ **EA,JH**

This accurate, well-written, well-illustrated book describes the major points in our current knowledge of the sun. Brief descriptions of the causes of day, night, and the seasons open the book. The interior and surface layers of the sun are described, as are sunspots, solar magnetism, flares, and the corona. A map of total eclipses for the 1990s is included. One strong point is the book's clear statements regarding the dangers of observing the sun directly. Projects for readers include how to make a sundial and how to observe sunspots and partial solar eclipses by projection.

Lampton, Christopher. *The Sun.* (Illus.; a First Bk.) NY: Watts, 1982. 71pp. $7.90. 81-21991. ISBN 0-531-04390-8. Glossary; index; C.I.P. ▶ **EA,JH**

Accurately discusses the formation, composition, and movement of the sun and explains the importance of this star to life on earth. After an outline of the relationship of ancient civilizations to the sun, the author describes its structure, violent nature as illustrated by solar flares and sunspots, and how it affects the weather on earth. Photographs enhance the text.

Petty, Kate. *The Sun.* (Illus. by Mike Saunders; from the First Library Series.) NY: Watts, 1985. 32pp. $9.40. 85-50512. ISBN 0-531-10027-8. Index. ▶ **K,EP**

Here, the young reader is given an introduction to the sun and its mysteries, composition, and importance in our lives. The illustrations are colorful and lifelike, especially the illustration of what the inside of the sun looks like. The "Look Back and Find" section at the end presents questions and answers paired with pictures from the text. Some questions are not answered, encouraging the reader to look back and find the answer in the body of the text.

Simon, Seymour. *Stars.* (Illus.) NY: Morrow, 1986. 32pp. $13.00. 85-32012. ISBN 0-688-05855-8. ▶ **EI,EA,JH**

Nebulas, red giants, white and black dwarfs, black holes, pulsars, quasars, and galaxies are described, and many are pictured here. However, the level of abstraction of both pictures and text exceeds that of Simon's books on the various planets and the sun. *Stars* includes outstanding photographs from various observatories and astronomical research centers, but it also includes diagrams and renderings that lack the drama and clarity of photographs. Many new words are introduced and explained in the text, but with varying levels of success. However, description of the stages through which a star ages is among the best in astronomy books for children.

Simon, Seymour. *The Sun.* (Illus.) NY: Morrow, 1986. 30pp. $13.00. 85-32018. ISBN 0-688-05857-4. C.I.P. ▶ **EP,EI**

A vivid, dramatic portrait of the sun. The book's extraordinary visual and textual introduction imparts a sense of the grandeur and power of this most important star. The NASA color photographs stand on their own without labels or other descriptors. Simon makes clear several difficult concepts such as the size of the sun, its distance from the earth, and how the sun burns without extinguishing itself. His book can be read for its picture-book value, with the text adding whatever the younger reader can grasp. For older children, the text will enhance the visual, giving a beautiful portrait of our sun.

530 Physics

See also 621 Applied physics.

Ardley, Neil, and Eric Laithwaite (Series Consultant). *Force and Strength.* (Illus.; an Action Science Bk.) NY: Watts, 1984. 32pp. $9.90. 83-51443. ISBN 0-531-03777-0. Index. ▶ **EA**

Section topics include strength and weakness, strong structures, forces in balance, center of gravity, fun with forces, increasing forces, pulleys, and pressure power. Each section contains experiments with instructions, cautions, and explanations. The equipment used comes from common household items. Well written, well illustrated, and well bound; use of this book requires understanding of intangibles, numbers, and measurement.

Dank, Milton. *Albert Einstein.* (Illus.) NY: Watts, 1983. 122pp. $8.90. 82-23853. ISBN 0-531-04587-0. Index; C.I.P. ▶ **EA,JH**

In addition to presenting a straightforward account of Einstein's life and contributions, Dank provides valuable supplements: a list of books for further reading and the appendices that introduce readers to the classical and relativistic concepts of space and time. The archival photographs of Einstein that are included are particularly enjoyable. A professional, pleasant biography that exhibits an obvious appreciation for its subject.

Gaskin, Carol. *Journey to the Center of the Atom!* (Illus. by Walter P. Martishius; from the Explorer Series.) NY: Scholastic, 1987. 128pp. $2.25. ISBN 0-590-40336-2. ▶ **EA,JH**

Journey to the Center of the Atom has three outstanding attributes: the scientific knowledge presented is accurate and concise; the story is entertaining; and the mystery-adventure novel approach adds a unique twist by allowing multiple endings. The book demands an adequate understanding of powers of ten as the reader and Professor Parton are reduced in size to discover the true nature of quarks as the basic building blocks of all materials in the universe. This book could excite young people about the atom, subatomic particles, and the nature of high-energy physics. Highly recommended.

Laithwaite, Eric. *Force: The Power Behind Movement.* (Illus.; from the Science at Work Series.) NY: Watts, 1986. 32pp. $10.90. 85-52047. ISBN 0-531-10181-9. Glossary; index. ▶ **EA,JH**

Looks at the basic principles of science and engineering in such a manner that readers might discover their practical applications in the machines and buildings around them. Two-page layouts are devoted to such aspects of force as gravity, inertia, friction, wheels, levers and gears, inclined planes, and expansion. Each topic is accompanied by exceptional photographs and sketches. This readable little volume should prove a valuable supplement for the science room at the upper-elementary level and a quick reference for the independent reader in junior high school.

Rabiza, F., and trans. by Alexander Repyev. *Space Adventures in Your Home.* (Illus.) Moscow: Mir Publishers (dist. by Imported Publications), 1983. 192pp. $5.95. ISBN 0-8285-2785-7. ▶ **EI,EA,JH**

This collection of experiments in physics to be done with apparatus constructed by the experimenter is suitable for classroom use with younger children and may be performed by older children with suitable supervision. The experiments, covering mechanics, heat, and optics, will teach a great deal of physics, and by constructing the apparatus, children will learn various elementary mechanical, electrical, and craft skills. A return to the worthwhile, simple, and sound way that science was taught 40 years ago.

Vowles, Andrew. *The EDC Book of Amazing Experiments You Can Do at Home.* (Illus. by Tim O'Halloran and Terry Wink.) Tulsa: EDC Publishing, 1985. 32pp. $5.95 (paper). ISBN 0-88110-197-4 (paper). ▶ **EI,EA**

These experiments cover 16 different physical science topics: current and static electricity, electromagnets, magnifying lenses, upside-down images, sinking and floating, color, center of gravity, action and reaction, inertia, chemical reaction, heat flow, pulleys, ice to water to ice, air pressure, and sound. Brief biographies of Bell, Edison, Cavendish, Einstein, Fleming, Franklin, Newton, Pasteur, and Orville and Wilbur Wright are offered. The directions and many illustrations will provide safe and successful experiments. A useful resource for the parent or teacher illustrating science principles and a good supplement for special students or for small-group activities in the classroom.

Whyman, Kathryn. *Forces in Action.* (Illus.; from the Science Today Series.) NY: Gloucester, 1986. 32pp. $10.40. 85-81665. ISBN 0-531-17021-7. Glossary; index. ▶ **EI,EA**

Whyman's slender, delightful, and beautifully illustrated *Forces in Action* covers natural and man-directed forces. After the uncontrolled forces of wind, water, and gravity are introduced, the concepts of pushing, pulling, and twisting are illustrated, and friction is introduced. The so-called elementary machines—inclined plane, pulley, and lever—are described and examples are given.

531–536 Mechanics; sound; heat
See also 621 Applied physics.

Ardley, Neil, and Eric Laithwaite (Series Consultant). *Making Things Move.* (Illus.; an Action Science Bk.) NY: Watts, 1984. 32pp. ea. $9.90 ea. 83-50854. ISBN 0-531-03771-1. Index. ▶ **EI, EA**

Sound and Music. 83-51442. ISBN 0-531-03776-2.

Section topics in *Making Things Move* include force, air pressure, and magnets, gravity, the force of friction, action and reaction, motors on the move, momentum, inertia, rotation and oscillation, centrifugal force, gyroscopes, and acceleration. Each section contains experiments using common household items with instructions, cautions, and explanations. Section topics in *Sound and Music* include producing sound, hearing sound, penetrating sounds, transmitting sounds, amplifying sounds, pitch, sound reflections, speed of sound, and musical sounds. The musical sounds section discusses instruments based on strings, reeds, tubes, diaphragms, and horns; it also covers harmonics. Experiments use common household items and are adequately explained. Both of these well-written, well-illustrated volumes require readers to understand intangibles, numbers, and measurement.

Kettelkamp, Larry. *The Magic of Sound, revised edition.* (Illus. by Anthony Kramer.) NY: Morrow, 1982. 80pp. $8.50. 82-6510. ISBN 0-688-01492-5. Index; C.I.P. ▶ **EI,EA**

Sound, its propagation through a material, its production and reproduction, and its uses in industry and medicine are clearly and simply described. The book's four chapters are well organized and are filled with good experiments to illustrate the various aspects of sound. All but one of the suggested experiments can be done without adult supervision or assistance. The techniques of sound reproduction of records or tape cassettes are clearly presented through illustrations. Similarly, explanations of how some common means of communication work will also interest young readers.

Santrey, Laurence. *Heat.* (Illus. by Lloyd Birmingham; from the Venture into Reading Series.) Mahwah, NJ: Troll, 1985. 32pp. ea. $7.59 ea.; $1.95 ea. (paper). 84-2711. ISBN 0-8167-0306-X; 0-8167-0307-8 (paper). C.I.P. ▶ **EI**

Magnets. (Illus. by Joseph Veno.) 84-2597. ISBN 0-8167-0140-7; 0-8167-0141-5 (paper).

Heat successfully introduces thermodynamics to the mid-elementary reader. It begins with an engaging experiment to show that "heat," in common parlance, is a relative concept. This leads to a discussion of thermometers. Heat is defined and the laws of thermodynamics are given. The book teaches that heat moves—by conduction, convection and radiation—and that it changes matter at the chemical level, in the basic functions of our bodies. *Magnets* describes magnetism as a mystery. After some history and definitions, polarity is introduced, and the absence of magnetism is ascribed to the disorder of molecules (which are not defined). Oersted's and Faraday's work showing the relationship of electricity to magnetism leads to a discussion of electromagnetism and its application in lifting, synchrotrons (termed atom smashers), and dynamos. This volume in the Venture into Reading Series does not mention the recent discovery that some animals carry magnets and may use magnetism to navigate.

Ward, Alan. *Experimenting with Surface Tension and Bubbles.* (Illus. by Zena Flax.) London: Batsford/Dyrad (dist. by David & Charles), 1985. 48pp. $12.95. ISBN 0-8521-9621-0. Index. ▶ **EA,JH**

The book begins with a brief description of surface tension and gives directions for fun activities that illustrate that phenomenon. Each activity's black-and-white line drawings give a general idea of the equipment or apparatus involved. Teachers could use these activities as attention-catchers in science classes, but those with minimal science background will not find the additional information they may need if their students begin to ask questions about what is happening or why. For those who agree that children should have fun with science and should be able to explore, this book is ideal for personal or classroom libraries.

537 Electricity

See also 621. 381 Electronic engineering and computers.

Ardley, Neil, and Eric Laithwaite (Series Consultant). *Discovering Electricity.* (Illus.; an Action Science Bk.) NY: Watts, 1984. 32pp. $9.90. 83-50853. ISBN 0-531-03770-3. Index. ▶ **EI,EA**

Topics covered include electric charge, electrical effects, batteries, currents, switches, resistors, series and parallel connections, heating and lighting, and electricity and water. The section on electrical effects discusses static electricity and lightning; another covers alternating and direct current, charge, currents, electrons, electric fields, lightning, static electricity, and voltage. Each section contains experiments with instructions, examples (possibly including a caution), and explanations. The equipment usually comes from common household items. Well written, illustrated, and bound, the book uses no math; however, it does require that the reader understand intangibles.

Brandt, Keith. *Electricity.* (Illus. by Chuck Harriton; from the Venture into Reading Series.) Mahwah, NJ: Troll, 1985. 32pp. $7.59; $1.95 (paper). 84-2705. ISBN 0-8167-0198-9; 0-8167-0199-7 (paper). C.I.P. ▶ **EI**

Through a logical and elementary presentation on electricity, this book defines electricity as an action. The author discusses atoms and subatomic particles to show that electricity is the movement of electrons. Franklin's lightning experiment is cited, but there is no mention of the personal hazard that was involved. Oersted's discovery that electricity produces magnetism and Faraday's that magnets in motion induce currents are also discussed, as are batteries. The attractive illustrations are more decorative than instructive.

Cooper, Alan. *Electricity.* (Illus; from the Visual Science Series.) Morristown, NJ: Silver Burdett, 1983. 48pp. $13.00. 83-50223. ISBN 0-382-06715-0. Glossary; index. ▶ **JH**

This well-done and interesting text, with liberal illustrations, presents the world of electricity and magnetism. The coverage of each topic is much like an entry in an encyclopedia. The figures are well done, and the photographs are well chosen and current (to 1982). A generous list of references for additional reading is provided, as well as a list of dates and events in the history of electricity. This "miniencyclopedia" on 20 topics in electricity and magnetism is particularly suitable for young readers who have experience with the subject—others would probably find the text difficult to understand.

Vogt, Gregory. *Electricity and Magnetism.* (Illus.; a First Bk.) NY: Watts, 1985. viii + 86pp. $9.40. 85-10565. ISBN 0-531-10038-3. Glossary; index; C.I.P. ▶ **EA, JH**

The author does a good job of reviving some of the mysteries of these fundamental forces of nature that have fascinated inquiring minds for centuries. Vogt reviews the historical development of our understanding of magnetism and its related phenomenon, electricity, clearly showing how one scientist builds on the discoveries of another to advance the frontier of scientific knowledge. He does a good job of explaining the fundamentals in fairly easy-to-understand terms. The book's strongest point is its many interesting experiments in the fundamentals of electricity and magnetism, which should prove both educational and fun. Somewhat lacking in explanatory diagrams, however.

Whyman, Kathryn. *Electricity and Magnetism.* (Illus.; from the Science Today Series.) NY: Gloucester, 1986. 32pp. $10.40. 85-81664. ISBN 0-531-17020-9. Glossary; index. ▶ **EI,EA**

In *Electricity and Magnetism*, Whyman introduces an important field of applied science to young readers. She deals with natural and man-made electricity, how it is conveyed from place to place, permanent and electromagnets, and some applications of electromagnetism. The language is reasonably simple, and the book is attractively illustrated.

540 Chemistry

See also **Manufacturing Technologies** section.

Cobb, Vicki. *Chemically Active! Experiments You Can Do at Home.* (Illus. by Theo Cobb.) NY: Lippincott, 1985. 154pp. $11.50. 83-49490. ISBN 0-397-32079-5. Index; C.I.P. ▶ **EI,EA,JH**

This interesting and thoughtful introduction to chemistry for elementary and junior-high students is presented as a series of laboratory experiments followed by an explanation of chemical theory. The experiments, designed to introduce concepts such as the nature of matter, chemical reactions, and electrical aspects of matter, vary from simple to somewhat sophisticated, giving students a choice. All necessary materials are readily available, and directions are given for required equipment. Safety suggestions are also provided.

Mebane, Robert C., and Thomas R. Rybolt. *Adventures with Atoms and Molecules, Book II: Chemistry Experiments for Young People.* (Illus.) Hillside, NJ: Enslow, 1987. 96pp. $13.95. 85-10177. ISBN 0-89490-164-8. Index; C.I.P. ▶ **EA,JH**

This book of chemistry experiments is accessible to sixth graders but is also an excellent reference for teacher demonstrations for grade levels from about third grade on. The student reader will get a better understanding of molecular theory with adult help, but many bright children will learn a great deal by reading and doing the experiments on their own. The title of each experiment asks a question that states the purpose of the experiment, and each investigation involves common items found in the home or school. The experiments are simple and fun and clearly demonstrate the principle under consideration and the processes of science. Also useful in college laboratory courses designed for elementary education majors.

Sabin, Louis. *Marie Curie.* (Illus. by Allan Eitzen; from the Venture into Reading Series.) Mahwah, NJ: Troll, 1985. 32pp. $7.59; $1.95 (paper). 84-2654. ISBN 0-8167-0162-8; 0-8167-0163-6 (paper). C.I.P. ▶ **EI,EA**

Marie Curie discusses the life and work of Marie and Pierre Curie, who discovered radioactivity and polonium and radium, two radioactive elements that have been of great value to medical science. It was the Curies' work that led to much of our current understanding of the structure of atoms. The dramatic story of their lives will hold the attention of all young readers.

550 Earth sciences
See also 371.42 Careers.

Bains, Rae. *Rocks and Minerals.* (Illus. by Richard Maccabe; from the Venture into Reading Series.) Mahwah, NJ: Troll, 1985. 32pp. $7.59; $1.95 (paper). 84-8644. ISBN 0-8167-0186-5; 0-8167-0187-3 (paper). C.I.P. ▶ **EI,EA**

This book discusses the three major classes of rocks, then clarifies what a mineral is for children or anyone who would like a quick and simple explanation. The two-page color drawing of a volcano and the accompanying text should be particularly helpful to curious young readers. Rocks from each major class that can be easily illustrated and described are included.

Challand, Helen. *Activities in the Earth Sciences.* (Illus. by Len Meents.) Chicago: Childrens Press, 1982. 93pp. $7.95. 82-9444. ISBN 0-516-00506-5. Index; C.I.P. ▶ **EA,JH**

Challand provides readers with 78 simple activities that demonstrate earth science concepts in geology, astronomy, and meteorology. All can be easily accomplished by students, and most require readily available materials. Each activity is described in three or four paragraphs. Although the activities provided are found in other sources, their compilation into a single volume provides teachers with a valuable and ready reference for suggesting projects for class demonstrations.

Fradin, Dennis Brindell. *Disaster! Floods.* (Illus.; from the Disaster Series.) Chicago: Childrens Press, 1982. 64pp. ea. $7.50 ea. 82-9402. ISBN 0-516-00856-0. Glossary; index; C.I.P. ▶ **EA**

Disaster! Fires. 81-9404. ISBN 0-516-00855-2.

Disaster! Hurricanes. 81-38553. ISBN 0-516-00852-8.

Disaster! Tornadoes. 81-12277. ISBN 0-516-00854-4.

This attractive, well-illustrated series provides vivid descriptions of some major disasters. The emphasis is on first-hand, human-interest accounts. Hurricane, flood, and tornado forecasting and early warning systems are discussed, as are fire and flood prevention. Safety precautions are covered. Each book includes a long list of famous American and foreign disasters, and no major errors of fact were noted. Useful collateral reading for upper elementary and lower junior-high school students.

Langley, Andrew. *Under the Ground.* (Illus.) NY: Bookwright, 1986. 32pp. $9.40. 85-71730. ISBN 0-531-18049-2. Glossary; index. ▶ **EA**

Under the Ground attempts in 32 pages to touch on many things that are found underground. The illustrations are attractive, the type is large, and the reading level is appropriate to children in intermediate grades. Among the topics discussed are animals, natural underground phenomena—earthquakes, "precious gems," caves, fossil fuels—and man-made underground structures and their uses. The author has been careless in explaining some scientific ideas and words. This book can be read to primary children to stimulate an interest in soils and the earth, but it does not provide the accuracy and depth appropriate to older children.

Lye, Keith. *The Earth.* (Illus.; from the Silver Burdett Color Library Series.) Morristown, NJ: Silver Burdett, 1983. 49pp. $14.00. 83-50390. ISBN 0-382-06727-4. Index. ▶ **EA,JH**

Excellent color photographs and illustrations combine with a text that effectively develops its subject to make this book a valuable preview of what young students can expect to learn when they pursue studies in the earth sciences. The information is not presented in textbook style; the book could, however, serve as an excellent supplement in upper elementary and lower secondary classes. The author has chosen his material from around the world, and this global perspective is extremely valuable.

McConnell, Anita. *The World Beneath Us.* (Illus.; from the World of Science Series.) NY: Facts On File, 1985. 64pp. $9.95. 84-1654. ISBN 0-8160-1068-2. Glossary; index; C.I.P. ▶ **EA,JH**

This book offers a tour of some of the more glamorous topics in the earth sciences. Even very young readers will enjoy the illustrations, and older children can find inspiration for special research projects. As a collection of short discussions that are not linked to one another, the volume is unsuitable as a classroom text, but it is quite useful as an introduction to individual topics such as volcanoes, fossils, the geologic timetable, plate tectonics, mining, remote sensing, and earthquake predictions.

Pasachoff, Jay M., Naomi Pasachoff, and Timothy M. Cooney. *Scott, Foresman Earth Science.* (Illus.) Glenview, IL: Scott, Foresman, 1983. 498pp. $12.77. ISBN 0-673-13724-4. Glossary; index. ▶ **JH**

Well-chosen color photographs and drawings illustrate this amazingly complete, simply written, earth science text for elementary school students. The topics are illustrated by events such as the eruption of Mount St. Helens, sinkhole formation in Florida, and the accidental draining of a lake into a salt mine in Louisiana. Each chapter provides experiments for students to verify the principles discussed, and each unit ends with a discussion of careers. This text should excite the interest of students, teachers, and parents.

Quinn, Kaye. *Planet Earth.* (Illus. by the author; from the Adventures in Science Series.) San Jose, CA: Enrich Corp., 1986. 32pp. $2.95 (paper). ISBN 0-86582-353-7 (paper). ▶ **EI**

In this earth science activity book, black-and-white drawings and type are bold and easy to read and follow. Pages are perforated for easy removal. The only activities promoted are those that can be done with paper and pencil or crayons, but this is not a drawback, for it provides students with the opportunity to become involved in learning without too much teacher control or supervision. The activities promote language skills with scrambled words, word searches, and other devices as well as much useful knowledge of the earth. The presentation has a few minor flaws, but the value of the activities outweighs the drawbacks.

Webb, Angela. *Air.* (Illus.; photographs by Chris Fairclough; a TalkAbout Bk.) NY: Watts, 1987. 32pp. ea. $9.90 ea. 87-50234. ISBN 0-531-10369-2. ▶ **K,EP**

Sand. 87-50233. ISBN 0-531-10370-6.

Soil. 87-50232. ISBN 0-531-10371-4.

Water. 87-50231. ISBN 0-531-10372-2.

These delightful books are designed to increase very young readers' awareness of the world around them. With pictures on nearly every page, each book leads the reader through exploratory activities of blowing bubbles, making mud pies, sifting sand, and pouring water. Air and Sand show young children engaged in the suggested activities, enabling children who cannot yet read to construe from the picture the intent of the caption or the suggested activity. Soil and Water do not make the same use of such inspiring photographs; they present scenic photographs or shots of items referred to in the large-type captions. Adults may need to help very young children interpret the activities in these two books. Overall, however, the concepts of exploring substances through everyday experiences as presented in these four books will intrigue young children and prompt them to make further discoveries on their own.

551.2–.3   Volcanoes; earthquakes; glaciers

Bramwell, Martyn. Glaciers and Ice Caps. (Illus.; from the Earth Science Library Series.) NY: Watts, 1986. 32pp. ea. $9.90 ea. 84-52046. ISBN 0-531-10178-9. Glossary; index. ▶ EA,JH

Volcanoes and Earthquakes. 85-52045. ISBN 0-531-10177-0.

In these two volumes from the Earth Science Library Series, each pair of facing pages elaborates on a single topic using colorful photographs and diagrams closely correlated to the adjacent text. The glossaries provide meaty, complete explanations and serve as good supplements to the text in which new words are printed in bold type and explained by the context. The attractive format, large type, and abundant illustrations will entice young readers; however, the vast amount of science presented would limit these books' use to the more knowledgeable intermediate and junior high students.

Branley, Franklyn M. Volcanoes. (Illus. by Marc Simont; a Let's-Read-and-Find-Out Science Bk.) NY: Crowell, 1985. 32pp. $11.50. 84-45344. ISBN 0-690-04451-8. ▶ EP,EI

Volcanoes is an elementary book about volcanoes that is surprisingly ambitious in scope. The connection between earthquakes and volcanoes is explained, as is the role geologists play in studying them. All the modern ideas of plate tectonics are used as a framework for the explanations and are presented well. There are colorful drawings on each page; several illustrations of cross-sections of the earth nicely illustrate the relationship of plate boundaries and volcanoes. An excellent book for classroom or home use.

Curran, Eileen. Mountains and Volcanoes. (Illus.) Mahwah, NJ: Troll, 1985. 32pp. $9.98; $2.50 (paper). 84-8638. ISBN 0-8167-0347-7; 0-8167-0348-5 (paper). ▶ K,EP

This beautifully illustrated book gently introduces some very solid science to young readers by inviting them to observe the details of a familiar setting. By means of a limited vocabulary and unusually appealing illustrations, young readers are directed to observe with care and are encouraged to think for themselves. Little adult guidance is needed for the child to succeed in answering the book's open-ended questions. The illustrations, while clear enough to avoid confusing young readers, are visually appealing and intricate enough to satisfy older children. Can uniquely and significantly serve remedial readers.

Fradin, Dennis Brindell. *Disaster! Earthquakes.* (Illus.) Chicago: Childrens Press, 1982. 63pp. $7.50. 81-12263. ISBN 0-516-00853-6. Glossary; index; C.I.P. ▶ **EA,JH**

This book begins by recounting the events that occurred during a severe earthquake in 1980 in Italy and the remarks of a few survivors. Descriptions of other major earthquakes that caused severe property damage and many deaths are also included. The text focuses on the causes of earthquakes, the causes of the death and destruction associated with earthquakes, the techniques for predicting earthquakes, and the safety procedures recommended for those who are caught in a quake. It is replete with attactive color, as well as black-and-white, photographs and illustrations. Although the reading level makes this accurate book appropriate for upper elementary school students, less able readers will benefit from the photographs.

Fradin, Dennis Brindell. *Disaster! Volcanoes.* (Illus.) Chicago: Childrens Press, 1982. 64pp. $7.50. 81-12294. ISBN 0-516-00851-X. Glossary; index; C.I.P. ▶ **EI,EA,JH**

This accurate, sturdily constructed book begins by describing the events that preceded, happened during, and followed the May 18, 1980, eruption of Mount St. Helens. Also included are accounts of several historically recorded, disastrous volcanoes; names and locations of important volcanoes; a description of the Ring of Fire; and photographs of volcanoes on Mars and Io. Some positive results of volcanoes, such as the formation of land and fertile soil, are given to provide readers with a different point of view. Interesting color and black-and-white photographs and illustrations increase the book's appeal.

Gilbreath, Alice. *Ring of Fire: And the Hawaiian Islands and Iceland.* (Illus.; from the Ocean World Library Series.) Minneapolis: Dillon, 1986. 96pp. $10.95. 85-6971. ISBN 0-87518-302-6. Glossary; index; C.I.P. ▶ **EA,JH**

Ring of Fire describes several common types of volcanic eruptions and their products. It focuses on the circum-Pacific volcanic belt, the Hawaiian Islands, and Iceland as examples of subduction, plume, and sea-floor spreading center volcanics, respectively. Krakatoa and Parícutin are featured in some detail. Other sections note instruments that monitor volcanic activity, use of volcanic energy to heat buildings and generate electricity, and attempts to control the progress of lava eruptions. The book is well written and is illustrated with spectacular photographs, most in color. A few minor errors do not detract seriously from the book's value. A list of activities to learn more about volcanoes, a glossary of technical terms, and a list of related readings are included.

Lambert, David. *Earthquakes and Volcanoes.* (Illus.; from the Topics Series.) NY: Bookwright, 1986. 32pp. $10.40. 85-73660. ISBN 0-531-18058-1. Glossary; index; C.I.P. ▶ **EI, EA**

This attractively illustrated little book covers the topics of earthquakes and volcanoes concisely but completely. It opens with descriptions of earthquakes and the destruction they cause and briefly discusses a few of the great earthquakes and quake-produced tidal waves. It then proceeds to a discussion of volcanoes, mentioning the Mt. Pelée, Krakatoa, and Mount St. Helens eruptions. Attempts to predict earthquakes and to protect buildings by earthquake-proof construction are discussed. An up-to-date and reasonably accurate introduction to the topics for young children.

Lauber, Patricia. *Volcano: The Eruption and Healing of Mount St. Helens.* (Illus.) NY: Bradbury, 1986. iv + 60pp. $14.95. 85-22442. ISBN 0-02-754500-8. Index; C.I.P. ▶ **EA,JH**

The author has done a masterful job in integrating narrative and illustrations dealing with the volcanic activity on Mt. St. Helens in particular and the Cascade Range in general. The most impressive parts may be the discussions of the recovery processes of plant and animal life, specifically, how they managed to survive and how new food webs begin to form. The narrative closes with a discussion of the Ring of Fire surrounding the Pacific Ocean. One will have to work hard to find another publication that does the job as well as this one does.

Marcus, Elizabeth. *All About Mountains & Volcanoes.* (Illus. by Joseph Veno, A Question & Answer Bk.) Mahwah, NJ: Troll, 1984. 30pp. $8.59; $1.95 (paper). 83-4834. ISBN 0-89375-969-4; 0-89375-970-8 (paper). C.I.P. ▶ **EA,JH**

This book examines how mountains can be formed, erosion, and how mountains affect weather. Its question-and-answer format is easy to follow and provides concise explanations of the subject. The text is accurate and readable, and the diagrams are excellent. The book is recommended for middle-grade students and for academically deficient junior-high students.

Radlauer, Ruth, and Lisa Sue Gitkin. *The Power of Ice.* (Illus.; photographs by Lisa Sue Gitkin; an Elk Grove Bk.) Chicago: Childrens Press, 1985. 48pp. $11.95. 85-5714. ISBN 0-516-07839-9. Glossary; index; C.I.P. ▶ **EA,JH**

This book represents the notes of one of the authors who spent two summers as a teen-age research assistant on the glaciers of Alaska. The writing style actively involves the reader in the study of this icebound landscape. Most of the information deals with modern glaciers, but there are brief references to continental ice sheets and how they helped form the landscapes of large portions of the earth's surface. Discussion of the native plants and animals supplements the information on glaciers. New and important technical terms, in bold type, are clearly defined in footnotes and in the glossary. Excellent color photographs and maps.

551.46 Oceanography and underwater exploration

See also 331.91 Waterbodies and water supply; 574.92 Marine biology and ecology.

Bramwell, Martyn. *Oceans.* (Illus.; from the Franklin Watts Picture Atlas Series.) NY: Watts, 1984. 38pp. $10.90. 84-51227. ISBN 0-531-04835-7. Glossary; index. ▶ **EI**

This concise introduction to the oceans provides appropriate illustrations and diagrams. The shape of the ocean basins is presented as a consequence of movements of land masses and accompanying volcanism. Next comes a description of the surface currents and how tides are produced. Specific features of the major oceans, including people, wildlife, and resources, are discussed.

Use of the oceans for trade and of their resources for food are mentioned, as are extractions of oil, gravel, and minerals. The subjects of abuse of the ocean and of the need for informed stewardship are touched on. Recommended as general interest reading to children in grades three and four.

Driggs, Lorin (Ed.). *The Voyage of the* Mimi: *The Book.* (Illus.; a Bank Street College Project in Science and Mathematics.) NY: Holt, Rinehart and Winston, 1985. 160pp. $9.95. ISBN 0-03-000753-4. Glossary. ▶ **EA,JH**

Based on the PBS television series of the same name, this book is a chronicle of the adventures of the young crew of the ketch *Mimi*, chartered by a woman marine biologist for whale studies in the Gulf of Maine. The voyage is recreated using paintings of action highlights and snippets from the script. Each episode also has a set of activities and a separate "expedition" by one of the PBS cast members to sites such as the New England Aquarium, the New Alchemy Institute, the weather station on Mt. Washington, and the Marine Biological Laboratory in Woods Hole. The expeditions are illustrated with good color photographs. The activities range from a simple board game to a nicely explained problem on analyzing transect census samples of whale abundance data. Useful but somewhat fragmented, this attractively produced multiauthor and multi-artist effort was too ambitious to really succeed as an independent book.

Elting, Mary. *Mysterious Seas.* (Illus. by Fiona Reid.) NY: Grossett & Dunlap, 1983. 77pp. $7.95. 83-47614. ISBN 0 448-18960-7. Glossary; index. ▶ **EI,EA,JH**

Elting does a good job of informing the reader about a huge variety of interesting, thought-provoking, and little-known facts and unsolved mysteries of life in the oceans. A good glossary, index, and pronunciation guide greatly enhance the overall effectiveness of the book as a learning tool. Helpful illustrations.

Gilbreath, Alice. *The Continental Shelf: An Underwater Frontier.* (Illus.; from the Ocean World Library Series.) Minneapolis: Dillon, 1986. 104pp. $10.95 ea. 85-6942. ISBN 0-87518-301-8. Glossary; index; C.I.P. ▶ **EI,EA**

River in the Ocean: The Story of the Gulf Stream. 96pp. 85-6883. ISBN 0-87518-297-6.

After an overview of the geology and ecology of the continental shelf, Gilbreath introduces us to animals, from fishes to mammals to birds, that depend on the shelf for life. Several chapters deal with natural resources such as oil, minerals, and protein. The remainder of the book describes the dangers of pollution and future plans for the development of the shelf. The political, social, and economic ramifications of shelf expolitation are presented so that children can grasp their significance.The glossary and index provide the chance to sharpen skills; a bibliography and selected projects encourage further investigation. While discussing the formation and integrity of the Gulf Stream current and its effect on the climate of surrounding land masses in *River in the Ocean*, the author presents some basic physics and chemistry. The history of the exploration of the current is a good introduction to the science of oceanography. Some of the more important, well-known, or visually prominent organisms in the ocean are introduced, and the role of nutrients and plankton in the food web is explained. The book is factually accurate, technically correct, and provides enough source and supplemental material to make additional study easy to initiate. Informative, introduces several sciences and their practical application, and provides excellent learning aids.

Nixon, Hershell H., and Joan Lowery Nixon. *Land Under the Sea.* (Illus.; a Skylight Bk.) NY: Dodd, Mead, 1985. 62pp. $8.95. 85-7041. ISBN 0-396-08582-2. Index; C.I.P. ▶ EI,EA

An excellent, general introduction to the discovery and exploration of the unique lands beneath the sea. With appropriate language, the authors relate our ever-increasing knowldege of the trenches and mountains, shelves and shores, plates and plateaus of the underwater world. The early explorers and their contributions as well as modern scientists and their most recent discoveries are discussed. Scientific concepts and terminology are clearly defined and carefully developed. Plate tectonics, underwater volcanism, ocean floor spreading and fracturing, and mineral formation are explained in the context of the physical forms they create. Much information is presented, but the spacing of the text and the variety of illustrations—numerous black-and-white photographs, diagrams, and charts—make the book approachable for the young reader.

Oleksy, Walter. *Treasures of the Deep: Adventures of Undersea Exploration.* (Illus.) NY: Messner, 1984. 189pp. $9.79. 83-22088. ISBN 0-671-42269-3. Index; C.I.P. ▶ EA,JH

Describes a number of undersea ventures, including treasure hunts, searches, archeological expeditions, and unusual activities such as a quest for the Loch Ness monster. The coverage is broad, the pictures are relevant, and the text is written in a style that will appeal to young teenagers. Olesky gives a concise but complete historical overview, and then traces all efforts to make discoveries. The style is somewhat suspenseful, but transmits information while it entertains.

Sabin, Francene. *Oceans.* (Illus. by June Goldborough; from the Venture into Reading Series.) Mahwah, NJ: Troll, 1985. 32pp. $7.59; $1.95 (paper). 84-8590. ISBN 0-8167-0216-0; 0-8167-0217-9 (paper). C.I.P. ▶ EI,EA

After describing the earth's oceans and naming and locating each on the globe, Sabin explains how seawater became salty. The topography of the ocean floor is discussed in words and pictures, as are tides and currents and their effects. Brief mention of the ocean food chain, the water cycle, and the fact that we look to the ocean for oil and minerals completes the book.

Weiss, Malcolm E. *One Sea, One Law? The Fight for a Law of the Sea.* (Illus.) NY: Harcourt Brace Jovanovich, 1982. vi + 120pp. $10.95. 81-47535. ISBN 0-15-258690-3. Index; C.I.P. ▶ JH

A law of the sea is the organizational device that the author uses to present a great deal of accurate and interesting information concerning current and future ocean resource exploitation and pollution issues. The book also includes an exccllent, brief history of many aspects of oceanography. Some technical terms are not defined, but students with some background in earth or environmental science should not have any problems.

551.48 Hydrology

See also 333.91 Waterbodies and water supply.

Dickinson, Jane. *Wonders of Water.* (Illus. by Rex Schneider; a Question &

Answer Bk.) Mahwah, NJ: Troll, 1984. 32pp. $8.59; $1.95 (paper). 82-17388. ISBN 0-89375-874-4; 0-89375-875-2 (paper). C.I.P. ▶ **EA**

Using a question-and-answer format, this book explains the water cycle and the uses of water. Topics include evaporation and condensation, freezing, erosion by water, flood prevention, and how people use water. Transportation, recreation, manufacturing, energy, and irrigation are also discussed. Because it focuses on both the natural science aspect of water—the water cycle—and the social science aspect of water—how people use water—the book will be useful as a reference for either social studies or science classes.

Emil, Jane. *All About Rivers.* (Illus. by Joseph Veno; a Question & Answer Bk.) Mahwah, NJ: Troll, 1984. 32pp. $8.59; $1.95 (paper). 83-4868. ISBN 0-89375-980-5; 0-89375-979-1 (paper). C.I.P. ▶ **EA,JH**

This question-and-answer book examines the geological features of rivers. Topics covered are how and where a river begins, drainage basins, glaciers, the Continental Divide, ages of rivers, erosion, river mouths such as deltas and estuaries, flooding and its prevention, and the importance of keeping rivers clean. The text provides basic factual information about rivers and includes many colorful diagrams.

Santrey, Laurence. *Rivers.* (Illus. by Lynn Sweat; from the Venture into Reading Series.) Mahwah, NJ: Troll, 1985. 32pp. $7.59; $1.95 (paper). 84-8818. ISBN 0-8167-0210-1; 0-8167-0211-X (paper). C.I.P. ▶ **EI,EA**

How rivers form from a trickle and grow and how they are classified are the topics of the first half of this book. Basic river concepts for elementary students, such as deltas and estuaries, hydropower and irrigation, are included. At the end, the author mentions food chains and how the pollution of many rivers has occurred.

551.5–.6 Meteorology; climatology; atmosphere

Adler, David. *World of Weather.* (Illus. by Ray Burns; a Question & Answer Bk.) Mahwah, NJ: Troll, 1984. 32pp. $8.59; $1.95 (paper). 82-17398. ISBN 0-89375-870-1; 0-89375-871-X (paper). C.I.P. ▶ **EA,JH**

This basic weather information book briefly describes tornadoes and hurricanes, two examples of how wind can be dangerous, and evaporation and condensation. The book then explains forms of precipitation and has a brief discussion of lightning. Weather forecasting, including how cloud types can be used to predict weather, is discussed in the last section. More emphasis could have been placed on the scientific concepts; however, the presentation is interesting and the illustrations are colorful and show situations that are familiar to children. Appropriate for middle-grade students and slow junior high readers.

Asimov, Isaac. *How Did We Find Out About the Atmosphere?* (Illus. by David Wool; from the How Did We Find Out? Series.) NY: Walker, 1985. 64pp. $9.85. 84-27125. ISBN 0-8027-6588-2. Index; C.I.P. ▶ **EI,EA,JH**

Asimov covers the growth of information concerning the atmosphere from about 500 BC to the present. In addition to a general chronology, he includes material on atoms and pressure, gases, molecules and heights, noble gases and ions, and other worlds. Readers learn of the scientist who enlarged each fledgling concept, the questions that led to experiments, the conclusions, and the remaining questions that led to further study. The text is interesting, and the vocabulary relatively simple. Interesting black-and-white drawings illustrate the text.

Brandt, Keith. *Air.* (Illus. by Raymond Burns; from the Venture into Reading Series.) Mahwah, NJ: Troll, 1985. 32pp. $7.59; $1.95 (paper). 84-2608. ISBN 0-8167-0130-X; 0-8167-0131-8 (paper). C.I.P. ▶ **EI,EA**

This well-illustrated, simply written book explores the qualities of air and examines such concepts as gravity, atmospheric pressure, and weather. It also describes the various layers of the earth's atmosphere. Brandt presents basic information in clear, concise, straightforward prose, giving readers a quick overview of the topic.

Branley, Franklyn M. *Air Is All Around You, revised edition.* (Illus. by Holly Keller; a Let's Read and Find Out Science Bk.) NY: Crowell, 1986. 32pp. $11.50; $3.95 (paper). 85-45405. ISBN 0-690-04502-6; 0-06-445048-1 (paper). ▶ **EP**

This volume describes the various properties of air and how air takes up space and is dissolved in water. The two "try it" experiments, along with the very friendly illustrations, would effectively convey to a child the "realness" of air. However, the book states its facts blandly, in large type, and with an abundance of free space.

Branley, Franklyn M. *Flash, Crash, Rumble, and Roll.* (Illus. by Barbara and Ed Emberley; a Let's Read and Find Out Bk.) NY: Crowell, 1985. 32pp. $11.50. 84-45333. ISBN 0-690-04424-0. ▶ **K,EP**

Flash, Crash, Rumble, and Roll is about thunderstorms, lightning, and thunder. Good, concise explanations are given for the causes of thunder and lightning, helping to demystify these scary phenomena for young children. The explanations are enhanced by excellent examples and colorful illustrations. Several pages are devoted to precautions children can take to prevent being hit by lightning. A good read-along book—an excellent choice for both classroom and home.

Branley, Franklyn M. *Snow Is Falling.* (Illus.; a Let's Read and Find Out Science Bk.) NY: Crowell, 1986. 32pp. $11.25. 85-48256. ISBN 0-690-04547-6. C.I.P. ▶ **K,EP**

This book affords small children the opportunity to read about scientific information in a vocabulary that does not require additional explanation. Colorful illustrations of snowflakes, animal homes, floods, and recreational uses of snow provide a focal point for children to ask questions. Branley deals with many concepts that are generally not pointed out to children, which add to the reality of the book and make it a good choice.

Jacobs, Una. *Sun Calendar.* (Illus. by the author.) Morristown, NJ: Silver Burdett, 1986. ii+37pp. $8.96; $5.75 (paper). 85-30317. ISBN 0-382-09217-1; 0-382-09220-1 (paper). Index; C.I.P. ▶ **EI,EA**

This superbly illustrated book describing seasonal changes that occur in living and nonliving things is packed with interesting information about day and night and morning evening animals. Although the material presented is essentially accurate, there is a lack of continuity and depth, and the book is valuable primarily for its illustrations. A major error occurs in the description of the relationship between water vapor and clouds, and no attempt is made overall to portray the processes of science.

Jefferies, Lawrence. *Air, Air, Air.* (Illus. by Lewis Johnson; a Question & Answer Bk.) Mahwah, NJ: Troll, 1984. 32pp. $8.59; $1.95 (paper). 82-15808. ISBN 0-89375-880-9; 0-89375-881-7 (paper). C.I.P. ▶ **EA**

To help readers understand that air is everywhere, the book outlines a simple demonstration, describes the results, and explains the phenomenon. The discussion on the composition of air includes the role of oxygen in burning, how plants use carbon dioxide, and short descriptions of helium, argon, and nitrogen gases. The weight of air (atmospheric pressure) is also discussed, and several investigations using readily available materials are described. The conclusion focuses on the relationship between wind and weather.

Jones, Philip. *The Forces of Nature.* (Illus.; from the World of Nature Series.) Chicago: Childrens Press, 1982. 64pp. $11.95. 81-38473. ISBN 0-516-00623-1. Index; C.I.P. ▶ **EA,JH**

Full-color photographs and their explanatory captions make up this book that examines some of the physical forces of the earth and atmosphere. Clouds, storms, rain, wind, snow and ice, thunder and lightning, as well as violent storms, are all pictured in excellent photographs taken all over the world. The formation of the earth is described and shown graphically, and the effects of earthquakes and volcanoes are illustrated by the destruction that they cause. Overall, the lack of text is adequately compensated for by illustrations that should be interesting to young students.

Lambert, David. *The Seasons.* (Illus., an Easy-Read Fact Bk.) NY: Watts, 1983. 32pp. $8.90. 82-62987. ISBN 0-531-04620-6. Glossary; index. ▶ **EI,EA**

Useful supplemental reading for elementary science classes, this book briefly describes the seasons and illustrates climatic and seasonal effects in different latitudes and regions. It is nicely illustrated with photographs and drawings. The book's major fault is that it is just a fact book. There is only one suggested activity for students, and by implication, the book conveys the message that science is product, not process.

Lambert, David. *Weather.* (Illus.; an Easy-Read Fact Bk.) NY: Watts, 1983. 32pp. $8.90. 82-62988. ISBN 0-531-04621-4. Glossary; index. ▶ **EA,JH**

This accurate, informative, and well-written book could be used as resource material for a school project by a bright ten-year-old or as a quick summary by an adult who wants to obtain a rudimentary but accurate understanding of most weather phenomena. The illustrations are clear and useful.

Oleksy, Walter. *Nature Gone Wild!* (Illus.; a Jem Bk.) NY: Messner, 1982. 63pp. $9.29. 82-60645. ISBN 0-671-44007-1. Index; C.I.P. ▶ **EA,JH**

Shows the forces and destructive powers of nature through vivid descriptions of property damage and eyewitness accounts of loss of home and loved ones. The devastation caused by tornadoes in Georgia, the cyclones in Bangladesh, the Alaskan earthquake, the Johnstown flood, hurricane Agnes, the Chicago fire, the eruption of Mount St. Helens is so overwhelming that it leaves one speechless. Photographs and many human-interest anecdotes help young readers to envision the magnitude of natural forces.

Seymour, Peter. *How the Weather Works.* (Illus. by Sally Springer; a Science Action Pop-up Bk.) NY: Macmillan, 1985. 10pp. $6.95. ISBN 0-02-782110-2. ▶ EI

This book explores the world of weather. Four double-thick pages are filled with facts and fun, including the familiar components of weather—temperature, clouds, wind, thunder/lightning, rain, snow, and forecasting. Key words are italicized, and pronunciation guides are provided. The excellent design engineering of the pop-ups, pull tabs, and lift-ups results in a windmill that turns, moving charts, and a quiz that will help young readers "predict" weather.

Paleontology and Physical Anthropology

See also 575 Organic evolution and genetics.

Arnold, Caroline. *Trapped in Tar: Fossils from the Ice Age.* (Illus.; photographs by Richard Hewett.) NY: Clarion (Ticknor & Fields), 1987. 57pp. $12.95. 86-17614. ISBN 0-89919-415-X. C.I.P. ▶ EI,EA

Trapped in Tar is a black-and-white photographic essay with accompanying text focusing on the exhibits and research of the George C. Page Museum of the Rancho La Brea tar pits discoveries in Los Angeles. Approximately one-third of the book is devoted to the history of the discovery and the techniques used to excavate, prepare, and study the fossils. Another third describes some of the organisms that have been found—mammoths, sloths, bison, dire wolves, saber-tooth cats, bears, birds, snails, pine cones, seeds, pollen, and a single human skull. The book concludes with speculations on why the large ice-age mammals became extinct. Contains a wealth of information on the methods used by paleontologists to learn about ancient life.

Bains, Rae. *Prehistoric Animals.* (Illus. by Alexis Batista; from the Venture into Reading Series.) Mahwah, NJ: Troll, 1985. 32pp. $7.59; $1.95 (paper). 84-2735. ISBN 0-8167-0296-9; 0-8167-0297-7 (paper). C.I.P. ▶ EI

The illustrations do much to enhance the narrative, offering glimpses of many animals, from trilobites to lacewings in amber. These pictures provide visual verification for the increase in complexity of organisms over hundreds of millions of years. However, such phrases as "[dinosaurs] ruled the earth" should have been deleted and generic names italicized, even for this young readership.

Dixon, Dougal. *Time Exposure: A Photographic Record of the Dinosaur Age.* (Illus.; photographs by Jane Burton.) NY: Beaufort, 1984. 96pp. $14.95. 83-25741. ISBN 0-8253-0217-X. Glossary; index; C.I.P. ▶ EI,EA,JH

Although this book's focus is the dinosaurs of the Mesozoic period, its coverage is much broader. The introduction briefly exposes readers to plate tectonics, paleogeography, the evolution of plant and animal life, reptilian taxonomy, convergent evolution, the restoration of fossil animals and the reconstruction of their behavior, and the history of paleontology. The book consists of entertaining descriptions of 35 fossil genera acting in their natural environmental setting. Burton's color photographs of Steve Kirk's art provide realistic depictions of the animals in lively action. The text is accurate, easy to read, and supplemented by tables.

Lauber, Patricia. *Dinosaurs Walked Here and Other Stories Fossils Tell.* (Illus.) NY: Bradbury, 1987. 56pp. $15.95. 86-8239. ISBN 0-02-754510-5. Index; C.I.P. ▶ **EI,EA,JH**

Lauber relates the prehistoric stories revealed by paleontologists around the world. In comparing the rock record to a diary, she emphasizes the importance of fossils in our "reading" of the earth's past. She also creates vivid scenarios to demonstrate plausible scientific interpretations of fossil finds. How specific fossil evidence changes our thinking about the past and how fossil footprints have revealed details of dinosaurs that were previously misunderstood are discussed. The writing is clear, concise, and accurate. Best of all are the exceptional and abundant illustrations. Looking at these pictures is like examining outstanding fossil collections or stepping back in time to the days of the dinosaurs.

Rydell, Wendy. *Discovering Fossils.* (Illus. by Ray Burns; a Question & Answer Bk.) Mahwah, NJ: Troll, 1984. 32pp. $8.59; $1.95 (paper). 83-4832. ISBN 0-89375-973-2; 0-89375-974-0 (paper). C.I.P. ▶ **EA,JH**

This book summarizes how humankind first came to understand the importance of fossils and explains how scientists date fossils and identify matching rock layers. Some of the great fossil discoveries, such as the woolly mammoth in Siberia and the remains from the La Brea tar pits, are interestingly presented. How readers can hunt fossils, what tools they will need, and what types of fossils they might find are described. The questions that the book asks are relevant, and the text is accurate and flows smoothly.

Sabin, Louis. *Fossils.* (Illus. by Richard Maccabe; from the Venture into Reading Series.) Mahwah, NJ: Troll, 1985. 32pp. $7.59; $1.95 (paper). 84-2716. ISBN 0-8167-0228-4; 0-8167-0229-2 (paper). C.I.P. ▶ **EI**

Interesting and fun reading, this straightforward text emphasizes the importance of paleontology in understanding earth's history and explains the formation of fossils in rock, ice, amber, and tar. Sabin makes clear the fact that a fossil can be whole or only part of a plant or animal and may even be just a footprint. He outlines the methods used to reclaim bones discovered deep in the ground and tells how this study helps scientists draw conclusions about prehistoric events. The illustrations are what make the book fun.

567.91 Dinosaurs

Aliki. *Dinosaurs Are Different.* (Illus.; a Let's Read and Find Out Science Bk.) NY: Crowell, 1985. 32pp. $11.50. 84-45332. ISBN 0-690-04456-9. ▶ **EP,EI,EA**

This useful book explains, in a simple and easy-to-follow presentation, how dinosaurs are different from each other in both structure and appearance. In simplified terms, the scientific method of classifying the different types of dinosaurs is laid out. The author notes fundamental points in the classification of these ancient reptiles and traces their evolution and basic skeletal similarities without unnecessary complications. This book is excellent in its organization and treatment of the material. The illustrations are fairly good and do a reasonable job of supplementing the text.

Cohen, Daniel. *Dinosaurs.* (Illus. by Jean Zallinger.) NY: Doubleday, 1986 (released in 1987). 41pp. $8.95. 85-29306. ISBN 0-385-23414-7. C.I.P. ▶ EI,EA

Dinosaurs illustrates various dinosaurs and reconstructs the dinosaurs' milieu. Topics as diverse as continental drift, geologic time, dinosaur classification, dinosaur social life, dinosaur metabolism, the relationship between dinosaurs and birds, reptiles contemporary with the dinosaurs, and the meteorite/asteroid extinction hypothesis are covered. Throughout, the book explains how scientists are able to reconstruct the world of the dinosaurs. For controversial issues, such as the terminal Cretaceous extinction hypotheses, the author presents various theories in a balanced manner. The profuse, exceptional, color illustrations will intrigue even very young children.

Cohen, Daniel. *Monster Dinosaur.* (Illus.) NY: Lippincott, 1983. 179pp. $9.95. 82-48460. ISBN 0-397-31953-3. Index; C.I.P. ▶ EA,JH

A find for any classroom, library, or home with young people who want to learn everything they can about dinosaurs and other earthly monsters. Cohen covers the history of the dinosaur's discovery and popularity and describes the early scientific rivalry of paleontologists Cope and Marsh; questions whether all dinosaurs were reptiles, coldblooded, and prehistoric; explores historic monster sighting; and ends the book by mentioning famous dinosaurs in ancient myths and modern literature. In elementary language, this self-described "fun" book provides a literary and cinematic history of the dinosaur.

Dixon, Dougal. *The First Dinosaurs.* (Illus.; from the New Dinosaur Library Series.) Milwaukee: Gareth Stevens, 1987. 32pp. ea. $13.26 ea. 87-6460. ISBN 1-55532-283-2. Glossary; index; C.I.P. ▶ K,EP,EI

Hunting the Dinosaurs and Other Prehistoric Animals. 87-6461. ISBN 1-55532-284-0.

The Jurassic Dinosaurs. 87-6462. ISBN 1-55532-285-9.

The Last Dinosaurs. 87-6463. ISBN 1-55532-286-7.

Each of the four books in this colorfully illustrated series about dinosaurs closes with a list of "fun facts" that are actually not trivia but as important from a scientific standpoint as the information in the main text. *The First Dinosaurs* juxtaposes pictorial representations of the dinosaurs with human beings to give readers an idea of each animal's size. Although the illustrations and text are accurate with regard to current thinking, the presentations and descriptions are somewhat simplistic. *Hunting the Dinosaurs* explains some of the processes paleontologists use to study and reconstruct extinct reptiles. While accurate and up to date, the text tends to jump from topic to topic in no apparent order, with a sometimes questionable selection of information included. While *The Jurassic Dinosaurs* covers some creatures that are not commonly depicted, it is understandably far from exhaustive. The author occasionally throws in a term or description that makes the text somewhat inconsistent for the targeted audience. *The Last Dinosaurs* deals with some of the later Cretaceous dinosaurs but is not complete enough to stand on its own as an extensive source of information about these ancient reptiles. The series as a whole is an interesting introductory source that requires supplementation for a balanced picture of the dinosaurs.

Gibbons, Gail. *Dinosaurs.* (Illus. by the author.) NY: Holiday House, 1987. 30pp. $12.95. 87-364. ISBN 0-8234-0657-1. C.I.P. ▶ **K,EP,EI**

The large, colorful pictures using soft earth tones will lure teacher and child alike. The author/illustrator is a charming raconteur with a style that is leisurely and relaxed but with facts that are trustworthy. She uses few words, but includes the proper names and pronunciations of the dinosaurs and compares and defines terms to clarify for children how they lived millions of years ago. She introduces fossils and paleontologists, emphasizing the importance of footprints and dinosaur remains buried in the earth and the putting together of dinosaur parts to make the whole skeleton. Finally, she excites us with the theories of why dinosaurs have disappeared from the earth.

Hopkins, Lee Bennett (Ed.). *Dinosaurs.* (Illus. by Murray Tinkelman.) NY: Harcourt Brace Jovanovich, 1987. 48pp. $12.95. 86-14818. ISBN 0-15-223495-0. Index; C.I.P. ▶ **K,EP,EI,EA,JH**

Through a few well-crafted lines of short poems, none taking more than a page, a young reader (or listener) can imagine how dinosaurs lived, died, ruled the earth, and simply passed their time. A couple of poems ponder the "What if?" questions of living in the dinosaurs' time and environment or their living in ours. Each poem is accompanied by an imaginative black-and-white illustration.

Kaufmann, John. *Flying Giants of Long Ago.* (Illus. by the author; from the Let's Read and Find Out Science Bks. Series.) NY: Crowell, 1984. 32pp. $9.95. 81-43881. ISBN 0-690-04219-1. C.I.P. ▶ **EI,EA,JH**

This delightful book focuses on the size of ancient flying animals. The attractive illustrations include unique methods of comparing animal size. The book is written for elementary school children, but the illustrations can be used by any age group. Hobbyists will find this book interesting, and it can be used as extra reading for a class on animals.

Knight, David C. *"Dinosaurs" That Swam and Flew.* (Illus. by Lee J. Ames.) Englewood Cliffs, NJ: Prentice-Hall, 1985. 64pp. $11.95. 84-24787. ISBN 0-13-214693-2. Index; C.I.P. ▶ **EP,EI**

This interesting book shows some of the less famous ancient reptiles. The author does a good job of explaining the origin and characteristics of various air- and water-dwelling reptiles from the age of dinosaurs. The information is detailed and accurate except that the author lists *Pteranodon* as the largest flying reptile instead of *Quetzalcoatlus*, the Texas pterosaur. Excellent black-and-white drawings.

Lambert, David. *The Age of Dinosaurs, revised edition.* (Illus.; an All-About Bk.). NY: Random House, 1987. 24pp. $5.99; $2.95 (paper). 86-26082. ISBN 0-394-98975-9; 0-394-88975-4 (paper). Index; C.I.P. ▶ **EI,EA**

This introduction to dinosaurs and other prehistoric reptiles is a revised edition, and, overall, the changes are improvements. Changes to the text are few. The illustration, all in color and the same as those in the original edition, range from adequate to good. The book does have some deficiencies but is better than many others in this price range.

McGuinness, Doreen. *Dinosaurs.* (Illus. by the author; a Blackie Press-Out Bk.) NY: Bedrick/Blackie Books, 1983. 10pp. $4.95. ISBN 0-216-91425-6. ▶ **K,EP,EI**

The Blackie Press-Out Book Series features thick cardboard animals printed on glossy, washable finish that are meant to be pressed out and stood up or reinserted in their proper settings on individual pages. The dinosaurs are brontosaurus, tyrannosaurus, pteranodon, hypsilophodon, triceratops, and stegosaurus. The accompanying text merely states that they "lived long ago." The illustrated backgrounds include properly primitive trees and plants. For any elementary-age child who wants to learn the names of six varied dinosaurs, since taking the book apart and putting it together as if it were a puzzle should stimulate learning.

Milton, Joyce. *Dinosaur Days.* (Illus. by Richard Roe; a Step 2 Bk.). NY: Random House, 1985. 48pp. $5.99; $2.95 (paper). 84-17861. ISBN 0-394-97023-3; 0-394-87023-9 (paper). ▶ **EP,EI**

The opportunity for young readers to learn about dinosaur natural history is good in this copiously illustrated book. Aids to the pronunciation of names are included in the text along with a literal translation of the scientific names. Fascinating and well-presented material.

Most, Bernard. *Dinosaur Cousins?* (Illus. by the author.) NY: Harcourt Brace Jovanovich, 1987. 32pp. $12.95. 86-18485. ISBN 0-15-223497-7. Glossary; C.I.P. ▶ **EP,EI,EA,JH**

Dinosaur Cousins? is a fascinating, odd, and ultimately quite clever book. Simplified color drawings of a specific dinosaur on one page face a contemporary unrelated animal on the next. The reader is then invited to compare the two animals. Minimal captions inspire the reader to consider the form, function, and life-styles of numerous little-known dinosaurs. A clever representation of adaptation in different animals.

National Geographic Society (Eds.). *Dinosaurs: Giant Reptiles.* (Illus.; a Wonders of Learning Kit.) Washington, DC: National Geographic Society, 1986. $28.95. (30 booklets; 1 narration cassette; teacher's guide; activity sheets.) ▶ **K,EP**

This well-made learning kit contains a teacher's guide folder with ample background information and suggestions for teaching. The instructions for using the kits are clear and concise and should ensure that both the content and skill objectives are met by pupils. In addition to several fundamental but easily understood content objectives, skill objectives, such as eye-hand coordination, reinforcement of concepts, applying information, counting, following directions, and creative expression are stressed in the work of the activity sheets. Even teachers who normally shy away from science will have no difficulty teaching from these kits.

Ranger Rick Magazine. *Ranger Rick's Dinosaur Book.* (Illus.) Washington, DC: National Wildlife Federation, 1984. 96pp. $12.95. 84-14680. ISBN 0-912186-54-2. Index; C.I.P. ▶ **EA,JH**

Dramatic photographs and artwork are carefully integrated with the informative text in this lively unfolding of the age of dinosaurs. Each double-page spread emphasizes a different topic. Time and size scales are rendered in children's terms. Consistently, the evidence on which modern speculations are built is presented. Parallels with modern animals are drawn to suggest possible physical and social behaviors.

Sattler, Helen Roney. *Baby Dinosaurs.* (Illus. by Jean Day Zallinger.) NY: Lothrop, Lee & Shepard, 1984. 32pp. $10.25. 83-25631. ISBN 0-688-03817-4. C.I.P. ▶ K,EP

An accurate summary of available data on dinosaur eggs, infants, and juveniles. Sattler also discusses the behavioral relationships of adult dinosaurs and their offspring. The text is enhanced by 24 well-executed color illustrations. Parents and teachers will find that *Baby Dinosaurs* is an excellent introduction to the fascinating world of dinosaurs.

Sattler, Helen Roney. *Pterosaurs, the Flying Reptiles.* (Illus. by Christopher Santoro.) NY: Lothrop, Lee & Shepard, 1985. 48pp. $13.00. 84-4428. ISBN 0-688-03995-2. Index; C.I.P. ▶ EI,EA,JH

This comprehensive look at pterosaurs clearly examines why pterosaurs are classified as reptiles (and why some scientists think they shouldn't be), identifies characteristics of all pterosaurs, then details individual species. The color illustrations are outstanding, depicting the various pterosaurs soaring, feeding, and nesting in their individual habitats. The illustrations complement and expand the text, creating an attractive unity. The book concludes with a brief discussion of the possible causes of pterosaur extinction. The integration of concise writing and detailed illustrations makes this an exceptionally fine book for elementary students.

569 Prehistoric mammals

See also 575 Organic evolution and genetics.

Gallant, Roy A. *The Rise of Mammals.* (Illus., A First Bk.) NY: Watts, 1986. 89pp. $9.40. 86-11161. ISBN 0-531-10206-8. Glossary; index; C.I.P. ▶ EA,JH

This book summarizes what is known about the age of mammals, the geologic era spanning the last 65 million years called the Cenozoic. The emphasis is on evolving mammals, shown against a backdrop of drifting continents, massive ice sheets, and erupting volcanoes. About 35 percent of the total text is devoted to human evolution and provides an account that is both more accurate and complete than that found in the best-selling high school biology textbook. An appendix provides a succinct comparison of evolution and creation science, with the religious nature of the latter clearly identified. Black-and-white photographs and drawings effectively illustrate the text, which presents the conclusions of science, but conveys nothing of the methods and logic used to reach these conclusions.

Lambert, David, and the Diagram Group. *The Field Guide to Early Man.* (Illus.) NY: Facts On File, 1987. 256pp. $18.95; $10.95 (paper). 86-29259. ISBN 0-8160-1517-1; 0-8160-1801-4 (paper). Index; C.I.P. ▶ EI,EA,JH

This is not a field guide but a concise and superbly illustrated museum guide and resource for students and teachers of human evolution featuring a singularly useful list of key museum collections of the world and their main exhibits. Relatively jargon-free yet accurate short descriptions of all but the very latest major fossil and archeological discoveries are provided. This high-quality compendium of facts is organized topically and chronologically. Does not deal with the methods of science.

Strachan, Elizabeth. *Prehistoric Mammals.* (Illus. by Peter Barrett et al.; from A Closer Look At Series.) NY: Gloucester, 1985. 32pp. $9.90. 84-62468. ISBN 0-531-17001-2. Glossary; index. ▶ **EA,JH**

Simple charts explain what a vertebrate is, the successive prehistoric ages, and the formation of fossils. With that background in place, the author unfolds the evolution of reptiles, birds, and mammals. Early humans and their discoveries are woven into the narrative. Finally, the author comments on the dominance of humans and how it results in increases or decreases in the populations of other mammals. This book exemplifies the type of writing for children that explains concepts so succinctly that it provides a painless way to learn.

Life Sciences

Bantock, Cuillin. *The Story of Life.* (Illus.) NY: Peter Bedrick, 1984. 45pp. $10.95. 83-25730. ISBN 0-911745-51-3. Index; C.I.P. ▶ **EA**

The text and the high-quality illustrations in this delightful book catch and hold the reader's interest. Offered are a wide variety of fascinating aspects of biology presented in two-page sections of text and illustration that allow the reader to browse through the book at leisure. The unifying concept seems to be the variety of ways that life forms seek to survive and reproduce. A good addition to school and home libraries; adults as well as children will enjoy it.

Burton, Robert, and Maurice Burton. *The Beginnings of Life.* (Illus.; from The World of Science Series.) NY: Facts On File, 1986. $9.95. 64pp. 84-1654. ISBN 0-8160-1070-6. Glossary; index; C.I.P. ▶ **EA,JH**

Readers are taken on a trip through the many different ways that all living things reproduce. Excellent color photographs and interesting and readable text cover the reproduction of plants and animals, heredity, genetics, and evolution. Difficult or new terms are explained. While this book's treatment of an important process is broad, some of the sections are limited because of space. Fortunately, that does not detract from the presentation.

Seddon, Tony, and Jill Bailey. *The Living World.* (Illus.) NY: Doubleday, 1986 (released 1987). 160pp. $12.95. ISBN 0-385-23754-5. Glossary; index. ▶ **EI,EA,JH**

The Living World starts with the rhetorical question, "Did you know that humans share the world with 3×10^{33} other living things?" and continues to pose many questions about animals and plants (answers are provided). The authors' answers to questions of "why" are teleological. Examples are generally of "wild" plants and animals, and they are described as to form, function, geography, food, reproduction, behavior, evolution, habitat, and interactions. The broad scope of the book, its profuse and relevant illustrations, and its questions and answers make it outstanding as a learning resource, but its objectivity is blurred by teleological explications.

574.5 Ecology of organisms

See also 500.1 Natural history; 581.1–.5 Plant physiology and ecology.

Dethier, Vincent G. *The Ecology of a Summer House.* (Illus.) Amherst: University of Massachusetts Press, 1984. ix + 133pp. $15.00; $7.95 (paper). 83-18007. ISBN 0-87023-421-8; 0-87023-422-6 (paper). C.I.P. ▶ **EA,JH**

This charming and informative book presents the fauna and, to some extent, the flora that share the author's summer bungalow in Maine. The characters are the insects, birds, and small mammals of the northeastern United States, and through the eyes of an experienced biologist, their interrelationships and lives are revealed. The author presents a detailed yet carefully wrought picture of prey and predator, each playing its role in the ecology of his summer home. A well-thought-out reading list concludes this cornucopia of information on behavior and life histories.

Hess, Lilo. *Secrets in the Meadow.* (Illus.) NY: Scribner's, 1986. 64pp. $13.95. 85-43350. ISBN 0-684-18525-3. Glossary; index; C.I.P. ▶ **EI,EA**

Using excellent black-and-white photographs, the author provides young readers with many insights into animal diversity, behavior, life cycle, and adaptation. Scientific terms are given in italics and defined in the glossary. Insects and mammals and their place in the community are emphasized. The content is generally accurate, except for an error in classifying centipedes with spiders.

Rinard, Judith E. *The World Beneath Your Feet.* (Illus.; from the Books for Young Explorers Series.) Washington, DC: National Geographic Society, 1985. 34pp. $10.95. 85-13642. ISBN 0-87044-561-8. C.I.P. ▶ **EI**

This well-organized, beautifully designed pictorial essay about the unobserved abundance of life beneath our feet in a forest will sharpen the observational skills of youngsters, making them more aware of living things around them. The book calls for the reader's active participation by posing questions. In one instance, the reader is asked to search for plants and animals in an illustration showing a rotting log. An answer key identifying the organisms is presented later. A two-page section provides additional details about forest organisms and suggests interesting activities. An appealing, enjoyable volume.

574.5263 Ecology of aquatic environments

See also 331.91 Waterbodies and water supply; 551.46 Oceanography and underwater exploration; 574.92 Marine biology and ecology.

Court, Judith, with Joyce Pope (Series Ed.). *Ponds and Streams.* (Illus.; from the Action Science Series.) NY: Watts, 1985. 32pp. $9.90. 84-52006. ISBN 0-531-04952-3. Glossary; index. ▶ **EA**

An excellent children's book on small freshwater systems. Pond and stream ecosystems are not only described well, but methods of study suitable for this age group are discussed in great detail. The students' interest is piqued with the aid of many first-rate drawings, and simple devices are described so that not only the organisms but the total environment may be easily studied. There is even a section on making one's own pond, along with a section on pollution.

Instructions are given for observing the various life forms and for growing some of them. A book to take into the field again and again; this is participatory science at its best.

Curran, Eileen. *Life in the Pond.* (Illus.) Mahwah, NJ: Troll, 1985. 32pp. $9.98; $2.50 (paper). 84-16285. ISBN 0-8167-0452-X; 0-8167-0453-8 (paper). ▶ **K,EP**

This beautifully illustrated book gently introduces some very solid science to young readers by inviting them to observe the details of a familiar setting. By means of a limited vocabulary and unusually appealing illustrations, young readers are directed to observe with care and are encouraged to think for themselves. Little adult guidance is needed for the child to succeed in answering the book's open-ended questions. The illustrations, while clear enough to avoid confusing young readers, are visually appealing and intricate enough to satisfy older children. Can uniquely and significantly serve remedial readers.

Michl, Reinhard. *A Day on the River.* (Illus. by the author.) Woodbury, NY: Barron's, 1985. 28pp. $6.95. 85-18551. ISBN 0-8120-5715-5. ▶ **EP,EI,EA**

Michl shares childhood memories in this nature picture book that contains outstanding watercolors (including an 18″ × 24″ foldout poster) and many two-page and several text-free illustrations. Young readers will be stimulated by the adventures of three boys who set out in a boat for a day alone to explore the river. Although the book has been translated from German, 15 of the 16 species illustrated are commonly encountered here. Children may need help with some words; reading aloud and flipping pages to check the map and identification guide are recommended.

Rockwell, Jane. *All About Ponds.* (Illus. by Joseph Veno; a Question & Answer Bk.) Mahwah, NJ: Troll, 1984. 31pp. $8.59; $1.95 (paper). 83-4853. ISBN 0-89375-971-6; 0-89375-972-4 (paper). C.I.P. ▶ **EA,JH**

Depicts the ecological succession of a pond. The illustrations provide colorful representations of the ecosystem as a whole and of the individual organisms living within the ecosystem. The book will help students understand the pond as an ecosystem and the process of ecological succession.

Sabin, Francene. *Swamps and Marshes.* (Illus. by Barbara Flynn; from the Venture into Reading Series.) Mahwah, NJ: Troll, 1985. 30pp. $7.59; $1.95 (paper). 84-2717. ISBN 0-8167-0280-2; 0-8167-0281-0 (paper). C.I.P. ▶ **EI,EA**

Sabin describes swamps, marshes, bogs, and the animal and plant life found in them and explains the formation and importance of these wetlands. The text is generally accurate; the illustrations are colorful but lack detail. Greater attention to detail would have made this a better book. Still, it is an acceptable and inexpensive introduction to wetlands which could be considered—especially by libraries with few or no holdings on swamps and marshes—for readers in the primary grades.

Sabin, Francene. *Wonders of the Pond.* (Illus. by Leigh Grant.) Mahwah, NJ: Troll, 1982. 32pp. $7.89; $1.95 (paper). 81-7407. ISBN 0-89375-576-1; 0-89375-577-X (paper). C.I.P. ▶ **K,EP,EI**

This book takes a logical and well-planned look through a pond and describes a variety of animals that inhabit ponds created by beavers. Although specific plant life is only occasionally mentioned, the author does stress that plants support animal life and are a necessary part of pond life. The language is clear and can be easily explained to a small child. Scientific words are phonetically respelled. The illustrations are colorful, accurate, and charming and are detailed enough to be used in a classroom. Recommended for a school or public library.

Ziefert, Harriet. *Trip Day.* (Illus. by Richard Brown; from the Mr. Rose Series.) Boston: Little, Brown, 1987. 64pp. $7.95. 86-2697. ISBN 0-316-98765-4. C.I.P. ▶ **EP,EI**

This excellent book follows an elementary class on a field trip to a local pond and returns with them to the classroom to observe the organisms collected from the pond water. The presentation of science is clear and accurate and gives a level of detail appropriate for primary age students. The story presents a lot of information and ideas beyond scientific fact. Classroom teachers will find the book very useful in initiating discussions, about both scientific ideas and the broader concepts presented.

574.5264–.5267 Ecology of land environments

Althea. *Polar Homes.* (Illus. by Barbara McGirr.) NY: Cambridge University Press, 1984. 24pp. $5.50; $1.95 (paper). ISBN 0-521-25501-5; 0-521-27511-3 (paper). Glossary; index. ▶ **EP,EI**

Explores the habits, food, and homes of animals that live in the coldest places on earth, the two polar regions. Some of the vocabulary will require assistance for early primary grade readers. The information on the penguin, walrus, and less familiar phalarope will be interesting enough that young readers will want to tackle the material. The information is accurate, and the book discusses each animal in terms of just a few facts, leaving much opportunity for further research by those who are interested. Four-color illustrations depict each animal mentioned. A simple but good choice for beginning readers.

Catchpole, Clive. *The Living World: Deserts.* (Illus. by Brian McIntyre; from the Dial Books for Young Readers Series.) NY: Dutton, 1983. 32pp. $10.95 ea. 83-7757. ISBN 0-8037-0035-0. C.I.P. ▶ **EI,EA**

The Living World: Grasslands. (Illus. by Peter Snowball.) 1984. 24pp. 83-27123. ISBN 0-8037-0082-2.

The Living World: Mountains. (Illus. by Brian McIntyre.) 1984. 24pp. 83-25273. ISBN 0-8037-0086-5.

Deserts is an excellent introduction to a biome that is largely misunderstood. Deserts differ greatly, a point well made here. Selections of flora and fauna from different kinds of deserts are well chosen, accurately presented, and colorfully illustrated. The one possible flaw in this otherwise fine book is that the format is for the young reader, but the reading level is junior high. *Grasslands* takes readers on a quick trip through the major grassy plains of the world, with the emphasis on animal life. The text and pictures are excellent, providing more depth and detail than the usual animal picture book for children. The specialization of grass and the reasons that it dominates in certain climates are not included, but children will learn about a major ecological setting and several facts about animals that live and die in the grasslands. The colorful, eye-catching pictures of flowers, animals, and vistas that are associated with mountains around the world highlight and enhance this educational, general-awareness book. Primarily about animals that live on mountains, *Mountains* also includes some information on mountain plants and insects. The author does not describe mountains or the major ecological divisions on mountains, making it difficult for young readers to appreciate differences in plants and animals in these divisions.

Curran, Eileen. *Life in the Forest.* (Illus.) Mahwah, NJ: Troll, 1985. 32pp. $9.98; $2.50 (paper). 84-16455. ISBN 0-8167-0446-5; 0-8167-0447-3 (paper). ▶ **K,EP**

Life in the Meadow. 84-12384. ISBN 0-8167-0343-4; ISBN 0-8167-0344-2 (paper).

These beautifully illustrated books gently introduce some very solid science to young readers by inviting them to observe the details of a familiar setting. By means of a limited vocabulary and unusually appealing illustrations, young readers are directed to observe with care and are encouraged to think for themselves. Little adult guidance is needed for the child to succeed in answering the books' open-ended questions. The illustrations, while clear enough to avoid confusing young readers, are visually appealing and intricate enough to satisfy older children. Can uniquely and significantly serve remedial readers.

George, Jean Craighead. *One Day in the Alpine Tundra.* (Illus. by Walter Gaffney-Kessel.) NY: Crowell, 1984. 44pp. $9.95. 82-45590. ISBN 0-690-04325-2. Index; C.I.P. ▶ **EP,EI,EA**

One Day is about a boy's adventure on an alpine tundra on a stormy day. It describes the components of the alpine tundra ecosystem—physical factors as well as producers and consumers. Twenty plant and eighteen animals species are accurately described in their natural habitats, as are weather conditions and geologic changes. Handsomely illustrated and of high instructional value, the book is easy to read and interesting enough to stimulate children to explore ecosystem ecology.

George, Jean Craighead. *One Day in the Prairie.* (Illus. by Bob Marstall.) NY: Crowell, 1986. 42pp. $11.95. 85-48254. ISBN 0-690-04564-6. Index; C.I.P. ▶ **EA,JH**

Through this book the reader spends a day on the prairie observing nature through the eyes of characters such as a boy, a buffalo, and a prairie dog. Reading much like a novel, this book captures both the long day of the prairie, as well as the continual and abundant activity of nature. Nearly 40 different animals are mentioned, each having an important role in the story and in the life of the prairie. This book also provides some indication of what the prairie was once like and how it has changed. While the book might be too difficult for independent reading by young elementary students, the story is quite appropriate for children of all ages.

Hughes, Jill. *Arctic Lands, revised edition.* (Illus. by R. Coombs, D. Cordery, and M. Wilson; A Closer Look At Bk.) NY: Gloucester, 1987. 32pp. ea. $10.40 ea. 86-82809. ISBN 0-531-17036-5. Glossary; index. ▶ **EA,JH**

Deserts, revised edition. (Illus. by Roy Coombs and Maurice Wilson.) 86-82810. ISBN 0-531-17037-3.

In *Arctic Lands*, the reader is led through the changes in plant and animal growth and behavior during changes of seasons in arctic lands. After an explanation of the tundra, the author describes plant development and strategies for survival during the brief summer in the tundra's clime. Resident animals are depicted in terms of their adaptations for keeping out the cold and finding food. *Deserts* emphasizes the lack of water and the heat, clarifies the nature of hot deserts, and shows the ecological fit and adaptations to this harsh environment of many plants, animals, insects, and birds. In each book the many detailed illustrations and clear text blend with and augment each other.

Langley, Andrew. *Jungles.* (Illus.; from the Topics Series.) NY: Bookwright, 1987. 32pp. $10.40. 86-70971. ISBN 0-531-18111-1. Glossary; index. ▶ **EI,EA,JH**

This book, with its excellent text and outstanding photographs, provides an attractive introduction for understanding jungle ecosystems and their importance to the stability of the earth's land, water, and living systems.

Lerner, Carol. *A Forest Year.* (Illus.) NY: Morrow, 1987. 48pp. $11.75. 86-9741. ISBN 0-688-06413-2. Glossary; index; C.I.P. ▶ **EA**

Although this is a well-done, beautifully illustrated children's nature book that presents facts, it involves none of the processes of science. It does provide a broad picture through words and excellent illustrations of a few of the changes in the life of the forest through the four seasons. The major vertebrate groups plus insects and other invertebrates are presented. Clearly aimed at a general but young audience, this book might best serve as a "coffee-table" book for 10–12-year-olds.

National Wildlife Federation. *Wonders of the Jungle.* (Illus.) Washington, DC: National Wildlife Federation, 1986. 95pp. $12.95. 86-17966. ISBN 0-912186-72-0. Index; C.I.P. ▶ **EI,EA,JH**

This book provides excellent analysis of complex jungle ecosystems. Outstanding photographs supply direct experiences with the beauty of jungle creatures.

Rydell, Wendy. *All About Islands.* (Illus. by Ray Burns; a Question & Answer Bk.) Mahwah, NJ: Troll, 1984. 32pp. $8.59; $1.95 (paper). 83-4833. ISBN 0-89375-975-9; 0-89375-976-7 (paper). C.I.P. ▶ **EA,JH**

Using a question-and-answer format, this book explains how various types of islands are formed. A possible succession of life on a newly formed volcanic island is recounted, as well as current efforts to protect island ecosystems. The book has a readable narrative style, and colorful pictures illustrate each page.

Sabin, Francene. *Wonders of the Forest.* (Illus. by Michael Willard.) Mahwah, NJ: Troll, 1982. 32pp. $7.89; $1.95 (paper). 81-7401. ISBN 0-89375-572-9; 0-89375-573-7 (paper). C.I.P. ▶ **K,EP,EI**

This book describes a northern deciduous forest in terms that young children can easily understand. Sabin describes how the different plants and animals interact throughout the seasons, introducing terms such as canopy, understory, shrub, and herb layers; migration and hibernation; and bacteria and fungi. The illustrations are well done and accurate.

Sabin, Louis. *Wonders of the Desert.* (Illus. by Pamela Baldwin Ford.) Mahwah, NJ: Troll, 1982. 32pp. $7.89; $1.95 (paper). 81-7397. ISBN 0-89375-574-5; 0-89375-575-3 (paper). C.I.P. ▶ **K,EP,EI**

A great deal of information about desert plants and animals is clearly presented and beautifully and colorfully illustrated. Many different animals, such as gecko lizards, scorpions, roadrunners, jackrabbits, and coyotes, are illustrated and discussed, and many of their special adaptations to the desert environment and features are well described. A good resource for students and teachers; recommended for classroom, school, and public libraries.

Sanders, John. *All About Deserts.* (Illus. by Patti Boyd; a Question & Answer Bk.) Mahwah, NJ: Troll, 1984. 32pp. $8.59; $1.95 (paper). 83-4857. ISBN 0-89375-965-1; 0-89375-966-X (paper). C.I.P. ▶ **EA**

After mentioning how much of the world is desert and where the deserts are located, this readable book describes how deserts were formed and how they are alike. It also introduces the concept of the desert as an ecosystem and shows examples of animals and plants that have adapted to it. The final sections explain the relationship of humankind to the desert environment. Vivid illustrations help readers become aware of the extremes that are present in the desert.

Wood, John Norris. *Nature Hide & Seek: Jungles.* (Illus. by Kevin Dean and John Norris Wood; from the Nature Hide & Seek Series.) NY: Knopf, 1987. 20pp. $8.95. 86-21450. ISBN 0-394-87802-7. C.I.P. ▶ **EP,EI**

Here are five jungle scenes printed in full color on stiff stock, each a foldout like a Japanese screen about two feet wide when opened, illustrating African, Australian, Indian, South American, and Southeast Asian jungles. Partly hidden in each picture are 41 species of animals readers are challenged to find and identify using detailed keys interspersed between each foldout. Through this captivating format, the book tells of animal beauty and diversity and shows some of the countless strategies, structural and behavioral, by which animals have managed to survive in the fiercely competitive world of the jungle. Conservation messages occasionally appear.

574.92 Marine biology and ecology

See also 551.46 Oceanography and underwater exploration; 574.5263 Ecology of aquatic environments.

Amos, William H. *Exploring the Seashore.* (Illus.; a Book for Young Explorers.) Washington, DC: National Geographic, 1984. 32pp. $12.95 (series set of four). 84-11464. ISBN 0-87044-526-X. C.I.P. ▶ **EP,EI**

In this short but informative book, the author shows and describes rocky shores, salt marshes, mud flats, and sandy shores and conveys a sense of the dynamic nature of the sea's edge. The excellent color photographs include a wide variety of plants and animals commonly found at the shore.

Bierce, Rose (Ed.). *The Ocean: Consider the Connections.* (Illus.) Washington, DC: Center for Environmental Education, 1985. 98pp. $2.00 (paper). ISBN 0-96152-940-7 (paper). ▶ **EP,EI**

This activity book is compiled from the educational materials of major U.S. aquariums and marine centers. Included are word games, art projects, experiments, brief narratives, and simple but concise marine definitions. The material on currents, weather, waves, and tides; on adaptation, including camouflage, color, shape, and body features; and on aquanaut Scott Carpenter's Sealab are most noteworthy. The experiments demonstrating salinity and temperature currents, shoreline erosion, and oil spill cleanup are excellent. The book even includes Gyotaku (Japanese fish printing). Recommended for parents and elementary school teachers.

Curran, Eileen. *Life in the Sea.* (Illus.) Mahwah, NJ: Troll, 1985. 32pp. $9.98; $2.50 (paper). 84-16190. ISBN 0-8167-0448-1; 0-8167-0449-X (paper). ▶ **K,EP**

This beautifully illustrated book gently introduces some very solid science to young readers by inviting them to observe the details of a familiar setting. By means of a limited vocabulary and unusually appealing illustrations, young readers are directed to observe with care and are encouraged to think for themselves. Little adult guidance is needed for the child to succeed in answering the book's open-ended questions. The illustrations, while clear enough to avoid confusing young readers, are visually appealing and intricate enough to satisfy older children. Can uniquely and significantly serve remedial readers.

Glaser, Michael. *Driftwood.* (Illus. by the author.) Fiskdale, MA: Knickerbocker, 1985. 32pp. $3.95 (paper). 85-50601. ISBN 0-911635-01-7 (paper). ▶ **K,EP,EI**

Glaser takes us through a rhythmic and visually exciting journey of the life cycle of a tree. The tree falls into the sea, gets ripped apart branch by branch, then travels past all the contents of the sea to come to rest on a shore to become driftwood; it might yet become more when the human element is introduced. This is a thought-provoking book that acquaints young children with the mysteries and wonders of the sea. The illustrations are simple black-and-white line sketches with a touch of color for the sea.

Glaser, Michael. *The Nature of the Seashore.* (Illus.) Fiskdale, MA: Knickerbocker, 1986. 16pp. $3.95 (paper). ISBN 0- 911635-02-5 (paper). Observation kit included. ▶ **K,EP**

This delightful field-trip guide for the youngest beachcombers or naturalists comes with a field kit that includes magnifier, magnet, and collecting dish. The author asks young readers (and attending teachers and parents) to use all their senses to "see" the wonders of the seashore—sand, wind, waves, and animal and plant life. Those who complete the simple exercises will never again view the seashore as only a tanning spa or swimming hole.

Lambert, David, and Anita McConnell. *Seas and Oceans.* (Illus.; from the World of Science Series.) NY: Facts On File, 1985. 64pp. $9.95. 84-1654. ISBN 0-8160-1064-1. Glossary; index; C.I.P. ▶ **JH**

One of those rare science books that does an excellent job of explaining a fascinating yet mysterious subject—in this case, the seas and oceans. The many excellent and detailed photographs complement and balance the readable text, but the subjects are not discussed in depth. Teachers will want a copy for the classroom or library; students will not be able to put it down.

Malnig, Anita. *Where the Waves Break: Life at the Edge of the Sea.* (Illus.; a Carolrhoda Nature Watch Bk.) Minneapolis: Carolrhoda, 1985. 48pp. $12.95. 84-9614. ISBN 0-87614-226-9. Index; C.I.P. ▶ **EI,EA,JH**

The excellent photographs illustrate the tremendous variety of life in the intertidal zone. The examples are from both the East and West Coasts and span tropical to temperate climate zones. The text is somewhat choppy, but it presents a great deal of information and a number of concepts with a limited number of words. Interested third and fourth graders can enjoy the pictures, but might have difficulty with some of the concepts in the text. Well indexed.

Pope, Joyce. *The Seashore.* (Illus.; from the Action Science Series.) NY: Watts, 1985. 32pp. $9.90. 84-52005. ISBN 0-531-04951-5. Glossary; index. ▶ **EA**

The author attempts to make study of seashore organisms an active enterprise by suggesting a suite of equipment items that could be used in methods of study. Different kinds of shores, ranging from rocky to sandy, are examined from the point of view of the differing life forms that have adapted to these environments. The pictures are well done, and the coverage is broad enough to make this a useful book both in the classroom and in the field.

Sibbald, Jean H. *Sea Babies: New Life in the Ocean.* (Illus.; from the Ocean World Library Series.) Minneapolis: Dillon, 1986. 88pp. $10.95. 85-7039. ISBN 0-87518-305-0. Glossary; index; C.I.P. ▶ **EP,EI,EA**

This fascinating book explains in a lively and interesting fashion some unusual methods of reproduction used by marine dwellers and how they enhance the survival of the animals. Major points include the significance of laying millions of eggs, aspects of parental care among ocean fish and mammals, and the phenomenon of animals leaving the ocean proper and moving to shore to lay eggs or traveling up rivers to spawn. Some typographical errors; however, when the value of the book and the wealth of information it provides are considered, these shortcomings are minor.

Tayntor, Elizabeth, Paul Erikson, and Les Kaufman. *Dive to the Coral Reefs.* (Illus.; a New England Aquarium Bk.) NY: Crown, 1986. 36pp. $12.95. 86-4565. ISBN 0-517-56311-8. C.I.P. ▶ **EI**

A factually accurate, visually beautiful introduction to coral reef ecology presented at a level understandable to young children. The narrative accompanies a team of New England Aquarium scientists and divers as they explore reefs off the coast of Jamaica. The biology of the coral is explained, then other reef organisms are discussed. The book concludes with a mention of the destruction of reefs by souvenir collectors and coastal development. The abundant full-page color photographs, which always relate to the accompanying text, are worthy of anyone's coffee table.

Wood, John Norris. *Nature Hide & Seek: Oceans.* (Illus. by Mark Harrison.) NY: Knopf, 1985. 22pp. $8.95. 85-73. ISBN 0-394-87583-4. ▶ **K,EP,EI,EA**

A delightful surprise awaits young readers in this highly recommended and well-organized book about the sea. Heavy printing stock is used throughout, and pairs of cutout pages fold over those parts of the illustrated scenes where sea animals are hidden. The backs of these pages provide brief descriptions, interesting bits of information, and full illustrations of the hidden animals. All 47 camouflaged animals are fun to find, and some are difficult even for adults to locate. Six habitats are represented, including European waters, coral reefs, Australian waters, the Sargasso Sea, and the deep ocean.

575 Organic evolution and genetics
See also **Paleontology and Physical Anthropology** section.

Benton, Michael. *The Story of Life on Earth: Tracing Its Origins and Development Through Time.* (Illus.) NY: Warwick, 1986. 93pp. $13.90. 85-52281. ISBN 0-531-19019-6. Glossary; index. ▶ **EA,JH**

In Benton's well-organized, handsomely produced book, full-color illustrations depict ancient environments, fossil preservation, the earth's formation, plate tectonics, and the chemical theory of life's origin. Important sections cover new findings from the Ediacaran and Burgess Shale fossil faunas to the Nemesis death-star theory of dinosaur extinction and human evolution. Difficult concepts, such as radiometric dating, correlation of strata by fossils, and varying rates of evolution, are brought within the reader's grasp. Sentences are kept generally short but without talking down. The care and effort expended in preparing this book are readily apparent, although there are a few minor errors.

Cole, Joanna. *The Human Body: How We Evolved.* (Illus. by Walter Gaffney-Kessel and Juan Carlos Barberis.) NY: Morrow, 1987. 64pp. $11.75. 86-23679. ISBN 0-688-06719-0. Index; C.I.P. ▶ **EA,JH**

The interesting story of human evolution is punctuated by fascinating explanations of the development of specific parts of the human body. Not only are descriptions of the development of the brain, foot, hair, eyes, hands, opposable thumb, skull and jaw clear and simple, but the reasons behind the development of these body parts are rivetingly imparted. Ideas are also portrayed through many beautiful sketches. Graphics depict 3.5 million years of evolution and specific time periods of species dominance. These aids clearly tie together the entire presentation, giving the reader a realistic, overall perspective. Highly recommended.

Cork, Barbara, and Lynn Bresler. *The Young Scientist Book of Evolution.* (Illus.) Tulsa: EDC Publishing, 1985. 32pp. $12.95; $4.95 (paper). ISBN 0-88110-219-9; 0-86020-867-2 (paper). Glossary; index. ▶ **EA,JH**

The authors have managed to present evolution in a manner both interesting and convincing. In a book packed with illustrations and clear, understandable concepts, they cover 30 separate topics. This book has something for intelligent readers of all ages. The colorful illustrations will interest the young reader, who may have to puzzle over some of the words. The older student will find a wealth of ideas to supplement books in science and biology. Since some biology texts often skim over evolution, this book is a valuable supplement.

Gallant, Roy A. *From Living Cells to Dinosaurs.* (Illus. by Anne Canevari Green; a First Bk.) NY: Watts, 1986. 96pp. $9.90. 86-11111. ISBN 0-531-10207-6. Glossary; index; C.I.P. ▶ **EA,JH**

Packed with information on the origin of life, the rise of living cells, and the evolution of early cell life into highly advanced plants and organisms, the seven chapters cover significant advances, beginning with prebiotic life and ending with the fall of the dinosaurs some 70 million years ago. Text and illustrations overflow with simple yet accurate information on earth's historical past. Particularly impressive is the author's ability to explain some advanced biological concepts in a simple, straightforward, and interesting way. A supplement to class work or just a good science book to read for information and fun.

Jaspersohn, William. *How Life on Earth Began.* (Illus. by Anthony Accardo.) NY: Watts, 1985. 48pp. $9.90. 85-10557. ISBN 0-531-10030-8. C.I.P. ▶ EI,EA

The author traces the development of cells and the evolution of many-celled plants and animals such as worms, sponges, jellyfish, clams, corals, and crablike creatures through fish, amphibians, reptiles, birds, and mammals to *Homo sapiens*. The major theme is biochemical evolution influenced by chance and by change over very long time periods. The author in almost free-verse form has written clearly about evolution as a model for creation of life on earth. This book could serve as a beginning volume for teaching biochemical evolution and probably should be a part of elementary biology courses.

Stein, Sara. *The Evolution Book.* (Illus.) NY: Workman, 1986. ii + 389pp. $11.95. 84-40682. ISBN 0-89480-927-X. Index; C.I.P. ▶ EA,JH

The Evolution Book attempts to put a great deal of information from different science disciplines into an evolutionary perspective. It teaches some facts and theories about evolution; presents information from other branches of science, from genetics to geology to animal behavior; and provokes the reader to think about why things are the way they are and how they got that way. Each section includes experiments and projects. The drawings, photographs, and layout are outstanding. Recommended for the school library, as an addition to the classroom, and for the family to use at home.

576 Microbiology

Bains, Rae. *Louis Pasteur.* (Illus. by Dick Smolinski; from the Venture into Reading Series.) Mahwah, NJ: Troll, 1985. 32pp. $7.59; $1.95 (paper). 84-2748. ISBN 0-8167-0148-2; 0-8167-0149-0 (paper). C.I.P. ▶ EI,EA

Louis Pasteur tells of the life and work of one of the world's foremost early microbiologists whose research resulted in so many useful findings, including those that led to pasteurization, now the standard method for killing disease-carrying bacteria in milk, cheese, and other foods. Pasteur's story is told simply but dramatically and is illustrated by excellent color drawings. Highly recommended for every young reader.

Sabin, Francene. *Microbes and Bacteria.* (Illus. by Alexis Batista; from the Venture into Reading Series.) Mahwah, NJ: Troll, 1985. 32pp. $7.59; $1.95 (paper). 84-2749. ISBN 0-8167-0232-2; 0-8167-0233-0 (paper). C.I.P. ▶ EI,EA

Microbes and Bacteria explores the world of invisible plants, animals, and bacteria as well as rickettsiae and viruses, telling how these microbes live and how some are wonderfully beneficial while others are extremely harmful. Many forms are shown in color as they would be seen under high-powered microscopes. The story of the founding of microbiology by Anton van Leeuwenhoek using primitive, homemade instruments is briefly told.

580   Botanical sciences
See also 371.3 Methods of instruction; **Agriculture** section.

Coldrey, Jennifer. *Discovering Flowering Plants.* (Illus.; by Wendy Meadway; from the Discovering Nature Series.) NY: Bookwright, 1987. 47pp. $10.40. 86-62101. ISBN 0-531-18098-0. Glossary; index. ▶ EA,JH

This excellent book forms part of the 15-book *Discovering Nature* series, which may well be one of the finest series of children's nature books to be published in the past few years. The volume is extremely well organized, clearly written, and scientifically accurate. Large, colorful, well-chosen photographs and diagrams to be found throughout make *Discovering Flowering Plants* visually attractive and appealing while greatly enhancing and illustrating points made in the text. Although written for children in grades five through eight, the book is remarkably thorough and provides enough detail to be of value to senior high school students and, indeed, the general public.

Cork, Barbara. *Mysteries & Marvels of Plant Life.* (Illus. by Ian Jackson et al.) Tulsa: Educational Development Corp., 1984. 32pp. $7.95; $4.95 (paper). ISBN 0-86020-756-0; 0-86020-753-6 (paper). Index. ▶ **EA,JH**

A potpourri of facts about the plant world that is appropriate for supplemental use only. Record-breaking facts are given, true-or-false boxes are scattered throughout, and there are many excellent, colorful illustrations.

Curran, Eileen. *Look at a Tree.* (Illus.) Mahwah, NJ: Troll, 1985. 32pp. $9.98; $2.50 (paper). 84-8843. ISBN 0-8167-0349-3; 0-8167-0350-7 (paper). ▶ **K,EP**

This beautifully illustrated book gently introduces some very solid science to young readers by inviting them to observe the details of a familiar setting. By means of a limited vocabulary and unusually appealing illustrations, young readers are directed to observe with care and are encouraged to think for themselves. Little adult guidance is needed for the child to succeed in answering the book's open-ended questions. The illustrations, while clear enough to avoid confusing young readers, are visually appealing and intricate enough to satisfy older children. Can uniquely and significantly serve remedial readers.

Florian, Douglas. *Discovering Trees.* (Illus.; from the Discovering Series.) NY: Scribner's, 1986. 32pp. $10.95. 85-22143. ISBN 0-684-18566. C.I.P. ▶ **EI,EA**

Discovering Trees gives a detailed look at the life cycle of a tree. Colorful illustrations show different types of leaves and their corresponding trees. Tree families, seeds, cones, flowers, and fruit are all covered, as are climate, natural habitat, and transplanting trees from one part of the world to another. The author ends with a discussion of the importance of trees and our responsibility to reduce pollution to maintain nature's ecological balance. This book is simple yet very informative and will encourage children to develop their classification skills.

Gibbons, Gail. *The Seasons of Arnold's Apple Tree.* (Illus. by the author.) NY: Harcourt Brace Jovanovich, 1984. 28pp. $13.95. 84-4484. ISBN 0-15-271246-1. C.I.P. ▶ **EP**

A simple, flowing text and colorful pictures combine to create an educational and delightful book. Gibbons follows the changes in an apple tree from the spring through the winter while telling about a young boy who plays near and in the tree. Some youngsters may have difficulty with the many new terms introduced; however, the adventure aspect and the special features (such as the apple pie recipe) will undoubtedly hold interest. Through this general-awareness book, children should gain a better understanding of the four seasons, the seasonal changes in trees, and, especially, the growth of apples.

Heller, Ruth. *Plants That Never Ever Bloom.* (Illus. by the author.) NY: Grosset & Dunlap, 1984. 40pp. $6.95. 84-080502. ISBN 0-488-18964-X. ▶ **K,EP**

Heller adequately and accurately covers the range of nonflowering plants with an enjoyable writing style. Perhaps the most striking feature of the book is its illustrations, for they are exotic, bold, and fascinating and should appeal to all readers. This is a book that all teachers should have and one that all children will enjoy reading.

Lauber, Patricia. *From Flower to Flower: Animals and Pollination.* (Illus.; photographs by Jerome Wexler.) NY: Crown, 1986 (released in 1987). 64pp. $13.95. 86-4566. ISBN 0-517-55539-5. Index; C.I.P. ▶ **EA**

Flower to Flower describes the role of animals in pollination. Particular emphasis is placed on the part played by bees, although other insects and animals are featured. The pollination process and adaptation of plants to attract specific pollinators are well described. The black-and-white photographs are excellent quality, but some color photographs would have enhanced the overall presentation.

Lerner, Carol. *Pitcher Plants: The Elegant Insect Traps.* (Illus. by the author.) NY: Morrow, 1983. 63pp. $10.50. 82-12514. ISBN 0-688-01717-7. Glossary; index; C.I.P. ▶ **EA,JH**

In this outstanding botany book for children, the illustrations are excellent and the technical data accurate and appropriate. Lerner discusses the eight species of *Sarracenia*, plants that grow only in North America. She examines the leaf structures that help the plants obtain nutrients that are lacking in their environments, the devices with which they trap their victims, and the special relationships that exist between the *Sarracenia* and their insect parasites. *Pitcher Plants* should be available in school libraries for students from the fourth grade to junior high school.

Leutscher, Alfred, and Joyce Pope (Series Consultant). *Flowering Plants.* (Illus.; from the Action Science Series.) NY: Watts, 1984. 32pp. $9.90. 84-51178. ISBN 0-531-03814-9. Glossary; index. ▶ **EI,EA**

This beautiful book on flowering plants is highly recommended for school and public libraries. The printing, layout, and illustrations are superb. The sections on plant life, including nutrition, physiology, and pollination, and on collecting plants, making herbaria, and studying and enjoying plants are nicely done. The language throughout is lucid.

Mabey, Richard. *Oak & Company.* (Illus. by Clare Roberts.) NY: Greenwillow, 1983. 28pp. $9.00. 82-15618. ISBN 0-688-01993-5. C.I.P. ▶ **EA,JH**

Mabey condenses the life cycle of the oak into half of this slim volume, and includes a delicate weaving of the fabric of interdependencies and successional order in a biotic community. The rest of the book is devoted to excellent illustrations of many of the community members. Long and often complex sentences will tax the reading ability of the younger audience; however, their interest will be sustained by the illustrations. Appropriate for all school and public libraries and for classrooms, for every page holds a complete "mini-lesson" in ecology.

Marcus, Elizabeth. *Amazing World of Plants.* (Illus. by Patti Boyd; a Question

& Answer Bk.) Mahwah, NJ: Troll, 1984. 32pp. $8.59; $1.95 (paper). 83-4836. ISBN 0-89375-967-8; 0-89375-968-6 (paper). C.I.P. ▶ **EA,JH**

This book examines the great variety that exists among plants, describes flowering plants, then goes on to conifers, ferns, mosses, algae, and fungi and the many ways that we use plants. In explaining photosynthesis, the author gives the mistaken impression that plants use carbon dioxide but not oxygen. Nevertheless, the subject is interestingly and accurately presented. Helpful for middle-grade and junior-high students who have difficulty concentrating or who have poor reading skills.

Pohl, Kathleen (Adaptor). *Morning Glories.* (Illus.; from the Nature Close-ups Series.) Milwaukee: Raintree, 1987. 32pp. ea. $15.33 ea. 86-26256. ISBN 0-8172-2711-3. Glossary; C.I.P. ▶ **EI,EA**

Sunflowers. 86-26228. ISBN 0-8172-2710-5

Morning Glories is devoted to the life cycle of morning glories, with special emphasis on the climbing and blossoming of the family Convolvulaceae. Magnificent color photographs combined with succinct prose may motivate the readers to grow some of these flowers themselves. Pollination is made clear through enlarged color photographs of the pistil, stigma, and stamens. Also pictures are the effects of pollutants on leaves and blossoms. A useful book for teaching plant life cycles, pollination, observation of adaptations for climbing, and variety in color of blooms. Outstanding photographs of every stage in the sunflower's life, from germination through the autumn harvest of its seeds, make up most of *Sunflowers;* the words used to describe these processes seem almost unnecessary. Sunflowers as a part of the Soviet Union's economy and their role as a health food in the United States are also covered. Little is said about the use of sunflowers in feeding and attracting wild birds, however.

Romanova, Natalia. *Once There Was a Tree.* (Illus. by Gennady Spirin.) NY: Dial, 1985. ii + 26pp. $10.95. 85-6730. ISBN 0-8037-0253-3. C.I.P. ▶ **K,EP**

This simple story of the life cycle of a tree starts with a mature tree cut down by a woodsman. Most of the book deals with the stump and the many creatures—bark beetle, ants, bear, titmouse, frog, earwig—that claim ownership by using it as a home or place to find food. At the end, a new tree grows in the stump's place. The book, translated from the Russian, reads like a Russian saga in miniature, and emphasizes the theme that "the tree belongs to all, because it grows from the earth that is home for all."

Schnieper, Claudia. *An Apple Tree Through the Year.* (Illus.; photographs by Othmar Baumli; a Carolrhoda Nature Watch Bk.) Minneapolis: Carolrhoda, 1987. 48pp. $12.95. 87-7997. ISBN 0-87614-248-X. Glossary; index; C.I.P. ▶ **EP,EI**

As the year's activities are traced, the reader finds lots of excellent four-color photographs and a clearly written text. Here and there, a new tidbit of information pops up—items that most books leave out. A separate chapter on grafting, although somewhat out of step with the rest of the book, is very informative. Readers, however, should be aware that the book's orientation is distinctly European, which can cause some confusion since the people and even the animals shown in the photographs might be unfamiliar to American audiences.

Selsam, Millicent E. *Mushrooms.* (Illus.; photographs by Jerome Wexler.) NY: Morrow, 1986. 48pp. $11.75. 85-18953. ISBN 0-688-06248-2. Index; C.I.P. ▶ **K,EP,EI,EA**

This volume explains the nature of the predominant mushroom (*Agaricus campestris bisporas*) commercially cultivated and sold in the United States and includes an interesting history of growing mushrooms and their use as food. The distinguishing traits of mushrooms are described, and different types of wild mushrooms are introduced; the book cautions against randomly picking and eating mushrooms. The illustrations and photographs are very good, and the text type is large, easy to read, and accurate. A good science reference for elementary students.

Wexler, Jerome. *From Spore to Spore: Ferns and How They Grow.* (Illus. by the author.) NY: Dodd, Mead, 1985. 48pp. $9.95. 84-3496. ISBN 0-396-08317-X. Index; C.I.P. ▶ **EA,JH**

More information is packed into this simple, straightforward, readable book than in many a dull textbook chapter. Even photosynthesis is simply and clearly discussed. This is mainly an account of fern reproduction and growth, accompanied by interesting reproductive comparisons with the higher, more common plants with which the reader may be familiar. All forms of fern propagation are extensively but simply covered and exceedingly well illustrated at each step. After taking an hour or less to read this book, one could easily go into the field with a useful knowledge of ferns.

Zoological Sciences

590.74 Zoos

Cajacob, Thomas, and Teresa Burton. *Close to the Wild: Siberian Tigers in a Zoo.* (Illus.; photographs by Thomas Cajacob; a Nature Watch Bk.) Minneapolis: Carolrhoda, 1986. 48pp. $12.95. 85-29299. ISBN 0-87614-227-7. Glossary; C.I.P. ▶ EI,EA

The best feature of this book is the 57 color photographs of Siberian tigers. Most of the pictures were taken at the Minnesota Zoo, which appears to provide its tigers with nearly perfect natural settings. The life of tigers in the wild and in a zoo and problems associated with keeping tigers in captivity are presented well in both text and illustration. A fine addition to any children's library.

Cutchins, Judy, and Ginny Johnston. *The Crocodile and the Crane: Surviving in a Crowded World.* (Illus.) NY: Morrow, 1986. x+54pp. $11.75. 86-5339. ISBN 0-688-06304-7. Glossary; index; C.I.P. ▶ EI,EA

Focuses on six captive breeding programs for rare and endangered species and their successes. Fairly sophisticated vocabulary is used to describe how zoologists have carefully structured appropriate mating, birthing, and survival training environments within zoos. The book sounds much like a television documentary script. Throughout, there is a strong emphasis on the detrimental impact of expanding human populations and unscrupulous hunters. Should provide valuable insights and could be a good, solid starting point for discussion on a timely topic.

591 Zoology

See also 371.3 Methods of instruction; 636 Care of domesticated animals.

Boorer, Michael. *Animals.* (Illus.; from the Silver Burdett Color Library Series.) Morristown, NJ: Silver Burdett, 1983. 49pp. $14.00. 83-50388. ISBN 0-382-06725-8. Index. ▶ EI,EA,JH

Essentially a colorful picture book with extensive captions, this adaptation of a British work provides an attractive introduction to the larger members of the animal kingdom, with representatives drawn from all over the world. Exclusively metric measures of whale lengths and a few of the British phrases may need translation. Overall, the material is well organized, and the illustrations are good.

Buxton, Jane Heath. *Baby Bears and How They Grow.* (Illus.; a Book for Young Explorers.) Washington, DC: National Geographic Society, 1986. 34pp. ea. $10.95 (set). 86-2481. ISBN 0-87044-634-7. C.I.P. ▶ **EP**

McCauley, Jane R. *Animals and Their Hiding Places.* 86-12848. ISBN 0-87044-642-8.

McGrath, Susan. *Saving Our Animal Friends.* 86-5177. ISBN 0-87044-635-5.

Young readers will enjoy this large-format book about the lives of young black, polar, and grizzly bears. They will discover how the three kinds of bears grow up, what they feed on, and how they play and explore their surroundings. The text is accurate, but the author glosses over the fact that the young are born, nurse, and grow during the mother's winter dormancy. Heavily illustrated with outstanding color photographs. Children will discover why they don't see more wildlife in woods and fields by reading *Animals and Their Hiding Places.* Well illustrated by color photographs and a few drawings, the text shows how some animals hide to hunt, to escape detection by enemies, and to seek shelter from heat and cold. Readers will also learn how animals camouflage or disguise themselves to avoid discovery. Good natural science writing for young children. *Saving Our Animal Friends* opens by acquainting readers with animals in the zoo and the care given to injured birds and mammals. The text then quickly moves to the wild, where the meeting of humans and animals is less than cordial. Photographs show what happens to animals when humans take over their habitat. The book ends with suggestions on how young readers can help wildlife. This excellent book should simulate the beginnings of a conservation ethic in children.

[*Editors' note:* The fourth title in this set, *Animals That Live in Trees,* was adjudged by its reviewer to be only acceptable rather than recommended.]

Chinery, Michael (Ed.). *Dictionary of Animals.* (Illus.) NY: Arco, 1984. 379pp. $17.95. 84-716. ISBN 0-668-06155-3. Glossary; index; C.I.P. ▶ **EI,EA,JH.**

This attractive book, which is something of a dictionary as well as an encyclopedia, provides brief one- to two-paragraph descriptions of more than 2,000 vertebrate and invertebrate animal species. The book is generously illustrated, with at least one color photograph per page, many quite striking. The descriptions are simple enough for elementary school children, yet enough information is given to be useful to advanced students and a broad adult audience. A valuable reference for any school or public library and any family that enjoys a day at the zoo.

Crow, Sandra Lee. *The Wonderful World of Seals and Whales.* (Illus.; a Bk. for Young Explorers.) Washington, DC: National Geographic Society, 1984. 32pp. ea. $12.95 (series set of four). 84-14893. ISBN 0-87044-527-8. C.I.P. ▶ **EP,EI,EA**

Rinard, Judith E. *What Happens at the Zoo.* 84-14876. ISBN 0-87044-524-3.

Windsor, Merrill. *Baby Farm Animals.* 84-16668. ISBN 0-87044-525-1.

Through beautiful and informative photographs, *The Wonderful World of Seals and Whales* gives the young reader many facts about the lives of these marine mammals. The text is somewhat disjointed; there is a middle and an end but no beginning. The inclusion of a simple, general overview of marine mammals would have helped. Nevertheless, in a restricted space, Crow has done a creditable job. In *What Happens at the Zoo*, large, vivid photographs give an overview of the many activities. Typical zoo animals are featured, and various zoo personnel are shown weighing, feeding, and cleaning the animals. The informative text and reader questions will encourage discussion and further investigation. Both browsers and serious readers will find this book interesting. Using large, vivid, informative photographs, the first part of *Baby Farm Animals* introduces ducklings, piglets, calves, foals, chicks, goslings, goat kids, and lambs. However, in the middle, the book loses its focus and emphasizes different types of farms and the mature animals that live on each. The final double-page spread attempts to tie both segments together by featuring text and illustrations about a young boy's 4-H project—raising a lamb. Valuable for its magnificent photographs and accurate and informative text.

[*Editors' note:* The other title in this four-book set is *Exploring the Seashore*.]

Goaman, Karen, and Heather Amery. *Mysteries & Marvels of the Animal World.* (Illus. by David Quinn et al.) Tulsa: Educational Development Corp., 1984. 32pp. $7.95; $4.95 (paper). ISBN 0-86020-752-8; 0-86020-751-X (paper). Index. ▶ **EA,JH**

A brief encyclopedia of the weird and wonderful in the animal world. The information provided ranges from the trivial to the important, but will appeal to the intended audience. Although initially published in England, the book's scope is global.

Kaufman, Joe. *Joe Kaufman's Slimy, Creepy, Crawly Creatures.* (Illus. by the author; a Golden Bk.) Racine, WI: Western, 1985. 48pp. $7.95. 84-82577. ISBN 0-307-15776-8. ▶ **EP,EI,EA**

Fun and full of the kinds of facts that children enjoy, *Creatures* looks at some fish, amphibians, reptiles, molluscs, insects, and, briefly, some other invertebrates. Morphology, behavior, and habitats are described and many examples presented. The text, though condensed, is carefully written and brings out the salient features of each animal group. The profuse illustrations are colorful and often amusing, with humans figuring in many of them. Large type and format make this book a good choice for a class or school library general awareness text.

Laycock, George. *Eye on Nature: A Photographer's Introduction to Familiar Wildlife.* (Illus. by the author.) Englewood Cliffs, NJ: Prentice-Hall, 1986. xii + 162pp. $9.95 (paper). 86-4880. ISBN 0-668-06542-7 (paper). Index; C.I.P. ▶ **EA,JH**

This book of stories, many of which first appeared in *Boys' Life* magazine, covers wildlife lessons, mammals, birds, reptiles, fish, and invertebrates, with mammals and birds the focus of about 75 percent of the stories. The book is well illustrated with excellent black-and-white photographs, many by the author. He also manages to get a bit of humor into the text, which is handled very effectively. All in all, an enjoyable and interesting book.

May, John, and Michael Marten. *The Book of Beasts.* (Illus.) NY: Viking, 1982. 192pp. $12.95 (paper). 82-40374. ISBN 0-670-17915-9 (paper). Index. ▶ **EI,EA,JH**

This delightful book is a "who's who" animal encyclopedia of unusual facts about both common and little-known mammals, birds, reptiles, amphibians, fishes, and invertebrates. Some biological concepts such as hibernation, growth rate, migration, symbiosis, and locomotion are also presented. Some of the concepts may be difficult for younger readers, but the theme of diversity and uniqueness in the animal kingdom should instill in and feed readers' interest in zoology. Many excellent color illustration complement the accurate text.

National Wildlife Federation. *Animals Up Close.* (Illus.; from Your Big Backyard See and Do Nature Series.) Washington, DC: National Wildlife Federation, 1985. $12.95. 12 (8 x 11") cards; 2 Story-Starter booklets; teacher's activity guide. ▶ **K,EP**

Animals Up Close is a set of 12 large cards, each with an outstanding, close-up color photograph of a common animal (several mammals, birds, an insect, and so on). On the back of each card is a series of ten facts and questions to be used by teachers to encourage children to observe the animal more closely. The booklets picture parallel children's and animals' activities to stimulate young students to develop their own stories. The teacher's guide provides an abundance of suggestions. The whole package is well planned, providing an excellent means to introduce preschool and elementary children to science and animal life.

Silver, Donald M. *The Animal World.* (Illus. by Patricia J. Wynne.) NY: Random House, 1987. 112pp. $11.99; $8.95 (paper). 86-3894. ISBN 0-394-96650-3; 0-394-86650-9 (paper). Index; C.I.P. ▶ **EA,JH**

This book is a very effective, basic introduction to the animal world. After a brief look at one-celled animals, the author begins to explore the oceans where life first appeared. With a nice ecological approach throughout, he works his way through sponges, stinging animals, some unusual animals, mollusks, worms, and into the arthropods and the interesting subjects of insects, spiders, and crustaceans. A little more than half the book is then spent on the vertebrates, where appropriate animals depict the fishes, amphibians, reptiles, birds, and mammals. Overall, this book contains a tremendous amount of factual information presented in an interesting format. The color illustrations are excellent and accurate and are the key to the book's success.

Simon, Seymour. *101 Questions and Answers About Dangerous Animals.* (Illus. by Ellen Friedman.) NY: Macmillan, 1985. vi + 88pp. $10.95. 84-42975. ISBN 0-02-782710-0. Index; C.I.P. ▶ **EI,EA**

These 101 questions that children in grades three through six might ask about the habits and behavior of dangerous animals are answered; comments are brief, well stated, and to the point. The simple illustrations and easy-to-read style will hold the interest of youngsters.

Taylor, Ron. *50 Facts About Animals.* (Illus.) NY: Warwick, 1983. 32pp. $8.90. 82-51264. ISBN 0-531-09208-9. Index. ▶ **EA**

A book of isolated but interesting facts about fish, birds, reptiles, insects, and mammals. The book is meant to be a stimulus for young readers or general audiences and, as such, is very successful. Words such as marsupial, evolution, and metamorphosis are introduced indirectly but as a natural follow-up to the context. Skimpy index, excellent color illustrations; a book for libraries and homes.

591.042 Endangered species
See also 590.74 Zoos.

Benirschke, Kurt, and Andy Warhol. *Vanishing Animals.* (Illus.) NY: Springer-Verlag, 1986. x + 99pp. $49.50. 86-21983. ISBN 0-387-96410-X. C.I.P. ▶ EI,EA,JH

Vanishing Animals combines the talents of a leading conservationist and a ranking artist. This excellent, extremely attractive, well-written account focuses on several lesser known and "less glamorous" animal species that now border on extinction. The introduction traces the history of the conservation movement and the extinction of species since the 1800s. The body of the book gives in-depth, sound scientific information on each animal. The most remarkable illustrations are Warhol's 16 superb color prints—silkscreen over collage—prepared specifically for this volume.

Robinson, Sandra Chisholm. *The Last Bit-Bear.* (Illus. by Ellen Ditzler.) Boulder, CO: Roberts Rinehart, 1984. 44pp. $3.95 (paper). 84-060440. ISBN 0-911797-09-2 (paper). ▶ K,EP,EI

"Clover," a so-called bit-bear, "Fish," "Rat," and "Wolf" wander across the country seeking a mate or an unpolluted environment or both. They learn that the "other animal" is the cause of their problems. This animal pollutes and destroys their food supply and even destroys their kin. In the end, when the animals accidentally meet a boy, they do not recognize him as the other animal. The boy directs them to the haven of a nearby national park. The book's epilogue explains that Clover is the last of his species and will never find a mate. The message is not the subtle one we expect to find in a true fable, and it will not be overlooked by young readers. Fine-lined, black-and-white drawings give the animals personality and humor.

591.1–.4 Animal physiology, anatomy, and development
See also 636 Care of domesticated animals.

Cole, Joanna. *A Dog's Body.* (Illus.; photographs by Jim and Ann Monteith.) NY: Morrow, 1986. 48pp. $11.75. 85-25885. ISBN 0-688-04154-X. C.I.P. ▶ EA,JH

Written in a pleasantly straightforward, conversational style, this book is scientifically accurate, usefully illustrated (34 beautiful photographs, 4 excellent diagrams), and appropriately titled. It covers anatomy, physiology, and behavior and achieves this comprehensiveness within 48 pages by singling out accurately and precisely the features that make a dog a dog.

Cole, Joanna. *Large as Life: Daytime Animals Life Size.* (Illus. by Kenneth Lilly.) NY: Knopf, 1985. 32pp. $11.99. 85-4301. ISBN 0-394-87188-X. C.I.P. ▶ EI,EA,JH

Large as Life: Nighttime Animals Life Size. 85-7593. ISBN 0-394-87189-8.

These remarkable, oversize books depict animals in large-as-life, museum-quality paintings. The 10 featured animals in *Daytime Animals* share diurnal nature, an interesting existence, and a size that permitted each to be illustrated in its real-life size. A brief but authoritative text accompanies each double-page spread, highlighting one aspect of the animal's life. Although the well-written text is interesting, accurate, and informative, it is almost incidental to the beautiful illustrations. Coffee-table material that will be respected on the science shelves as well. Cole's reputation for accurate and well-written informational books for young readers is further enhanced in *Nighttime Animals*, a volume on interesting aspects in the lives of 10 nocturnal animals. Lilly has rendered the animals in detailed paintings, with each animal the same size as in real life. The last four pages give more specific information about each animal. This book will be a favorite with both the casual reader and the one who is seeking accurate scientific information. A superb offering.

Freeman, Dan. *Beautiful Bodies.* (Illus.) NY: Peter Bedrick, 1984. 45pp. $10.95. 83-25723. ISBN 0-911745-52-1. Index; C.I.P. ▶ **EA**

This is a fascinating book about the structural diversity found in nature. The familiar structure-function approach is offered in a good combination of text and high-quality illustration; 19 topics are covered in two pages each. Recommended for school libraries and homes, as both children and adults will enjoy browsing through this almost coffee-table book.

Goor, Ron, and Nancy Goor. *All Kinds of Feet.* (Illus.; a Let's-Read-and-Find-Out Science Bk.) NY: Crowell, 1984. 48pp. $10.95. 83-45239. ISBN 0-690-04384-8. C.I.P. ▶ **EP,EI**

Although children are the primary audience, adults will enjoy presenting this book to children and discussing it with them. The photographs are excellent, and the text effectively establishes the relationship between structure and function. That is, feet reflect the dynamics of the medium—land, water, and air—in hoof, flipper, and wing. The book also generates ideas about dispersal of animals into different environmental situations, about animal locomotion, and about eating behavior.

Hirschi, Ron. *Headgear.* (Illus.; photographs by Galen Burrell.) NY: Dodd, Mead, 1986. 64pp. $12.95. 85-20407. ISBN 0-396-08673-X. Glossary; index; C.I.P. ▶ **EI,EA**

This book describes the horns and antlers of North American mammals. Its well-written and accurate narrative details the characteristics of the headgear of each species and briefly discusses habitats and behavior. Forty superb color photographs closely follow the text. There are no tables, charts, maps, artwork, or diagrams—just interesting reading and beautiful pictures. The final chapter describes Indian folklore associated with these antlered and horned ungulates and ends with a comment on the need for conservation.

Isenbart, Hans-Heinrich. *Birth of a Foal.* (Illus.; photographs by Thomas David; a Carolrhoda Nature Watch Bk.) Minneapolis: Carolrhoda, 1986. 48pp. $12.95. 85-17406. ISBN 0-87614-239-0. Glossary; C.I.P. ▶ **EA,JH**

Birth of a Foal describes horse development from conception to weaning. The book is beautifully, profusely, even redundantly illustrated with excellent color photographs. Two pages of drawings illustrate the stages of fetal development and birth. Concise text, mostly relevant, is associated with each illustration. The photographs depict the birth in explicit detail. Suitable for inquisitive children, age ten and older, for information, reference, and classroom use.

Lauber, Patricia. *What Big Teeth You Have!* (Illus. by Martha Weston.) NY: Crowell (Harper & Row), 1986. iv + 60pp. $11.50. 85-47902. ISBN 0-690-04506-9. Index; C.I.P. ▶ **EA,JH**

Amply illustrated with black-and-white line drawings, the book contains much information on a variety of animals, their teeth, and the relationship of tooth type to living habits. Animals discussed include wolves, horses, and chimps; humans; elephants, hippos, and walruses; beavers, bats, and whales; gators, snakes, and sharks; and dinosaurs. While the author presents much information about the relationship of teeth to the kinds of food the animals eat, she also identifies some questions for which science does not yet have answers.

Peters, David. *Giants of Land, Sea and Air, Past and Present.* (Illus.; a Sierra Club Bk.) NY: Knopf, 1986. vi + 73pp. $12.95. 86-2719. ISBN 0-394-87805-1. Glossary; index; C.I.P. ▶ **EA,JH**

This informative book effectively illustrates the comparative sizes of a wide variety of large animals. Each animal is represented on the same scale (1 inch = 22.5 inches). A man and woman, also drawn to scale, appear on every two-page spread to provide a familiar basis for comparison. The illustrations are very detailed and interesting. The scientific and common names of each animal are given, with their classification of order, class, and phylum. A description of the creature's general characteristics and behavior is included. An illustrated time chart of animal evolution facilitates interpretation of the text information on extinct species.

Robinson, Marlene M. *What Good Is a Tail?* (Illus.) NY: Dodd, Mead, 1985. 48pp. $10.95. 85-6979. ISBN 0-396-08487-7. Index; C.I.P. ▶ **EP,EI**

What Good Is a Tail? is meant to challenge children to look afresh at that most functional part of an animal, its tail. Through examples—everything from beavers to mot-mots and mules to seahorses—the author presents a variety of tails and then asks how they are used. This method of presentation makes this book good for reading aloud by a teacher because it gives the students a chance to consider answers that address both identity and function. The plentiful black-and-white photographs are of good quality.

Sibbald, Jean H. *Strange Eating Habits of Sea Creatures.* (Illus.) Minneapolis: Dillon, 1986. 111pp. $11.95. 85-11621. ISBN 0-87518-349-2. Glossary; index; C.I.P. ▶ **EI**

This book's strength lies in its cutting across taxonomic classifications (species names are included in an appendix) and dealing with organisms that have common feeding strategies; these range from filter feeders and carnivores to the exotic behavior of animals that "farm" their prey and electroshockers that stun their prey. No attempt was made to include familiar freshwater species, which is unfortunate; also, a listing of the common animals associated with each feeding strategy might have allowed young naturalists to make more connections with their own experiences. Nevertheless, the ideas are well organized, adequately documented, and supported by a clear, concise text and colorful photographs.

591.5   Animal ecology and behavior

Gilmore, Jackie. *Year at Elk Meadow.* (Illus.; drawings by Susan Strawn.) Boulder, CO: Roberts Rinehart, 1986. 16pp. $3.95 (paper). ISBN 0-911797-24-6 (paper). ▶ **EI,EA**

In describing seasonal adaptations in wildlife behavior over a one-year period,

Gilmore begins with animal activities near the end of a long winter. Although this book tells a very basic story, Gilmore's language is unusually rich and evokes clear, detailed images of the events that occur as animals emerge from hibernation and elk migrate back to their meadow, reproduce and migrate out again. This well-written book has excellent science content and literary quality.

Hirschi, Ron. *One Day on Pika's Peak.* (Illus.; photographs by Galen Burrell.) NY: Dodd, Mead, 1986. 48pp. $10.95. 86-2069. ISBN 0-396-08778-7. Index; C.I.P. ▶ **K,EP,EI,EA**

The weasel is featured in this book in which more than 40 high-quality color photographs illustrate a 44-page text about animal life in the mountains. The sparse text is informative and touches on everything from climate and hibernation to animal signs and predation. The delicate subject of how the mother weasel feeds her carnivorous family is handled very well in both words and pictures. Hunter and prey are treated with a balanced appreciation for both and a nonjudgmental view of the interactions, setting this apart from many children's books that emphasize the cute and cuddly.

Hughey, Pat. *Scavengers and Decomposers: The Cleanup Crew.* (Illus. by Bruce Hiscock.) NY: Atheneum, 1984. 56pp. $11.95. 83-17474. ISBN 0-689-31032-3. Glossary; index; C.I.P. ▶ **EI**

This is an interesting book with an unfortunate subtitle. It describes the habitat and the animals that feed off dead animals and plants. What the book lacks in pictures it makes up for in information. Teachers will find this book useful in building interest in this topic in young children.

Lilly, Kenneth. *Animal Builders.* (Illus.) NY: Random House, 1984. 10pp. ea. $2.95 ea. 83-61970. ISBN 0-394-86373-9. ▶ **K**

Animal Climbers. 83-61968. ISBN 0-394-86374-7.

Animal Jumpers. 83-61969. ISBN 0-394-86375-5.

Animal Runners. 83-61971. ISBN 0-394-86376-3.

Animal Swimmers. 83-61967. ISBN 0-394-86377-1.

This series of five beautifully illustrated and sturdy books is for preschoolers who are just beginning to be interested in books and nature. The books are also appropriate for beginning readers because of the one-sentence-per-page format, large type, and simple yet accurate vocabulary. In *Animal Builders,* harvest mice build grass nests, squirrels build twig nests in trees, beavers construct a dam, weaverbirds make huge nests, and swallows make mud nests. These animals are not often found in children's books, and they are not depicted as cute, cuddly creatures but as clever, even elegant creatures and strong, hard workers. In *Animal Climbers,* the koala, loris, orangutan, leopard, and raccoon illustrate different climing abilities and styles. Each animal is shown in a natural setting, but with minimum background detail that does not detract from the focus of discussion. *Animal Jumpers* includes the salmon, an extremely capable jumper in the animal kingdom not often found even in nature books for children. *Animal Runners* and *Animal Swimmers* are just as attractive and interesting and complete a highly recommended set.

National Geographic Society. *The Secret World of Animals.* (Illus.; from the Books for World Explorers Series.) Washington, DC: National Geographic Society, 1986. 104pp. $6.95. 86-5141. ISBN 0-87044-575-8. Index; C.I.P. ▶ **EA**

This easy-to-read, colorful book replete with beautiful photographs describes the world of animals—their "shelters, hiding places, and nurseries." The book's design is attractive, and young readers will find it quite informative. It suffers, however, from some unevenness; the authors of each of the five chapters approach the subject from a slightly different vantage point, creating some overlap in themes and discussions. Teachers at the fourth- through sixth-grade levels may find it useful for a specific science unit on hibernation or animal shelters.

Pringle, Laurence. *Animals at Play.* (Illus.) NY: Harcourt Brace Jovanovich, 1985. x + 70pp. $12.95. 85-901. ISBN 0-15-203554-0. Index; C.I.P. ▶ **EA,JH**

For young people interested in a serious discussion about animal play, this is a very good introduction. The first chapter introduces the concept of play and the problem of defining play behavior. The following chapters describe the play of dogs, cats, primates (including humans), and other species. Accompanying black-and-white photographs add much detail to the vivid descriptions, some taken directly from ethological reports. The book ends with a valuable chapter on theoretical approaches to play that is intended to stimulate thought about its adaptive purposes. An attractive, well-organized, stimulating presentation of an interesting aspect of animal behavior suitable for above-average readers.

591.52 Animal adaptations to specific environments

Cloudsley-Thompson, John, et al. (Contributors.) *Nightwatch: The Natural World from Dusk to Dawn.* (Illus.; photographs by Jane Burton and Kim Taylor.) NY: Facts On File, 1983. 190pp. $24.95. 83-14040. ISBN 0-87196-271-3. Glossary; index; C.I.P. ▶ **EA,JH**

The subject here is the nocturnal world of animals, and the succession of startling images reveals each story in a way that the text can only approximate. With night strobe and underwater photographs, the books reveals the worlds of owls, bats, moths, nocturnal mammals, and deep sea fishes in an immediate and gripping way. Each photograph is accompanied by an informative caption, and the text is interesting and clear. Accurate but not comprehensive, the book would be inappropriate as a reference.

Leon, Dorothy. *The Secret World of Underground Creatures.* (Illus.) NY: Messner, 1982. 96pp. $8.29. 82-8185. ISBN 0-671-42403-8. Index; C.I.P. ▶ **EA,JH**

Introduces young readers to the fascinating animals that make their homes or take shelter underground. Leon discusses some of the evolutionary reasons animals use the underground region for shelter and includes instructions on how to observe and photograph animals in their habitats. Illustrated with black-and-white photographs and simple line drawings.

MacClintock, Dorcas. *African Images.* (Illus. by Ugo Mochi.) NY: Scribner's, 1984. xiv + 158pp. $14.95. 84-10565. ISBN 0-684-18089-8. Glossary; index; C.I.P. ▶ **EI,EA,JH**

Beautifully organized, this book covers eight African habitats, discussing the typical mammals and birds that live there. These written images are not meant to be complete or authoritative; rather, they represent personal selections that serve to lead the reader to further investigation of these animals, their behavior, and their ecologies. The illustrations are paper cutouts that show the shadow images of the animals. Technically accurate, these cutouts offer an artistic image that no painting or photograph could ever capture. A highly selective but accurate and informative introduction to a large subject.

McClung, Robert M. *Mysteries of Migration.* (Illus.) Champaign, IL: Garrard (1607 North Market St., Box A, 61820), 1983. 64pp. $7.22. 82-15740. ISBN 0-8116-2950-3. Index; C.I.P. ▶ **EA,JH**

McClung describes the migration of selected species of mammals, birds, reptiles, amphibia, fishes, and arthropods. Migration routes are clearly illustrated. The sentences are short, the language is clear, and the illustrations are profuse. Includes occasional movements without return (for example, lemmings, locusts) as well as seasonal round-trip travels between feeding and breeding grounds.

Pollock, Jean Snyder, and Robert Pollock. *Common Campground Critters of the Mountain West: A Children's Guide.* (Illus.) Boulder, CO: Roberts Rinehart, 1987. 20pp. $3.95 (paper). ISBN 0-911797-32-7 (paper). ▶ **K,EP**

This booklet describes common animals that can be found at almost any campground. Eight mammals and seven birds are described. Each description includes either a color or black-and-white photograph, a short write-up of the animal's sounds, its living and eating habits, differences between two apparently similar animals, and the national parks where the animal can be found. A map of the 12 western states, showing the location of the 11 national parks referred to in the text, is provided.

Powzyk, Joyce. *Tasmania: A Wildlife Journey.* (Illus.) NY: Lothrop, Lee & Shepard, 1987. 32pp. $11.75. 86-7288. ISBN 0-688-06459-0. Glossary; C.I.P. ▶ **EA**

Like Australia, Tasmania has a diverse fauna, much of which is unfamiliar to those outside Australia, Tasmania, and New Zealand. The excellent text describes animals found in the five habitats of Tasmania. Each page depicts one or two animals in an appropriate environmental setting. Especially interesting are the Tasmanian devil, the forester kangaroo, and the Tasmanian wolf, which may be extinct. The book ends with a slightly misleading and somewhat inaccurate evolutionary tree showing the relationship of the animals described to each other.

Powzyk, Joyce. *Wallaby Creek.* (Illus.) NY: Lothrop, Lee & Shepard, 1985. 32pp. $11.75. 84-29757. ISBN 0-688-05692-X. C.I.P. ▶ **EA,JH**

This slender gem describes a dozen animals of the Queensland rain forest in Australia. Both the narrative and the lovely watercolor illustrations will appeal to a broad range of readers. Text and illustration accurately portray this unique habitat. The presentations of the animals are refreshingly free of anthropomorphism. The book will find most use as source material for secondary school and above-average middle school readers.

Pringle, Laurence. *Wolfman: Exploring the World of Wolves.* (Illus.) NY: Scribner's, 1983. 71pp. $12.95. 82-19144. ISBN 0-684-17832-X. Index; C.I.P. ▶ **EA,JH**

A remarkably excellent, easy-to-read adventure story about the life, tribulations, and success of animal biologist David Mech. After his study of wolf/ moose predator relations on Isle Royale in Lake Superior, Mech went on to northern Minnesota to investigate the largest populations of wolves in the United States outside of Alaska. Here, radio tracking enabled him to conduct a thorough scientific study of wolf/deer predator relations. Black-and-white photographs, maps, and line drawings add considerable interest to the text. An adventure story in the strictest sense, this book will excite young readers and encourage them to follow Mech's path.

Sanders, John. *All About Animal Migrations.* (Illus. by Ray Burns; a Question & Answer Bk.) Mahwah, NJ: Troll, 1984. 31pp. $8.95; $1.95 (paper). 83-6630. ISBN 0-89375-977-5; 0-89375-978-3 (paper). C.I.P. ▶ **EA,JH**

This book's question-and-answer format provides readers with clear, accurate, and succinct information about animal migration. The book explains why animals migrate, while noting that not all the reasons for migration are completely understood.

Selberg, Ingrid. *Nature's Hidden World.* (Illus. by Andrew Miller; a Pop-Up Bk.) NY: Philomel Books, 1984. 14pp. $9.95. ISBN 0-399-20973-5. C.I.P. ▶ **K,EP,EI**

Each of the six double-page scenes that make up this beautifully color-illustrated book has pop-up figures as well as other figures controlled by pull tabs of animals not initially apparent. The six scenes are English landscapes rich in detail, inviting visual exploration. The questions and answers concerning one of the animals in each scene seem designed more to be read to children than by them. Adults and young children will have fun exploring this book together.

591.53 Animal communication

Patterson, Francine. *Koko's Kitten.* (Illus.; photographs by Ronald H. Cohn.) NY: Scholastic, 1985. 32pp. $9.95. 85-2311. ISBN 0-590-33811-0. C.I.P. ▶ **EI,EA**

This is a most welcome, well-written, and scientifically accurate book for children on animal communication. The author tells how she taught American sign language to Koko, a female gorilla, and how Koko then requested a cat, refused a toy cat, expressed pleasure on being presented with a live kitten, and indicated the proper signs for sorrow and anger when her pet was killed by a car. Excellent color photographs.

Sattler, Helen Roney. *Fish Facts & Bird Brains: Animal Intelligence.* (Illus. by Giulio Maestro; a Lodestar Bk.) NY: Dutton, 1984. 127pp. $10.95. 83-20805. ISBN 0-525-66915-9. Index; C.I.P. ▶ **EA,JH**

Sattler presents anecdotal gleanings from ethologists' previously published accounts of scientific studies of animal behavior and intelligence, including amazing studies of chimpanzees, crows, elephants, and planarians (flatworms). The book also gives details on how to test one's own pet for intelligence, and links the benefits of animal studies to human learning. A reading list cites articles and books by many of the scientists involved.

592–595 Invertebrates

Buholzer, Theres. *Life of the Snail.* (Illus. by the author; from the Nature Watch Series.) Minneapolis: Carolrhoda, 1987. 34pp. $12.95. 86-21544. ISBN 0-87614-246-3. Glossary; index; C.I.P. ▶ EI,EA,JH

Buholzer has observed, over a period of years, the habits of three common species of land snail in an outdoor enclosure made to resemble the natural habitat. The author describes many aspects of the snails' behavior throughout the year but is careful to point out that behavior in the wild may differ. The book is illustrated with many color photographs taken by the author, both at night and during the day. Overall, an excellent, carefully written book, with morphology and scientific processes clearly explained.

Climo, Shirley. *Someone Saw a Spider: Spider Facts and Folktales.* (Illus. by Dirk Zimmer.) NY: Crowell, 1985. 128pp. $11.50. 85-45340. ISBN 0-690-04435-6. ▶ EA,JH

This lighthearted look at an often misunderstood creature combines facts with legends, myths, and folktales about spiders. A variety of topics are covered, including spiders and insect control, spider courtship, and spider silk. The chapters are followed by a section on facts, figures, and spider trivia.

Johnson, Sylvia A. *Crabs.* (Illus. by Atsushi Sakurai; a Lerner Natural Science Bk.) Minneapolis: Lerner, 1982. 48pp. $8.95. 82-10056. ISBN 0-8225-1471-0. Glossary; index; C.I.P. ▶ EA,JH

This book is handsomely produced, beautifully illustrated with superb color photographs on every page, and written in a lively style that is packed with information. It is readable, scientifically accurate, amazingly comprehensive for its brevity, and entertaining. Johnson covers basic crab morphology, feeding, larval growth, molting, and the ecological importance of crabs. If your library is buying only one children's book on ocean life this year, then *Crabs* should be a top candidate.

Morris, Dean. *Spiders.* (Illus.; Read About Animals Library, accompanying study guide.) Milwaukee: Raintree, 1977. 47pp. $10.69; $6.95 (paper). 77-8115. ISBN 0-8393-0004-2; 0-8393-0288-6. Glossary; index; C.I.P. ▶ EI,EA,JH

Spiders develops the ability to use diagrams and labeled pictures. The book contains a drawing of a garden spider with body parts labeled, and the skill card instructs the reader on how to use it. *Spiders* is also a colorful and informative book that contains drawings of different spiders and describes web-building, hunting, diving, mating, and reproduction. Index, a pronunciation key, glossary, and a partially annotated bibliography complete the book. Recommended particularly for its illustrations and accuracy.

Selsam, Millicent E., and Joyce Hunt. *A First Look at Spiders.* (Illus. by Harriett Springer; from the First Look At Series.) NY: Walker, 1983. 32pp. $7.95. 82-42530. ISBN 0-8027-6480-0. C.I.P. ▶ K,EP

This satisfactory introduction to spiders provides background for further discussion about types of spiders and the strategies they use. Selsam presents material that allows students to distinguish between spiders and other arthropods and gives information on the various groups of spiders. Hunting strategies and the types of webs built by web-building spiders are included.

Shale, David, and Jennifer Coldrey. *The Man-of-War at Sea.* (Illus.; photographs by Oxford Scientific Films; from the Animal Habitat Series.) Milwaukee: Gareth Stevens, 1987. 32pp. $9.95. 86-5719. ISBN 1-55532-091-0. Glossary; C.I.P. ▶ **EI,EA,JH**

Everything one needs to know about the fascinating Portuguese man-of-war is contained in this excellent little book. The superb photographs are accompanied by a very good text, which, with some minor exceptions, is accurate, interesting, and informative. The book describes in adequate detail the complex structure of these animals, their behavior in the open ocean, and the means by which they capture their prey. The text is an expanded version of *The World of a Jellyfish* written by the same authors for a younger audience, and the publishers use the same photographs in both versions.

Shale, David, and Jennifer Coldrey. *The World of the Jellyfish.* (Illus.; photographs by Oxford Scientific Films; from the Where Animals Live Series.) Milwaukee: Gareth Stevens, 1987. 32pp. $9.95. 86-5719. ISBN 1-55532-091-0. Glossary; C.I.P. ▶ **K,EP**

Describes the Portuguese man-of-war with appropriate, carefully written text and superb color photographs. While the man-of-war is not strictly a jellyfish, as the book points out, it is commonly included with true jellyfish, and it is more photogenic than most. This is a simplified version of *The Man-of-War at Sea* written by the same authors (above) and the the publishers use the same photographs in both versions. A good introduction to jellyfish and to the tropical oceanic plankton.

595.7 Insects

See also 638 Insect culture.

Brewer, Jo, and Dave Winter. *Butterflies and Moths: A Companion to Your Field Guide.* (Illus.) NY: PHalarope (Prentice Hall), 1986. xiii + 194pp. $24.45. 86-3182. ISBN 0-13-108846-7. Glossary; index. ▶ **EA,JH**

There is little to criticize and much to praise in this introduction to the natural history of butterflies and moths and the methods used to observe and study them. Remarkably accurate in its statements of facts, the book is interesting and easy to understand. Throughout, it is apparent that the authors have first-hand knowledge of their subjects. They cover all the essential categories of lepidopteran biology—subjects that the field identification manuals usually neglect. Their encouragement of children in the pursuit of nature studies centering on moths and butterflies is especially commendable.

Cole, Joanna. *An Insect's Body.* (Illus.; photographs by Jerome Wexler and Raymond A. Mendez.) NY: Morrow, 1984. 48pp. $9.50. 83-22027. ISBN 0-688-02771-7. C.I.P. ▶ **EA**

Using a combination of photographs and line drawings, this book covers insect anatomy well. The photographs are good, and many provide a feeling of action that is usually associated with crickets and other insects. The labeling of the photographs enhances the content. Children already interested in insects will find this book useful.

Fischer-Nagel, Heiderose, and Andreas Fischer-Nagel. *Life of the Butterfly.* (Illus.; a Carolrhoda Nature Watch Bk.) Minneapolis: Carolrhoda, 1987. 48pp.

$12.95. 86-23217. ISBN 0-87614-244-7. Glossary; index; C.I.P. ▶ **EP,EA,EI**

This book is an absolute joy to look at and contains a wealth of interesting information. The reader is drawn in by the magnificent photographs. The text is well organized and, in clear language, explains the metamorphosis and other aspects of the peacock butterfly's existence.

Fischer-Nagel, Heiderose, and Andreas Fischer-Nagel. *Life of the Ladybug.* (Illus.; a Nature Watch Bk.) Minneapolis: Carolrhoda, 1986. 48pp. $12.95. 85-25467. ISBN 0-87614-240-4. Glossary; C.I.P. ▶ **K,EP,EI**

In this profusely illustrated book, the high-quality color photographs provide excellent material for nonreading students, and the text is appropriate for fourth or fifth graders to read on their own. The syntax is not always clear, however, and some of the science could be improved. Only the outstanding photography boosts this book into the "recommended" category.

Florian, Douglas. *Discovering Butterflies.* (Illus.; from the Discovering Series.) NY: Scribner's, 1986. 32pp. $10.95. 85-2312. ISBN 0-684-18439-7. C.I.P. ▶ **EI,EA**

Florian takes readers through this insect's journey from larva to butterfly, beginning with life inside the egg and continuing with hatching of the larva, molting, growth of the caterpillar, and cocoon spinning of the pupa to the final emergence of the butterfly. Next come explanation of the butterfly's body parts, butterfly history, and number and descriptions of butterfly species. Each example is accompanied by a color illustration. The author ends by relating the value of butterflies to humans: their role in pollination and their usefulness to scientists as monitors of environmental pollution. Very informative and well organized.

Heymann, Georgianne (Adaptor). *Aphids.* (Illus.; a Nature Close-Ups Bk.) Milwaukee: Raintree. 1987. 32pp. $10.99; $6.95 (paper). 86-28017. ISBN 0-8172-2717-2; 0-8172-2735-0 (paper). Glossary; C.I.P. ▶ **EA,JH**

This superbly color-illustrated book is accompanied by an uneven, often difficult text that presents an excessive number of new concepts and many new terms that are mentioned but not developed further. However, the complex relationships among aphids and other insects, involving mutualism, predation, and parasitism, are well described and illustrated. The vivid, close-up photographs carry the text over rough spots.

Johnson, Sylvia A. *Beetles.* (Illus. by Isao Kishida; a Lerner Natural Science Bk.) Minneapolis: Lerner, 1982. 48pp. $8.95. 82-7230. ISBN 0-8225-1476-1. Glossary; index; C.I.P. ▶ **EI,EA**

Beetles is a clearly and concisely written and well-illustrated general introduction to the Coleoptera. It outlines life history, structure and development, and other topics such as male and female morphology, flight, feeding variations, and environment. Readers are introduced to a small selection of the numerous beetle families, including some of the more commonly seen and economically important ones, and the sheer diversity found in the group is emphasized. The text is liberally illustrated with excellent color photographs, mainly of live specimens.

Johnson, Sylvia A. *Fireflies.* (Illus.; photographs by Satoshi Kuribayashi; a Lerner Natural Science Bk.) Minneapolis: Lerner, 1986. 48pp. $12.95. 86-26. ISBN 0-8225-1485-0. Glossary; index; C.I.P. ▶ **EA,JH**

Adapted from a Japanese book, *Fireflies: The Secret of Their Light*, Johnson's text is readable and interesting. Many excellent color photographs follow the text and show close-ups of the firefly life cycle. Clear explanations and illustrations reveal light-pulse signaling, larval development, feeding, molting, pupal development, adult emergence, and the "secret of the firefly's fire"—bioluminescence. This is a great book, and if younger children cannot manage some of the vocabulary—no matter; the illustrations alone tell the story.

Johnson, Sylvia A. *Mantises.* (Illus. by Satoshi Kuribayashi; from the Lerner Natural Science Bks. Series.) Minneapolis: Lerner, 1984. 48pp. $8.95. 83-23889. ISBN 0-8225-1458-3. Glossary; index; C.I.P. ▶ **EI,EA**

Wasps. (Illus. by Hiroshi Ogawa.) 83-23847. ISBN 0-8255-1460-5.

The complete and detailed life story of the mantis—its life cycle, range, habitat, anatomy, predators, prey and method and special physical characteristics for catching prey, and the incomplete metamorphosis of the mantis compared to the complete metamorphosis of other insects—are all covered in *Mantises*. The color photographs on every page are excellent and a useful supplement to the descriptive text. A useful reference for elementary school and public libraries, primary-grade biology classes, or simply for young science buffs. *Wasps* tells the detailed life story of the wasp in sequence: the building of the nest, the first eggs and larvae, which are nurtured by the foundress of the colony, the activities of these first adults, the growth of the colony, the reproduction of more eggs and their development, the communal life or social aspect of the wasp colony, and hibernation. The color photographs on each page are excellent. Useful for reference and collateral reading at the primary school level.

O'Toole, Christopher. *Discovering Ants.* (Illus. by Wendy Meadway; from the Discovering Nature Series.) NY: Bookwright, 1986. 46 pp. $10.40. 85-73663. ISBN 0-531-18056-5. Glossary; index. ▶ **EI,EA**

Discovering Bees and Wasps. (Illus.; photographs from Oxford Scientific Films.) 85-72247. ISBN 0-531-18047-6.

Discovering Ants contains an impressive amount of sound information about ants and their varied life-styles. The good photographs and illustrations are tied together by a minimal narrative, but in some cases, there is a gap of several pages between the text and the relevant picture. Also, the narrative does not flow very smoothly and is telegraphic in places. Despite these minor shortcomings, *Discovering Ants* should be a great stimulator of student interest. *Discovering Bees and Wasps* is indeed a guide to discovery of bees and wasps. The minimal narrative ties together truly outstanding photographs. The breadth of coverage is good and conveys the diversity of the group, but the narrative, a commentary on the photographs, is so brief as to be cryptic in many places. The brief bibliography should be useful because the excellent photographs should whet the appetite of young readers.

O'Toole, Christopher. *Discovering Flies.* (Illus. by Wendy Meadway; from the Discovering Nature Series.) NY: Bookwright, 1987. 46pp. $10.40. 86-71272. ISBN 0-531-18097-2. Glossary; index. ▶ **EA,JH**

Extremely well organized, clearly written, and scientifically accurate, this volume is from an outstanding series of children's nature books. Large, colorful, well-chosen photographs and diagrams make *Discovering Flies* visually attractive and appealing while greatly enhancing and illustrating points made in the text. New scientific terms are set in boldface type and are defined in the glossary. For children in grades five through eight, but provides enough detail to be of value to senior high students and, indeed, the general public.

Patent, Dorothy Hinshaw. *Mosquitos.* (Illus.) NY: Holiday House, 1986. 40 pp. $11.95. 86-45387. ISBN 0-8234-0627-X. Index; C.I.P. ▶ **EP,JH**

This book contains concise descriptions of the larva, pupa, and adult stages in the life of a mosquito. Feeding and reproductive functions are also explained. Each stage of the life cycle is pictured and described in terms of the changes in structure and function that are taking place as the mosquito develops into the adult form. The second half of the book includes discussions of why mosquito bites itch, how mosquitoes carry diseases, and methods of controlling mosquito populations. The black-and-white photographs outshine the words because most of them are highly magnified images. An interesting reference for elementary students and their teachers.

Petty, Kate. *Bees and Wasps.* (Illus. by Tony Swift and Norman Weaver; a Small World Bk.) NY: Gloucester, 1987. 29pp. $9.90. ISBN 0-531-17048-9. Index. ▶ **EP,EI**

This well-presented book considers the life and work of the colonial honeybee, bumblebees, solitary bees, common and solitary wasps, and wasps without stingers. It ends with a brief summary of the importance of bees and wasps to people, predominantly as pollinators. The text is clear, concise, and illuminated by many excellent, accurate, and detailed color illustrations. It could serve as an introductory text, general-awareness text, or collateral reading.

Pope, Joyce. *Insects.* (Illus.; from the Action Science Series.) NY: Watts, 1984. 32pp. $9.90. 84-51177. ISBN 0-531-03815-7. Glossary; index. ▶ **EA**

A nicely done and delightful book for young people and adults who would like to learn about insects. The printing, layout, and illustrations are superb. There are sections on what insects are and how they live and feed themselves, how to watch them, and how to make insect collections. This book should be added to the collections of schools and public libraries.

Porter, Keith. *Crickets and Grasshoppers.* (Illus. by Wendy Meadway; a Discovering Nature Bk.) NY: Bookwright, 1986. 46pp. $10.40. 86-70990. ISBN 0-531-18096-4. Glossary; index. ▶ **EA**

An excellent introduction to straight-winged insects. The characteristics of insects and of crickets and grasshoppers are briefly described and pictured in gorgeous photographs from Oxford Scientific Films. Such outstanding features of these insects as their acoustic behavior and the extraordinary biology of plague locusts are also briefly discussed and illustrated. The print is large and the words simple and well chosen. Porter informs his young readers clearly and without condescension.

Porter, Keith. *Discovering Butterflies and Moths.* (Illus. by Wendy Meadway; from the Discovering Nature Series.) NY: Bookwright, 1986. 46pp. $10.40. 85-73664. ISBN 0-531-18055-7. Glossary; index. ▶ **EP,EI**

A sufficient variety of Lepidoptera is mentioned and illustrated to present the order and give a balanced view. Youngsters may find the information on classification in the first few pages a bit difficult and boring due to the introduction of too many new terms, but after reading the rest of the book on insect parts, growth, feeding, behavior, and other informative points, young readers may be glad to come back to the first chapter to see how these beautiful creatures are sorted. Beautifully illustrated and clearly written in simple, well-formed sentences; a welcome addition to a primary-level library.

Saintsing, David. *The World of Butterflies.* (Illus.; photographs by Oxford Scientific Films; from the Where Animals Live Series.) Milwaukee: Gareth Stevens, 1987. 32pp. $9.95. 86-5706. ISBN 1-55532-097-X. Glossary; C.I.P. ▶ **EP,EI,EA**

The World of Butterflies is a good introduction to the life of butterflies. All of the excellent illustrations are photographs, except the drawing of a food web. Topics include anatomy, feeding, reproduction, migration, enemies, camouflage, habitat destruction, and insecticide use. There is no explanation of the difference between butterflies and moths.

Seymour, Peter. *Insects: A Close-up Look.* (Illus. by Jean Cassels Helmer; a Science Action Pop-Up Bk.) NY: Macmillan, 1985. 10pp. $6.95. ISBN 0-02-782120-X. ▶ **EI**

Four double-thick pages with pop-ups, pull tabs, and lift-ups will get young children involved in exploring the world of grasshoppers, ants, butterflies, and other insects. Where insects live, what they eat, how they move, and the process of metamorphosis are covered. A degree of completeness is sacrificed due to the limited number of pages, but this book provides an excellent introduction to the world of insects.

Whalley, Paul, and Mary Whalley. *The Butterfly in the Garden.* (Illus.; photographs by Oxford Scientific Films; from the Animal Habitats Series.) Milwaukee: Gareth Stevens, 1987. 32pp. $9.95. 86-5705. ISBN 1-55532-093-7. Glossary; C.I.P. ▶ **EI,EA,JH**

The Butterfly in the Garden is a good introduction to the life of butterflies. The text is organized in the same way and around the same illustrations as in *The World of Butterflies* by the same publisher. Topics include anatomy, feeding, reproduction, migration, enemies, camouflage, and impact of habitat destruction and insecticide use. Mentions that butterflies are an indicator of the health of the biological community and gives suggestions of making the local environment safer for butterflies and, therefore, for many other organisms.

Yajima, Minoru. *The Firefly.* (Illus.; photographs by Yukoh Sato; from the Nature Close-ups Series.) Milwaukee: Raintree, 1986. 32pp. ea. $10.99 ea.; $6.95 .ea (paper). 85-28193. ISBN 0-8172-2535-8; 0-8172-2560-9 (paper). Glossary; C.I.P. ▶ **EA,JH**

Hasegawa, Yo. *The Grasshopper.* (Illus.; photographs by Hidekazu Kubo. 85-28228. ISBN 0-8172-2536-6; 0-8172-2561-7 (paper).

Nanao, Jun. *Life of the Ant.* (Illus.; photographs by Satoshi Kuribayashi. 85-28198. ISBN 0-8172-2539-0; 0-8172-2564-1 (paper).

Oda, Hidetomo. *The Ladybug.* (Illus.; photographs by Nanao Kikaku. 85-28199. ISBN 0-8172-2538-2; 0-8172-2563-3 (paper).

These four books on insects are by Japanese authors and photographers and are uniformly excellent in text and illustration. The illustrations are largely colored photographs, most of which are of exceptional clarity and some of which are of rare beauty. The illustrations take somewhat more than half the space of each book and provide a good balance to the well-written descriptions. The information is accurate and is presented in a direct, clear, and appealing style, neither cute nor pedantic.

597 Fishes

Blassingame, Wyatt. *Wonders of Sharks.* (Illus.) NY: Dodd, Mead, 1984. 96pp. $9.95. 84-10097. ISBN 0-396-08463-X. Index; C.I.P. ▶ **EA,JH**

Dispels the myth of sharks as terrifying creatures by presenting facts from scientific studies. Topics covered include the scientific definition of sharks, evolution, food finding tactics, reproduction, why sharks occasionally attack humans, how sharks are kept from beaches, intelligence, shark-dolphin relationships, sport fishing for sharks, legends, what to do when you see a shark, the man eaters, and the harmless species. Well written and contains a great deal of fascinating, reliable information; good for pleasure reading and useful for reports.

Bunting, Eve. *The Sea World Book of Sharks.* (Illus.; photography by Flip Nicklin.) NY: Harcourt Brace Jovanovich, 1984. 79pp. $6.95 (paper). 84-12950. ISBN 0-135-271952-0 (paper). Index; C.I.P. ▶ **EI,EA,JH**

A splendidly illustrated, lively, and empathetic portrayal of the lives of sharks. The author helps to debunk mystique based on ignorance while cultivating the mystique that stems from true wonder and awe based on a fuller understanding of these marvelous creatures. Each of the many color photographs is appropriate and well placed. A short general bibliography makes the book a good starting point for extended library research on sharks.

Casey, Horton. *Fish.* (Illus.; from the Insight Series.) NY: Gloucester Press, 1983. 37pp. $9.90. 83-80461. ISBN 0-531-03474-7. Glossary; index. ▶ **EI,EA,JH**

Well written, concise, and interesting as well as accurate. The excellent layout is designed to present a simple but comprehensive introduction to the wide world of fish. The text is divided into 17 subtopics that cover all the basic information, such as environment, classification, and diet. Beautifully illustrated with good-quality color pictures. Very good index.

Cole, Joanna. *Hungry, Hungry Sharks.* (Illus. by Patricia Wynne; from the Step into Reading Series.) NY: Random House, 1986. 48pp. $5.99; $2.95 (paper). 85-2218. ISBN 0-394-97471-9; 0-394-87471-4 (paper). C.I.P. ▶ **EP**

This little book, with its well-presented and significant natural history content, is a refreshing introduction to reading. The format is clear and attractive, the illustrations are neat but not gaudy, and the style is natural and unstilted. The content is accurate, and, as far as it goes, comprehensive, sampling the diversity, feeding, reproduction, ecology, and physiology of sharks, and providing enough information to whet the appetite as reading becomes more facile. Useful in the classroom, at home, and for general awareness.

Green, Carl R., and William R. Sanford. *The Great White Shark.* (Illus.; from the Wildlife Habits and Habitat Series.) Mankato, MN: Crestwood, 1985. 48pp. $9.95. 85-14936. ISBN 0-89686-281-X. Glossary; index; C.I.P. ▶ **EP,EI,EA**

Green and Sanford tell the fascinating and true tale of an unborn great white shark getting so hungry that it ate one of its nearby "brothers." The life cycle of the animal is given, together with its importance to man its interrelationships with its surroundings. The illustrations are average, but the storyline is interesting enough to hold attention.

Reed, Don C. *Sevengill: The Shark and Me.* (Illus. by Pamela Ford Johnson; A Sierra Club Bk.) NY: Knopf, 1986. xii + 125pp. $11.95. 86-2727. ISBN 0-394-86926-5. Index; C.I.P. ▶ **EA,JH**

This recounting of an aquarium diver's experiences with captive sevengill sharks will engross students from grades five to nine. There is much drama here along with a fair amount of good shark biology. Both the tedium and the exhilaration of working in a large public aquarium are well expressed. This book is only slightly marred by a few technical inaccuracies concerning the sensory systems of sharks and a preposterous suggestion that sharks hold the key to a cure for AIDS. The illustrations are not very helpful.

Schmitz, Siegfried. *Fish Calendar.* (Illus. by Jürgen Ritter.) Morristown, NJ: Silver Burdett, 1986. ii + 37pp. $8.96; $5.75 (paper). 86-4003. ISBN 0-382-09239-2; 0-382-09240-6 (paper). Index; C.I.P. ▶ **EA,JH**

Although life cycles and fishes in the summer are contrasted with those in the winter, to call this a "fish calendar" is inappropriate. This book is a calendar only in the sense that a wide variety of fishes and their natural histories are presented. Young readers should find the construction of a garden pond and an indoor aquarium interesting. The illustrations are excellent.

597.6–.9 Amphibians and reptiles

Green, Carl R., and William R. Sanford. *The Cobra.* (Illus.; from the Wildlife Habits and Habitat Series.) Mankato, MN: Crestwood, 1986. 48pp. $9.95. 85-19469. ISBN 0-89686-289-5. Glossary; index; C.I.P. ▶ **EI,EA**

Discussions of the various kinds of cobras and other venomous snakes; their physical differences, life cycles, habitats, and behavior; the mythical and religious stories about them; and how snakes are milked for venom comprise this elementary introduction to the cobra. The book provides some general information about snakes, animal behavior, ecology, and the relationships of animals to humans. The quality and value of the photographs are uneven.

Green, Carl R., and William R. Sanford. *The Rattlesnake.* (Illus.) Mankato, MN: Crestwood House, 1984. 47pp. $8.95. 83-20865. ISBN 0-89686-247-X. Glossary; index; C.I.P. ▶ **EI,EA,JH**

This book provides encyclopedic coverage by including chapters stressing shedding, fangs and rattles, habitat and size, life cycle, economic use, and myths. The writing is clear and interesting, and errors are few and minor. Except for two, the photographs are good and relate to the text. A map shows the combined distribution of all North American rattlesnakes and is accurate at a gross level.

Johnson, Sylvia A. *Snakes.* (Illus.; photographs by Modoki Masuda; a Lerner

Natural Science Bk.) Minneapolis: Lerner, 1986. 48pp. $12.95. 87-7162. ISBN 0-8225-1484-2; Glossary; index; C.I.P. ▶ **EA,JH**

Tree Frogs. 86-2721. ISBN 0-8225-1467-2.

An attractive and carefully constructed book, translated from the Japanese, *Snakes* is an excellent introduction to snake biology and diversity. The accurate text is highly readable and well organized. Snakes are first shown to be reptiles, and various harmless and venomous species are briefly introduced. A section on anatomy precedes a fairly detailed discussion of snake locomotion. A section on sense organs and their use in food capture is followed by a description of snake venoms. A discussion of reproduction concludes the text. *Tree Frogs* is a beautifully illustrated book centered on the Japanese forest tree frog, *Rhacophorus arboreus*, with clear writing and none of the stylistic oddities that often appear in translations. The first section introduces general frog adaptations and adaptation for arboreal life. The second section follows the life cycle of this tree frog from hibernation through mating to egglaying; then it follows the development, hatching, growth and metamorphosis of tadpoles. The photographs are superb in depicting frog life history, attractiveness, and reproduction. Unfortunately, the book's emphasis on a single species belies the generality of its title and neglects the diversity in the life styles and body forms of the hundreds of other species of tree frogs.

Lambert, David. *Reptiles.* (Illus.) NY: Gloucester (dist. by Watts), 1983. 37pp. $9.90. 83-80462. ISBN 0-531-03475-5. Glossary; index. ▶ **EI, EA**

This easy-to-read book covers such topics as how reptiles breed, their methods of defense, and unusual behavior. The section on snakes shows how snakes use their muscles to move and to kill prey. Richly illustrated with attractive drawings; useful in natural history classes for the elementary grades.

Linley, Mike. *Discovering Frogs and Toads.* (Illus.; from the Discovering Nature Series.) NY: Bookwright, 1986. 47 pp. $10.40. 85-73666. ISBN 0-531-18053-0. Glossary; index. ▶ **EI,EA**

The answers to questions about frogs and toads sought by young inquiring minds are presented here in a direct and well-organized manner. The author writes to children and not down to them. The words toad and frog are used almost interchangeably in this book. A fine introduction to the subject with excellent color photographs.

McCarthy, Colin. *Poisonous Snakes.* (Illus.; a First Sight Bk.) NY: Gloucester, 1987. 32pp. $10.90. 87-80464. ISBN 0-531-17053-5. Index. ▶ **EI,EA**

This book offers a sound introduction to snake biology and variety. Each topic is explained in two or three paragraphs, which are usually accompanied on the same page by a color illustration depicting some aspect of the topic and on the facing page by a full-page color photograph of an appropriate snake. The text is interesting and generally accurate, but with a few minor overgeneralizations. The photographs are attention-grabbers and are well produced. Could be easily used in a classroom to introduce younger elementary students to snakes and snake biology without frightening them.

National Geographic Society (Eds.). *Reptiles and How They Grow.* (Illus.; a Wonders of Learning Kit.) Washington, DC: National Geographic Society, 1986. $28.95. (30 booklets; 1 narration cassette; teacher's guide; activity sheets.) ▶ **K,EP**

This well-made learning kit contains a teacher's guide folder with ample background information and suggestions for teaching. The instructions for using the kits are clear and concise and should ensure that both the content and skill objectives are met by pupils. In addition to several fundamental but easily understood content objectives, skill objectives, such as eye-hand coordination, reinforcement of concepts, applying information, counting, following directions, and creative expression are stressed in the work of the activity sheets. Even teachers who normally shy away from science will have no difficulty teaching from these kits.

Sabin, Louis. *Reptiles and Amphibians.* (Illus. by Nancy Zink-White; from the Venture into Reading Series.) Mahwah, NJ: Troll, 1985. 32pp. $7.59; $1.95 (paper). 84-8445. ISBN 0-8167-0294-2; 0-8167-0295-0 (paper). C.I.P. ▶ **EI,EA**

Packed with information about the origin of and similarities and differences between reptiles and amphibians. Hibernation and body-temperature fluctuations are explained; dinosaurs and their descendents are described; many species of lizards, snakes, and turtles, their methods of locomotion, and their life cycles are included. Reads like a textbook, but the text is often broken by large colorful illustrations. Useful for research by young students because the sizes of both the type and the books themselves are less inhibiting and easier to handle than an encyclopedia.

Scott, Jack Denton. *Alligator.* (Illus.; photographs by Ozzie Sweet.) NY: Putnam's, 1984. 64pp. $11.95. 84-9927. ISBN 0-399-21011-3. C.I.P. ▶ **EA,JH**

This sympathetic, fairly comprehensive exposition of the problems that are associated with more than 100 years of the harvesting and poaching of alligators traces the development and effects of recent conservation laws designed to protect them. Woven into the narrative, which presents the life history and habits of alligators in an interesting manner, are discussions of some prevalent misconceptions. Photographer Sweet creates an excellent pictorial study in black and white of these surviving prehistoric "lizards." The vocabulary and sentence length make *Alligator* difficult for young readers.

Serventy, Vincent. *Crocodile and Alligator.* (Illus.; photographs by the author; from the Animals in the Wild Series.) NY: Scholastic, 1986. 24pp. $1.95 (paper). ISBN 0-590-40198-X (paper). ▶ **EP,EI**

Short comments and excellent photographs make this interesting reading for youngsters. Scientific facts about crocodiles and alligators, as well as their similarities and differences, will fascinate. The photographs follow the text closely, each illustrating a particular natural history feature. Designed to show these reptiles in their natural surroundings and to describe their life and struggle for survival, this book succeeds well. It should find a place in all public libraries and elementary schools.

598 Birds

See also 636 Care of domesticated animals.

Austin, Oliver L., Jr. *Birds of the World: A Survey of the Twenty-Seven Orders and One Hundred and Fifty-Five Families.* (Illus. by Arthur Singer.) NY: Golden Press, 1983. 317pp. $24.95. 82-83715. ISBN 0-307-46645-0. Index. ▶ **EA,JH**

This beautifully illustrated coffee-table book is aimed at a general audience. Singer's paintings are spectacular. The organization is basically phylogenetic, proceeding from a general evolutionary discussion of birds to specific descriptions of each of the orders, from the most primitive kiwis of New Zealand to the burgeoning order of perching birds. The book was first published in 1961, so, while the descriptions of the birds are still generally accurate, the status of some threatened groups is now different. The use of British common names is occasionally jarring.

Boulton, Carolyn, and Joyce Pope (Series Consultant). *Birds.* (Illus.; from the Action Science Series.) NY: Watts, 1984. 32pp. $9.90. 84-50015. ISBN 0-531-04634-6. Glossary; index. ▶ **EA**

This excellent book on birds should be fun to use at home, especially during the summer months. The printing, layout, and illustrations are superb. There are sections on how birds fly, adaptations for flying in air, and how birds nest. Bird watching and the simple equipment needed are also explained. Highly recommended for school and public libraries.

Curran, Eileen. *Birds' Nests.* (Illus.) Mahwah, NJ: Troll, 1985. 32pp. $9.98; $2.50 (paper). 84-8658. ISBN 0-8167-0341-8; 0-8167-0342-6 (paper). ▶ **K,EP**

This beautifully illustrated book gently introduces some very solid science to young readers by inviting them to observe the details of a familiar setting. By means of a limited vocabulary and unusually appealing illustrations, young readers are directed to observe with care and are encouraged to think for themselves. Little adult guidance is needed for the child to succeed in answering the book's open-ended questions. The illustrations, while clear enough to avoid confusing young readers, are visually appealing and intricate enough to satisfy older children. Can uniquely and significantly serve remedial readers.

Givens, Janet Eaton. *Just Two Wings.* (Illus. by Susan Elayne Dodge.) NY: Atheneum, 1984. 28pp. $8.95. 83-2710. C.I.P. ▶ **K**

The short, simple, question-and-answer text about birds introduces a variety of topics, such as the changing seasons, preparation for migration, the advantages birds take of prevailing winds, different thoughts on directional finding of migratory birds, reasons for migration, birds that don't migrate, the return to the north for nesting, some of the kinds of information that can be gleaned by banding birds, and instinct. The black-and-white line drawings on every page are excellent. A fun book for kindergarten classes and homes that have a bird feeder by the window.

National Geographic Society. *The Wonder of Birds.* (Illus.) Washington, DC: National Geographic Society, 1983. 280pp. $39.95. 83-12141. ISBN 0-87044-470-0. Index; C.I.P. ▶ **EA,JH**

This book's photographs and captions alone tell fine stories, and the authoritative, if romanticized, text offers novices and veteran birders readable and accurate information about how birds live. Several well-known ornithologist-writers contribute chapters that celebrate birds, describe their diversity, and trace their habits through the year. *Birds* includes a list of bird-watching locales by state and province, four paper-thin records of bird songs, and a map of migration routes over North and South America.

Perrins, Christopher M., and Alex L. A. Middleton (Eds.). *The Encyclopedia of*

Birds. (Illus.) NY: Facts On File, 1985. xxxi + 464pp. $35.00. 84-26024. ISBN 0-8160-1150-8. Glossary; index; C.I.P. ▶ **EP,EI,EA,JH**

This superb book describes the anatomical, physiological, behavioral, and ecological adaptations of bird families worldwide. A condensed strip of information on the geographical distribution, habitat, plumage, voice, nests, eggs, and size range prefaces the discussion of each family. Spectacular studies on particular aspects of bird biology are treated in special boxes, and the consequences of human activities on the birds (and vice versa) are included in each article. The illustrations include color photographs and paintings.

Santrey, Laurence. *Birds*. (Illus. by Pamela Johnson; from the Venture into Reading Series.) Mahwah, NJ: Troll, 1985. 32pp. $7.59; $1.95 (paper). 84-2731. ISBN 0-8167-0192-X; 0-8167-0193-8 (paper). C.I.P. ▶ **EI,EA**

The reader learns that the first bird, *archaeopteryx*, looked more like a lizard than a bird but had wings and feathers, then that modern birds, quite different in appearance and structure from this ancestor, all share several characteristics, including feathers, wings, beaks, warm-bloodedness, and the ability to lay hard-shelled eggs. Feeding habits, habitats, reproduction, nesting, and singing are discussed. Bird flight and feather structure are briefly described; the discussion of migration is particularly good. The illustrations are well done and attractive. Of value for classroom or reference use.

Selsam, Millicent E., and Joyce Hunt. *A First Look at Bird Nests*. (Illus. by Harriett Springer; from the First Look At Series.) NY: Walker, 1984. 32pp. $9.85. 84-15238. ISBN 0-8027-6565-3. Index; C.I.P. ▶ **K,EP,EI**

A well-written and illustrated book that tells about nests and the birds that build and use them. The pictorial representations of nests are accompanied by text that points out "clues" to the nest owner. The reader is advised to look at the nest location, at its size and shape, and at the material used in construction. The presentation encourages children to use their powers of observation and reasoning to put the textual clues and the bird and nest illustrations together. This type of "science" for young children makes sense; it teaches them to note differences and similarities and to correlate observations.

Wolff, Ashley. *A Year of Birds*. (Illus.) NY: Dodd, Mead, 1984. 26pp. $10.95. 83-27470. ISBN 0-396-08313-7. C.I.P. ▶ **K,EP**

Each month, a different group of birds visits Ellie's house, as shown in a series of 12 large, multicolored illustrations accompanied by single sentences in large print. Beginning readers will be inspired to read the names of the birds as well as the names of the months. How the seasons change is emphasized by changes in animal and plant life, changes in Ellie's activities and clothing, and changes in Ellie's mother, who is clearly quite pregnant in May and holding an infant by July.

598.3–.4 Water birds

Ahlstrom, Mark E. *The Canada Goose*. (Illus.) Mankato, MN: Crestwood House, 1984. 47pp. $8.95. 83-24015. ISBN 0-89686-243-7. Glossary; index; C.I.P. ▶ **EI,EA,JH**

This book provides a detailed summary of the habits of this well-known bird.

The first chapter explains migration, breeding and wintering grounds, flyways, and flight information. Readers then learn about the goose's senses, diet, communication, and locomotor abilities. The third chapter describes a year in the life of a goose. The text, index, and glossary are accurate, and the writing is generally good. The illustrations are good to excellent and closely match the text. This book will give young bird watchers or hunters a better appreciation of the extraordinary Canada goose.

Coldrey, Jennifer. *Penguins.* (Illus.: photographs by Douglas Allan et al.; from the Nature's Way Series.) London, England: André Deutsch (dist. by Elsevier-Dutton), 1983. 32pp. $9.95. ISBN 0-233-97524-1. ▶ **K,EP,EI,EA**

In color closeups, the book shows Adélie penguins parading, mating, and hatching; rockhoppers performing daring gymnastics on craggy rocks; and majestic king and emperor penguins brooding their young on their feet and "tobogganing" across snow and ice. Although the book explains that the penguins' natural enemies stalk and kill them, it also depicts the vast breeding colonies of penguins. Young children will delight and learn from the photographs alone, and older children will gain insights from the lucid and complete text.

Coldrey, Jennifer. *The Swan on the Lake* (Illus.; photographs by Oxford Scientific Films; from the Animal Habitats Series.) Milwaukee: Gareth Stevens, 1987. 32pp. $9.95. 86-5719. ISBN 1-55532-091-0. Glossary; C.I.P. ▶ **EI,EA,JH**

This small book gives a detailed account of swans. The many superb color photographs are accompanied by an interesting and accurate text that describes swans' habitats, different kinds of swans, how they swim and fly, feeding, courtship and mating and nesting habits, growth of the young, and the effective self-defense methods of the adult birds. The ravages of man are also described. The text is an expanded version of *The World of Swans* (below) written by the same author for a younger audience.

Coldrey, Jennifer. *The World of Swans.* (Illus.; photographs by Oxford Scientific Films; from the Where Animals Live Series.) Milwaukee: Gareth Stevens, 1987. 32pp. $9.95. 86-5721. ISBN 1-55532-095-3. Glossary; C.I.P. ▶ **K,EP,EI**

Superb color photographs marvelously illustrate these beautiful and majestic animals going about their daily business of feeding, preening, flying, nesting, and caring for young. Their formidable reputation for aggressively defending their territory and nesting sites is also discussed. The text is interesting and accurate, complementing the photographs nicely.

Featherly, Jay. *Ko-hoh: The Call of the Trumpeter Swan.* (Illus.; a Carolrhoda Nature Watch Bk.) Minneapolis: Carolrhoda, 1986. 48pp. $12.95. 85-30955. ISBN 0-87614-288-9. Glossary; C.I.P. ▶ **EI,EA**

Interesting details about the nature and life cycle of these elegant birds are described in this substantive and engaging book. Its spirited and graceful style reflects the writer's obvious affection for these lovely waterfowl; however, the text is also exceptionally clearly written and carefully organized. The many photographs have been strategically chosen and placed to illustrate and extend the text. The story of the trumpeter swan is a conservation success story; in 1932, there were only 69 known individuals, but today there are over 10,000. Young readers can learn from this book that not all is unremitting gloom in the fight to preserve our natural habitat.

Lewis, Naomi. *Puffin.* (Illus. by Deborah King.) NY: Lothrop, Lee & Shepard, 1984. 28pp. $11.00. 83-23864. ISBN 0-688-03783-6. C.I.P. ▶ **EI,EA**

Lewis presents a wealth of information about the life and habits of a young puffin born in a rabbit burrow off the coast of Scotland. The book follows the bird into adulthood and describes courtship and the feeding of the offspring. Lewis writes in a straightforward, engaging style without sentimentality. Superb color illustrations by Deborah King.

McNulty, Faith. *Peeping in the Shell: A Whooping Crane Is Hatched.* (Illus. by Irene Brady.) NY: Harper & Row, 1986. 58pp. $10.95. 85-45837. ISBN 0-06-024134-9. C.I.P. ▶ **EI,EA**

McNulty has combined the natural history of whooping cranes, experiments in animal behavior, and avian embryology into one highly readable book. The illustrations are crisp and accurate. Part one provides a brief account of how whooping cranes live and why only 50 remain alive today. Part two describes the almost heroic effort of an ornithologist to induce egg laying in a female whooping crane by simulating the energetic crane mating dance. Parts three and four describe the hatching of this egg in detail. Both author and scientist become emotionally involved with their subject, belying the stereotype of the dispassionate researcher.

Stone, Lynn M. *The Penguins.* (Illus.; from the Wildlife Habits & Habitat Series.) Mankato, MN: Crestwood, 1987. 47pp. $10.95. 87-646. ISBN 0-89686-326-3. Glossary; index; C.I.P. ▶ **EI,EA,JH**

The Penguins is concise and information-packed. The introduction and first chapter discuss the history of these birds: discovery, name origin, relationship to similar birds, and fossil records. Chapters two and three (the most interesting) deal with the (mostly emperor) penguins' habitat, anatomy, daily and seasonal habits, and life cycle. The last chapter brings out a little more history and touches on the penguins' future in captivity and in the wild. Good color photographs; however, a more detailed map of Antarctica with regions labeled to show where different penguins live is needed.

Todd, Frank S. *The Sea World Book of Penguins.* (Illus.; photographs by the author; from the Sea World Series.) NY: Harcourt Brace Jovanovich, 1984. 96pp. $12.95; $6.95 (paper). 84-12983. ISBN 0-13-271949-0; 0-13-271951-2 (paper). Index; C.I.P. ▶ **EA,JH**

This delightful, information-packed book contains many color photographs that are splendid, well placed, and very well captioned. The author delightfully summarizes some of the amazing adaptations of penguins to their aquatic habitats. A good chapter on the special problems and rewards of maintaining penguins in zoos is followed by a concise summary of the status of penguins in the wild. The author's personal experiences shine through in this captivating, authoritative introduction that is sure to fascinate young naturalists.

598.5–.9 Land birds

Dewey, Jennifer Owings. *Clem: The Story of a Raven.* (Illus. by the author.) NY: Dodd, Mead, 1986. 128pp. $11.95. 85-27440. ISBN 0-396-08728-0. C.I.P. ▶ **EA**

This book successfully blends science and anecdote in a tale that can be read aloud to accurately inform and nurture its audience. As a "found" nestling, Clem joins a human family just before the arrival of their baby. We learn about a domestic community of related ecologies—family, domesticated animals, neighborhood, climate, and landscape.

Heilman, Joan Rattner. *Bluebird Rescue.* (Illus.) NY: Lothrop, Lee & Shepard, 1982. 48pp. $9.00. 81-17191. ISBN 0-688-00894-1. Glossary; C.I.P. ▶ **EA,JH**

Heilman carefully details the problems that bluebirds face and explains how the birds' behavior patterns are interrupted by human activities—including the introduction of the house sparrow and starling. She shows us how we can aid this beautiful bird by building and managing correctly dimensioned bird houses and gives clear descriptions and diagrams. The book is a practical and attractive guide, and it carries an accurate ecology story. It can be the springboard for classroom nature lessons, as well as a source for an extended parent-child activity.

Lavine, Sigmund A., and Vincent Scuro. *Wonders of Turkeys.* (Illus.) NY: Dodd, Mead, 1984. 64pp. $9.95. 84-1638. ISBN 0-396-08333-1. Index; C.I.P. ▶ **EA**

This book focuses on the interactions of wild and domestic turkeys with humankind and covers turkeys in literature, art, and folklore. How turkeys are domesticated and used as a food source are also covered, but the book does not give the natural history of the turkey or a detailed look at anatomy and physiology. Nevertheless, it is a fairly comprehensive and accurate treatment with many interesting and often obscure facts. Good black-and-white photographs.

598.91 Birds of prey

Green, Carl R., and William R. Sanford. *The Peregrine Falcon.* (Illus.; from the Wildlife Habits and Habitat Series.) Mankato, MN: Crestwood, 1986. 48pp. $9.95. 86-2670. ISBN 0-89686-271-2. Glossary; index; C.I.P. ▶ **EA,JH**

Beginning with a dramatic illustration and a fictional account of the first free flight of a peregrine falcon raised and trained for release by a young girl and her naturalist uncle, the authors go on to describe the three subspecies of peregrines and their behavior, migrations, diet, and life history. They also explain how DDT almost led to the extinction of these magnificent birds. A final chapter describes the ancient sport of falconry and its modern equivalent—raising falcons for release into the wild. The illustrations are stunning and well chosen to complement the text.

Hunt, Patricia. *Snowy Owls.* (Illus.; a Skylight Bk.) NY: Dodd, Mead, 1982. 62pp. $7.95. 82-7361. ISBN 0-396-08073-1. Index; C.I.P. ▶ **EI,EA**

In this delightful and informative book, many aspects of the natural history and ecology of the snowy owl are described, including their external morphology, habitat, feeding and hunting behavior, territory, mating habits and reproduction, enemies, competitors and prey, and evolution. Of particular interest is a discussion of the relationship between snowy owls and lemming population cycles. A note about owls in myth and legend ends the book. The text is accurate without being technical and avoids the anthropomorphism often found in children's natural history books. Illustrated with 16 full-page and 3 half-page black-and-white photographs.

Selsam, Millicent, and Joyce Hunt. *A First Look at Owls, Eagles, and Other Hunters of the Sky.* (Illus. by Harriett Springer; from the First Look Series.) NY: Walker, 1986. 32pp. $10.95. 86-7738. ISBN 0-8027-6625-0. Index; C.I.P. ▶ **K,EP,EI**

As an introduction to the classification of owls, eagles, hawks, falcons, and vultures, this is an excellent book for young children. It is suitable as a read-aloud book for preschool, kindergarten, and the early primary grades. It is also appropriate for beginning readers. The vocabulary is simple but accurate. The illustrations do exactly what they should: illustrate characteristics useful in classification. Of particular value are the silhouettes of eagles, hawks, and falcons in flight.

Tejima. *Owl Lake.* (Illus.) NY: Philomel Books, 1987. 36pp. $13.95. 86-25173. ISBN 0-399-21426-7. C.I.P. ▶ **K,EP,EI**

A simple yet poetic story line translated from the Japanese chronicles one night in the life of a Blakiston's fish owl. But the text is just the *basso continuo* for this book's delightful series of woodcuts, which portray the moods and textures of the environment in which this owl lives and hunts food for his family. North American readers should be made aware that this peculiar fish-eating owl is unknown in the Western Hemisphere; it is found only on the artist's home island of Hokkaido and adjacent areas of the Asian mainland.

599 Mammals

599.2 Marsupials

Arnold, Caroline. *Kangaroo.* (Illus.; photographs by Richard Hewett.) NY: Morrow, 1987. 48pp. $11.75. 86-18103. ISBN 0-688-06480-9. C.I.P. ▶ **EI**

In this true story, Sport, a kangaroo, is orphaned after his mother is killed by hunters. Fortunately for Sport, the Meltons adopt him and nurse him back to health. Sport is released into a wildlife reserve when he is able to care for himself. *Kangaroo* focuses on raising Sport but also manages to describe the origins of marsupials and the different species of kangaroos without burdening the story with excessive detail. The author is clearly sensitive to the plight of marsupials but is not melodramatic. The book needs at least a hint of humor to lighten its somber tone, however.

Arnold, Caroline. *Koala.* (Illus.; photographs by Richard Hewett.) NY: Morrow, 1987. 48pp. $11.75. 86-18092. ISBN 0-688-06478-7. Index; C.I.P. ▶ **K,EP,EI**

This book traces the life cycle of a specific koala female and the natural history of the species. With a simple text and 39 excellent photographs, the book covers such topics as Australian settlement by humans, endangered species and koala preserves, scientific names, varieties of koalas, physical character-istics of sexes of koalas including marsupial traits, Australian flowers and eucalyptus-tree varieties, and the aborigine origin of the name "koala." The unstated, underlying principles of ecology and conservation are supported by the story line, which leads to the transport of the young koala to the San Francisco Zoo in an effort at conservation.

Gelman, Rita Golden. *A Koala Grows Up.* (Illus. by Gioia Fiammenghi.) NY: Scholastic, 1986. 32pp. $2.50 (paper). ISBN 0-590-30563-8 (paper). ▶ **EP,EI**

Extremely well illustrated, this pleasing account of the life of a koala weaves scientific facts within a charming story. The language is simple and clear, and the material is well organized and will introduce young children to the world of natural science. A good supplementary reader for students who are beginning to learn English as a foreign language. Highly recommended for all public libraries and elementary schools.

Irvine, Georgeanne. *Sydney the Koala.* (Illus. by Ron Garrison; from the Zoo Babies Series.) Chicago: Childrens Press, 1982. 20pp. $5.95. 82-0452. ISBN 0-516-09304-5. Index; C.I.P. ▶ **K,EP,EI**

Using a first-person, narrative style, Sydney the baby Koala tells the story of the first days in his life at the zoo. The book is sturdily bound and has large type and superb color photographs. This delightful "playful aid" should motivate young children to learn about animal life.

Rue, Leonard Lee, III, with William Owen. *Meet the Opossum.* (Illus. by Leonard Lee Rue III; a Skylight Bk.) NY: Dodd, Mead, 1983. 62pp. $7.95. 83-14033. ISBN 0-396-08221-1. Index; C.I.P. ▶ **EA,JH**

The opossum, the only marsupial in North America, is one of the continent's most successful mammals. This book dispels misunderstandings and provides an almost encyclopedic reference on the opossum's physical features, range and spread, reproduction, life of the young in the pouch, behavior, foods, home and habitat, and human relations. Prosaic writing style, well illustrated with a range map and 29 outstanding photographs, and well indexed, increasing its reference value.

Sanford, William R., and Carl R. Green. *The Kangaroos.* (Illus.; from the Wildlife Habits & Habitat Series.) Mankato, MN: Crestwood, 1987. 47pp. $10.95. 86-32881. ISBN 0-89686-322-0. Glossary; index; C.I.P. ▶ **EI,EA,JH**

After a thorough overview of different kangaroo species, their anatomy, abilities, and habits, the second and third chapters of this book follow the daily routines of a mob of grey kangaroos and detail the life cycle of a joey, from birth to self-reliance. The fourth chapter is a serious discussion of the kangaroo as a natural resource worth conserving but one often in conflict with sheep ranchers and modern society. In the last chapter, the reader is taken on a kangaroo hunt and follows the action through the eyes of a naturalist and of a hunter just doing their jobs. It is here that the reader comes to understand why these engaging creatures need to be managed if they are to exist in balance with humans.

Selsam, Millicent E., and Joyce Hunt. *A First Look at Kangaroos, Koalas, and Other Animals with Pouches.* (Illus. by Harriett Springer; from A First Look At Series.) NY: Walker, 1985. 32pp. $9.95. 85-3126. ISBN 0-8027-6600-5. Index; C.I.P. ▶ **K,EP**

Like other books in this series, this one aims to develop young readers' powers of observation by helping them distinguish among the characteristic of various species. Concentrating on the pouched mammals of Australia, the book presents the distinguishing features of the wombat, tiger cat, cuscus, long-nosed bandicoot, and koala. Important scientific terminology is presented with easily understood definitions and pronunciation guides. The black-and-white illustrations would have been more appealing in color.

599.32   Rabbits and hares

Bare, Colleen Stanley. *Rabbits and Hares.* (Illus. with photographs by the author.) NY: Dodd, Mead, 1983. 96pp. $8.95. 82-45992. ISBN 0-396-08127-4. Index; C.I.P. ▶ **EA,JH**

The author, whose black-and-white photographs illustrate the book, does a fine job outlining the natural history of wild rabbits and hares, as well as providing information necessary for the successful maintenance of these animals in captivity. Basic lagomorph biology is well covered, and for the potential home breeder, there is a well-illustrated survey of the many breeds available. Valuable to both school and public libraries and in the home reference library of any young reader interested in rabbits.

Feder, Jan. *The Life of a Rabbit.* (Illus. by Tilman Michalski; from the Animal Lives Series.) Chicago: Childrens Press, 1982. $6.95. 82-9750. ISBN 0-516-08934-X. Index; C.I.P. ▶ **K,EP,EI**

Originally published in Europe, this book is a useful addition to children's natural science collections, although it does consider primarily Old World species that live in the wild. The first section tells in story form about the everyday life of rabbits and the problems of finding food, avoiding predators, caring for offspring, and dealing with seasonal changes. A second part examines behavior and habitat in greater detail. The two-page "Interesting Facts" and the truly lovely color illustrations are worthy of particular note.

Porter, Keith. *Discovering Rabbits and Hares.* (Illus.; a Discovering Nature Bk.) NY: Bookwright, 1986. 47pp. $10.40. 85-73665. ISBN 0-531-18054-9. Glossary; index. ▶ **EI**

This book not only corrects the notion that hares and rabbits are rodents but actually distinguishes between the two in a satisfactory, nontechnical way. The subject matter, though rather broad in scope, is presented in easy-to-read sentences, and the well-chosen color photographs nicely supplement the text. The subject matter, photographs, and readability make this book a good introduction to the subject of lagomorphs.

Tarrant, Graham. *Rabbits.* (Illus. by Tony King; a Natural Pop-Ups Bk.) NY: Putnam's, 1984. 9pp. $6.95. 83-4633. ISBN 0-399-21005-9. ▶ **K,EP**

This pop-up book is well written, readable, and colorful but lacks durability. The lengthy summary on the final page may provide more information than a young child may desire or be able to understand. The book does provide the person reading to the child with some details that will be useful in answering questions or adding to the main text. Appealing grey-brown rabbits are shown digging burrows, slipping into holes to escape predators, wiggling their ears, and munching on garden vegetables. The information is accurate, and the brightly colored pictures are appropriate.

599.323 Rodents

Bailey, Jill. *Rats and Mice.* (Illus. by Wendy Meadway; a Discovering Bk.) NY: Bookwright, 1987. 46pp. $10.40. 86-62100. ISBN 0-531-18099-9. Glossary; index. ▶ **EI,EA**

This little book with its excellent photographs introduces many members of the largest order of mammals. As in other books in this series, there is a rather odd use of boldface—for trivial rather than important words. The variety of forms, habits, and habitats among rats and mice is described, as is their economic importance—as agricultural pests, health hazards, and experimental animals in biological research. The book ends with a brief discussion of mice and rats and their kin as pets.

Davies, Adrian. *Discovering Squirrels.* (Illus.; from the Discovering Nature Series.) NY: Bookwright, 1987. 46pp. $10.40. 86-71273. ISBN 0-531-18100-6. Glossary; index. ▶ **EA,JH**

This excellent book is extremely well organized, clearly written, and scientifically accurate. Large, colorful, well-chosen photographs and diagrams to be found throughout make *Discovering Squirrels* visually attractive and appealing while greatly enhancing and illustrating points made in the text. Although written for children in grades five through eight, the book provides enough detail to be of value to senior high school students and, indeed, the general public.

Feder, Jan. *The Life of a Hamster.* (Illus. by Tilman Michalski; from the Animal Lives Series.) Chicago: Childrens Press, 1982. $6.95. 82-12768. ISBN 0-516-08933-1. Index; C.I.P. ▶ **K,EP,EI**

Originally published in Europe, this book is a useful addition to children's natural science collections, although it does consider primarily Old World species that live in the wild. The first section tells in story form about the everyday life of hamsters and the problems of finding food, avoiding predators, caring for offspring, and dealing with seasonal changes. A second part examines behavior and habitat in greater detail. The two-page "Interesting Facts" and the truly lovely color illustrations are worthy of particular note.

Fischer-Nagel, Heiderose, and Andreas Fischer-Nagel. *Inside the Burrow: The Life of the Golden Hamster.* (Illus.; a Carolrhoda Nature Watch Bk.) Minneapolis: Carolrhoda, 1986. 48pp. $12.95. 86-2591. ISBN 0-87614-286-2. Glossary; C.I.P. ▶ **EI**

The authors display both love and respect for this tiny animal in a charming story about the life-style of the golden hamster in the wild. They describe the burrow's components, the hamster's nocturnal ways and habit of gathering and hoarding food, and its mating and parenting activities. Readers follow newborn hamsters as they grow from blind, naked infants through increasing independence to adulthood. Remarkable color photographs reinforce the text on every page. Reference is made throughout to keeping hamsters as pets, and the final pages give careful directions for caring for a hamster in a cage.

Graham, Ada, and Frank Graham. *We Watch Squirrels.* (Illus. by D.D. Tyler.) NY: Dodd, Mead, 1985. 64pp. $9.95. 85-7075. ISBN 0-396-08740-X. Index; C.I.P. ▶ **EA**

Behaviors explained include nut gathering and hiding, nesting, and response to weather. Clearly written descriptions of the physical appearance of the squirrel are given. The strength of the book, however, is in the detailed illustrations, which, unfortunately, are not placed close to supporting text. Although the book appears simple, it contains a wealth of information. As a resource for a student project or as a reference, it is excellent.

Green, Carl R., and William R. Sanford. *The Porcupine.* (Illus.; from the Wildlife Habits and Habitat Series.) Mankato, MN: Crestwood, 1985. 48pp. $9.95. 85-7899. ISBN 0-89686-280-1. Glossary; index; C.I.P. ▶ **EI,EA**

The Porcupine will alleviate some worries and dispel some myths that children may have about this medium-size rodent. Fascination with the nature of the modified hairs (the quills) will hold the young reader's attention—as will the statement (with caveats) that young porcupines can be semi-domesticated and kept as pets. Predators, reproductive cycle, and habitat are other topics covered in relative detail. Color photographs are plentiful.

Lavine, Sigmund A. *Wonders of Woodchucks.* (Illus.) NY: Dodd, Mead, 1984. 72pp. $9.95. 84-1637. ISBN 0-396-08332-3. Index; C.I.P. ▶ **EA,JH**

Covers a number of aspects of woodchucks: their place among the mammals; Groundhog Day and similar legends; body features, behavior, and seasonal life cycle; how woodchucks benefit humans by turning the soil and providing food; and how humans try to control woodchucks when they harm fields and gardens. The book will arouse sympathy for animals while explaining the problems that can develop between country folk and wildlife. The illustrations—photographs, drawings, and old prints—are well chosen.

Oxford Scientific Films. *Grey Squirrel.* (Illus. by George Bernard and John Paling.) NY: Putnam's, 1982. 31pp. $8.95. 32-411. ISBN 0-399-20906-9. C.I.P. ▶ **EI,EA,JH**

This is a picture book, with 26 of its 31 pages consisting of outstanding color photographs and terse captions that depict aspects of grey squirrel life. The four-page text is an informative and accurate summary of the natural history of grey squirrels. The book was written for readers in Britain, where the species is generally considered an alien nuisance rather than an important game animal as in the United States.

Rue, Leonard Lee, III, with William Owen. *Meet the Beaver.* (Illus. with photographs by the author.) NY: Dodd, Mead, 1986. 78pp. $10.95. 86-13456. ISBN 0-396-08782-5. Index; C.I.P. ▶ **EA,JH**

Physical characteristics, behavior, diets, and other aspects of beavers' natural history are presented in this book by an excellent writer who has extensive first-hand experience studying beavers in the wild. This work provides a comprehensive summary of the life of beavers, including their enemies and interaction with humans. Thirty-five very good black-and-white photographs complement the text. Considerable factual data are accurately presented in a readable, flowing style.

Ryder, Joanne. *Chipmunk Song.* (Illus. by Lynne Cherry.) NY: Lodestar (Dutton), 1987. 32pp. $10.95. 86-19786. ISBN 0-525-67191-9. C.I.P. ▶ **EA**

The reader is asked to imagine himself as a chipmunk. The text and illustrations combine to form a powerful image as the reader feels himself emerging from his/her burrow onto the forest floor to look for food while constantly on the alert for danger. After successfully avoiding a foraging hawk, the reader is made to feel that fall has begun, bringing with it the task of collecting and storing food for the winter. Overall, this book is charming and should excite young people to explore further topics such as hibernation, camouflage, and predation.

599.4 Bats

Green, Carl R., and William R. Sanford. *The Little Brown Bat.* (Illus.; from the Wildlife Habits and Habitat Series.) Mankato, MN: Crestwood, 1986. 48pp. $9.95. 85-22345. ISBN 0-89686-267-4. Glossary; index; C.I.P. ▶ EI,EA

The Little Brown Bat is easy, interesting reading, and the illustrations are clear and to the point. The authors give an excellent description of the external anatomy and features of that bat, its feeding habits, long life span, and usual habitats. Some of the many bat predators are described. In one chapter, the entire life cycle of the bat is detailed from hibernating adult to newborn infant and on to the next period of hibernation. Finally, the authors chip away at the myths that have long given the bat its bad name, relating how bats contribute to medical studies, engineering projects, and radiation-related research.

Hopf, Alice L. *Bats.* (Illus.; photographs by Merlin D. Tuttle; a Skylight Bk.) NY: Dodd, Mead, 1985. 64pp. $8.95. 84-28712. ISBN 0-396-08502-4. Index; C.I.P. ▶ EA

This interesting, comprehensive, and accurate summary of the natural history of bats is clearly written at a vocabulary level suitable for fifth and sixth graders. Scientific nomenclature is used and explained as the different species of bats are identified. Sharp black-and-white photographs of common and unusual bats supplement the description of their physical and behavioral characteristics and natural environment.

Johnson, Sylvia A. *Bats.* (Illus.; photographs by Modoki Masuda; a Lerner Natural Science Bk.) Minneapolis: Lerner, 1985. 48pp. $10.95. 85-15999. ISBN 0-8225-1461-3. Glossary; index; C.I.P. ▶ EI,EA,JH

The emphasis here is on the positive aspects of bats (from a human point of view) and why their conservation is so important. The author describes the characteristics of bats, their habits and important role as pollinators and seed dispersers. Also discussed are the mechanics of bat flight, feeding habits, location of insect prey, development of young, and hibernation in temperature climates. There is an important section on how bats interact with people as well as their role in the transmission of disease, especially rabies. Excellent illustrations, many in color. Highly recommended for its accurate, well-organized and clear message.

Makool, Ann. *Batty's Up: A Story About Bats for Children of All Ages.* (Illus. by Sylvia Henderson-Halton.) Necedah, WI: Central Wisconsin Printing, 1983. 20pp. (paper). ▶ EP,EI,EA

Batty's Up is a nicely written book about bats. Robb, a second or third grader, is grumbling about a homework assignment to write an essay about an animal. His problem is solved when he encounters "Batty," a talking brown bat who has made Robb's garage its home. Batty talks about himself and his relatives and a number of deep subjects, such as rabies, habitat destruction, extinction, hibernation, living in houses, vocalization, echolocation, migration, folklore, and much more. The story flows naturally, and aside from the bat's ability to talk, the narrative is scientifically accurate. There is nothing cute or sentimental about this story. Highly recommended.

599.5 Cetaceans

Bright, Michael. *Saving the Whale.* (Illus.; from the Survival Series.) NY: Gloucester, 1987. 32pp. $10.90. 87-80459. ISBN 0-531-17061-6. Index. ▶ EI,EA,JH

While this book is comprised mainly of pictures, the reader's consciousness is raised precisely because of the vivid photographs and accompanying text. The book presents several facets of whaling, including reasons for hunting whales, the problem of overfishing, survival profiles of various species, a description of whalers and the industry, protection, and efforts being undertaken to stem the slaughter.

Green, Carl R., and William R. Sanford. *The Humpback Whale.* (Illus.; from the Wildlife Habits and Habitat Series.) Mankato, MN: Crestwood, 1985. 48pp. $9.95. 85-9645. ISBN 0-89686-274-7. Glossary; index; C.I.P. ▶ EP,EI,EA

Although the illustrations are not outstanding, many interesting facts can be learned from this informative book about the "gentle giants of the sea." It will have served its purpose if some of its young readers, when they grow up, decide to take part in the worldwide effort to save whales and other endangered creatures.

Patent, Dorothy Hinshaw. *Dolphins and Porpoises.* (Illus.) NY: Holiday House, 1987. 89pp. $14.95. 87-45332. ISBN 0-8234-0663-6. Index; C.I.P. ▶ EA,JH

A well-organized, general introduction to dolphins and porpoises. The coverage is primarily natural history but with considerable input from knowledge gained from captive specimens. This latter source also provides most of the intelligence-testing studies and many interesting and amusing anecdotes (such as dolphins training people). Reliance on empirical data is stressed, and that is important given the anthropomorphic treatment often accorded these animals and the public's strong feelings about them in general. Also laudable is the use of metric equivalents for all English system measurements. Sixty-five good photographs effectively complement the well-written text. No maps or color photographs.

Patent, Dorothy Hinshaw. *Whales: Giants of the Deep.* (Illus.) NY: Holiday House, 1984. 90pp. $12.95. 84-729. ISBN 0-8234-0530-3. Glossary; index; C.I.P. ▶ EA,JH

Well written and illustrated, instructive, accurate, appealing, and provides excellent coverage of the topic. Explains clearly and logically "everything you wanted to know about whales" without getting bogged down in academic details, yet does not skirt issues and problems. This interesting, packed-with-facts reference will delight middle- and intermediate-grade students and their teachers.

Rinard, Judith E. *Dolphins: Our Friends in the Sea.* (Illus.; from the Books for

Young Explorers Series.) Washington, DC: National Geographic Society, 1986. 104pp. $6.95. ISBN 0-87044-609-6. Index. ▶ **EP,EI,EA,JH**

Dolphins is a visual book; 81 full-color, fully captioned pictures tell the story while the well-written text stands ready to elucidate. Somewhat overly romantic and highly anthropomorphic, *Dolphins* also contains large doses of good science. In addition to some strong, up-to-date factual material, it shows what scientists actually do with these toothed whales. Because of the dramatic visual appeal, this book is suitable for very young readers, while the written text, though simple, is authoritative and might appeal to many secondary school students.

Smith, Elizabeth Simpson. *A Dolphin Goes to School: The Story of Squirt, a Trained Dolphin.* (Illus. by Ted Lewin.) NY: Morrow, 1986. x + 86pp. $11.75. 85-28407. ISBN 0-688-04816-1. Index; C.I.P. ▶ **EI**

This enjoyable and informative account of training dolphins for public performances sustains interest by focusing on the capture, care, and training of an individual bottlenose dolphin, Squirt, and some of his cohorts. The subject was researched through visits to Squirt's school and discussions with his trainer and others. The illustrations are well done and support the text.

Stidworthy, John. *A Year in the Life: Whale.* (Illus. by Jeane Colville; from A Year in the Life Series.) NY: Silver Burdett, 1987. 32pp. $7.96; $4.95 (paper). 86-31427. ISBN 0-382-09446-8; 0-382-09455-7 (paper). Index; C.I.P. ▶ **EA,JH**

Kaska, a sperm whale, is featured in this book. Seasonal temperatures, ocean currents, and food supply are shown as affecting migration toward the equator in autumn and toward the poles in spring. Other topics include breathing and diving phenomena, group social structure, herding harems, courtship and mating, rivalry among males, deep-sea feeding, and echolocation. Little-known details are provided on whale parasites and predators and pack behavior to protect the young and injured.

599.6 Elephants

Hoffman, Mary. *Animals in the Wild: Elephant.* (Illus.; a Random House Pictureback.) NY: Random House, 1984. 22pp. $1.50 (paper). 83-21257. ISBN 0-394-86553-7 (paper). CIP. ▶ **K,EP,EI**

The struggle of elephants, largest of all land animals, to survive in their natural surroundings is shown through beautiful photographs and simple, factual prose. In only four or five lines of text per page, Hoffman introduces young readers to some of the techniques that elephants use to survive, and she provides good, simple descriptions of the animal, its habits, habitat, and characteristics.

Lane, Margaret. *The Elephant.* (Illus. by David Wright; an Early Bird Bk.; from the Animal World Series.) NY: Random House, 1985. 28pp. $1.95. 84-17929. ISBN 0-394-86695-9. ▶ **K,EI**

Written to be read to preschool children by parents or teachers; also suitable for children in upper primary grades to read by themselves. The well-written, accurate text presents considerable information in a very few pages. Outstanding illustrations capture the nature of the elephant and its habitat.

Stidworthy, John. *A Year in the Life: Elephant.* (Illus. by Rosalind Hewitt; from A Year in the Life Series.) NY: Silver Burdett, 1987. 32pp. $7.96; $4.95 (paper). 86-31463. ISBN 0-382-09447-6; 0-382-09456-5 (paper). Index; C.I.P. ▶ **EA,JH**

An adult East African female elephant named Mbili is featured in this book. The focus is on Mbili's seasonal movements as influenced by water availability. Other topics include her physical characteristics, daily routines such as skin care and keeping cool, individual and herd defense, food gathering, courtship and mating, and family life. There is good coverage of the communal life among herd females and young. Overall, the information is accurate, the purpose clear, and the material well organized.

599.725 Horses and zebras
See also 636 Care of domesticated animals.

Arnold, Caroline. *Zebra.* (Illus.; photographs by Richard Hewett.) NY: Morrow, 1987. 48pp. $11.75. 87-1503. ISBN 0-688-07067-1. Index; C.I.P. ▶ **EI**

This excellent book describes the social organizational and reproductive behavior of zebras. Their classification, interactions, and structural and functional adaptations for survival are emphasized. Their habitats in a large open-air wildlife park in New Jersey and on the African plains are explored. The author effectively introduces the ecological principle of the balance of nature in the prey-predator relationship. The evolutionary principle, survival of the fittest, is well illustrated and discussed in the example of zebras and lions. Arnold provides accurate, quality information.

Dinneen, Betty. *Striped Horses: The Story of a Zebra Family.* (Illus. by Stefen Bernath.) NY: Macmillan, 1982. 85pp. $9.95. 82-7786. ISBN 0-02-732200-9. C.I.P. ▶ **EI,EA,JH**

An engaging story of a zebra family that lives in Nairobi National Park, Kenya. The scope of zebra natural history is well developed in a "year of the zebra" format. The story also tells of a research team studying zebra, so readers understand how this kind of information is gathered. Easy to read, intensely interesting and exciting, with outstanding illustrations.

Irvine, Georgeanne. *Zelda the Zebra.* (Illus.; from the Zoo Babies Series.) Chicago: Childrens Press, 1982. 20pp. $5.95. 82-4576. ISBN 0-516-09306-1. Index; C.I.P. ▶ **K,EP,EI**

As in other books in this series, Zelda the baby zebra tells her story using a first-person, narrative style. The story attracts readers' attention and gives them information about zebras, as do the outstanding color photographs taken at the San Diego Zoo. At the back of the book is a concise list of facts about the zebra, including where it lives, its herd structure, diet, and species characteristics. A useful resource for children seeking answers for an assignment and for pleasure reading.

Pope, Joyce. *Horses, revised edition.* (Illus. by Peter Barrett; A Closer Look At Bk.) NY: Gloucester, 1987. 32pp. $10.40. 86-82690. ISBN 0-531-17039-X. Glossary; index. ▶ **EA,JH**

Horse enthusiasts will enjoy *Horses.* The many detailed illustrations and clear text blend with and augment each other. There are many drawings of all kinds of horses, zebras, and asses. Origins of horses are traced to tarpans or Prze-walski's horses. Other topics are horse's gaits, horse's teeth, and advantages of social life in the herd. A short, illustrated essay explains the differences among asses, hemoines (half-asses), mules, and donkeys. The volume also deals with the influence of humans on these animals.

Scuro, Vincent. *Wonders of Zebras.* (Illus.) NY: Dodd, Mead, 1983. 64pp. $9.95. 83-14053. ISBN 0-396-08277-0. Index; C.I.P. ▶ **EA,JH**

An interesting and readable account of zebras, from their evolution, taxonomy, and physical characteristics to their behavior, natural habitat, and history as captives. Well organized and accurate, with an adequate index and 43 black-and-white photographs and drawings. The role of zoos and other conservation efforts are discussed. Should inform and interest readers from grades five through seven who enjoy equines or wildlife in general.

599.734 Boars and pigs
See also 636 Care of domesticated animals.

Ahlstrom, Mark E. *The Wild Pigs.* (Illus.; from the Wildlife Habits and Habitat Series.) Mankato, MN: Crestwood, 1986. 48pp. $9.95. 86-2282. ISBN 0-89686-272-0. Glossary; index; C.I.P. ▶ **EI,EA**

The descriptions of these animals, their habits and habitats, are quite good and hold one's interest. Much scientific knowledge is imparted in a thorough and interesting way. Young children may have difficulty understanding the scientific terms, but the small index/glossary at the end of the book is very helpful. Perhaps the weakest feature of the book is the photography—a number of the pictures are so low contrast as to be unclear. Still, young readers should be able to gather much information from the volume.

Nicholson, Darrel. *Wild Boars.* (Illus.; photographs by Craig Blacklock; a Nature Watch Bk.) Minneapolis: Carolrhoda, 1987. 48pp. $12.95. 87-677. ISBN 0-87614-308-7. Glossary; index; C.I.P. ▶ **EA,JH**

A group of wild boars recently installed on a farm in west central Minnesota is the subject of this book. Clear distinctions are made among the pig-like peccaries and the many kinds of true pigs of the old world. Among the latter are wild boars, feral pigs or domesticated pigs gone wild, and the current hybrids portrayed in this book. Large, full-color, close-up photographs make this a beautiful photoessay on a unique animal. The animal's high intelligence and amazing adaptability are emphasized. Topics include physical characteristics, seasonal behavior, diet, shelter, aggressiveness, mating, rearing of young, and interacting with humans.

599.735 Ruminants

Ahlstrom, Mark E. *The Elk.* (Illus.; from the Wildlife Habits and Habitat Series.) Mankato, MN: Crestwood, 1985. 48pp. $9.95. 85-11667. ISBN 0-89686-278-X. Glossary; index; C.I.P. ▶ **EP, EI, EA**

Here the story of the elk is well told, the illustrations are apt, and the facts presented are generally accurate. However, the writing style is somewhat ir-ritating, with the word "you" and the future tense being used excessively. The story of the animals' lives, the relationships between elk and humans, and the need to care properly for the herds to avoid extermination are all presented.

Ahlstrom, Mark E. *The Moose.* (Illus.; from the Wildlife Habits and Habitat Series.) Mankato, MN: Crestwood, 1985. 48pp. $9.95. 85-26931. ISBN 0-89686-279-8. Glossary; index; C.I.P. ▶ **EI, EA**

This attractive, well-illustrated book is marred only by the lack of a personal touch, as interesting facts are presented in a straightforward but dry style. Recommended for libraries reaching young nature lovers.

Ahlstrom, Mark E. *The Mule Deer.* (Illus.; from the Wildlife Habits and Habitat Series.) Mankato, MN: Crestwood, 1987. 47pp. $10.95. 87-614. ISBN 0-89686-324-7. Glossary; index; C.I.P. ▶ **EI, EA, JH**

The Mule Deer is long on habitat and short on habits of the animal. Nearly half the book is devoted to a dry, encyclopedic listing of the ranges of the seven subspecies of mule deer. The rest covers the living habits of the mule deer, provides a history of its names and ancestors, and gives a brief account of the rut, birth, and migration. The most interesting sections describe the growth of the mule deer's antlers, the shape of the subspecies' tails, and the functions of the various scent glands. Many informative color photographs. The book's overall tone indicates that the author is more hunter than naturalist. Suitable for reference.

Ahlstrom, Mark E. *The Sheep.* (Illus.) Mankato, MN: Crestwood, 1984. 47pp. $8.95. 83-25215. ISBN 0-89686-248-8. Glossary; index; C.I.P. ▶ **EA, JH**

A good, brief summary of the habits and distribution of the wild sheep of North America. The present state of populations and efforts to preserve them are pointed out, aided by a distribution map. The color photographs are excellent. A useful reference for elementary and junior-high students.

Arnold, Caroline. *Giraffe.* (Illus.; photographs by Richard Hewett.) NY: Morrow, 1987. 48pp. $11.75. 87-1502. ISBN 0-688-07069-8. Index; C.I.P. ▶ **EI**

Arnold describes the natural habitat of giraffes as well as their food habits and social and reproductive behavior as observed in a large, open-air wildlife park in New Jersey. The origin of the giraffes and their functional adaptations to the environment are also discussed. Scientific information, such as the giraffe's body measurements and its oversize heart and lungs, are accurate and interesting. Well written and well illustrated with 40 excellent color photographs.

Aronsky, Jim. *Deer at the Brook.* (Illus. by the author.) NY: Lothrop, Lee & Shepard, 1986. 28pp. $11.75. 84-12239. ISBN 0-688-04099-3. C.I.P. ▶ **K, EP**

The text of this book describes a family of deer that comes to a brook to drink, eat, and sun itself. Though the text is sparse, the many illustrations of gentle, soft-eyed deer should fascinate very young readers and teach them about the appearance and behavior of deer and the natural environment of a stream. Colorful, realistic, and uncluttered, each drawing has little surprises to delight children, such as a frog peeking out of the reeds, a bird building a nest in a tangle of branches, or a fish snapping at a mayfly.

Green, Carl R., and William R. Sanford. *The Bison.* (Illus.; from the Wildlife Habits and Habitat Series.) Mankato, MN: Crestwood, 1985. 48pp. $9.95. 85-6624. ISBN 0-89686-275-5. Glossary; index; C.I.P. ▶ **EI, EA**

Bison begins with a chapter that dwells on the carnage that nearly destroyed this largest North American mammal. Subsequent chapters cover the physical traits and habits of the bison, the reproductive year, and a consideration of the bison's image as etched in the American consciousness. Conservation efforts are covered in detail appropriate for grade school readers. Numerous color photographs enhance this attractive, informative book. Appropriate for elementary school libraries and children's departments of public libraries.

Lane, Margaret. *The Giraffe.* (Illus. by David Wright; an Early Bird Bk.; from the Animal World Series.) NY: Random House, 1985. 28pp. $1.95. 84-11795. ISBN 0-394-86696-7. ▶ **K, EI**

This book, written to be read to preschool children by parents or teachers, is also suitable as a "read-by-myself" book for children in grades three and four. The well-written, accurate text presents considerable information in few words. The illustrations, well integrated with the text, are outstanding. The artist has captured the personality of the giraffe and the nature of its habitat in a manner rarely achieved in children's books.

Leslie-Melville, Betty. *Daisy Rothschild: The Giraffe That Lives with Me.* (Illus.) NY: Doubleday, 1987. vi + 42pp. $12.95. 86-29070. ISBN 0-385-23895-9. Index; C.I.P. ▶ **EI, EA**

This delightful children's book tells how the author and her husband raised a rare Rothschild giraffe (the largest of the three different species of giraffe in Kenya). It is also a story of the growth of mutual trust and love that illuminates several basic facts for children about the problems of dealing with baby wild animals in general and giraffes in particular. How the author and her husband establish the African Fund for Endangered Wildlife winds up this lovely tale of animal/human friendship. The large color photographs more than adequately illustrate Daisy's story. The accurate facts, the wonderful story line, and the beautiful photographs make this a recommended book.

McClung, Robert M. *Whitetail.* (Illus. by Irene Brady.) NY: Morrow, 1987. 82pp. $11.75. 86-18183. ISBN 0-688-06126-5. ▶ **EI, EA, JH**

McClung does an outstanding job of presenting the life history of the white-tailed deer in story form for children. This is not another "Bambi" book. *Whitetail* is factual, presenting ecological detail and introducing the reader to environmental problems white-tailed deer face. There are some moral messages that come across clearly: bow hunting, snowmobiles, and free-ranging dogs are detrimental to deer; poaching is wrong. The value of hunting as a population management tool is presented, but so are arguments against hunting.

Patent, Dorothy Hinshaw. *Buffalo: The American Bison Today.* (Illus.; photographs by William Muñoz.) NY: Ticknor & Fields (Houghton Mifflin), 1986. ii + 74pp. $12.95. 85-25483. ISBN 0-89919-345-5. Index; C.I.P. ▶ **EI, EA, JH**

This delightful book will fit nicely in an elementary school library. It is packed with facts about buffalo life, habitat, and interactions among buffalo and with humans. Black-and-white photographs abound and, with the text, cover buffalo life from birth to death, through all seasons. The book also describes how the Indians hunted and used the buffalo; the subsequent decline of the buffalo with overhunting and pioneer settlement; and the current status of the buffalo in Yellowstone and other reserves.

Sanford, William R., and Carl R. Green. *The Cape Buffalo.* (Illus.; from the Wildlife Habits & Habitat Series.) Mankato, MN: Crestwood, 1987. 47pp. $10.95. 86-32859. ISBN 0-89686-321-2. Glossary; index; C.I.P. ▶ **EI, EA, JH**

The opening dialogue between a hunter and his guides erases the notion the reader might have of the Cape buffalo as just another member of the *Bovidae* family (milk cows, water buffalos, American bison). Evidently, "m'bogo" has earned its reputation as the most dangerous animal to hunt, for it is smart, fearless, and has no intention of becoming a trophy. This effective beginning is followed by a chapter on the physical characteristics that make this animal so ferocious. There is also a clear, concise discussion, with illustration, of how this animal's four-chambered stomach works. The next several chapters detail daily routines, habitat, symbiotic releationships, and social structure within the herd. The authors succeed in getting across the point that the Cape buffalo's major threat today is people.

599.74 Carnivores

BEARS

Ahlstrom, Mark E. *The Black Bear.* (Illus.; from the Wildlife Habits and Habitat Series.) Mankato, MN: Crestwood, 1985. 48pp. $9.95. 85-22872. ISBN 0-89686-276-3. Glossary; index; C.I.P. ▶ **EI, EA**

In addition to the usual facts about physical traits and habits, Ahlstrom discusses why the black bear, of all the bears native to North America, is so successful in avoiding the endangered species list. He also deals with the history, range, senses, and intelligence of the black bear. Readable and filled with eye-pleasing color photographs, *Bear* covers much information useful for the young reader or writer of school reports.

Ahlstrom, Mark E. *The Polar Bear.* (Illus.; from the Wildlife Habits and Habitat Series.) Mankato, MN: Crestwood, 1986. 48pp. $9.95. 85-30900. ISBN 0-89686-268-2. Glossary; index; C.I.P. ▶ **EA, JH**

The author quickly captures his reader's interest with two vivid descriptions of encounters between polar bears and people (both ending badly for the bears). Two chapters then describe the biology and natural history of these "lords of the ice." Tracking methods, movements of bears living on the ice, their migrations, behavior (especially their seal hunting techniques), and biology (such as their ability to meet their fresh-water needs by eating blubber) are understandably presented.

Irvine, Georgeanne. *Nanuck the Polar Bear.* (Illus.; from the Zoo Babies Series.) Chicago: Childrens Press, 1982. 20pp. $5.95. 82-9463. ISBN 0-516-09302-9. Index; C.I.P. ▶ **K, EP, EI**

Using a first-person, narrative style, Nanuck the polar bear cub tells a story that attracts readers' attention and gives them information. The outstanding color photographs were taken at the San Diego Zoo. At the back of the book is a concise list of facts about the polar bear, including where it lives, its family structure, diet, and species characteristics. For children seeking answers for an assignment, this section is a real bonus. For both pleasure reading and information.

Johnston, Ginny, and Judy Cutchins. *Andy Bear: A Polar Cub Grows Up at the Zoo.* (Illus.; photographs by Constance Noble.) NY: Scholastic, 1986. 60pp. $2.95 (paper). ISBN 0-590-40157-2 (paper). ▶ **EI, EA, JH**

This is a delightful account of a polar bear cub born in a zoo and rescued from the male bear that threatened to kill it despite the mother's presence. The little bear then grows up in a human household. When he grows too large and destructive to be kept indoors, he is sent back to the zoo, where the zoo custodian visits him in his cage until he adjusts to life away from "home." The photographs, in color and black and white, follow the narration admirably.

Nentl, Jerolyn Ann. *The Grizzly.* (Illus.) Mankato, MN: Crestwood, 1984. 47pp. $8.95. 83-22354. ISBN 0-89686-245-3. Glossary; index; C.I.P. ▶ **EA, JH**

This book provides a map of the grizzly's present distribution and a good description of their characteristics and habits, with great emphasis on their incompatibility with people. The color photographs are excellent. A suitable reference for elementary and junior high students.

Patent, Dorothy Hinshaw. *The Way of the Grizzly.* (Illus.; photographs by William Muñoz.) NY: Clarion, 1987. 65pp. $12.95. 86-17562. ISBN 0-89919-383-8. Index; C.I.P. ▶ **JH**

This is a slim book with an ample number of black-and-white photographs of reasonable quality and easy-to-read, anecdotal text about the awesome grizzly bear. Some of the subject matter—for example, the brief section on hibernation and metabolism—may require concentrated effort but probably not of such an intensity as to turn the young reader away. On the whole, the material appears to be factually correct, serving as a reasonable introduction to the life and times of the North Americn grizzly.

CANIDS

Ahlstrom, Mark E. *The Coyote.* (Illus.; from the Wildlife Habits and Habitat Series.) Mankato, MN: Crestwood, 1985. 48pp. $9.95. 85-24290. ISBN 0-89686-277-1. Glossary; index; C.I.P. ▶ **EA, JH**

Ahlstrom's report of training coyotes, without the use of poison, to hate even the smell of lambs, is fascinating. He gives an accurate picture of the daily life of the coyote, his loyalty to his mate, and the care coyote parents give their young. Although a bit dark, the photographs are good.

Korschunow, Irina, and trans. by James Skofield. *The Foundling Fox: How the Little Fox Got a Mother.* (Illus. by Reinhard Michl.) NY: Harper & Row, 1984. 48pp. $12.50. 84-47631. ISBN 0-06-023243-9. C.I.P. ▶ **K, EP, EI**

This story describes a fox pup left alone when a hunter kills its mother, and a mother fox, with pups of her own, that adopts the abandoned one. The illustrations are excellent, lively, and full of color. The language is straightforward and easy to read but not too simplified. This is a good book for adults to read to young children and for developing readers to tackle on their own.

Leighner, Alice Mills. *Reynard: The Story of a Fox Returned to the Wild.* (Illus.; photographs by the author.) NY: Atheneum, 1986. vi + 48pp. $11.95. 85-26848. ISBN 0-689-31189-3. C.I.P. ▶ **EI, EA**

This is the fascinating story of how Reynard, a red fox, was raised by volunteers of Wildcare, an organization that cares for orphaned wild animals. The text details the steps taken in a domesticating milieu to create an animal that could survive in the wild. The reader is given a great deal of information about the characteristics and habits of the red fox, which has learned to survive despite human encroachment on its territory. The numerous superb black-and-white photographs depicting Reynard's training greatly enhance and support the text. Recommended as a good source of information but especially for its photographs.

Schnieper, Claudia. *On the Trail of the Fox.* (Illus. with photographs by Felix Labhardt; a Carolrhoda Nature Watch Bk.) Minneapolis: Carolrhoda, 1986. 48pp. $12.95. 86-6893. ISBN 0-87614-287-0. Glossary; index; C.I.P. ▶ **EA**

Students will learn from this book that not all is known about even an animal as familiar as the red fox, despite ongoing attempts to track and observe the animal in the wild. In this way, the exciting prospect of future study is revealed to an interested student. Basic facts about sharp fox senses, interesting fox habits, and the yearly cycle of fox life are illustrated with lively and appealing color photographs on each page. The text has been translated from the original German and presents a great deal of information in a straightforward if somewhat dry fashion.

Thompson, Bruce, and the staff of the Teton Science School. *Looking at the Wolf: Biology.* (Illus.) Boulder, CO: Roberts Rinehart, 1987. 16pp. $3.95 (paper). ISBN 0-911797-24-6 (paper). ▶ **JH**

This small booklet is packed with information about the biology of wolves. The authors manage to discuss the evolutionary history of wolves, wolf behavior, the wolf pack social system, and similarities and differences between wolves and domestic dogs. The writing throughout is clear, concise, and, at times, enjoyable. The text is complemented by a series of excellent and informative illustrations. The book's clear discussion of evolution and its avoidance of anthropomorphism would make it a valuable addition to any library's section on North American wildlife.

CATS

Ammann, Katherine, and Karl Ammann. *Cheetah.* (Illus.; foreword by Stefanie Powers.) NY: Arco, 1985. 136pp. $29.95. 84-70999. ISBN 0-668-06259-2. ▶ **EA, JH**

Based on a two-year study in Kenya's Mara Game Reserve, this book is a clear introduction to and summary of basic cheetah biology, especially hunting and family behaviors. Although not trained animal behaviorists or photographers, the Ammanns have produced a book of stunning photographs and charming narrative. Fully illustrated with color photographs, the text shines with clarity, factuality, and anecdotal interest.

Green, Carl R., and William R. Sanford. *The Bengal Tiger.* (Illus.; from the Wildlife Habits and Habitat Series.) Mankato, MN: Crestwood, 1986. 48pp. $9.95. 85-31411. ISBN 0-89686-270-4. Glossary; index; C.I.P. ▶ **EI, EA**

This book should be particularly appealing to those who want an accurate and detailed description of the tiger. The account moves along easily and is interspersed with interesting anecdotes. Younger children will be fascinated by the pictures, each of which is an excellent photograph. The size and format of the book will appeal to young children, and the text moves along at a smooth, appropriate pace.

Hoffman, Mary. *Animals in the Wild: Tiger.* (Illus.; a Random-House Pictureback.) NY: Random House, 1984. 22pp. $1.50 (paper). 83-19236. ISBN 0-394-86556-1 (paper). C.I.P. ▶ **K, EP, EI**

Through beautiful photographs and simple, factual prose, this book introduces young readers to some of the techniques that tigers use to survive. There are only four or five lines of text per page, but the good, simple descriptions of each animal, its habits, habitat, and characteristics, supplement the photographs that dominate each page.

Hughes, Jill. *Lions and Tigers, revised edition.* (Illus. by Peter Barrett et al.; from A Closer Look At Series.) NY: Gloucester, 1985. 32pp. $9.90. 84-62467. ISBN 0-531-17000-4. Glossary; index. ▶ **EI, EA, JH**

Just right for intermediate-grade students and useful for junior-high students who find reading difficult, this generously illustrated, large-type book would serve well as a research source. Lions, tigers, jaguars, the various leopards, and cheetahs are differentiated by geographical location, size, coloration, and social habits. Special adaptations, such as excellent night vision and sensory nerves attached to whiskers, are discussed. The author touches on the effect hunting and human settlement development have had on their numbers.

Irvine, Georgeanne. *Sasha the Cheetah.* (Illus. by Ron Garrison; from the Zoo Babies Series.) Chicago: Childrens Press, 1982. 20pp. $5.95. 82-9450. ISBN 0-516-09303-7. Index; C.I.P. ▶ **K, EP, EI**

Sasha the baby cheetah tells the story of the first days in her life at the zoo. A good read-aloud book with superb color photographs that will appeal to readers of all ages. This delightful, sturdily bound, large-type book will motivate young children to learn about animal life.

Lane, Margaret. *The Lion.* (Illus. by David Nockels; an Early Bird Bk.; from the Animal World Series.) NY: Random House, 1985. 28pp. $1.95. 84-11634. ISBN 0-394-86697-5. ▶ **K, EI**

This book, written to be read to preschool children by parents or teachers, is also suitable for children in upper primary grades. The illustrations, well integrated with the text, are outstanding and capture the personality of the lion and the nature of its habitat. The well-written, accurate text presents considerable information in few words and is sure to provoke queries from children.

Nentl, Jerolyn Ann. *The Wild Cats.* (Illus.) Mankato, MN: Crestwood, 1984. 47pp. $8.95. 83-22506. ISBN 0-89686-249-6. Glossary; index; C.I.P. ▶ **EA, JH**

A good, brief treatment of the life histories and georgraphic distribution of the wild cats of the Western hemisphere. Emphasis is placed on the lynx, bobcat, and mountain lion, with briefer treatment of the jaguar, ocelot, jaguarundi, and margay. Excellent color photographs, many of them taken in the wild, give a good idea of the appearance of the cats.

Stidworthy, John. *A Year in the Life: Tiger.* (Illus. by Priscilla Barrett; from A Year in the Life Series.) NY: Silver Burdett, 1987. 32pp. $7.96; $4.95 (paper). 86-31425. ISBN 0-382-09444-1; 0-382-09454-9 (paper). Index; C.I.P. ▶ **EA, JH**

A six-year-old female tiger, Mohini, is the focus of this fine book. Maps show tiger distribution worldwide as well as in central India, where Mohini lives. There is also a detailed look at Mohini's local environment. There is emphasis on the relationship of the changing annual climate to the tiger's hunting shifts between forest and grassland. Other topics include the tiger's solitary life, courtship and mating behavior, rearing of cubs, and protection.

MARINE CARNIVORES

Bare, Colleen Stanley. *Sea Lions.* (Illus.; photographs by the author; a Skylight Bk.) NY: Dodd, Mead, 1986. 64 pp. $9.95. 85-16276. ISBN 0-396-08719-1. Index; C.I.P. ▶ **EI,EA**

Through the descriptions of anatomy, behavior, and yearly cycle of sea lions, readers will learn about their adaptations for life in a watery world. Bare describes birth, feeding, migration, diving depths, longevity, learning ability in captivity, enemies, and diseases. The writing style is easy, and the book's treatment of "man as friend" and "man as enemy" is sensitive without being sentimental. *Sea Lions* will instill a sense of humaneness while at the same time cautioning that wildlife may on occasion harm as well as benefit the interests of people.

Green, Carl R., and William R. Sanford. *The Walrus.* (Illus.; from the Wildlife Habits and Habitat Series.) Mankato, MN: Crestwood, 1986. 48pp. $9.95. 85-17509. ISBN 0-89686-273-9. Glossary; index; C.I.P. ▶ **EA,JH**

Presents a superficial but interesting discussion of walrus biology, a description of a typical year in the life of a walrus, their daily life, the effects of human activity, and some problems of maintaining these huge animals in oceanaria. The 19 well-chosen four-color illustrations are crisply reproduced. The natural history is solidly based on observation and is presented at a middle- to upper-elementary reading level. Some carelessness with scientific nomenclature, but the book is still a useful supplementary reader.

Irvine, Georgeanne. *Wilbur and Orville the Otter Twins.* (Illus. by Ron Garrison; from the Zoo Babies Series.) Chicago: Childrens Press, 1982. 20pp. $5.95. 82-9451. ISBN 0-516-09305-3. Index; C.I.P. ▶ **K,EP,EI**

Using a first-person, narrative style, Wilbur and Orville tell the story of their first days of life at the zoo. A fine book for reading to small children; older siblings or parents will also enjoy the superb color photographs. Young children will want to learn about animal life after reading this book.

MUSTELIDS

Lavine, Sigmund A. *Wonders of Badgers.* (Illus.) NY: Dodd, Mead, 1985. 64pp. $9.95. 84-25941. ISBN 0-396-08581-4. Index. ▶ **EA,JH**

An extensive review of the available information on a relatively unknown and somewhat unpopular animal. The information is accurate and very interesting, especially the chapter on myths surrounding the badger. The book also covers the badger's physical characteristics and its behavior and relationship to man. Well illustrated with black-and-white photographs and line drawings.

RACCOONS AND THEIR RELATIVES

Hoffman, Mary. *Animals in the Wild: Panda.* (Illus.; a Random House Pictureback.) NY: Random House, 1984. 22pp. $1.50 (paper). 83-19283. ISBN 0-394-86555-3 (paper). C.I.P. ▶ **K**

Panda contains outstanding photographs that portray the panda in real life surroundings. The print is large and encourages pre-readers to learn left-to-right eye-hand coordination. Although the short, descriptive sentences are directed to the preschool and kindergarten levels, the excellent photographs could be used to expand older children's knowledge of pandas.

Leslie, Robert Franklin. *Ringo, the Robber Raccoon: The True Story of a Northwoods Rogue.* (Illus. by Leigh Grant.) NY: Dodd, Mead, 1984. 143pp. $10.95. 83-25505. ISBN 0-396-08323-4. C.I.P. ▶ **EA,JH**

A blend of fiction and Leslie's actual adventures with "Ringo, the Robber Raccoon." The book is scientifically accurate, except for the anthropomorphic descriptions of the animal/human interactions. The first-person narrative of the author's daily activities in the wilderness includes descriptions of numerous plants and animals, and techniques of field biology and concepts of ecology are introduced in a subtle way. Suitable for classroom use.

McDearmon, Kay. *Giant Pandas.* (Illus.; a Skylight Bk.) NY: Dodd, Mead, 1986. 62pp. $8.95. 85-20641. ISBN 0-396-08736-1. Index; C.I.P. ▶ **EI**

Black-and-white photographs taken in zoos show us pandas in a variety of poses, a panda habitat in China, panda "relatives," and predators on panda cubs. There is interesting information about pandas in captivity and how they are captured. We learn about the joint Chinese-American project to study the behavior of pandas in the wild and what can be done to protect this rare animal. There is unevenness to the text, and cute pictures and phrases are interspersed with quite detailed information on panda biology, making it unclear exactly who the intended audience is.

Nentl, Jerolyn Ann. *The Raccoon.* (Illus.) Mankato, MN: Crestwood, 1984. 47pp. $8.95. 83-21072. ISBN 0-89686-246-1. Glossary; index; C.I.P. ▶ **EA,JH**

The life history of the raccoon is given in brief, illustrated by excellent color photographs. There is a distribution map for this animal in North America. The book is a helpful reference for elementary and junior high students, in spite of a few typographical errors.

Schlein, Miriam. *Project Panda Watch.* (Illus. by Robert Shetterly.) NY: Atheneum, 1984. 87pp. $11.95. 84-2914. ISBN 0-689-31071-4. Glossary; index; C.I.P. ▶ **EA,JH**

This well-written little book clues children in to the difficulties that scientists face trying to increase our knowledge of pandas and their habits. Schlein describes an expedition to panda country (in China) and the techniques that have been used to study pandas in their native habitat. The author also does a fine job of relating the life of pandas in zoos. The photographs are particularly good and reveal the panda's delightful nature.

599.8 Primates

Anderson, Norman D., and Walter R. Brown. *Lemurs.* (Illus.) NY: Dodd, Mead, 1984. 63pp. $9.95. 84-8097. ISBN 0-396-08454-0. Index; C.I.P. ▶ **EA,JH**

Describes the physical characteristics, habits, and habitats of the wild lemurs found in the forests of Madagascar. Attractive color photographs are generously used throughout. A concern for the uncertain future of the lemur is well expressed, and measures to protect and preserve them are discussed. *Lemurs* can be used as a classroom reference or simply for the joy of reading.

Fitzpatrick, Michael. *Apes, revised edition.* (Illus. by Richard Orr; A Closer Look At Bk.) NY: Gloucester, 1987. 32pp. $10.40. 86-82691. ISBN 0-531-17038-1. Glossary; index. ▶ **EA,JH**

Good quality, detailed illustrations and clear text blend and augment each other in a book that presents a wealth of information. Drawings and line diagrams nicely show the similarities and differences among prosimians, gibbons, monkeys, chimpanzees, orangutans, and gorillas. The life patterns of each emerge from the text and habitat drawings.

Green, Carl R., and William R. Sanford. *The Gorilla.* (Illus.; from the Wildlife Habits and Habitat Series.) Mankato, MN: Crestwood, 1986. 48pp. $9.95. 85-9991. ISBN 0-89686-269-0. Glossary; index; C.I.P. ▶ **EI,EA**

Green and Sanford have provided a wealth of technical information about gorillas in this excellently written and illustrated book. The text is easily read, contains useful definitions and references, and is enhanced by the accompanying color photographs and descriptions. The excellent section on a day with a mountain gorilla includes details of their daily activities of feeding and play. Also described are the intricacies of training gorillas to use Ameslan (American sign language). An excellent addition to any elementary library.

Hoffman, Mary. *Animals in the Wild: Monkey.* (Illus.; a Random House Pictureback.) NY: Random House, 1984. 22pp. $1.50 (paper). 83-21158. ISBN 0-394-86554-5 (paper). C.I.P. ▶ **K**

This book on monkeys is an excellent introduction to their different life styles; vivid illustrations help listeners understand how these animals struggle to survive in their natural surroundings. The book can be used by teachers and parents to develop listening skills in preschool and kindergarten children.

Irvine, Georgeanne. *Alberta the Gorilla.* (Illus.; from the Zoo Babies Series.) Chicago: Childrens Press, 1982. 20pp. $5.95. 82-94456. ISBN 0-516-09301-0. Index; C.I.P. ▶ **K,EP,EI**

Using a first-person, narrative style, Alberta the baby gorilla tells the story of being raised by her keeper and how she was treated much as a human baby. The story attracts readers' attention and is a ploy for giving children information about gorillas. The book's outstanding color photographs were taken at the San Diego Zoo. At the back of the book is a concise list of facts about the gorilla, including where it lives, its family structure, diet, and species characteristics. For both pleasure reading and information.

Lane, Margaret. *The Chimpanzee.* (Illus. by Denise Finney; an Early Bird Bk.; from the Animal World Series.) NY: Random House, 1985. 28pp. $1.95. 84-11698. ISBN 0-394-86694-0. ▶ **K,EI**

This well-written, accurate text presents considerable information in few words. The outstanding illustrations capture the personality of the chimpanzee and the nature of its habitat in a manner rarely achieved in children's books. The book is written to be read to preschool children by parents or teachers and is sure to provoke queries, so adults should be ready with answers. One deficiency: the book is unnecessarily sexist, with the female appearing only as a mother.

McClung, Robert M. *Gorilla.* (Illus. by Irene Brady.) NY: Morrow, 1984. 92pp. $11.00. 84-718. ISBN 0-688-03875-1. C.I.P. ▶ **EA,JH**

An accurate and interesting account of the natural history of gorillas in a fictional format, with a heavy emphasis on the continuing exploitation of this species by humans. The human characters include scientists who are studying the gorilla band and poachers who ambush the band, shoot many of its members, and capture two infants. An eloquent statement of the gorilla's precarious position in Africa which also conveys a wealth of information about the animal's natural history. The black-and-white pen drawings are disappointing.

Technology

See also 371.3 Methods of instruction.

McKie, Robin. *Technology: Science at Work.* (Illus.; from the Franklin Watts Science World Series.) NY: Watts, 1984. 40pp. $9.90. 84-50609. ISBN 0-531-04838-1. Glossary; index. ▶ **EA**

This excellent overview of applied science for elementary school readers could also be enjoyed by interested adults, although they will find little in-depth information. Each subject is dealt with in short descriptions placed next to several relevant color drawings. The eight general areas covered are oil refining, electricity, computers, space satellites, manufacturing, transportation, agriculture, and medicine.

608 Inventions and inventors

Cohen, Peter Zachary. *The Great Red River Raft.* (Illus. by James Watling.) Niles, IL: Whitman, 1984. 39pp. $9.22. 84-3568. C.I.P. ▶ **EI,EA**

This story rich in American folklore tells of a little-known riverman, Henry Miller Shreve, who invented the snagboat which cleared the Red River of a 200-mile logjam, thereby opening the way for steamboat travel to Texas. The book describes life in the 19th century as boatmen worked to get cargo from the North to the South, but it is primarily an inspirational story of how one man succeeded in accomplishing what others, including the U.S. Army, had failed to do. The illustrations capture the flavor of the times; the dialogue is true to life. This book is useful also in the study of American history or folklore.

Cosner, Shaaron. *The Light Bulb.* (Illus.; from the Inventions That Changed Our Lives Series.) NY: Walker, 1984. 64pp. $10.85. ISBN 0-8027-6527-0. Index; C.I.P. ▶ **EA,JH**

This book describes how, with the financial assistance of J.P. Morgan and a group of bankers, the Edison Electric Light Co. was established along with the first scientific research laboratory to develop the incandescent light bulb.

Dempsey, Michael (Ed.). *The Illustrated Encyclopedia of Invention, Vols. 1– 25.* (Illus.; from the Growing Up with Science Series.) Westport, CT: Stuttman, 1984. 2304pp. $183.54 (set). 82-63047. ISBN 0-87475-830-0. Index; C.I.P. ▶ EA

The purpose of this 25-volume set is "to introduce children to the fascinating and challenging world of science." Volumes 1 through 22 are alphabetically arranged and describe scientific inventions and discoveries of interest to children. Written to facilitate understanding by young readers, every page contains pictures or labels as well as "how-it-works" diagrams. Volume 23 describes discoveries and inventions from a historical perspective with ample drawings that illustrate various stages of development. Volume 24 contains biographies of scientists. Included in Volume 25 are 40 science projects and an expanded index of all 25 books. Information appropriate for upper-elementary grades through junior-high level is clearly written and graphically illustrated in elaborate color. Stimulating for the young, this set should find a place at school or home.

Mitchell, Barbara. *Click! A Story About George Eastman.* (Illus. by Jan Hosking Smith; a Carolrhoda Creative Minds Bk.) Minneapolis: Carolrhoda, 1986. 56pp. $8.95. 86-2672. ISBN 0-87614-289-7. C.I.P. ▶ EI,EA

Over five decades after Eastman's death, Mitchell has written an informative, charming biography. She recounts Eastman's impoverished childhood, initial interest in photography, business ventures, most noted contributions to amateur photography, and philanthropic endeavors and personal adventures. The natural dialogue makes the book good for reading aloud even to first and second graders. The black-and-white drawings are detailed and focus the reader's imagination on a vivid trip back in time. Overall, this is an excellent biography: smooth dialogue; short, simple paragraphs; engaging illustrations; all important milestones in Eastman's life covered. Only the ending is abrupt and dangling.

Mitchell, Barbara. *Shoes for Everyone: A Story About Jan Matzeliger.* (Illus. by Hetty Mitchell; a Carolrhoda Creative Minds Bk.) Minneapolis: Carolrhoda, 1986. 64pp. $8.95. 86-4157. ISBN 0-87614-290-0. C.I.P. ▶ EI

Jan Matzeliger was a young Afro-Dutch ship's engine room mechanic when he arrived in Philadelphia from Suriname in 1873. Although he was well trained, machining was not a black trade in the post-Civil War North. Eventually he did obtain a job with a shoemaker. Soon his spare time was consumed by the dream of mechanizing the remaining manual-labor step in the burgeoning industry—attaching the sole to the upper around a form known as the "last." His new lasting machine removed the last bottleneck in shoe manufacture and made good shoes affordable by the average worker in the new industrial society. The demand for black history in elementary school curricula has spawned some pretentious claims to black biography. Mitchell has avoided this trap and has written a gentle story about perseverance in a less integrated society.

Mitchell, Barbara. *We'll Race You, Henry: A Story About Henry Ford.* (Illus. by Kathy Haubrich; a Carolrhoda Creative Minds Bk.) Minneapolis: Carolrhoda, 1986. 56pp. $8.95. 86-2691. ISBN 0-87614-291-9. C.I.P. ▶ EP,EI

Reading programs in elementary schools need biographies that hold the interest of younger readers. That requires a distinctive biographical form that emphasizes the early life of an important person, often leaving room for only a contrived explanation of that person's later importance. Mitchell has successfully bridged that difficulty in this book about Ford and his early interest in designing and building a practical, affordable automobile and the assembly line to produce it in volume. This biography presents lessons in advertising and industrial economics with an enthusiastic directness that should hold young readers.

National Geographic Society. *How Things Work.* (Illus.; from the Books for Young Explorers Series.) Washington, DC: National Geographic Society, 1983. 104pp. $8.75. 81-47894. ISBN 0-87044-425-5. Glossary; index; C.I.P. ▶ **EI,EA,JH**

This fine book explains the physical principles behind the operation of devices such as bicycles, clocks, smoke detectors, cameras, and calculators. Technically correct without sacrificing ease of comprehension, the materials are useful through junior high school. The diagrams are so clear and the material so interesting that children and adults both should find the content fascinating. Activities folder, wall poster, duplication masters for classroom use, and a useful index.

National Geographic Society. *Small Inventions That Make a Big Difference.* (Illus. by Joseph H. Bailey and John Huehnergarth; from the Books for World Explorers Series.) Washington, DC: National Geographic, 1984. 104pp. $6.95. 83-23770. ISBN 0-87044-498-0. Index; C.I.P. ▶ **EA,JH**

This interesting and informative books on inventions and inventors is designed to delight, inform, and entertain young people. The book presents its information in three parts: inventors, a story of plastics, and a description of inventions from A to Z. Included are brief descriptions of many small and sometimes important inventions, together with brief historical notes. Loaded with lush and colorful pictures and delightful illustrations, the book also includes a set of duplicating masters, activities, and games. Informative and educational— its quality and value are unsurpassed.

Pollard, Michael. *The House That Science Built.* (Illus.; from the Discovering Science Series.) NY: Facts On File, 1987. 48pp. $10.95. 87-80099. ISBN 0-8160-1780-8. Glossary; index. ▶ **K,EP,EI,EA**

This excellent book gives an easy-to-understand yet technically correct introduction to many of the technologies used in and around the house. It covers the building and its materials, the utilities, furnishings and appliances, food and cooking, and electronics. Woven throughout the text are little excursions to side topics that deliver important messages on safety, health and cleanliness, conservation, the cost of running a home, and the tradeoffs between convenience and cost of buying and running appliances. The language is simple and flows easily and the excellent illustrations will stimulate questions. There are a few terms common in Great Britain but not in the United States.

Provensen, Alice, and Martin Provensen. *Leonardo da Vinci: The Artist, Inventor, Scientist.* (Illus.) NY: Viking, 1984. 12pp. $14.95. 83-26005. ISBN 0-670-42384-X. ▶ **EI,EA,JH**

This book is six double-page panels with three-dimensional "stand-ups," turnable diagrams that reveal two scenes each, and an ingenious lift-and-pull page that illustrates da Vinci's flying machine. Terse, entertaining text on each page describes the man and his various activities in art, invention, engineering, and astronomy. This book is a technical masterpiece; each manipulative piece works well, and each is unique. Although classroom use by unsupervised children will shorten the book's life considerably, it would be a treasure for repeated browsing by individual owners.

Siegel, Beatrice. *The Sewing Machine.* (Illus.; from the Inventions That Changed Our Lives Series.) NY: Walker, 1984. vii + 56pp. $10.85. 83-40397. ISBN 0-8027-6532-7. Index; C.I.P. ▶ **EA,JH**

This book begins with the first workable sewing machine built by Walter Hunt in 1840, then traces the development of Hunt's ideas by Elias Howe, and the spread of the machine in industrial settings in the United States. Also covered are Howe's patenting and marketing problems.

Medicine

See also 371.3 Methods of instruction; 371.42 Careers.

Berenstain, Stan, and Jan Berenstain. *The Berenstain Bears Go to the Doctor.* (Illus.; a First Time Bk.) NY: Random House, 1985. 32 pp. (with cassette tape.) $4.95 (paper). 81-50043. ISBN 0-394-84835-7 (paper). C.I.P. ▶ **EP,EI**

In this book and cassette tape set, the Bears visit the doctor for the children's checkup. It is heartening that the family physician they visit is a woman. However, there are some flaws. In particular, the pictorial depiction of a "shot" shows a syringe enlarged out of proportion, perhaps needlessly arousing anxiety in children. Also, the rapidity of the narrator's voice on the audio cassette makes it difficult for a young child to keep up.

Hautzig, Deborah. *A Visit to the Sesame Street Hospital.* (Illus.) NY: Random House, 1985. 32pp. $4.99. 84-17852. ISBN 0-394-87062-X. ▶ **EP,EI**

Sesame Street characters take a tour through a hospital prior to a tonsillectomy for one of their number. The Illustrations are colorful, detailed, and realistic. A useful book for parents and children to read together to encourage questions that can be answered before and during a hospital visit or stay.

Jacobs, Francine. *Breakthrough: The True Story of Penicillin.* (Illus.) NY: Dodd, Mead, 1985. 128pp. $10.95. 84-26037. ISBN 0-396-08579-2. ▶ **EA,JH**

Recounts one of the most significant events of the 20th century—the discovery and development of penicillin. Alexander Fleming's role in its discovery and Howard Florey and Ernst Chain's role in its development are clearly portrayed. Readers will gain insight into the context of scientific discovery and development, because Jacobs places these pioneers in their social and historical settings.

Lambert, Mark. *Medicine in the Future.* (Illus.; from Tomorrow's World Series.) NY: Bookwright, 1986. 48pp. $10.90. 85-73671. ISBN 0-531-18078-6. Glossary; index. ▶ **EA,JH**

This well-constructed book presents recent medical technology via a number of excellent photographs, most in color, good illustrations, and a concise but clear text. Topics range from the use of the endoscope to view the internal anatomy of the body without major surgery to the use of monoclonal antibodies to fight cancer. One interesting section focuses on alternative approaches such as homeopathy, osteopathy, and acupuncture. Both factually correct and interesting reading.

Reit, Seymour. *Some Busy Hospital!* (Illus. by Carolyn Bracken; a Golden Bk.) NY: Western, 1985. 40pp. $6.95. 83-83310. ISBN 0-307-15600-1. ▶ **K,EP**

For the child preparing for hospitalization, the book provides information in a calm manner, and it shows patients behaving appropriately. Both children and adults are shown as patients. The scope of procedures is realistic, and the male and female health care personnel are portrayed as caring and professional and from diverse ethnic backgrounds. This reassuring book also suggests professions within the allied health fields to which a child can aspire other than the usual doctor and nurse.

Wolfe, Bob, and Diane Wolfe. *Emergency Room.* (Illus.) Minneapolis: Carolrhoda, 1983. 39pp. $7.95. 82-19878. ISBN 0-87614-206-4. C.I.P. ▶ **EI,EA,JH**

This matter-of-fact book includes case histories that enliven the recitation of the step-by-step procedures of modern emergency rooms. Black-and-white photographs offer good explanations without overdramatization. *Emergency Room* contains some minor inaccuracies; however, these are not so serious that elementary and early junior high school students cannot benefit from the overall presentation.

611–612   Human anatomy and physiology

See also 617.6 Teeth and their care; 618.4 Childbirth; pregnancy; 649.65 Sex education.

Asimov, Isaac. *How Did We Find Out About Blood?* (Illus. by David Wool; from the How Did We Find Out . . . ? Series.) NY: Walker, 1986. 63pp. $10.85. 86-15844. ISBN 0-8027-6647-1. Index; C.I.P. ▶ **EI,EA**

The text and its numerous helpful illustrations and diagrams introduce the reader to the sometimes agonizingly slow process of how scientists and physicians have gained an understanding of the circulatory system. Chapters on the heart, circulation, red cells, white cells, platelets, and plasma give a historical perspective and offer brief insight into the people who contributed to some of what we know about blood. Most biochemical and physiological aspects of the circulatory system either are briefly alluded to or are omitted; however, enough information is included to give a well-organized and easily understandable introduction to this interesting system.

Daly, Kathleen N. *Look at You!: A Book About How Your Body Works.* (Illus. by Kathy Allert; a Golden Learn About Living Bk.) NY: Western, 1986. 32pp. $4.95. 84-82594. ISBN 0-307-10398-6. ▶ **K,EP,EI**

For the inquisitive child who asks questions about parts of the body, this book provides the answers. It starts with a baby learning to move different parts of its body skillfully and continues on to simplified descriptions of the functions of bones and joints, muscles, lungs, eyes, ears, tongue, and teeth. Unfortunately, the circulatory and nervous systems are omitted, but the material covered is accurate, easy to read, and answers some of the most common questions asked by children.

Elting, Mary. *The Macmillan Book of the Human Body.* (Illus. by Kirk Moldoff.) NY: Aladdin (Macmillan), 1986. 80pp. $15.95; $8.95 (paper). 85-24204. ISBN 0-02-733440-6; 0-02-043080-9 (paper). Glossary; index; C.I.P. ▶ **EA,JH**

Written for middle school through high school grades, this book presents "the physical characteristics and functions of the various parts of the body." The text is actually more comprehensive than that because it includes a discussion of biological clocks and how enzymes and the immune system work. The book even closes with a sensitive treatment of human sexuality. The real kudos go to the illustrations, however, which are delicately contrived, attractive and instructive, and reproduced in full color. Overall, the presentation is generally accurate and can be easily assimilated by its intended audience.

Gaskin, John. *Breathing.* (Illus.) NY: Watts, 1984. 32pp. 83-50855. ISBN 0-531-03768-1. Glossary; index. ▶ **EI**

Movement. 84-50022. ISBN 0-531-04633-8.

Breathing explains the action of breathing and how it takes place in an environment of air—principally oxygen—to keep our bodies alive. It also explains that although breathing is an automatic function, making sounds for speech is an intentional act that involves the mouth, lips, tongue, and teeth. Other facts imparted by this instructive book are that particles in the air and smoke pollute the environment, which can impair breathing, and that mountain climbers, deep water divers, and astronauts require additional oxygen supplies. The illustrations support the text. In *Movement,* exercise is described to the young reader: push, pull, stretch, lift, swing extremities in a slow or fast rhythm. We learn that movement depends on muscles that are attached to bones assembled into a skeletal structure and that a covering of skin and a padding of fat protect the assemblage as well as the nerves. The illustrations depict the bones of the skeleton. The joints that serve to connect bones are also explained, as is how muscles can move the bones through shortening and lengthening.

Iveson-Iveson, Joan. *Your Eyes.* (Illus. by Bill Donohoe; from the All About You Series.) NY: Bookwright, 1985. 25pp. $8.90. 84-73572. ISBN 0-531-18014-X. Glossary; index. ▶ **EP,EI**

Your Nose and Ears. 1986. 26pp. 85-71729. ISBN 0-531-18042-5.

Your Eyes will help children appreciate vision and understand the physical structures involved in seeing. The description of the anatomy of the eye is clear and would be understandable to a bright seven- or eight-year-old. The author gives a fine description of the operation of the eye, but the concept of image inversion is introduced too abruptly. There is a brief but valuable presentation about ethnic differences in the appearance of the exterior and related structures of the eye. In the discussion of eye protection, the author could have given stronger warning about harmful accidents. The only real negative, however, is the tendency of the author to sensationalize. *Your Nose and Ears* presents a complicated subject in a simple but accurate form. The lucidity of the description of how the middle ear operates is such that young readers should never forget it. The illustrations and accompanying text are equally good for the nose and ear. The discussion of the value of smell as a major factor in distinguishing taste is clear and understandable. The distinction between congenital and acquired deafness is good, especially as it relates to speech problems.

Iveson-Iveson, Joan. *Your Hands and Feet.* (Illus. by Bill Donohoe; from the All About You Series.) NY: Bookwright, 1986. 26pp. $9.40. 85-71728. ISBN 0-531-18041-7. Glossary; index. ▶ **K,EP,EI**

Your Skin and Hair. 85-72746. ISBN 0-531-18043.3.

Your Hands and Feet is well thought out and superbly organized. The author has done an excellent job in getting difficult subject matter across using simple-to-understand terminology. The illustrations are well done and strategically placed, although the color photographs are of poor quality. *Your Skin and Hair* is a well-organized book that explains the anatomy of skin and hair, how they function, and how to care for them. The illustrations, especially those that describe the anatomical features of the hair and skin, are quite good and enhance the text significantly. The text is also supplemented by color photographs, which for the most part are appropriate but mediocre in quality.

Martin, Paul D. *Messengers to the Brain: Our Fantastic Five Senses.* (Illus.; from the Books for World Explorers Series.) Washington, DC: National Geographic Society, 1984. 104pp. $8.50. 82-45636. ISBN 0-87044-499-9. Glossary; index; C.I.P. Classroom activity folder. ▶ **EA**

An excellent introduction to sensory physiology for young readers. The opening overview chapter is followed by a discussion of the nervous system's role in interpreting sensory information and integrating different modalities. Subsequent chapters cover vision, taste and smell, hearing and balance, and touch. The information is current and written without dogmatism and with respect for the students' intelligence. The illustrations include electron micrographs, biological photographs, computer graphics, and diagrams. Throughout, peripheral sensory structures and the corresponding color-coded analytical centers in the brain are depicted to help students visualize the main theme while focusing on the detailed material in each chapter. Teachers are provided with a set of activities and suggestions to reinforce each chapter.

Moncure, Jane Belk. *Sounds All Around.* (Illus. by Lois Axeman; from the Five Senses Series.) Chicago: Childrens Press, 1982. 31pp. ea. $6.95 ea. 82-4516. ISBN 0-516-03252-6. C.I.P. ▶ **K,EP**

The Look Book. 82-4517. ISBN 0-516-03251-8.

A Tasting Party. 82-4411. ISBN 0-516-03253-4.

The Touch Book. 82-4154. ISBN 0-516-03254-2.

What Your Nose Knows! 82-9464. ISBN 0-516-03255-0.

Each of these books introduces one of the five senses by describing and illustrating a set of experiences that should seem real to young children. The text and especially the illustrations convey a warm feeling and good humor along with accurate information about animals, plants, people, and a variety of phenomena. *A Tasting Party* perhaps goes a bit overboard in its effort to include nutritional information, and it should caution readers that some leaves, seeds, and other items are not safe to taste. Nevertheless, these appealing books should be very useful in supplementing direct experiences used in teaching young children about their senses.

Pluckrose, Henry. *Hearing.* (Illus; photographs by Chris Fairclough; from the Think About Series.) NY: Watts, 1986. 32pp. ea. $9.40 ea. ISBN 0-531-10170-3. ▶ **K,EP**

Seeing. ISBN 0-531-10171-1.

Smelling. ISBN 0-531-10172-X.

Tasting. ISBN 0-531-10173-8.

Touching. ISBN 0-531-10174-6.

Any parent or primary teacher who wants a top flight teaching aid will find it in this set of books. The 113 vivid, full-page photographs seem to leap off the page. Their composition, color, selection, and appropriateness are excellent. The scant, direct text points the direction for discussion with very young children. *Seeing* covers how we use our eyes, the kinds of things we see, and does not forget sightlessness and aids for impaired vision. *Smelling* recalls delightful odors and repulsive stenches. *Hearing* includes sounds of outdoors and indoors, city and country, loud and soft, natural and mechanical. *Tasting* ranges from mouth-watering pictures of ice cream, freshly baked bread, and candy, to toothpaste and medicine. *Touching* begins with touching hands together and leads through the feel of rough and smooth, slippery and sticky, hard and soft, warm and cool, wet and dry. After a parent or teacher has established a memory bank of sensations, these beautiful books can come into their own.

Settel, Joanne, and Nancy Baggett. *Why Does My Nose Run? (and Other Questions Kids Ask About Their Bodies).* (Illus.) NY: Atheneum, 1985. ix + 83pp. $9.95. 84-21549. ISBN 0-689-31078-1. Index; C.I.P. ▶ **EP,EI,EA**

Uses a question-answer format to deal with typical questions that young children (approximately 6–10 years old) ask about their bodies. These questions range from why we get fevers or goose bumps to why a cut stops bleeding. Allergies, warts, moles, and what happens when you hit your funny bone are also covered. The answers are well organized, technically sound, and should satisfy even the most inquisitive child. The material and format will serve parents better than science teachers; however, the book would be an excellent addition to a classroom or school library.

Sharp, Pat. *Brain Power! Secrets of a Winning Team.* (Illus. by Martha Weston.) NY: Lothrop, Lee & Shepard, 1984. 56pp. $10.50. 83-14896. ISBN 0-688-02679-6. Index; C.I.P. ▶ **EI,EA**

Sharp has written a clever book about the brain. Its "winning team" approach and appealing illustrations are irresistible; it is also fun to read and informative. Almost every page has illustrations to clarify points and present more facts. Overall, an excellent resource for the classroom.

Smallman, Clare. *Outside-in: A Lift-the-Flap Body Book.* (Illus. by Edwina Riddell.) NY: Barron's, 1986. 32pp. $8.95. 86-7982. ISBN 0-8120-5760-0. C.I.P. ▶ **EP,EI**

This book familiarizes young readers with elementary physiology and anatomy in a stimulating, personalized manner. Fundamental aspects of the cardiorespiratory, gastrointestinal, and musculoskeletal systems are explained using examples and metaphors from the child's everyday world. With some illustrations, the reader lifts a flap to reveal an aspect of the child's internal anatomy. Some readers may be offended by the graphic presentation of internal and external anatomy, but the book is a useful attempt to help youngsters better understand how their body works.

Stafford, Patricia. *Your Two Brains.* (Illus. by Linda Tunney.) NY: Atheneum, 1986. x + 75pp. $11.95. 85-28575. ISBN 0-689-31142-7. Glossary; index; C.I.P. ▶ **EA,JH**

Although this text is aimed mainly at upper elementary and junior high students, the clear, accurate presentation is very suitable even for adult education classes. Many beautiful woodcuts punctuate the neurologically correct presentation of right brain–left brain functioning. The concept of brain preference is elucidated well, and a two-part test enables readers to determine which side of their brain is the stronger. There are discussions of right- and left-handedness and genius, and well-known but accurately presented descriptions of highly creative, famous individuals add to the usefulness of this little gem.

Vevers, Gwynne. *Skin and Bone.* (Illus. by Sarah Pooley; Vol. 1 of the Your Body Series.) NY: Lothrop, Lee & Shepard, 1983. 24pp. ea. $8.25 ea. 83-18757. ISBN 0-688-02820-9. Index; C.I.P. ▶ **EI,EA**

Blood and Lungs (Vol. 2). ISBN 0-688-02823-3.

Feeding and Digestion (Vol. 3). ISBN 0-688-02830-6.

Muscles and Movement (Vol. 4). ISBN 0-688-02825-X.

These four books are well-written, well-organized, technically accurate descriptions of human anatomy and physiology for elementary school children. Plentifully illustrated with excellent, colorful line drawings and cartoons that amplify the text, each book covers the gross anatomy, the microanatomy, and the physiology of the systems under discussion. Excellent as first textbooks for human biology and for use by parents in answering children's questions.

Ward, Brian R. *Birth and Growth.* (Illus.; from the Human Body Series.) NY: Watts, 1983. 48pp. $8.90. 82-50055. ISBN 0-531-04459-9. Glossary; index. ▶ **EA,JH**

Body Maintenance. 82-50056. ISBN 0-531-04457-2.

Birth and Growth handles the delicate subject of sexual reproduction in a straightforward manner, providing basic facts that will satisfy adolescent curiosity in an intelligent way. The book describes the male and female genital organs and their role in conception, development of the fetus, the process of birth, determination of the sex and characteristics of offspring, and the major stages of development of the individual after birth. Excellent diagrams and drawings; useful as a textbook, collateral reading, or reference for classrooms or libraries. *Body Maintenance* explains how the human body maintains the proper conditions for the numerous and complicated chemical reactions, including maintenance of temperature, blood pressure, and blood sugar levels. Focuses on the role played by hormones, the glands that produce them, and the hormone balance needed to maintain proper chemical conditions. The functions of certain organs, including the kidneys, are also explained. Excellent drawings and diagrams support a very readable text.

Ward, Brian R. *Food and Digestion.* (Illus.; from the Human Body Series.) NY: Watts, 1982. 48pp. $7.90. 82-500057. ISBN 0-531-04458-0. Glossary; index. ▶ **EI,EA,JH**

Full-page anatomical illustrations of the human digestive system complement each page, and a glossary offers additional explanations of biological and medical terms. Ward's factual presentation and its correlation to the functional digestive process, from receiving food in the mouth to metabolic transformation into absorbable particles, assists cognitive learning.

White, Lawrence B., Jr., and Ray Broekel. *Optical Illusions.* (Illus.; a First Bk.) NY: Watts, 1986. ii+93pp. $9.90. 86-10986. ISBN 0-531-10220-3. Index; C.I.P. ▶ **EP,EI,EA,JH**

This book has a wonderful evocative power too seldom seen. Young readers are invited to perform dozens of experiments by simply looking at optical illusions. The authors provide a great deal of good information about the process of "seeing." They point out that seeing and illusions are to be regarded at three levels: the physical stimulus (light), the visual organ (eye), and information processing (brain). The reader is left not only with a greater understanding of the visual process, but with a heightened awareness and sensitivity to the extraordinary embodied in the ordinary—the hallmark of real science.

616 Specific health problems

Cole, Joanna. *Cuts, Breaks, Bruises, and Burns: How Your Body Heals.* (Illus. by True Kelley.) NY: Crowell, 1985. 48pp. $10.25. 84-45335. ISBN 0-690-04437-2. Index; C.I.P. ▶ **EI,EA**

This book describes the body, comparing and contrasting it to a machine. The structure of the various types of cells and their role in healing are discussed in conjunction with inflammation, infection, sutures, scars, bruises, bumps, nosebleeds, broken bones, sprains, and burns. Cole has taken a complex subject and successfully presented it in simple language for young readers. The excellent illustrations are fun, informative, self-explanatory, and a useful adjunct to the text. A good addition to primary school libraries.

Delton, Judy. *I'll Never Love Anything Ever Again.* (Illus. by Rodney Pate.) Niles, IL: Whitman, 1985. 32pp. $9.25. 84-17271. ISBN 0-8075-3521-4. C.I.P. ▶ **EP,EI,EA**

This skillfully written story about a boy with allergies who must give away his dog is effectively told from the child's perspective. It realistically portrays the child's efforts to cope, which include talking with his mother about his feelings. Well-sketched pictures on each page enhance the text. A note of caution: this is an emotional story, so if a child is experiencing this type of stressful situation, the book should be read and discussed with an adult. Overall, an excellent book for its understanding presentation of the problems that a child with newly diagnosed allergies must face.

Dowdle, Walter, and Jack Lapatra. *Informed Consent: Influenza Facts and Myths.* Chicago: Nelson-Hall, 1983. ix+136pp. $22.95. 83-4099. ISBN 0-88229-741-4. Index; C.I.P. ▶ **JH**

This easy-to-read book says everything about influenza that nonscientists would want to know. It gives a fascinating review of influenza's influence on history from 415 BC to the present, explains the scientific jargon of influenza in lay terms (including genetic "wobble," antigenic drift, and antigenic shift), and deals with water birds and pigs as reservoirs and with contaminated water in transmission of influenza. Epidemiology; worldwide surveillance programs; signs, symptoms, and natural course of the illness; treatment, immunology, and the economic cost of society; and the benefits versus the risks of vaccination are all clearly explained.

Gilbert, Sara. *What Happens in Therapy.* NY: Lothrop, Lee & Shepard, 1982. 144pp. $8.63; $6.00 (paper). 81-15233. ISBN 0-688-01458-5; 0-688-01459-3 (paper). Glossary; index; C.I.P. ▶ **JH**

Gilbert aims for a specific audience—adolescents with emotional, family, and social problems. She sets out to help them begin to cope by perceiving that they need not be isolated by their personal problems, by showing them that assistance is available, and by offering them encouragement to take logical, positive steps to resolve their dilemmas. The author covers currently available types of psychotherapies with objectivity, evenness, and commendable depth without using unnecessary technical jargon. Could profitably be used as student collateral reading material or for oral book reports, and deserves a place in school libraries.

Hyde, Margaret O. *Know About Smoking.* (Illus. by Dennis Kendrick.) NY: McGraw-Hill, 1983. 78pp. $8.95. 82-14953. ISBN 0-07-031671-6; Index; C.I.P. ▶ **EA,JH**

A well-written, profusely illustrated book that is designed to convince kids not to smoke. The author uses role-playing dialogue effectively throughout the text to teach kids how to resist peer pressure. She covers health hazards and social problems related to smoking, and ends by suggesting various avenues of help for the person who has already started.

Nourse, Alan E. *Viruses, revised edition.* (Illus.; a First Bk.) NY: Watts, 1983. 64pp. $8.90. 82-16010. ISBN 0-531-04534-X. Glossary; index; C.I.P. ▶ **JH**

In clear prose, Nourse introduces readers to Jenner's and Pasteur's discovery of vaccination. The meaning and mechanism of immunity are simply but thoroughly described. This is followed by a review of current virus research, including the functions of the nucleic acids and the relationship between viruses and cancer.

617.6 Teeth and their care

See also 371.42 Careers.

Iveson-Iveson, Joan. *Your Teeth.* (Illus. by Bill Donohoe; from the All About You Series.) NY: Bookwright, 1985. 26pp. $8.90. 84-73573. ISBN 0-531-18013-1. Glossary; index. ▶ **EP,EI**

This book should make its audience aware of the importance and care of teeth. The author identifies ethnic differences and phenotypic variations in dentition and appearance of the teeth without making a fuss over the differences. The depiction and illustrations of a healthy and a damaged tooth are well done; unfortunately, the discussion about cleaning one's teeth is not. But overall, worthwhile for young readers.

Marsoli, Lisa Ann. *Things to Know About Going to the Dentist.* (Illus.; from the Look Before You Leap Series.) Morristown, NJ: Silver Burdett, 1985. 48pp.

$8.96; $4.95 (paper). 84-50439. ISBN 0-382-06781-9; 0-382-06961-7 (paper). Index; C.I.P. ▶ **EP**

This book answers the many questions that children have when preparing for a first visit to the dentist. In the tone of a kindly old dentist who nevertheless has kept up with modern techniques, Marsoli decribes the different staff members' roles and how patients can make their visits as painless as possible. The book addresses how to be comfortable with the many different procedures. Many illustrations show procedures that can't be seen by the patient who is undergoing them. The last few pages give a nice history of dentistry.

618.4   Childbirth; pregnancy

See also 611–612 Human anatomy and physiology.

Cole, Joanna. *How You Were Born.* (Illus.) NY: Morrow, 1984. 48pp. $10.25. 83-17314. ISBN 0-688-1710-X. C.I.P. ▶ **EP,EI,EA**

The author's intent was to relate the story of birth in a simple yet informative way, so the technical information is kept to a minimum: not even the words pregnant, fetus, or placenta are used. Some of the pictures, especially one showing an actual delivery, may be too graphic. Nevertheless, human birth is presented as a natural, happy occurrence, giving children a healthy outlook.

Girard, Linda Walvoord. *You Were Born on Your Very First Birthday.* (Illus. by Christa Kieffer; A Concept Bk.) Niles, IL: Albert Whitman, 1983. 28pp. $8.25. 82-13700. ISBN 0-8075-9455-5. C.I.P. ▶ **K,EP,EI**

An excellent introduction to pregnancy and childbirth for young readers. Realistically illustrated and clearly written, it portrays the details of uterine life. Two criticisms should be noted, however. First, the term uterus should have been introduced and used instead of "stomach," especially since other reasonably technical and accurate terms are used. Second, the book is oriented to the middle class, for whom the ideal is overjoyed parents who are both eager to participate in childbirth.

Engineering

See also 608 Inventions and inventors.

621 Applied physics

Boltz, C. L. *How Electricity Is Made.* (Illus,; from the How It Is Made Series.) NY: Facts On File, 1985. 32pp. $7.95. 84-21050. ISBN 0-8160-0039-5. Index; C.I.P. ▶ EA,JH

The author explores the phenomenon of naturally occurring static electricity and how it fits into the modern theory of the electron, then provides a detailed presentation of the making of electricity by means of energy from nuclear fission, water, wind, geysers, and the sun. The use of electricity in the home and its storage in dry cell and car batteries are clearly explained. Important dates and major discoveries are nicely tabulated; diagrams and illustrations enhance the work.

Freeman, John, and Martin Hollins. *Mechanics.* (Illus.; from the Visual Science Series.) Morristown, NJ: Silver Burdett, 1983. 48pp. $13.00. 83-50224. ISBN 0-382-06716-9. Glossary; index. ▶ JH

Broadly covers the subject of mechanics, from fundamental principles to familiar applications involving the human body and machines, and includes technical material that will be difficult for readers without some background knowledge of mechanics and machines. About half of the book is devoted to excellent figures and photographs. With interesting and effective textual and visual presentations, it is most suitable for young readers who already have an interest in mechanics, science, and/or mechanical engineering.

Gutnik, Martin J. *Simple Electrical Devices.* (Illus.; a First Bk.) NY: Watts, 1986. vi + 66pp. $9.40. 85-26369. ISBN 0-531-10127-4. Glossary; index; C.I.P. ▶ EA

A child interested in electricity and electrical devices will find a good historical outline in this book but only four pages on modern devices such as the vacuum tube, transistors, and the microchip. The excellent illustrations are selected from historical manuscripts. As the development of each electrical device is described, there is a project for the reader to do that mimics the original device. Although there is a safety note warning about hot wires, the caution is placed in the introduction where it might be overlooked. The vocabulary is somewhat difficult, but the technical words are in bold type and are defined in the glossary.

Hawkes, Nigel. *Nuclear Power.* (Illus.; from the Inside Story Series.) NY: Gloucester Press, 1984. 40pp. $9.90. 84-80511. ISBN 0-531-04870-5. Glossary; index. ▶ **EA,JH**

This book imparts information through elaborate, colorful diagrams and detailed captions. Only about one-eighth of the page space is devoted to true text. The information given is scrupulously accurate and unburdened by detail or extensive nomeclature. Numerical values are given in metric units accompanied by Imperial (not U.S.) equivalents. The visual impression of the book is dazzling, and the material, which covers the nuclear power cycle, is highly readable.

Zubrowski, Bernie. *Wheels at Work: Building and Experimenting with Models of Machines.* (Illus.; from The Boston Children's Museum Activity Book Series.) NY: Morrow, 1986. 112pp. $5.95 (paper). 86-12500. ISBN 0-688-06349-7 (paper). C.I.P. ▶ **JH**

This book offers fun, challenges, and excitement through experiments and guided discovery. It demonstrates how wheels, pulleys, gears, and so on help make real-life machines function. The black-and-white sketches are simple and clear and are accompanied by step-by-step explanations of proven, workable models. The fascinating background material shows how machines make life easier, and it gives concrete examples of machines used from early times to today. The book suggests that students keep a notebook just as scientists and engineers do to test designs for workability, endurance of parts, and efficiency.

621.366 Lasers

Barrett, N.S. *Lasers and Holograms.* (Illus.; from the Picture Library Series.) NY: Watts, 1985. 32pp. $9.40. 84-52000. ISBN 0-531-04946-9. Glossary; index. ▶ **EA,JH**

Copiously illustrated with color drawings and photographs, the text is simple, with large type for easy reading. Various uses of lasers and holograms are shown with short descriptions and illustrations. The book should interest students in grades five through eight, although some younger children may benefit from the pictures. The description and illustration of the making of a hologram are well done, but the concept is probably too difficult to be fully grasped from just an illustration.

Bender, Lionel. *Lasers in Action.* (Illus.; from the Tomorrow's World Series.) NY: Bookwright, 1985. 48pp. $10.40. 85-70450. ISBN 0-531-18021-2. Glossary; index. ▶ **EI,EA,JH**

This is a broad and interesting selection of the uses of lasers. Industrial, medical, earth sciences, and military uses, and uses in holography and communications are covered in enough detail to arouse interest in further study. The coverage is current and is enhanced by good pictures and adequate diagrams. Not too difficult for young readers, the book should prove entertaining to almost any age level.

Devere, Charles. *Lasers.* (Illus.) NY: Gloucester, 1984. 40pp. $9.90. 84-80510. ISBN 0-531-04869-1. Glossary; index. ▶ **EA**

Underlying principles are minimally explained in this description of laser uses. With only minor expansion of the material presented and minor changes in the language used, this could have been a delightful book for general audiences, but for its intended audience, it falls somewhat flat. In this book directed at a young audience, the author includes frighteningly clear descriptions of military lasers and space weapons intended to destroy nuclear missiles. The applications of lasers in medicine, measurement, and communications are appropriately described, and the color plates are beautiful. Recommended for anyone who enjoys picture books and has no need for strong reference material.

Filson, Brent. *Exploring with Lasers.* (Illus. by Brigita Fuhrmann.) NY: Messner, 1984. 95pp. $9.29. 84-14731. ISBN 0-671-50573-4. Glossary; index; C.I.P. ▶ **EA,JH**

Filson succeeds in bringing a complex subject to young readers without being superficial. The nature of light and quantum optics are discussed in the presentation of how a laser works. Also discussed are various laser applications in communications, medicine, art, science, industry, and the military. Holography is explained, and the text is supplemented with illustrations. A good resource for school libraries, despite some simple errors in metric conversions.

621.381   Electronic engineering and computers
See also 001.64 Electronic data processing.

Asimov, Isaac. *How Did We Find Out About Computers?* (Illus. by David Wool; from the How Did We Find Out About Series.) NY: Walker, 1984. 54pp. $8.85. 83-40401. ISBN 0-8027-6533-5. Index; C.I.P. ▶ **EA**

As brief history of how we learned to count and how we developed calculators and computers, this book is a pleasant and uncommon journey. Phonetic spelling and, in some cases, a description of the term's origin help students understand the terms of this high-technology field. From the inventions of thousands of years ago to present-day microchips, Asimov examines the work of important pioneers in this field. Appropriate for elementary school children and any adult wishing a glimpse of the computer's history, the book's collateral value is its bibliographical completeness.

Billings, Charlene W. *Microchip: Small Wonder.* (Illus.; A Skylight Bk.) NY: Dodd, Mead, 1984. 48pp. $7.95. 84-10179. ISBN 0-396-08452-4. Index; C.I.P. ▶ **EA,JH**

Billings explains microchips simply and directly, first in general terms and appearance, then in applications such as computers, calculators, watches, robots, video games, telephones, and pacemakers. Fabrication methods and operational concepts are explained and illustrated. Finally, future possibilities for microchips are predicted.

Herda, D. J. *Computer Maintenance.* (Illus.; a Computer-Awarenesss First Bk.) NY: Watts, 1985. 66pp. $9.40. 84-21882. ISBN 0-531-04905-1. Glossary; index; C.I.P. ▶ **EA,JH**

This book is a must for anyone working with computers. The do's and don't's are well illustrated for lay people; for example, there are explanations of why smoking and loud music may harm a computer. Diagnosis, remedies, and prevention of common problems are discussed.

Lachenbruch, David. *Television.* (Illus. by Tom Baldini; a Look Inside Bk.) Millwaukee: Raintree, 1985. 47pp. $11.64. 84-9914. ISBN 0-8172-1408-9. Glossary; index; C.I.P. ▶ **EA,JH**

This excellent book for children and adults is clearly written and superbly illustrated. From the history of television and a simplified, understandable description of how a color TV camera works to a discussion of how signals are transmitted and how a television set receives these signals, this book constantly retains the reader's interest. Accurate and well organized, *Television* will serve as rich entertainment and as an educational resource for all readers.

623–628 Nautical, civil, and sanitary engineering

Cobb, Vicki. *The Trip of a Drip.* (Illus. by Elliot Kreloff; from the How the World Works Series.) Boston: Little, Brown, 1986. x + 50pp. $11.95. 85-23960. ISBN 0-316-14900-4. C.I.P. ▶ **EA**

A straightforward account of how drinking water is usually obtained by rural dwellers from aquifers through wells and springs and by urban residents from surface water in rivers, lakes, and reservoirs. Water purification and sewage treatment are explained simply and well through diagrams and text. The number of scientific terms introduced seems unnecessarily large, but readers will probably skip over most of them. Most of the activities seem suitable for children to do at home without supervision, although some will probably lead only to confusion. Useful as a supplement to the curriculum and as independent reading.

Gibbons, Gail. *Fire! Fire!* (Illus, by the author.) NY: Crowell, 1984. 38pp. $9.95. 83-46162. ISBN 0-690-04417-8. C.I.P. ▶ **EI,EA,JH**

This instructive and entertaining book is about the different kinds of fire and the different kinds of firefighting. It also contains some other helpful information on fire and fire prevention. Ideally suited for elementary and junior-high students, this book could entertain young readers with its clear and colorful graphics while educating them. Well paced, accurate, and well organized, this book could be used in science, reading, and social studies classes and for general awareness.

Gibbons, Gail. *Tunnels.* NY: Holiday House, 1984. 30pp. $12.95. 83-18589. ISBN 0-8234-0507-9. C.I.P. ▶ **K,EP**

This book should help youngsters fulfill their fascination with tunnels through its visual presentation of simple and complex tunnels made by animals and people. The illustrations are bright, bold, and well labeled and show in detail how a tunnel is built, its parts, and the different types of tunnels—those that carry water, minerals, cars, trains, and/or people. The last page is a historical summary that provides a short account of tunnels from ancient times to the present. Written in a simple, easy style.

Gibbons, Gail. *Up Goes the Skyscraper!* (Illus. by the author.) NY: Macmillan, 1986. 32pp. $12.95. 85-16245. ISBN 0-02-736780-0. C.I.P. ▶ **K,EP,EI**

The many functions that go into the building of a skyscraper are identified without condescending to the reader. The straightforward language, aided by appealing color illustrations, conveys the integration of tasks needed for so complex a project. The book charts the orderly progression of events from the initial need for a building to its completion. The layout of the book is somewhat distracting, with some sentences carrying over and mixing in with illustrations on following pages.

Grey, Michael. *Ships and Submarines.* (Illus.; from the Modern Technology Series.) NY: Watts, 1986. 32pp. $10.40. 86-50034. ISBN 0-531-10201-7. Glossary; index. ▶ JH

This excellent review of the current state of ship technology deals with modern merchant shipping and its economic concerns. The text is clear, and most points are well illustrated with clear and attractive diagrams. Unusual or special vocabulary is defined. The book's failings are its lack of discussion of the economic dimensions of the shipping industry and an extremely weak closing chapter containing conjectures about the future of the industry.

Kingston, Jeremy. *How Bridges Are Made.* (Illus.; from the How It Is Made Series.) NY: Facts On File, 1985. 32pp. $7.95. 84-21054. ISBN 0-8160-0040-9. Index; C.I.P. ▶ EA,JH

Kingston presents explanations of basic bridge styles—beam, arch, suspension, and cantilever—and includes descriptions of the design, construction, and materials used. His examples enable us to compare such great engineering feats as the Roman massive stone bridge of the semicircular arch with Maillart's continuous single arch spanning an alpine gorge. Excellent illustrations clarify the stages of construction and techniques involved in handling various materials. Great bridges of the world and the world's longest bridges are also included.

Petty, Kate. *Submarines.* (Illus.) NY: Watts, 1986. 30pp. $9.40. 86-50275. ISBN 0-531-10256-4. ▶ EP,EI,EA

The captioned illustrations are colorful, interesting, and instructive, not only featuring types of submarines but also providing specific names of vessels. Sizes and uses of submarines are explored, and basic functions, such as diving and surfacing, are explained. While the typeface is large enough for second graders, the vocabulary and style are more appropriate for fourth graders. The book ends with a series of questions, some drawing readers back to the text to find the answers and some offering new information on the spot.

629 Transportation

Bushey, Jerry. *Monster Trucks and Other Giant Machines on Wheels.* (Illus.) Minneapolis: Carolrhoda, 1985. 40pp. $12.95. 84-23160. ISBN 0-87614-271-4. ▶ EI,EA

This beautifully illustrated book describes in accurate detail the world of large vehicles, including massive snow-blowers, log stackers, tree crushers, mine and other large trucks and earthmovers. Each section contains a full-color photograph with accompanying text. To the technologically conscious fifth or sixth grader, the book should be fascinating. For the ecologically sensitive, some of the content should be troubling.

Lambert, Michael, and Jane Insley. *Communications and Transport.* (Illus.; from The World of Science Series.) NY: Facts On File, 1986. 64pp. $9.95. 84-1654. ISBN 0-8160-1073-0. Glossary; index; C.I.P. ▶ **JH**

This book gives a short description of the history and technology of each of the major modes of transportation—road, railway, water, and air. The topic is introduced by a section on communications and ends with a look into the future. Well illustrated with many colorful and attractive pictures. Some terms are foreign to American readers, but each point is fully illustrated and labeled. Overall, an interesting, well-written, and informative summary of fascinating yet familiar technologies.

Marston, Hope Irvin. *Snowplows.* (Illus.) NY: Dodd, Mead, 1986. 48pp. $10.95. 86-8935. ISBN 0-396-08818-X. Glossary; index; C.I.P. ▶ **EP,EI,EA**

This interesting book describes snow moving and removal. Each page contains a black-and-white photograph and two or three short paragraphs of text. After some of the problems caused by snow are illustrated, various snow-moving devices are introduced, ranging from simple snow shovels and small snow blowers to plows and snow blowers of all sizes. Many of the machines will be new even to readers from the snowiest climes. The pictures are sharp, clear, and stimulating, and they greatly extend the text.

Tessendorf, K.C. *Look out! Here Comes the Stanley Steamer.* (Illus. by Gloria Kamen.) NY: Atheneum, 1984. 58pp. $11.95. 83-15661. ISBN 0-689-31028-5. C.I.P. ▶ **EA**

The book is most instructive from a historical perspective because it traces the development of the Stanley Steamer, one of America's outstanding automobiles. The story of how the Stanley brothers developed the steamer is well told, moving quickly but pleasantly. Attention to detail makes readers almost intimate observers. We come to know the Stanley brothers in a personal way while learning a great deal about how this mechanical device worked.

629.13 Aerodynamics; aircraft types; aviators

Ardley, Neil, and Eric Laithwaite (Series Consultant). *Air and Flight.* (Illus.; an Action Science Bk.) NY: Watts, 1984. 32pp. $9.90. 83-51441. ISBN 0-531-03775-4. Index. ▶ **EI,EA**

This book presents information and activities on air and flight. Topics include what air is, expanding air, air pressure, air seals, lifting liquids, the power of air, moving air, wings, and measuring the air. Each section contains experiments with instructions, cautions, and explanations. Well written, well illustrated, and well bound.

Ayres, Carter M. *Soaring.* (Illus.; from the Superwheels & Thrill Sports Series.) Minneapolis: Lerner, 1986. 40pp. $8.95. 85-23667. ISBN 0-8225-0442-1. C.I.P. ▶ **EA,JH**

The fine illustrations and the lucid, exciting text make this book a good introduction to the sport of soaring. Scant historical background is included, but the sufficient scientific and technical background that the author does provide is well integrated into the how-to and excitement of soaring. The information is accurate and well organized.

Briggs, Carole S. *Ballooning.* (Illus.; from the Superwheels & Thrill Sports Series.) Minneapolis: Lerner, 1986. 48pp. $8.95. 86-7365. ISBN 0-8225-0441-3. C.I.P. ▶ **EA,JH**

This well-illustrated book is a good introduction to the sport of ballooning for youngsters of perhaps 11 to 15 years of age. The author combines modest but good sections on the history and scientific uses of balloons with the main text, which is devoted to the sport of ballooning.

Chadwick, Roxane. *Amelia Earhart: Aviation Pioneer.* (Illus.; from The Achievers Series.) Minneapolis: Lerner, 1987. 56pp. ea. $7.95 ea.; $4.95 ea. (paper). 87-4241. ISBN 0-8225-0484-7; 0-8225-9515-X (paper). C.I.P. ▶ **EA**

Anne Morrow Lindbergh: Pilot and Poet. 87-4242. ISBN 0-8225-0488-X; 0-8225-9516-8 (paper).

These well-illustrated books emphasize the personal lives of Anne Lindbergh and Amelia Earhart, providing much anecdotal information. The technical and intellectual achievements of these women are not dealt with in great detail, but their lives are adequately described at a level appropriate for an elementary school-age audience. Little science is presented.

Gibbons, Gail. *Flying.* (Illus.) NY: Holiday House, 1986. 32pp. $12.95. 85-22027. ISBN 0-8234-0599-0. C.I.P. ▶ **K,EP**

Flying is the type of book that preschool and kindergarten classrooms can benefit from, although some of the vocabulary is beyond the independent reading level of the intended audience. The illustrations are colorful, attractive, and accurate. They depict the various stages of flight from balloons to space ships in a way that would appeal to young readers and help them understand the material. Much of the more technical vocabulary is illustrated clearly in the drawings. A good book for classrooms and libraries.

Gunston, Bill. *Aircraft.* (Illus.; from the Modern Technology Series.) NY: Watts, 1986. 32pp. $10.90. 85-51643. ISBN 0-531-10135-5. Glossary; index. ▶ **EI,EA**

Excellent color photographs and simple diagrams are the major strength of this attractive book. It gives a good, if very brief, introduction to many modern aviation concepts. Its main thrust seems to be as an introductory review of the modern technology involved in aircraft design. The book would serve well as supplementary classroom material for an elementary science class that is emphasizing modern technology.

Hosking, Wayne. *Flights of Imagination: An Introduction to Aerodynamics.* (Illus.) Washington, DC: National Science Teachers Assoc., 1987. 56pp. $6.50. ISBN 0-87355-067-6. Glossary. ▶ **EI,EA,JH**

This book can be used by science teachers for many different grade levels. Elementary science teachers can help their students create different types of kites to fly, while senior-high science teachers and students can make and fly kites and study such variables as wind speed and lift or the ratio of the kite's weight to its area. Eighteen projects are clearly illustrated, and the materials called for are readily obtainable (trash bags, dowels, plastic tubing, and popsicle sticks). The book is suitable for independent use by middle and secondary school students. The information and the questions included with the projects in a "Think About It" section transform this book from a set of simple how-to activities into a useful teaching tool combining pupil hands-on activities with mathematics and science process skills.

Provensen, Alice, and Martin Provensen. *The Glorious Flight: Across the Channel with Louis Blériot.* (Illus. by the authors.) NY: Viking, 1983. 39pp. $13.95. 82-7034. ISBN 0-670-34259-9. C.I.P ▶ **K,EP**

This well-written and beautifully illustrated book chronicles the life of Louis Blériot, one of the great pioneers of aviation. Exposure to the development of Blériot's various aircraft should provide children with a sense of the stages one needs to go through to perfect a product. The soft-color illustrations are finely detailed and capture the feeling of the story. Well-researched, accurate history with a nice foreign flavor.

Rosenblum, Richard. *The Airplane ABC.* (Illus.) NY: Atheneum, 1986. v+32pp. $10.95. 85-28760. ISBN 0-689-31162-1. C.I.P. ▶ **K,EP**

Sticking strictly to the single theme of aircraft history, this alphabet book uses simple but elegant black-and-white illustrations to cover the alphabet from amphibian to zeppelin. Each entry relays a piece of aviation history or point of educational interest. Parents will enjoy reading this book to their older preschool children and discussing the illustrations and topics presented. Because it is a fun book, it might also be useful as a classroom supplement for readers who need extra stimulation.

Rosenblum, Richard. *The Golden Age of Aviation.* (Illus. by the author.) NY: Atheneum, 1984. 60pp. $11.95. 83-15652. ISBN 0-689-31034-X. C.I.P. ▶ **EA**

Rosenblum labels as golden the dozen years between Lindbergh's flight in 1926 and the eve of World War II because "pilots and airplanes would establish new records in distance, altitude, speed, and endurance, and then break their own records with new ones." In a simply told series of accounts but with a vocabulary that will challenge sixth-grade readers, the author describes many of the aircraft and events of the times. More than 60 pen-and-ink sketches that are appealing, if not technically rigorous, augment the text.

Williams, Brian. *Aircraft.* (Illus.; from the Modern Knowledge Library.) NY: Warwick, 1982. 48pp. $7.90. 76-13645. ISBN 0-531-01195-X. Glossary; index; C.I.P. ▶ **EA**

A fine example of how to simplify and condense some fairly complex subjects into language, photographs, and sketches that are readily understandable. Gliders, balloons, airships, warplanes of both world wars, supersonic flight, helicopters and autogyros, navigation, and aircraft recognition are all discussed. The artwork and photographs are excellent, and the book should provide many youngsters with joyous and informative reading.

629.4 Astronautics and astronauts

Barrett, N.S. *Astronauts.* (Illus.; from the Picture Library Series.) NY: Watts, 1985. 32pp. ea. $9.40 ea. 85-50156. ISBN 0-531-10002-2. Glossary; index; C.I.P. ▶ **EP,EI**

The Moon. 85-50157. ISBN 0-531-10003-0.

Spacecraft. 85-50160. ISBN 0-531-10006-5.

These books provide an attractive, visual way to introduce primary grade children to the world of space flight. Color photographs and drawings and large-print text provide accurate information. A surprisingly large number of ideas are at least mentioned in passing. In *Spacecraft,* there are lots of pictures of different craft and a detailed color diagram of the space shuttle. *Astronauts* shows pictures of U.S. and Soviet astronauts, briefly describes their training, and shows some examples of the work they do in space. *The Moon* is devoted entirely to the story of manned exploration of the moon. It provides a good, detailed diagram of the Apollo lunar module and its operation, a nice series of pictures of the lunar lander and of the astronauts on the moon's surface, and some closeups of the moon's surface.

Benford, Timothy B., and Brian Wilkes. *The Space Program Quiz & Fact Book.* (Illus.) NY: Harper & Row, 1985. xii + 257pp. $13.95; $8.95 (paper). 84-48816. ISBN 0-06-015454-3; 0-06-096005-1 (paper). Glossary; index; C.I.P. ▶ **EA,JH**

Questions and facts about American and Soviet space and related activities and history are organized into chapter titled "Manned Space Flights," "Nicknames, Code Names," "Messages and Quotes," "Dreamers and Pioneers," and "Unmanned Space Probes." Nearly 75 pages of appendices are crammed with information. There are brief biographies of the 127 persons selected as astronaut candidates between 1959 and 1980, tables of the flight data of missions, and diagrams and specifications of the flight vehicles. This book has educational value, is useful for reference, and is simply entertaining to read.

Berenstain, Jan, and Stan Berenstain. *The Berenstain Bears on the Moon.* (Illus.; a Bright & Early Bk.) NY: Random House, 1985. 45pp. $4.95. 84-20428. ISBN 0-394-87180-4. ▶ **K,EP**

The story tells of two bears and a puppy that travel to the moon, and it is nicely illustrated and reasonably scientifically sound. It deals with weightlessness and shows the use of pressurized suits on the moon, but the lunar landscape is unfortunately not accurately illustrated. The book also misrepresents a meteor shower as a compact bunching of material. However, as a read-aloud book for youngsters, this book is a delight. Its scientific shortcomings are not serious for the intended audience.

Berger, Melvin. *Space Shots, Shuttles, and Satellites.* (Illus.) NY: Putnam's, 1983. 80pp. $7.99. 83-19279. ISBN 0-399-61210-6. Glossary; index; C.I.P. ▶ **JH**

The book opens with "Becoming an Astronaut," which briefly describes requirements and training for the job. Three short chapters present a history of space flight. The section on the space shuttle is particularly well done; it provides a countdown, from the first inception of the shuttle idea at $T-12$ years to the end of the first flight of *Columbia* at about $T+54$ hours. The final section introduces various civilian and military uses of satellites, covers space shuttle flights up to June 1983, and mentions concerns such as the possible future overcrowding of satellites in geosynchronous orbits.

Berger, Melvin. *Space Talk.* (Illus.) NY: Messner, 1985. 96pp. $9.29. 84-22737. ISBN 0-671-54290-7. C.I.P. ▶ **EA,JH**

This excellent book clearly, accurately, and concisely defines, in alphabetical order, some 250 words primarily used in conjunction with space projects. It does not explain *why* things work, but its abundant lucid, concise definitions and large black-and-white photographs could be the beginning of many science projects. A good, general reference space-talk dictionary that is impressively complete.

Billings, Charlene W. *Space Station: Bold New Step Beyond Earth.* (Illus.; a Skylight Bk.) NY: Dodd, Mead, 1986. 64pp. $9.95. 85-20700. ISBN 0-396-08730-2. Index; C.I.P. ▶ **EI**

Here is a narrative of the challenge, design, purpose, and the experience of building and using a space station. The book introduces the "power tower" as NASA's design choice for the space station and gives the overall design and details of the living quarters. Illustrations show the construction equipment and techniques. Strategies and equipment to meet the problems of eating, keeping clean, loneliness, and communication are all discussed, as are precise details of the space suit. An explanation of what the space station will do and the future of space is attempted.

Branley, Franklyn M. *From Sputnik to Space Shuttles: Into the New Space Age.* (Illus.; a Voyage into Space Bk.) NY: Crowell, 1986. viii + 53pp. $11.95. 85-43186. ISBN 0-690-04531-X. Index; C.I.P. ▶ **EI**

This book explains that all orbiting objects are satellites, even the space shuttle. Most types of satellites—communications, military, earth viewing, space science, and even future ones—are covered. The accompanying black-and-white and color photographs are sharply reproduced and relate well to the text. This book was written for the general awareness and understanding of students who are familiar with space terminology. It would be good for book reports and outside class reading because it has many good illustrative examples and coverage of basic satellite concepts.

Cannon, Robert L., and Michael A. Banks. *The Rocket Book: A Guide to Building and Launching Model Rockets for the Space Age.* (Illus.; from the Science Education Series.) Englewood Cliffs, NJ: Prentice-Hall, 1985. xii + 224pp. $12.95 (paper). 85-587. ISBN 0-13-782244-8. Glossary; index; C.I.P. ▶ **EA,JH**

In 11 well-illustrated and attractive chapters, the authors move from a general introduction to advanced techniques and a variety of activities related to rocketry. A brief history adds interest. Along with detailed instructions for actually building a variety of rockets, there is an accompanying science education content. Lists of manufacturers and distributors of rocket kits and components, organizations devoted to rocketry, and periodicals are included. The authors have made every effort to make their book as complete as possible and yet keep the presentation suitable for children.

Dwiggins, Don. *Flying the Space Shuttles.* (Illus.) NY: Dodd, Mead, 1985. 64pp. $11.95. 84-23898. ISBN 0-396-08510-5. Glossary; index; C.I.P. ▶ **EA**

Assisted by 34 excellent color photographs, this book summarizes the purposes and experiences of contemporary manned space flight and answers many of the questions that young people ask about the daily routines of working, eating, sleeping, cleaning up, and so on in space. While the author has missed some easy pedagogical opportunities to teach the basics of mass, force, acceleration, momentum, pressure, and insulation, young readers may be stimulated to ask questions such as "Why does the fuel tank break up?" The few technical errors are forgivable.

Furniss, Tim. *Modern Technology: Space.* (Illus.) NY: Watts, 1985. 32pp. $10.40. 85-51185. ISBN 0-531-10087-1. Glossary; index. ▶ **EI,EA**

Topics such as space probes, the space shuttle, living in space, space telescopes, and military weapons in space permit the reader to explore new vistas of knowledge not often presented at this reading level. The section on space telescopes clearly and succinctly describes the use of the Hubble space telescope without overpowering the reader with a deluge of technological terms. The relief drawings of the first American spacelab and the Soviet Union's Salyut deserve special mention for their completeness and clarity.

Hartmann, William K., Ron Miller, and Pamela Lee. *Out of the Cradle: Exploring the Frontiers Beyond Earth.* (Illus.) NY: Workman, 1984. 190pp. $19.95; $11.95 (paper). 84-40316. ISBN 0-89480-813-3; 0-89480-770-6 (paper). Index; C.I.P. ▶ **EA,JH**

This book takes readers on an imaginary trip through our planetary system. The many colorful drawings and photographs are stunning, and every effort has been made to accurately portray, with camera-like clarity, the construction of a space city, space exploration by robots, a return to the moon, and a trip to asteroids and comets, Mars and its satellites, and the outer reaches of our solar system. Along the way, there are interesting discussions of the chemistry and geology of the planets, their moons, and the asteroids.

Haskins, Jim, and Kathleen Benson. *Space Challenger: The Story of Guion Bluford.* (Illus.) Minneapolis: Carolrhoda, 1984. 64pp. $8.95. 84-4251. ISBN 0-87614-259-5. Glossary; index; C.I.P. ▶ **EI,EA**

Space Challenger is an inspirational book that includes a brief biographical sketch of the first black astronaut and accounts of his adventures aboard the space shuttle *Challenger*. (The 21 black-and-white photographs and drawings depict his training and actual flight experiences.) This book will spark the imagination of most of its young readers and inspire them, regardless of sex, race, or socioeconomic class, to follow Bluford's lead—to define and work toward a personal goal in their lives and to ignore the unsolicited advice of others to lower one's sights.

Herda, D.J. *Research Satellites.* (Illus.; a First Bk.) NY: Watts, 1987. 71pp. $9.90. 86-24225. ISBN 0-531-10311-0. Glossary; index; C.I.P. ▶ **EA,JH**

The author provides a brief history of the theory behind launching an artificial satellite and early rockets and the first earth and interplanetary probes. Most of the remaining pages are devoted to only two classes of satellites: those for earth observation (Landsat, Seasat, and weather satellites) and those for communication. These sections are well written, providing the history and uses of each type of satellite listed. They most usefully demonstrate the extensive commercial utility of earth-orbiting satellites.

Hitchcock, Barbara. *Sightseeing: A Space Panorama.* (Illus.; a Borzoi Bk.) NY: Knopf, 1985. x + 107pp. $24.95. 85-40347. ISBN 0-394-54243-6. C.I.P. ▶ **EA,JH**

As a science book, *Sightseeing* is not very informative, but as a picture book, it is delightful. The 84 images taken by astronauts in the Gemini, Apollo, Skylab, and shuttle programs are first-rate. By far the most dramatic images are those of America's first space walker, the late Edward White II. The book is a faithful documentary of the wonders our astronauts have been privileged to see in their explorations of the earth-moon system.

Lampton, Christopher. *Space Science.* (Drawings by Anne Canevari Green; a Reference First Bk.) NY: Watts, 1983. 93pp. $8.90. 82-16108. ISBN 0-531-04539-0. C.I.P. ▶ **EA,JH**

This volume covers the field adequately with no major omissions of material, the definitions are clearly and simply written but with enough depth to be of value, and the book is accurate. Astronomical and physics terms, major figures in the history of astronomy and rocketry, space vehicles, and rocket travel are covered; however, some references to rocket travel date the book.

Maurer, Richard. *The NOVA Space Explorer's Guide: Where to Go and What to See.* (Illus.; a NOVA Kids' Bk.) NY: Clarkson N. Potter/WGBH Boston, 1985. x + 118pp. $15.95. 84-24905. ISBN 0-517-55752-5. Index; C.I.P. ▶ **EA**

Facts and figures give children an "up close and personal" tour of our solar system and beyond. The book blends human space flight and astronomy, putting the reader through the rigors of life aboard a space shuttle, walking in space, and viewing the earth from orbit. Sections that include rocketry and astronautics also note historic milestones. Facts about our nearby celestial neighbors are supplemented with data and images relayed by U.S. and Soviet space probes. The use of self-contained story boxes, copious color photographs, excellent graphs, and fresh layout schemes make this book a treasure.

O'Connor, Karen. *Sally Ride and the New Astronauts: Scientists in Space.* (Illus.) NY: Watts, 1983. 88pp. $8.90. 82-21844. ISBN 0-531-04602-8. Index; C.I.P. ▶ **EA,JH**

Ride and the other female astronauts are featured in early chapters, but the importance of teamwork among all astronauts is stressed as well. Most of the book describes the selection, training, and outfitting of astronauts and the special problems of weightlessness during flight. Illustrations are black-and-white photographs supplied by NASA; they should interest any reader.

Shulke, Flip, Debra Shulke, Penelope McPhee, and Raymond McPhee. *Your Future in Space: The U.S. Space Camp Training Program.* (Illus.) NY: Crown, 1986. 144pp. $14.95 (paper). 86-9003. ISBN 0-517-56418-1. Glossary; C.I.P. ▶ **EA,JH**

For junior and senior high school students looking to careers in space science, there is hardly a better primer than this stylish and highly readable book. The U.S. Space Camp in Huntsville, Alabama, is a dream come true for would-be astronauts. The authors' beautiful photographs show youngsters as they go about their simulated space tasks. The most fascinating chapter is on living in space, which examines the effects of zero gravity on the human body. To help explain the acronym-filled language used at the camp, the authors have thoughtfully added a glossary; they have also provided an appendix of space career centers.

Smolders, Peter, and trans. by Sidney Woods. *Living in Space: A Manual for Space Travelers.* (Illus.) Summit, PA: Tab, 1986. 186pp. $14.60 (paper). 86-5863. ISBN 0-8306-8480-8 (paper). Glossary; C.I.P. ▶ **EA,JH**

Smolders provides an accurate and comprehensive view of space life past and present and projects the forseeable future in a style that informs and, occasionally, even amuses. Space enthusiasts from upper grade school through retirement age should enjoy it. The many illustrations are beautiful and informative. Occasionally, however, the author fails to make clear what is accomplished fact, what is simple projection, and what is far speculation, and the British-English translation from the original Dutch introduces some unfamiliarities.

White, Jack R. *Satellites of Today and Tomorrow.* (Illus.) NY: Dodd, Mead, 1985. 120pp. $10.95. 85-6985. ISBN 0-396-08514-8. Index; C.I.P. ▶ **EA,JH**

White is remarkably successful here in covering the gamut of space activities; his success stems from his broad knowledge of the relevant science, engineering, and space technology applications and his facility for producing a graceful and readable text. Six main applications of satellites are discussed: communication, weather observation, navigation, astronomy, earth sciences, and surveillance (spying). Explanations of orbital physics, history of space activities, and satellite design are also included. A good introduction to many aspects of space activities.

629.892 Robots

Maccarone, Grace, Nancy Krulick, and Jolie Epstein. *Real Robots.* (Illus.) NY: Scholastic, 1985. 31pp. $2.50 (paper). ISBN 0-590-33670-3 (paper). ▶ **EP,EI**

Real Robots explains what robots are, what they're used for, and how they work. Generously illustrated with good color photographs—at least one on almost every page—so that the reader literally sees what is being described.

McKie, Robin. *Robots.* (Illus.; from the Modern Technology Series.) NY: Watts, 1986. 32pp. $10.90. 85-51644. ISBN 0-531-101363. Glossary; index. ▶ **EI,EA**

This book has excellent color photographs and simple diagrams that would serve well as supplementary classroom material. Although the text is brief, the author does a good job of explaining how robots work. He shows their strengths and limitations and how use of robots is shifting human jobs from the routine work of unskilled and skilled areas to more interesting technician-type jobs.

Radlauer, Ruth, and Carolynn Young. *Voyagers 1 & 2: Robots in Space.* (Illus.; from the Radlauer Geo Bks. Series.) Chicago: Childrens Press, 1987. 48pp. $11.95. 86-29922. ISBN 0-516-07840-2. Glossary; index; C.I.P. ▶ **EA,JH**

This book provides one-page treatments of several topics, each accompanied by a photograph or illustration on the facing page. A lot of information is given in the brief text, but readers will need to seek more detail from other sources. The book offers 15 "chapters" on robots in space, a description of how planetary pictures are made, and a brief look at the Voyager encounter with Uranus. Such staccato presentations introduce some points well but muddy others.

Rickard, Graham. *Robots.* (Illus.) NY: Bookwright, 1986. 32pp. $9.40. 85-73662. ISBN 0-531-18061-1. Glossary; index. ▶ **EI,EA**

The various types and uses of robots are competently described in this book. It points out that humans have long sought to build a mechanical "human being," and in discussing the modern robot, the author stresses that a robot is only as good as the program fed into it. Good illustrations accompany the text.

Storrs, Graham. *The Robot Age.* (Illus.; from Tomorrow's World Series.) NY: Bookwright Press, 1985. 48pp. $10.90. 85-70451. ISBN 0-531-18020-4. Glossary; index. ▶ **EA,JH**

In this interesting history of robots, Storrs compares the automata devised 2000 years ago with the controllable machines first introduced in 1801 and subsequent improvements. Especially well done is Storrs' specific presentation of the many factors that have contributed to the improvement of robotics over the past 40 years. All outlined in some detail are types of robots, how robots obtain feedback from their environment, and their varied uses. The sociological consequences of widespread use of robots are also discussed.

Agriculture

See also 580 Botanical sciences.

Arnow, Jan. *Hay from Seed to Feed.* (Illus.) NY: Knopf, 1986. 40pp. $11.99. 86-2843. ISBN 0-394-96508-6. C.I.P. ▶ **EA**

This book uses excellent black-and-white photographs to outline the essential steps in haymaking: land preparation, seeding, harvesting, baling, and storing the hay. Incidences of insects and diseases are also included. The author's acquaintance with the farm owners adds an appealing personal touch.

Bellville, Cheryl Walsh. *Farming Today Yesterday's Way.* (Illus.) Minneapolis: Carolrhoda, 1984. 40pp. $8.95. 84-3215. ISBN 0-87614-220-X. Glossary; C.I.P. ▶ **EP,EI**

Describes the annual cycle of life on a small dairy farm in Wisconsin, where the power to run farm equipment is draft horses rather than modern farm tractors. It is the story of a compromise, where old methods—draft horse power—are combined with modern ones—milking machines and bulk tanks. As such, this book does not reflect typical modern farming methods in the United States and Canada. Suitable for juvenile readers who have little or no agricultural background; excellent black-and-white and color photographs.

Fyson, Nance Lui. *Feeding the World.* (Illus.; from the Today's World Series.) London, England: Batsford (dist. by David & Charles), 1984. 72pp. $14.95. ISBN 0-7134-4264-6. Index. ▶ **EA,JH**

A truly international survey of the food people grow, eat, and export. The discussion of factors that contribute to hunger is well balanced, and the lack of simple solutions is made clear. This book also presents nutritional patterns in different parts of the world, environmental and cultural patterns that affect food patterns, the effects of protectionist policies on food prices, problems of food production, storage, and transport, the pros and cons of pesticide use, and relative rates of population and food growth. Could serve as a social studies textbook, collateral reading, or simply fascinating pleasure reading.

Johnson, Sylvia A. *Potatoes.* (Illus.; photographs by Masaharu Suzuki; a Lerner

Natural Science Bk.) Minneapolis: Lerner, 1984. 48pp. $8.95. 84-5760. ISBN 0-8225-1459-1. Glossary; index; C.I.P. ▶ **EA,JH**

The many excellent and colorful photographs do much to enhance the accurate, detailed information on the potato plant's growth and development. Also included are the history and current uses of the potato. An effective effort has been made to explain the necessary botanical terms as they naturally occur in the text. Some experimentation and investigation by the reader are encouraged in the section on starch storage.

Mitchell, Barbara. *A Pocketful of Goobers: A Story About George Washington Carver.* (Illus. by Peter E. Hanson; a Carolrhoda Creative Minds Bk.) Minneapolis: Carolrhoda, 1986. 64pp. $8.95. 86-2690. ISBN 0-87614-292-7. C.I.P. ▶ **EI,EA**

This biography of agricultural scientist George Washington Carver tells his remarkable story accurately, sympathetically, and felicitously. Young readers will learn how, because of his genius, Carver rose to a place of honor in the agricultural community and, perhaps more important to him, among the black tenant farmers in Alabama and later among many of his fellow white citizens. The line drawings add appeal.

Patent, Dorothy Hinshaw. *Wheat: The Golden Harvest.* (Illus.; photographs by William Muñoz.) NY: Dodd, Mead, 1987. 62pp. $12.95. 85-32801. ISBN 0-396-08781-7. Glossary; index; C.I.P. ▶ **K,EP,EI**

This attractive reference on the growing, harvesting, and processing of wheat combines vivid information on food supply, nutrition, machine technology, and geography. A good pictorial description of an important food source and exactly where it comes from.

Pike, Norman. *The Peach Tree.* (Illus. by Robin and Patricia DeWitt.) Owings Mills, MD: Stemmer House, 1983. 32pp. $10.95. 83-4393. ISBN 0-88045-014-2. ▶ **K,EP**

This delightful little book tells a simple tale of planting and nurturing a peach tree. When the tree is attacked by aphids, the family that planted it introduces natural pest control in the form of ladybugs. The tree survives, thrives, and bears fruit. Beautifully illustrated.

Pohl, Kathleen (Adaptor). *Potatoes.* (Illus.; from Nature Close-ups Series.) Milwaukee: Raintree, 1987. 32pp. $15.33. 86-26239. ISBN 0-8172-2723-7. Glossary; C.I.P. ▶ **EI,EA**

Excellent close-up photographs supported by concise prose demonstrate the life cycle of potatoes. The print is oversize and the paper rugged and leather-like; clearly, the production of the book was conducted with young readers and prolonged school and library use in mind. The book tells how the first potatoes were planted by the Incas and that the practice was then brought to Europe by the Spanish. Close-up photographs lead the reader from the planting of seed potatoes to the development of roots and stems, leaves, flowers, and finally, a new crop of tubers.

Rahn, Joan Elma. *More Plants That Changed History.* (Illus. by the author.) NY: Atheneum, 1985. 125pp. $10.95. 84-21563. ISBN 0-689-31099-4. Index; C.I.P. ▶ **EA,JH**

This interesting and informative book consists of three stories: section one deals with plants for writing materials—papyrus and paper; section two concerns the trees that weep—the story of rubber; and section three discusses tea, tobacco, opium, and the China trade. Each section traces the use of the plants and introduces some of the people, places, and times involved. Simple line drawings are adequate and useful in developing each story. The stress placed on scientific names and definition of terms is helpful.

Rice, Karen. *Does Candy Grow on Trees?* (Illus. by Sharon Adler Cohen.) NY: Walker, 1984. 32pp. $9.95. 83-40407. ISBN 0-8027-6535-1. Index; C.I.P. ▶ **EA,JH**

Sugar, corn syrup, chocolate, vanilla, licorice, chicle, soybeans, peppermint, gum arabic, and cinnamon are all discussed in this book. In the process of describing how each ingredient is obtained from a plant, science concepts are explained, including how lecithin functions as an emulsifier, photosynthesis, and the relationship between a plant and the specific kind of organism that pollinates it. Often encourages the reader to examine a candy wrapper to find out which of the ingredients described in the book are in the candy. Large, clear illustrations and readable text.

635 Horticulture

Ehlert, Lois. *Growing Vegetable Soup.* (Illus. by the author.) NY: Harcourt Brace Jovanovich, 1987. 30pp. $10.95. 86-22812. ISBN 0-15-232575-1. ▶ **K**

Bright, colorful graphics and simple text are used to describe planting vegetables for soup. Readers learn that it is necessary to plant bean seeds for beans and tomato plants for tomatoes, not a trivial concept for young children. The conditions for growth are also listed.

Oechsli, Helen, and Kelly Oechsli. *In My Garden: A Child's Gardening Book.* (Illus.) NY: Macmillan, 1985. 32pp. $12.95. 84-21285. ISBN 0-02-768510-1. C.I.P. ▶ **EP,EI**

This book describes simple gardening techniques to children in an enjoyable and instructional way. How to plant and the different varieties of hardy vegetables to plant are described, along with different harvesting techniques. The text is clear and concise, and the book is an excellent resource for teachers of primary and early intermediate grades.

Sobol, Harriet L. *A Book of Vegetables.* (Illus.; photographs by Patricia A. Agre.) NY: Dodd, Mead, 1984. 48pp. $10.95. 84-5991. ISBN 0-396-08450-8. C.I.P. ▶ **K,EP,EI**

This book is a handsome treatment of the family Solanaceae—potatoes, tomatoes, peppers, and eggplant—and other vegetables. The author missed the opportunity to show plant phyletic relationships by presenting near relatives together in a comparative manner; however, this book has large, beautiful photographs, and the text is easy to read and factually correct.

636 Care of domesticated animals
See also 590.74 Zoos; 591.1–.4 Animal physiology, anatomy, and development; 599.725 Horses and zebras.

Ancona, George. *Sheep Dog.* (Illus.; photographs by the author.) NY: Lothrop, Lee & Shepard, 1985. 64pp. $11.75. 84-20100. ISBN 0-688-04118-3. C.I.P. ▶ **EA,JH**

A book with an unexpected and admirable ecological message. The author explains that sheep dogs are either herding dogs or guard dogs. Guard dogs, used for thousands of years in Europe, will guard sheep against predators, eliminating the need for poison and traps. The Livestock Dog Project at Hampshire College is promoting the study and introduction of these European guard dogs into the United States. Black-and-white photographs of the various breeds on the job, from puppies to adults, are abundant, and the text is sure to please the adolescent dog lover.

Bare, Colleen Stanley. *Guinea Pigs Don't Read Books.* (Illus.) NY: Dodd, Mead, 1985. 32pp. $10.95. 84-18707. ISBN 0-396-08538-5. C.I.P. ▶ **K,EP**

This book will be received with pleasure by teachers of young children for its quality photographs and simple text. It is especially valuable in a situation where a pet is to be introduced, either in the home or in the classroom. The author's purpose is to indicate that pets are lovable and gentle companions; this simple theme with regard to guinea pigs is particularly effective.

Bellville, Rod, and Cheryl Walsh Bellville. *Large Animal Veterinarians.* (Illus.) Minneapolis: Carolrhoda, 1983. 32pp. $7.95. 82-19750. ISBN 0-87614-211. C.I.P. ▶ **JH**

This book does a good job of presenting the work of a large-animal veterinarian. The photographs are generally informative and of good quality, although some could be clearer. Some readers may find that the parenthetic pronunciation of words detracts from the text, with many of the pronunciations difficult to interpret. Nevertheless, the book is recommended to junior-high students as a reasonable source of accurate information on large-animal practice.

Chase, Edith Newlin, and Barbara Reid. *The New Baby Calf.* (Illus. by Barbara Reid.) NY: Scholastic, 1986 (c.1984). 32pp. $8.95. 86-3931. ISBN 0-590-40457-1. ▶ **K**

The brief story of the first few days of a calf's life makes a charming book for children who are beginning readers. The illustrations shot from bas-relief sculptures in plasticine are charming and lend a most unusual touch. The narrative explains in simple terms the first days of a calf and how it nurses, grows stronger, plays, and gains independence. It contains no technical information, even of a simple nature.

Chiefari, Janet. *Kids Are Baby Goats.* (Illus.) NY: Dodd, Mead, 1984. 60pp. $9.95. 83-25342. ISBN 0-396-08316-1. Index; C.I.P. ▶ **EI,EA,JH**

This is a delightful description of the appearance, life cycle, and utility of dairy goats. Outstanding in its appeal, written in language simple and concise, and with excellent photographs, this book and its "heroine," Amy, will please children of all ages and be useful to them, their teachers, and their families.

Coldrey, Jennifer. *The Chicken on the Farm.* (Illus.; photographs by Oxford Scientific Films; from the Animal Habitats Series.) Milwaukee: Gareth Stevens, 1987. 32pp. $9.95. 86-5716. ISBN 1-55532-092-9. Glossary; C.I.P. ▶ **EI,EA,JH**

The Chicken on the Farm is a good introductory text, organized in the same way and even with some of the same wording as *The World of Chickens* (below). Covered here in an explanatory style are reproduction, anatomy, social behavior, feeding, predators and diseases, and the relationship of chickens to humans, including some history of that relationship. More discussion of bioethical issues would have been appropriate. *The Chicken on the Farm* could have profited from anatomical and embryological diagrams but uses basically the same photographs as the more elementary book.

Coldrey, Jennifer. *The World of Chickens.* (Illus.; photographs by Oxford Scientific Films; from the Where Animals Live Series.) Milwaukee: Gareth Stevens, 1987. 32pp. $9.95. 86-5718. ISBN 1-55532-096-1. Glossary; C.I.P. ▶ **EP,EI,EA**

The World of Chickens is a good introduction to the life of chickens. It shares all of its illustrations with *The Chicken on the Farm* (above). Except for the diagram of a food web, the illustrations are all excellent photographs. The book covers reproduction, feeding, predators, diseases, and the relationship of chickens to humans, including some history of that relationship. Young readers are also introduced to the bioethical issues posed by domestication.

Curran, Eileen. *Hello, Farm Animals.* (Illus.) Mahwah, NJ: Troll, 1985. 32pp. $9.98; $2.50 (paper). 84-8657. ISBN 0-8167-0345-0; 0-8167-0346-9 (paper). ▶ **K,EP**

This beautifully illustrated book gently introduces some very solid science to young readers by inviting them to observe the details of a familiar setting. By means of a limited vocabulary and unusually appealing illustrations, young readers are directed to observe with care and are encouraged to think for themselves. Little adult guidance is needed for the child to succeed in answering the book's open-ended questions. The illustrations, while clear enough to avoid confusing young readers, are visually appealing and intricate enough to satisfy older children. Can uniquely and significantly serve remedial readers.

Curtis, Patricia. *The Animal Shelter.* (Photographs by David Cupp.) NY: Dutton, 1984. xi + 163pp. $13.95. 83-8908. ISBN 0-525-66783-0. Index; C.I.P. ▶ **EA,JH**

Curtis discusses the problems that unwanted pets have to face and dramatizes the problems and decisions facing the people who are involved in the welfare and control of these animals. She does not suggest any real solutions other than to point out the value of educational programs. The volume has a strong educational value for youngsters, especially since it details the health and safety hazards that uncontrolled animals present.

Dunn, Judy. *The Little Puppy.* (Illus; photographs by Phoebe Dunn; a Random House Pictureback.) NY: Random House, 1984. 29pp. $4.99; $1.95 (paper). 84-2031. ISBN 0-394-9659-7; 0-394-86595-2 (paper). C.I.P. ▶ **K**

This charming story about a child selecting a puppy will help young children get an idea of what it is like to own a puppy. They will be fascinated by the large photographs and the story of this pup and his young owner. Set in large type, the text is easy to read, informative, and useful for developing listening and perception skills in preschool and kindergarten children.

Feder, Jan. *The Life of a Cat.* (Illus. by Tilman Michalski; from the Animal Lives Series.) Chicago: Childrens Press, 1982. 32pp. $6.95 ea. 82-12795. ISBN 0-516-08931-5. Index; C.I.P. ▶ **EI,EA**

The Life of a Dog. 82-9752. ISBN 0-516-08932-3.

These two beautiful, colorful books portray the highlights in the lives of a farm cat and a farmyard dog, respectively. The first part of each book presents a brief, simply written narrative of their roles in life. Large, striking, brightly colored illustrations that dominate each page support the text exceedingly well. The second part of each book offers basic factual information. The brief history of each animal, its physical characteristics, body language, behavior, and illustrations of several kinds of cats and dogs, as well as two pages of interesting facts, will intrigue young readers. The books are translations of *Die Katze* and *Der Hund.*

Foster, Sally. *A Pup Grows Up.* (Illus. by the author.) NY: Dodd, Mead, 1984. 60pp. $10.95. 83-25474. ISBN 0-396-08314-5. C.I.P. ▶ **EP,EI**

A Pup Grows Up consists of delightful pictures and brief descriptions of 15 breeds of dogs ranging in size from toy poodles to Great Danes. Development, temperament, innate behavior, training, and utility of each breed are concisely stated. The photographs are excellent, the sentences short, and the words familiar.

Gibbons, Gail. *The Milk Makers.* (Illus.) NY: Macmillan, 1985. 32pp. $12.95. 84-20081. ISBN 0-02-736640-5. ▶ **K,EP,EI**

Gibbons takes the reader step by step from cow to table in this brief text with large, attractive, four-colored drawings. Starting with dairy cows grazing, nothing is overlooked in the procedure, from the role of the calf, to the winter feed and shelter, the function of four stomachs, milking, milk handling, and the operation of a dairy. The text can be handled by most third graders, who will appreciate the phonetic pronunciation aids for the scientific names of the stomachs. Younger children studying foods, health, or community helpers can have the understandable text read to them at school or at home.

Lavine, Sigmund A., and Brigid Casey. *Wonders of Draft Horses.* (Illus.) NY: Dodd, Mead, 1983. 79pp. $9.95. 82-46002. ISBN 0-396-08138-X. Index; C.I.P. ▶ **EA,JH**

This well-organized, accurate, and interesting look at domestic draft horses examines the six major breeds, their current rise in popularity, and harnesses and other specialized equipment. It provides enough data for a clear understanding or a short school report. The book makes effective use of numerous drawings and black-and-white photographs. A good library reference acquisition.

Lavine, Sigmund A., and Vincent Scuro. *Wonders of Mules.* (Illus.) NY: Dodd, Mead, 1982. 64pp. $7.95. 82-4963. ISBN 0-396-08051-0. Index; C.I.P. ▶ **EA,JH**

This elementary treatise on mules presents an introduction to and an overview of this unique animal hybrid, some old lore and mulish "quirks," aspects of breeding for mule production, tips on keeping and care, and the role of mules in past wars and in the development of this country. The book is amply illustrated with 57 pictures distributed over 55 pages of text. An interesting addition to the scant literature on mules.

McPherson, Mark. *Caring for Your Cat.* (Illus.; photographs by Marianne Bernstein.) Mahwah, NJ: Troll, 1985. 48pp. $9.89; $2.50 (paper). 84-223. ISBN 0-8167-0115-6; 0-8167-0116-4 (paper). Index; C.I.P. ▶ **EI,EA**

Caring for Your Dog. 84-222. ISBN 0-8167-0113-X; ISBN 0-8167-0114-8 (paper).

Caring for Your Fish. 84-8563. ISBN 0-8167-0109-1; ISBN 0-8167-0110-5 (paper).

Choosing Your Own Pet. 84-226. ISBN 0-8167-0111-3; ISBN 0-8167-0112-1 (paper).

While the author seems to have mixed feelings about the natural independence of cats, *Caring for Your Cat* is on the whole a good tool to teach children how to care for their new pet. Individual breeds are not discussed in any depth; the emphasis is on the basic adjustment between the pet and its owner. Topics include grooming, illness, and pregnancy. The text is easy to read and aims to inform the animal-loving child (and perhaps the wary parent). The photographs are pleasant and plentiful. The author's obvious fondness for dogs and his desire that children should not only treat their pets well but try to understand them are evident in *Caring for Your Dog.* McPherson covers the gamut of dog care for children. His prose is fact-filled yet easy to read, and color photographs are plentiful, generally well chosen, and oriented to young readers. Although different breeds (and mixtures) are pictured, they are not discussed individually. *Caring for Your Fish* reminds readers how important and how fragile the artificial world of the aquarium is. Responsible children will be able to follow the rules for the necessary upkeep, and they will also learn a bit about the workings of tanks and hoses and about the basic chemistry of acidity and alkalinity. Goldfish, guppies, and freshwater and saltwater tropicals are covered. Through the many colorful photographs, young readers will learn how to enjoy the underwater world by noting individual traits of particular species. *Choosing Your Pet* covers all types of pets: rodents, rabbits, guinea pigs, cats, birds, fish, dogs, turtles, salamanders, snakes, and even "exotics." Dogs command the most coverage, while the other animals each receive brief treatment. The author neatly summarizes the pros and cons and basic concerns of owning each animal. Children will enjoy the many color photographs, and parents will appreciate the basic caveats and helpful hints on acclimating the pet to its new home.

Patent, Dorothy Hinshaw. *Baby Horses.* (Illus.; photographs by William Muñoz.) NY: Dodd, Mead, 1985. 64pp. $10.95. 85-1573. ISBN 0-396-08629-2. C.I.P. ▶ **K**

This attractive book describes, mainly through photographs, the activities of a foal from its birth in spring to its development of a winter coat in the fall. The color photographs are well chosen, and each is accompanied by a concise caption, the only text in the book.

Patent, Dorothy Hinshaw. *Draft Horses.* (Illus.; photographs by William Muñoz.) NY: Holiday House, 1986. viii + 86pp. $12.95. 85-21998. ISBN 0-8234-0597-4. Glossary; index; C.I.P. ▶ **EA,JH**

For city and country folk alike, this little primer is a revelation. Although it is printed in large type suitable for fourth to sixth graders the text is pitched toward seventh to ninth graders, parents and horse lovers of all ages will learn that there is much more to the world of horses than racing or riding. It informs the reader of the many breeds of draft horses and of their origins, derivations, and specific traits. Handsomely printed and bound; liberally illustrated with pleasing black-and-white photographs.

Patent, Dorothy Hinshaw. *Maggie: A Sheep Dog.* (Illus.; photographs by William Muñoz.) NY: Dodd, Mead, 1986. 48pp. $9.95. 85-20562. ISBN 0-396-08617-9. C.I.P. ▶ **K,EP**

In this clearly written story about a Hungarian Kuvasz, Maggie does not just herd sheep. She is raised with them, forms attachments to them, and protects them against predators. Numerous black-and-white photographs accompany the easy-to-read text. The book's strengths are in the quality of the photographs and the clarity and simplicity of the story. Its weaknesses are in its excessively negative portrayal of the coyote as vicious predator.

Roy, Ron. *What Has Ten Legs and Eats Corn Flakes? A Pet Book.* (Illus. by Lynne Cherry; a Clarion Bk.) NY: Ticknor & Fields, 1982. 48pp. $10.50. 82-1220. ISBN 0-89919-119-3. Index; C.I.P. ▶ **K,EP**

Three unusual pets—land hermit crabs, gerbils, and chameleons—are discussed in terms of their habits and care. The book is oriented to the situations and interactions a young child might have with such a pet. Drawings are detailed, accurate, and captivating. However, Roy's suggestions for pet care may not be the most efficient, and prices quoted for animals, housing, or feed are outdated.

Ziefert, Harriet. *Pet Day.* (Illus. by Richard Brown; from the Mr. Rose Series.) Boston: Little, Brown, 1987. 64pp. $7.95. 86-27421. ISBN 0-316-98766-2. ▶ **EP,EI**

In *Pet Day*, a class builds a terrarium for six different desert animals and learns about the birth of baby gerbils. Almost every sentence teaches a scientific fact, and the story is used as a vehicle for concepts such as sharing and honesty. The vocabulary is extensive. *Pet Day* has merit as a science book, but its utility as an educational tool goes beyond that.

638 Insect culture

See also 595.7 Insects.

Fischer-Nagel, Heiderose, and Andreas Fischer-Nagel. *Life of the Honeybee.* (Illus.; a Nature Watch Bk.) Minneapolis: Carolrhoda, 1986. 48pp. $12.95. 85-13960. ISBN 0-87614-241-2. Glossary; C.I.P. ▶ **EP,EI**

This informative and clearly written text is packed with facts about the honeybee. The vivid color photographs will hold the attention of young students who are being read to. Taxonomy, morphology, ecology, behavior, competition, and agriculture are covered thoroughly in a lucid writing style even when the subject is difficult. Entertaining and informative without sacrificing accuracy, this book represents the best of scientific literature available to young people.

Johnson, Sylvia A. *Silkworms.* (Photographs by Isao Kishida; a Lerner Natural Science Bk.) Minneapolis: Lerner, 1982. 48pp. $8.95. 82-250. ISBN 0-8225-1478-8. Glossary; index; C.I.P. ▶ **EI,EA,JH**

Packed with information on silkworm ethology, morphology, feeding habits, rearing, and silk production without being tedious, condescending, or trite. Color illustrations abound, and unfamiliar words are defined. The depth and breadth of coverage make this book interesting to a wide range of audiences and allow discussion on many levels so that repeated exposures continue to be rewarding. Teachers will find *Silkworms* a good science book to read to their classes in the lower grades or for assignment reading for fifth graders or older. A fine book that informs the novice without alienating the professional.

Tarrant, Graham. *Honeybees.* (Illus. by Tony King; a Natural Pop-Ups Bk.) NY: Putnam's, 1984. 9pp. $6.95. 83-8624. ISBN 0-399-21006-7. ▶ **K,EP**

A well-rounded, readable look at life inside a beehive. Like many pop-up books, this one is fragile and will have a short life. One feature that could have been improved is the movable format itself; there is little action in many of the pull tabs. The illustrations are bright, appealing, and appropriate. A nice introduction to natural history.

Home Economics
and
Family Living

641 Nutrition

See also 611–612 Human anatomy and physiology.

Berenstain, Jan, and Stan Berenstain. *The Berenstain Bears and Too Much Junk Food.* (Illus.; a First Time Bk.) NY: Random House, 1985. 32pp. $4.99. 84-40393. ISBN 0-394 87217-7. ▶ **EP,EI**

This fun book reminds us of a few bad habits that promote junk food, such as snacking at the movies or while watching television. A visit to Dr. Grizzly (a female) turns into an educational slide show on the anatomy and physiology of the nervous system, muscles, bones, and digestive tract, as well as an explanation of which foods help build and strengthen different parts of the body. Dr. Grizzly mentions the benefits of exercise as the Bear family leaves her office, and they decide to jog home. Mom has healthy snacks ready now for munching: nuts, raisins, frozen yogurt, and carrot sticks. A most enjoyable introduction to good nutrition and exercise for parents and children to read together.

Gaskin, John. *Eating.* (Illus.) NY: Watts, 1984. 32pp. 84-50021. ISBN 0-531-04632-X. Glossary; index. ▶ **EI**

The subject of eating introduces the principles of nutrition, the food groups, and where food is grown. We also learn why we feel hungry and about the process of digestion. The two pages of explanation about why you can feel sick to your stomach and how to take care of yourself when you do are particularly worthwhile. Appealing, multicultural illustrations help to explain the details of the text.

Peavy, Linda, and Ursula Smith. *Food, Nutrition & You.* (Illus.) NY: Scribner's, 1982. ix + 197pp. $12.95. 82-5694. ISBN 0-684-17461-8. Index; C.I.P. ▶ **JH**

This nicely written, modestly comprehensive introductory nutrition text should particularly interest junior-high school students, as well as general readers. In addition to covering the usual, requisite topics, the authors intersperse references to athletes, food merchandisers, and scientists throughout the text. The historical references are particularly well done. The volume is also suited as a reference in lower school or public libraries.

Seixas, Judith S. *Vitamins: What They Are, What They Do.* (Illus. by Tom Huffman.) NY: Greenwillow, 1986. 55pp. $10.25. 85-17761. ISBN 0-688-06065-X. C.I.P. ▶ **K,EP,EI**

An extremely pleasant, readable, and factually correct book on the value of various vitamins to the human body. Although the author describes the role of vitamin pills in a diet, she also stresses that a complete and varied diet is the best source of vitamins. The book's best feature is its presentation of vitamin interactions. Delightful black, white, and green illustrations are interspersed throughout the text. A book that is pleasant for both child and adult to read.

Ward, Brian R. *Diet and Nutrition.* (Illus.; from the Life Guides Series.) NY: Watts, 1987. 48pp. $10.90. 86-50357. ISBN 0-531-10259-9. Glossary; index. ▶ **EA**

This book introduces a variety of topics from the importance of food for its aethestic appeal to the poor health consequences of a diet of too much sugar, salt, fat, processed foods, additives, and artificial coloring. The book also outlines the diseases associated with the lack of certain nutrients in a diet. The section on weight watching briefly discusses feelings about body weight and defines the terms anorexic and bulimic. The illustrations are clear and colorful.

649   Child rearing
See also 306.7–.8 Relations of the sexes; marriage and family.

649.65   Sex education
See also 155.4 Child psychology; 618.4 Childbirth; pregnancy.

Aho, Jennifer Sowle, and John W. Petras. *Learning About Sexual Abuse.* (Illus. by Jennifer Sowle Aho.) Hillside, NJ: Enslow, 1985. viii + 87pp. $11.95. 84-26028. ISBN 0-89490-114-1. Index; C.I.P. ▶ **EA,JH**

This is an exceptionally well-written guide for school-age children, with comprehensive descriptions of what happens between children and adults in various situations involving different levels of sexual abuse. It does a powerful job of increasing awareness in children and adults that sexual abuse is against the law, that all children have rights to privacy, and that getting help begins by communicating with a trusted adult. Highly recommended for intermediate and middle-school staff, parents, counselors, and above all, children.

Girard, Linda Walvoord. *My Body Is Private.* (Illus. by Rodney Pate.) Niles, IL: Whitman, 1984. 26pp. $9.25. 84-17220. ISBN 0-8075-5320-4. C.I.P. ▶ **EP,EI,EA,JH**

This excellent book is told in the words of a young girl, perhaps nine, who learns, with support and encouragement by her parents, about privacy and saying no to touching she doesn't like. The writing is beautiful in its directness and accuracy, and accompanying illustrative drawings highlight the story. A "Note to Parents" provides valuable information about the incidence, nature, and frequency of sexual abuse and what parents can do for their children.

Johnson, Eric W. *People, Love, Sex, and Families: Answers to Questions That Preteens Ask.* (Illus. by David Wool.) NY: Walker, 1985. vi + 122pp. $13.95. 85-15381. ISBN 0-8027-6591-2. Index; C.I.P. ▶ **EA**

This sex education textbook is in the form of answers to questions submitted by students in the fourth through sixth grades. It covers human reproduction, contraception, abortion, homosexuality, sexually transmitted diseases, and masturbation and discusses human relationships in the chapters on love, sex, and families. The book has wide scope—perhaps too wide, for some may find several of the topics offensive, although the treatment is even-handed. Good reading ability is assumed. More and better illustrations in the chapter on reproduction would have enhanced the book. A good resource for those inquisitive not only about their bodies but about all the implications of being sexually active. For students who have not yet developed this curiosity, this book may be overwhelming.

Patterson, Sherri, et al. *No-No the Little Seal: A Story for Very Young Children That Tells About Sexual Abuse.* (Illus.; a Random House Pictureback Bk. from the Children's Book & Cassette Library.) NY: Random House, 1986. 32pp. $4.95. 86-617. ISBN 0-394-88054-4. C.I.P. ▶ **K,EP**

This story, using a picture book and audiocassette format, is about a young seal who is sexually abused by a favorite uncle. "No-No" feels sad and frightened when hugged too tightly and touched in "private places" by the uncle. After trying to run away, "No-No" is eventually persuaded by a friend to tell his/her parents about the abuse. "No-No" is also encouraged to say "No!" the next time he/she is touched in a "private place." This story does not make a clear distinction between appropriate and inappropriate touching. The colorful pictures and the songs should appeal to young children.

Wachter, Oralee. *No More Secrets for Me.* (Illus. by Jane Aaron.) Boston: Little, Brown, 1983. 47pp. $12.95. 83-12077. ISBN 0-316-91490-8. ▶ **K,EP,EI,EA,JH**

This well-written book alerts children to the fact that sometimes an adult may touch them in a way that makes them feel uncomfortable. Four stories describe the uncomfortable feelings of a child after an uncaring adult has touched him or her in a rough or abusive way. Each story has a happy ending—the upset child talks with a trusted adult and feels okay again. Should be in the children's section of public libraries and in the libraries of elementary, junior-high, and high schools everywhere.

Manufacturing Technologies

Anderson, Norman D., and Walter R. Brown. *Fireworks! Pyrotechnics on Display.* (Illus.) NY: Dodd, Mead, 1983. 79pp. $9.95. 82-45995. ISBN 0-396-08142-8. Index; C.I.P. ▶ **EA,JH**

Although the authors are clearly aiming for a young audience, older children and adults may enjoy browsing through *Fireworks!* The history of explosives and fireworks leads into a discussion of modern devices—sparklers, firecrackers, smoke bombs, rockets, snakes, and the big star-burst shells launched from mortars—and an explanation of the dangers of fireworks.

Bates, Robert L. *Stone, Clay, Glass: How Building Materials Are Found and Used.* (Illus.; An Earth Resource Bk.) Hillside, NJ: Enslow, 1987. 64pp. $11.95. 86-19692. ISBN 0-89490-114-3. Glossary; index; C.I.P. ▶ **EA,JH**

Strong on content, plain in style, this book describes the earth-science aspect of building materials. It's about natural materials used in their natural state—stone, clay, mud—as well as bulk materials that are modified to serve humans—glass, cement, and plaster—all treated in terms of their materials of origin. The author gives a microscopic to macroscopic account of each material: its chemical nature, geological and geographical origins, and any processing it undergoes. Fact follows meaty fact in a well-organized procession. Good for people who enjoy knowing what things are made of, how they act, and how they differ from similar things.

Cosner, Shaaron. *Rubber.* (Illus.; from the Inventions That Changed Our Lives Series.) NY: Walker, 1986. v + 56pp. $10.85. 86-5603. ISBN 0-8027-6653-6. Index; C.I.P. ▶ **EA,JH**

The story of rubber is told from early times to the space age and covers the finding and transplanting of gum trees, experiments to make rubber useful, and the myriad ways it has bettered our lives. The research is careful and comprehensive; the well-written narrative flows smoothly and makes the reader eager to learn more. Charles Goodyear, whose vulcanization process transformed rubber into a "miracle material,'" is portrayed colorfully and with great sensitivity.

Ford, Barbara. *Keeping Things Cool: The Story of Refrigeration and Air Conditioning.* (Illus.; from Inventions That Changed Our Lives Series.) NY: Walker, 1986. iv + 60pp. $10.95. 85-26549. ISBN 0-8027-6635-8. Index; C.I.P. ▶ **EA,JH**

Six chapters focus on the historical background of refrigeration, machine-made ice, frozen foods, the scientific air conditioner, refrigeration in the home, and new ways to keep things cool. Good-quality black-and-white photographs and the illustrations used frequently throughout the book greatly enhance one's understanding of the text. The information is accurate and of value to students interested in refrigeration technology, conducting research on the topic, or just generally interested in how an "invention that changed our lives" works.

Gibbons, Gail. *Fill It Up!: All About Service Stations.* (Illus.) NY: Crowell, 1985. 32pp. $9.95. 84-45345. ISBN 0-690-04439-9. ▶ **K,EP**

Fill It Up takes us through a typical 24-hour day at the local service station. We meet all the people who work there, and we learn in detail how a hydraulic lift works, how gasoline is stored and pumped, and how a flat tire is fixed. Brightly colored illustrations are integral to the text. Only one or two lines of text per page make this an excellent book to read along with a preschooler.

Haldane, Suzanne. *The See-through Zoo: How Glass Animals Are Made.* (Illus.; photographs by the author.) NY: Pantheon, 1984. 37pp. $9.95. 83-13122. ISBN 0-394-95497-7. C.I.P. ▶ **EA,JH**

This photographic essay on the art and technique of making glass animals is abundantly illustrated with black-and-white photographs of glassmaking tools, ingredients, and processes. After a brief introduction to the history of glassmaking and a discussion of the production of molten glass, the author takes us through the steps in the creation of a glass elephant. Technical terms are defined in simple, clear prose.

Högner, Franz. *From Blueprint to House.* (Illus.; a Start to Finish Bk.) Minneapolis: Carolrhoda, 1986. 14pp. $6.95. 86-17185. ISBN 0-87614-295-1. C.I.P. ▶ **K,EP**

From Blueprint to House describes planning and excavation for a house, pouring the foundation, raising the walls, installation of the wiring and plumbing, and painting the new structure. All this in eight pages of no more than nine lines of text per page. Opposite each page of text is a colorful and charming illustration depicting new vocabulary and concepts. Although the presentations are meant for young children, they may find the text too brief for the complex and unfamiliar processes presented. However, teachers and parents should find the book useful for introducing the subject to youngsters.

Kerrod, Robin. *Metals.* (Illus.; from the Visual Science Series.) Morristown, NJ: Silver Burdett, 1982. 48pp. $13.00. 82-50388. ISBN 0-382-06661-8. Glossary; index. ▶ **EA,JH**

This excellent introductory reference that covers the gamut of metal technology from mining to machining is loaded with dozens of excellent color photographs and diagrams that make the learning easy and enjoyable. Areas covered include mining, metal chemistry, corrosion, metal testing, smelting, refining, shaping, joining, and machining.

Lynch, Michael. *How Oil Rigs Are Made.* (Illus.; from the How It Is Made

Series.) NY: Facts On File, 1985. 32pp. $7.95. 84-21048. ISBN 0-8160-0041-7. Index; C.I.P. ▶ **EA,JH**

Lynch explains the conditions and processes of oil rig construction. He explains basic geological data and seismic surveys that help us find oil, and how different drilling procedures can be used to procure it, as well as how pipelines transport oil to the refineries. Excellent diagrams, charts, and photographs enhance the technical material and help make this an attractive exposition of the subject.

Mitgutsch, Ali. *From Graphite to Pencil.* (Illus. by the author; a Start to Finish Bk.) Minneapolis: Carolrhoda, 1985. 24pp. $5.95. 84-17469. ISBN 0-87614-231-5. C.I.P. ▶ **K,EP,EI**

The vocabulary in this beautifully illustrated book is on the level of a primary child and is clear enough for most children to understand with a minimum of adult intervention. An added interest factor is that the final product, the pencil, is a familiar item to children. A good book to add to a primary library as a basic introduction to nonfiction reading.

Mitgutsch, Ali. *From Lemon to Lemonade.* (Illus.; a Start to Finish Bk.) Minneapolis: Carolrhoda, 1986. 14pp. $6.95. 86-17201. ISBN 0-87614-298-6. C.I.P. ▶ **K,EP**

From Rubber Tree to Tire. 86-17170. ISBN 0-87614-297-8.

From Lemon to Lemonade describes how a bottled drink is made, from production to the liquid to labeling and distribution. All of this information is presented in eight pages of no more than nine lines of text per page. Opposite each page of text is a colorful and charming illustration depicting new vocabulary and concepts. Young children may find the text too brief for the complex and unfamiliar process presented, but teachers and parents can use the book to introduce the subject to youngsters. *From Rubber Tree to Tire* is a charming little book whose primary value lies in its illustrations. The content with regard to rubber making is light but perhaps sufficient for the intended age group.

Moxon, Julian. *How Jet Engines Are Made.* (Illus.; from the How It Is Made Series.) NY: Facts On File, 1985. 32pp. $7.95. 84-21049. ISBN 0-8160-0037-9. Index; C.I.P. ▶ **JH**

Excellent illustrations of the inside of a jet engine and its method of operation are followed by detailed explanations of the compressor, turbine, fuel control, combustion chamber, exhaust system, and how they are assembled. The description of automation and performance testing allows the reader to see the breadth of this industry. All technical words are carefully explained and illustrated.

Paterson, Alan J. *How Glass Is Made.* (Illus.; from the How It Is Made Series.) NY: Facts On File, 1985. 32pp. $7.95. 84-21047. ISBN 0-8160-0038-7. Index; C.I.P. ▶ **EA,JH**

Paterson explains the technical vocabulary of the trade and provides a variety of examples of glassmaking methods. Techniques devised by Syrian glassblowers of 2,000 years ago and still practiced today for fine, handmade glass are shown, as is the development of machine processes in the past 100 years that have provided us with glass products as diversified as marbles and bottles, chemical glassware, and fiber.

Perrins, Lesley. *How Paper Is Made.* (Illus.; from the How It Is Made Series.) NY: Facts On File, 1985. 32pp. $7.95. 84-1838. ISBN 0-8160-0036-0. Index; C.I.P. ▶ **EA,JH**

Clearly describes the different processes used to make paper and the many uses of paper and board that indicate the extent to which paper has become part of modern life. If you would like to turn your hand to papermaking or use paper to make a Samurai hat, see the "Things to Do" section in Perrin's useful book.

Shapiro, Mary J. *How They Built the Statue of Liberty.* (Illus. by Huck Scarry.) NY: Random House, 1985. 64pp. $9.99. 85-42720. ISBN 0-394-86957-5. C.I.P. ▶ **EA,JH**

The biggest drawback of this heavily illustrated text is the faintness of the pencil-toned sketches. However, the artwork itself is beautiful, and everything else is outstanding. Shapiro extensively researched the subject, and the results show. There were innumerable challenges involved in the building of the statue, and Shapiro describes them in a detailed, accurate, and comprehensive manner. Every library should order a reference copy of this book.

Geography and History

910 General geography and travel

Arnold, Caroline. *Land Masses: Fun, Facts, and Activities.* (Illus. by Lynn Sweat; and Easy-Read Geography Activity Bk.) NY: Watts, 1985. 32pp. $9.40. 74-19615. ISBN 0-531-04897-7. Glossary; index; C.I.P. ▶ **EI,EA**

This book suggests 12 interesting activities for children on five geography topics. The contents do not present sequential, planned learning, but rather provide a sampling of the topics. The illustrations are attractive; the materials for the projects are safe and typically available in an elementary school classroom. A teacher could capitalize on the hands-on aspects of the experiences to stimulate interest in geography.

Boase, Wendy. *Earth Voyager.* (Illus.) NY: Little Simon (Simon & Schuster), 1984. 31pp. $5.95. ISBN 0-671-50764-8. ▶ **EI,EA**

Boase examines unique characteristics of several unusual places on earth, covering the entire range of extremes from hottest to coldest, driest to wettest, highest to lowest, and so forth. Many colorful illustrations and several easy quiz questions, with answers that must be read in a mirror, contribute to making this an enjoyable reading experience. In addition, there is a two-page spread that contains a simple board game that ties the book's main ideas together. An interesting classroom supplement for an elementary natural science curriculum.

Knowlton, Jack. *Maps and Globes.* (Illus. by Harriet Barton.) NY: Crowell, 1985. 48pp. $9.95. 85-47537. ISBN 0-690-04457-7. C.I.P. ▶ **EP,EA**

Presents a difficult subject in a bright and lively folio format, with illustrations that greatly enhance the text. The first 18-page folio deals with the history of maps, their place in exploration, scale, and the advantages of globes over flat maps. The second folio discusses map language. Because of its physical format, the book can be spread out flat to allow students to trace the illustrations and follow the text. The ideas presented meet social studies objectives for lower elementary grades, and this presentation will be very helpful to teachers charged with introducing these concepts.

Lye, Keith. *Explorers.* (Illus.; from the Silver Burdett Color Library Series.) Morristown, NJ: Silver Burdett, 1983. 49pp. $14.00. 83-50391. ISBN 0-382-06728-2. ▶ **EA,JH**

In this picture book with wonderful color photographs and paintings, each topic is laid out on facing pages, and there is little text; most of the page is devoted to illustrations and descriptions of the topic. After a brief introduction that explains why, how, and where people explore, the reader gets a worldwide geography and history lesson.

Sabin, Francene. *Pioneers.* (Illus. by Hal Frenck; from the Venture into Reading Series.) Mahwah, NJ: Troll, 1985. 32pp. $7.59; $1.95 (paper). 84-2580. ISBN 0-8167-0120-2; 0-8167-0121-0 (paper). C.I.P. ▶ **EI**

Pioneers conveys, with lavish illustrations and easy-to-understand language, the mixed motivations of the American pioneers—from poor economic conditions to population pressures to a desire for excitement—in their movement westward. It also provides a sense of the problems these pioneers confronted and solved.

930 Ancient world

Caselli, Giovanni. *The First Civilizations.* (Illus.; from the History of Everyday Things Series.) NY: Peter Bedrick, 1985. 48pp. $12.95. 84-6179. ISBN 0-911745-59-9. C.I.P. ▶ **EA,JH**

This volume is packed with clearly presented information augmented by numerous color drawings. Twelve chapters divide the rise of civilization into chronological and geographical segments, beginning with "The Earliest Toolmakers" 4 million years ago and ending with "The Greeks at Home" about 2,400 year ago. The text focuses on European and circum-Mediterranean areas. The discussion emphasizes how life was lived at various times as revealed through archeological records. The illustrations add details about housing, dress, tools, and arts and crafts. Of particular interest are the sequences showing how ancient people made things.

Caselli, Giovanni. *A Roman Soldier.* (Illus. by Sergio; from The Everyday Life Of Series.) NY: Peter Bedrick, 1986. 30pp. $9.95. 86-4366. ISBN 0-87226-106-9. Glossary; C.I.P. ▶ **EI,EA**

A Viking Settler. (Illus. by Gino D'Achille.) 86-3302. ISBN 0-87226-104-2.

A Roman Soldier describes the activities of a young Roman soldier stationed on Hadrian's Wall, the northern frontier of Roman Britain in the early 3rd century. Topics include Roman military organization, recruitment and training of soldiers, their everyday round of activities, town life in Roman Britain, the relationship between the Romans and indigenous Celts, and Roman religious practices and beliefs. Attractively illustrated with numerous archeologically correct and visually engaging illustrations, this book would serve as an excellent starting point for a discussion and study of Roman Britain and of Roman military history. *A Viking Settler* describes the world of Viking farmers and merchants of the 10th century through the fictional adventures of a young boy, Egil, who lives in the Viking seaport settlement of Hedeby in Denmark. The reader is introduced to the geographic limits of the Viking world through the travels of Egil's merchant father. Careful attention is given to the accurate depiction of many aspects of Viking life, including the character of the farmstead, town life, and legal and social customs. The text is enhanced by numerous archeologically precise illustrations and maps, as well as an illustrated glossary dealing with Norse metal work, ship and house construction, tools, and the Runic alphabet.

Goor, Ron, and Nancy Goor. *Pompeii: Exploring a Roman Ghost Town.* (Illus.) NY: Crowell, 1986. ix + 118pp. $11.95. 85-47895. ISBN 0-690-04515-8. Index; C.I.P. ▶ JH

This book explores the historic eruption of Mt. Vesuvius in AD 79. It leads readers safely through the avalanche of ash, stone, and superheated gases that destroyed two major Roman cities, Pompeii and Herculaneum, and killed at least 2000 people. Described are the physical layout of the area of Pompeii that has so far been unearthed and the use of the recovered cultural materials to reconstruct Pompeiian social, political, commercial, and religious life. The brief text is accompanied by superb black-and-white photographs.

Hackwell, W. John. *Digging to the Past: Excavations in Ancient Lands.* (Illus. by the author.) NY: Scribner's, 1986. vi + 50pp. $13.95. 86-13115. ISBN 0-684-18692-6. Index; C.I.P. ▶ EA,JH

This attractive book describes how archeologists carry out an excavation and is based on the author's experiences in Jordan. The book takes us step by step through the progress of the dig. Hackwell stresses that archeologists aim to do more than simply fill museums with artifacts. They are interested in the life-styles and food systems of the inhabitants as well as in their waterworks, roads, and architecture. Environmental factors are also studied. About half of the book is composed of attractive black-and-white and color drawings.

Lauber, Patricia. *Tales Mummies Tell.* (Illus.) NY: Crowell, 1985. x + 118pp. $11.95. 83-46172. ISBN 0-690-04388-0. Index; C.I.P. ▶ EA,JH

This well-written and profusely illustrated book presents reasonably detailed descriptions of mummies, mummification processes, and the information to be obtained from the study of these phenomena. The geographic scope is worldwide, extending well beyond the usual treatment of the more famous Egyptian examples. Both human and animal mummies are treated with a refreshing and innovative approach that emphasizes what scientists can learn about ancient societies and life-styles. A useful addition to elementary and junior high school libraries.

Marston, Elsa. *Mysteries in American Archeology.* (Illus.; from the Walker's American History Series for Young People.) NY: Walker, 1986. xii + 116pp. $13.95. 85-20259. ISBN 0-8027-6608-0. Glossary; index; C.I.P. ▶ EA,JH

A well-organized and informative introduction to North American archeology that covers prehistory to the Contact Period. The "mysteries" of the title range from the Bering land bridge and the arrival of the first people to the North American continent through mound builders, the Anasazi, Cahokia, and medicine wheels, to who left the 16th(?)-century cannon on the Santa Barbara beach in 1981. The 41 archeological sites mentioned are shown on a map, and those open to the public are listed in an appendix.

Meyer, Carolyn, and Charles Gallenkamp. *The Mystery of the Ancient Maya.* (Illus.) NY: Atheneum, 1985. ix + 159pp. $11.95. 84-24209. ISBN 0-689-50319-9. Glossary; index; C.I.P. ▶ EA,JH

The accent here is on mystery, adventure, and the spectacular—the key ingredients that have attracted young men and women to archeology, especially Mayan archeology, for generations. Along with adventure, the authors serve up a smattering of information on the pre-Hispanic Maya. The major weakness of the work is the attempt to synthesize too much archeological, ethnohistoric, and ethnographic data in such a short text; the results are sometimes misleading or ambiguous, although the text is generally accurate. The illustrations are very good.

Santrey, Laurence. *Prehistoric People.* (Illus. by Dick Smolinski; from the Venture into Reading Series.) Mahwah, NJ: Troll, 1985. 32pp. $7.59; $1.95 (paper). 84-8464. ISBN 0-8167-0242-X; 0-8167-0243-8 (paper). C.I.P. ▶ **EI**

Prehistoric People provides an introduction to the concepts of culture and symbolic language. The activities of contemporary humans are linked to their biological needs. The development of tools, the use of fire, and the domestication of plants and animals are treated briefly in easy-to-read text and outstanding illustrations. Should make a nice addition to a young reader's collection.

A-V Materials

A-V Materials Annotations

The films, filmstrips, and videocassettes annotated in this volume are arranged alphabetically within Dewey Decimal categories. Each is indexed by title. Significant words in each Dewey category head are also included in a title and subject index, along with other words identifying specific topic areas covered. Producers and distributors are listed in an index which shows the address and phone number of each at the time this volume went to press.

The following information is given in each citation:

Films and videocassettes

[1] **Forces and Motion.** [2] *Guidance Associates,* [3] 1985. [4] (Part of the Children's Television Workshop Series.) [5] 60 min. [6] Color. [7] $895 (16mm); [8] $209 (¾-inch video); $179 (½-inch video); [9] $75 (rental). [10] o.n. CXR680. [11] Teacher's guide. [12] ▶ EI,EA,JH [16] Annotation

Filmstrips

[1] **Different.** [2] *National Geographic Society,* [3] 1986. [4] (From the Look, Listen, Explore Series.) [13] 2 color filmstrips; 55 frames ea. [14] 2 cassettes; 10–12 min. ea. [15] $61.95. [11] Teacher's guide. [12] ▶ K,EP [16] Annotation

1. Title of film, filmstrip, or videocassette
2. Producer or distributor
3. Copyright date
4. Title of series (if any); also, producer (if different from #2)
5. Running time, rounded to the nearest minute
6. Color (or black-and-white) print available
7. Cost* to purchase one 16mm print
8. Cost* to purchase one videocassette in either ½-inch or ¾-inch format
9. Cost* of renting film or videocassette. Rental period varies with each distributor. Rental fees can in some cases be applied toward purchase price
10. Film order number
11. Teacher's guide included

* *All purchase or rental prices listed are those supplied by the distributor at the time that the A-V materials first entered distribution.*

12. The grade or viewer level[s] as assigned by the subject-matter specialist who reviewed the film or filmstrip:

K	Kindergarten	EA	Grades 5 and 6
EP	Grades 1 and 2	JH	Grades 7–9
EI	Grades 3 and 4		

13. Number of filmstrips in set; number of frames per strip

14. Number of audiocassettes, if any; running time of each tape

15. Purchase price* of set; rental not available for filmstrips

16. Annotations are based on much longer reviews prepared by subject-matter specialists and published in **Science Books & Films**, the book and film review journal of the American Association for the Advancement of Science. Back issues of **SB&F** are available either from AAAS or from University Microfilms, Ann Arbor, MI 48106.

Films, filmstrips, and videocassettes should be ordered directly from the producer or distributor listed (*see* A-V Materials Distributors, pp. 331–335).

Philosophy and Related Disciplines

150 Psychology

153 Conscious mental processes

Decision Making: Values and Goals. *Barr Films*, 1982. (Part of the Decision Making Series.) 17 min. Color. $375 (16mm); $375 (video). o.n. A329. Teacher's guide. ▶ **EA,JH**

This film is the first of a three-part series on decision making. In all, six steps are discussed: knowing values, setting goals, expanding alternatives, seeking information, predicting outcomes, and taking action. This film examines the first two steps—value clarification and goal setting. Major points are interspersed between the film's running dialogue and effective portrayals of a young woman who agonizes over career choices. Since the exigencies of compromise, uncontrolled factors, and so forth are not explored, a dimension invariably involved in decision making is slighted. Nevertheless, because the logical, cognitive steps in decision making are effectively described, the film is an appropriate vehicle for initiating group discussion.

Decisions! Decisions! *Barr Films*, 1984. 18 min. Color. $395 (16mm); $395 (video); inquire for rental. Teacher's guide. ▶ **EI,EA,JH**

Decisions! Decisions! is an effective introduction to the principles of decision making. The film uses a five-point system: knowing what is important, considering all alternatives, gathering information, considering consequences, and making a decision and acting. The narrator is a college student working in an ice cream parlor, and she describes problems that have been encountered by the children who are customers. The application of the five-point system is illustrated in each case, but the trap of presenting the system as a rigid set of rules to be followed is carefully avoided. The emphasis is on looking for alternatives that might not be obvious and on the importance of making a decision and acting.

Problem Solving: Identifying the Problem. *Agency for Instructional Technology,* 1986. (From the Math Works Series.) 15 min. Color. $125 (video). Inquire for series and rental. Teacher's guide available. ▶ **EA**

This film encourages students to ask the following questions when trying to clarify a problem and attempt a solution: What do I know? What do I need to know? What is a related problem that I can solve? These themes are illustrated in four vignettes with a narrator intervening. One scene involves a textbook problem while the other three occur in settings unrelated to school. The teacher's guide offers good supplemental material.

Why Is It Always Me? *MTI Teleprograms Inc.,* 1983. 14 min. Color. $250 (16mm); $250 (video); $50 (one-week rental). Teacher's guide. ▶ **EA,JH**

Admirably straightforward, this brief film demonstrates a specific problem-solving approach to difficulties in human interaction. Mike, the protagonist, is helped to moderate his self-defeating anger through the five steps of IDEAL— an acronym for identifying the problem, describing the possible solutions, evaluating the alternatives, acting on a plan, and learning. Some viewers may find the film's concentration on anger a drawback, and without extensive discussion, the film will have little lasting impact despite its entertaining quality.

155.4–.5 Child and adolescent psychology

See also 362.7 Problems of and services to young people; 649.65 Sex education.

Anger: Handle with Care. *Barr Films,* 1982. 12 min. Color. $275 (16mm); $275 (video); inquire for rental. Teacher's guide. ▶ **EI,EA,JH**

Contrary to the information in the teacher's guide, this is not a film that shows children how to handle their anger; rather it does attempt to demonstrate that anger is an emotion that everyone experiences and that it is possible to deal with it constructively. This is accomplished by showing two different endings for each of the seven vignettes: one shows the result of letting anger get out of control, the other shows the result of controlling anger. The film does manage to capture the attention of its audience in a unique way, and it is a heuristic tool for introducing and discussing its subject. In addition, it is divided into segments that would allow a teacher or counselor to stop the film over an hour-long period for discussion and enhanced effect. Negatives: some technical aspects are deficient, with distracting acting and some unrelated dialog, and techniques for emotional control are omitted.

Being a Fat Child. *MTI Teleprograms Inc.,* 1984. (Prod.: "ABC News".) 15 min. Color. $275 (16mm); $250 (video); $50 (rental). o.n. AE16. ▶ **EA,JH**

This interesting film on obesity in adolescents focuses on the emotional and psychological pain that accompanies being overweight and presents some ways of coping with it. Causes such as heredity, stress, and contributing actions of well-meaning parents are discussed, but the most important point the film makes is that only self-discipline and motivation to change eating patterns will keep weight off once and for all. The film was originally aired on the television program "20/20". Although it is excellent, it is also very condensed and should be viewed more than once.

Change . . . Coping with Your Changing World. *Barr Films,* 1984. 21 min. Color. $465 (16mm); $465 (video). ▶ **JH**

This visually attractive film is an excellent introduction to the subject of change and could be a good springboard for extended class discussion. The content is nicely presented, showing the discussion between two adolescents and an older friend on attitudes toward change. As the film shows, the key to coping with change is to be prepared for it and to be willing to adapt.

Expectations: A Story About Stress. *Walt Disney Educational Media Co.*, 1985. 22 min. Color. $529 (16 mm); $397 (video); inquire for rental. Teacher's guide. ▶ EA,JH

Two complex examples of children under stress are drawn from the lives of Pauline and Carlos as they compete in a gymnastic event. Even though she has multiple stressors, Pauline can cope adequately because she is in control of these events and can capitalize on her strong internal motivation. Carlos, on the other hand, is controlled almost entirely by his parents. After Carlos succumbs to the stress and cannot perform in the gymnastic event, he tells his dad to cease his demands for athletic achievement. In both profiles, suitable outcomes are portrayed for young viewers. To profitably use this film with youngsters, a skilled discussion leader would be needed to bring out its best points.

Friends. *Barr Films*, 1983. 20 min. Color. $440 (16 mm); $440 (video); inquire for rental. Teacher's guide. ▶ EP,EI,EA

This is a pleasant story about two girls whose friendship is broken up when one moves away. The one who is left behind experiences a brief depression that is resolved when she visits a new girl in the neighborhood whom she had previously ignored. The new girl turns out to be physically handicapped and wheelchair bound in contrast to the old friend, who was an athlete. The emotional issues that the film raises (acceptance of individual differences, sharing, dealing with physical handicaps, and loss of a friend) are subtle for the intended young audience, and they may require considerable advance preparation for a meaningful discussion.

Life Changes Cause Stress. *Encyclopaedia Britannica Educational Corp.*, 1982. (Part of The Stress Series.) 3 color filmstrips, 60 frames (average) ea.; 3 cassettes, 10 min. ea. $81. Teacher's guide. ▶ EA,JH

This filmstrip set depicts situations often experienced by middle-grade to junior-high students, including changes in boy-girl interactions and alcohol, prescription drugs, cigarettes, and food abuse. The individuals portrayed face dilemmas and the difficult decisions needed to resolve those situations, a stress-producing process. The strength of the set lies in the development of outcomes and the testing of consequences regarding potential problem-solving actions. Viewers can identify similar situations in their own lives and model the decision-making process shown in the filmstrips.

Then One Year, revised. *Churchill Films*, 1984. 19 min. Color. $390 (16mm); $350 (video); inquire for rental. Teacher's guide. ▶ EA,JH

A resource to supplement instruction related to the emotional and physiological changes of adolescence, this film shows developmental scenes of boys and girls accompanied by upbeat music in keeping with the film's positive tone. Through accurate and explicit drawings and diagrams, students are exposed to the external and internal changes that accompany the transition to sexual maturity. A particularly positive feature is that the illustrations are amplified by the narration, which emphasizes the variability of growth spurts and the normality of such variations. The presentation of the controversial topic of masturbation is candid and objective; no value judgments are made.

The Wizard of No. *MTI Teleprograms Inc.*, 1984. 19 min. Color. $400 (16mm); $300 (video); $70 (rental). o.n. 4650M. ▶ JH

This film is a brief but effective dramatization of a young boy facing peer group pressures. It uses humorous dialogue between him and his imaginary friend— The Wizard of No—to give a taste of the classic developmental conflict between youthful desires and mature choices. The film's adolescent actor is believable, and the anti-tobacco and drug story is straightforward enough to make its logic obvious.

155.937 Death and dying

Coping with a Death in the Family. *Learning Tree Filmstrips*, 1982. 4 color filmstrips, 46–59 frames ea.; 4 cassettes, 8–10 min. ea. $72. o.n. LT1113. Teacher's guide. ▶ EA,JH

Coping with a Death in the Family, designed to help children and young adolescents understand the feelings that may be associated with the death of a relative, could be used in classes dealing with grief and loss. "Is It Normal to Feel This Way?" shows Sally, who does not feel grief at the loss of a grandmother whom she did not know. "Was It My Fault?" portrays Chris, who feels that is is his fault when his father is seriously injured at work and later dies after a period of hospitalization. "Accepting the Unacceptable" concerns Nita, who refuses to accept that her mother is dying. In "Going On without Them." Harry recalls the auto accident that killed his older brother. Because these topics are presented in a realistic manner with a focus on feelings, supportive preparation before viewing and discussion and counseling after viewing are essential to ensure successful assimilation of the material and resolution of feelings aroused by the filmstrips.

Death of a Goldfish. *Family Communications*, 1980. (Prod.: "Mister Rogers' Neighborhood".) 28 min. Color. $395 (16mm); $150 (video); $55 (rental 16mm, video free). Booklet available. ▶ K

This episode from the television program "Mr. Rogers's Neighborhood" attempts to pave the way for parents to discuss the subject of death with their preschool children. After finding a dead fish at the bottom of his aquarium, Mr. Rogers buries it, then goes on to talk of a pet dog that had died and to explain that machines do not die, only living things. *Death of a Goldfish* is tedious for anyone older than five; however, it is a good beginning for the very young to learn acceptance of the finality of death.

The Foundling. *Barr Films*, 1986. 22 min. Color. $520 (16mm); $520 (video). ▶ K,EP,EI,EA,JH

In *The Foundling*, we observe the painful process through which a boy comes to grips with the loss of his beloved dog and his guilt feelings for not using a leash. A replacement dog is suggested but refused for fear of betraying the first dog's memory. The boy's father stresses the valuable but difficult concept that we can't change what has happened and that it's "time to go on." Eventually the boy brings home an abandoned dog. This story is told quickly and interestingly enough to capture the attention of its intended young audience. It is also well suited to a large group in death education or a small counseling situation to bring out repressed or confused feelings.

170 Ethics

Ethics in the Computer Age. *Walt Disney Educational Media Co.*, 1984. 22 min. Color. $504 (16mm); $378 (video). Teacher's guide. ▶ **EA,JH**

In two brief sketches, this film dramatically conveys a strong and even frightening message about two common ethical problems associated with computers. The first sketch, on pirating, depicts two teen-agers who develop a new computer game, then take it to a software developer. The second story, about hacking, tells of a girl who puts off doing her term paper until the last minute. Her boyfriend obtains plenty of information for her by illegally entering an encyclopedia database. Sandwiched between these sketches are succinct comments on computer ethics from several experts. Should be seen especially by teens who see nothing wrong with copying disks or breaking into databanks.

Speaking of Harvey. *Pyramid Film & Video*, 1983. 8 min. Color. $210 (16mm); $210 (video); $40 (rental). ▶ **EA, JH**

An excellent presentation of the ethical issues involved in animal experimentation. While a young researcher performs an operation on a rabbit, he discusses his feelings about conducting research on live animals, including the humane treatment of laboratory animals, balancing the benefits of research with the harm to the animals, and the need for sensitivity to the welfare of the animals. The researcher's concern and sensitivity are conveyed through actions as well as words. Students viewing this film will be exposed to a balanced viewpoint, in which concern for animal welfare does not mean a complete rejection of research on live animals.

Social Sciences

303.483   Social change through science and technology
See also 621 Applied physics.

Decisions, Decisions, Decisions. *Agency for Instructional Technology*, 1983. (Part of the You, Me, and Technology Series.) 20 min. Color. $115 (video). Teacher's guide.   ▶ JH

Living with Technology.

These two films can be useful in science, social studies, and English classes to help students recognize the need to exert reasoned control over expanding technologies and not just accept them passively or react to them out of fear and suspicion. *Living with Technology* follows a middle-class family for a day, showing the impact of technology on their lives and how they cope with the resulting problems. *Decisions, Decisions, Decisions* describes some of the decisions that technology forces us to make and depicts a decision-making process that works much like a thermostat. The elements of a decision are input, output, feedback, and constraints, and the film uses them to construct a decision model. An excellent starting point for a class discussion and a follow-up homework assignment.

Inventors and the American Industrial Revolution. *Churchill Films*, 1984. 14 min. Color. $295 (16mm); $295 (video); inquire for rental. Teacher's guide.   ▶ EA, JH

This film provides a brief overview of the key inventions of the Industrial Revolution in the United States. Using old prints, pictures, and film clips, the film depicts inventions such as the cotton gin, steamboat, telephone, and airplane. The narration is comprised of quotes from older people who lived through the changes that these inventions brought. The film does not address the possible negative consequences of inventions, and overemphasizes the role of Thomas Edison.

306 Cultural anthropology

An Ancient Gift. *University of California Extension Media Center, 1983.* 18 min. Color. $315 (16mm); $240 (video); $32 (rental, 16mm). ▶ **EA, JH**

This film about the importance of the sheep to the Navajo people serves as an excellent introduction to the largest Indian tribe in the United States. The focus is on the importance of sheep to the individual family, beginning with the care of the sheep; wool and its processing into rugs; and the butchering of sheep for food. Although the focus on a single family provides continuity, the film is rich in narrative detail, providing much information on Navajo culture in general. One of the most comprehensive views available of a contemporary Indian tribe.

Children of Brunei. *Journal Films, Inc.,* 1982. (Part of the Children of the World Series.) 12 min. Color. $255 (16mm); $30 (3-day rental). Teacher's guide. ▶ **K,EP,EI,EA,JH**

Although the naive style of this film would draw snickers from senior-high students, the film's child narrators have considerable charm. The film shows the life-style and culture of these children, and it depicts a Borneo kingdom that has Islamic traditions that are more Malaysian than Indonesian. The traditional market economy, including fishing and boat building, the segregation of the sexes outside of the home, and the extended family system are covered.

Corn Is Life. *University of California Extension Media Center,* 1983. 19 min. Color. $330 (16mm); $250 (video); $33 (rental, 16mm). ▶ **EP,EI,EA,JH**

This film documents the importance of corn as a food and craft material to the Hopi of northeastern Arizona. Corn's life cycle, from planting through harvest, parallels the Hopi life cycle from birth to death. At each stage in a Hopi's life, corn is used ceremonially and as a vital part of subsistence. Excellent photography, clear narration by a Hopi, and traditional music all help make this an excellent film for viewers of all ages.

A Cowhand's Song: Crisis on the Range. *New Front Films Programming Services,* 1982. 28 min. Color. $475 (16mm); $375 (video); $55 (rental, 16mm); $45 (rental, video). ▶ **EA, JH**

This film depicts the way of life and seasonal cycle of activities of family ranchers in Surprise Valley in northern California. This way of life is described as being part of a modern range war that concerns conflicting demands on the use of public lands. Environmentalists charge that overgrazing is damaging the range and wildlife. Other competing interests include hunters, hikers, dirt bikers, oil and mining interests, and the military. The film focuses on how the family ranchers perceive their life, and this view is stated almost entirely in their own words. An outstanding look at a traditional way of life that is being threatened by new policies and developments and an important statement of one aspect of the land use controversies in the western United States.

It's a Small World. *Walt Disney Educational Media Co.,* 1986. 5 color filmstrips, 60–69 frames ea.; 5 cassettes, 7–9 min. ea. $169. Teacher's guide. ▶ **K,EP,EI**

The five cultures presented are beautifully illustrated, and the narration is appropriate for the intended age group. The interest of young students will be maintained throughout each segment's exploration of South American, Canadian Indian, Italian, African, and Japanese customs and traditions. The narration provides a well-developed and accurate account of each country and is fast paced, lively, and clear.

Suzhou. *University of California Extension Media Center,* 1981. (Part of the Cities of China Series.) 28 min. Color. $450 (16mm); $340 (video); $40 (rental, 16mm); $32 (rental, video). ▶ EA,JH

This ancient Chinese city of "6,000 bridges of stone," as described by Marco Polo, proudly retains its traditions in culinary and graphic arts, water trade, rice cultivation, fishing, silk making, tea collecting, and the performance of dramatic arts in lush city gardens. The film is generally effective in capturing the city of Suzhou as a "state of mind and way of life," not just a place. This is accomplished by focusing on some current human activities that have been molded by centuries of urban and rural social dialogue. The film is not a comprehensive view of life in this city.

Tighten The Drums: Self-Decoration Among The Enga. *Documentary Educational Resources, Inc.,* 1982. (Prod.: The Institute of Papua New Guinea Studies.) 58 min. Color. $750 (16mm); $70 (rental). ▶ EA,JH

This is a very nice mood film of some highland Papua New Guinea people who decorate their bodies with paint and feathers for a ceremony, but it is too long and has too little ethnographic meat for most teaching purposes. A brief introduction explains that all these designs are communication, but the film does not systematically demonstrate that claim. Most audiences will want more ethnographic information about the Enga, the ceremony, and the meanings of the decorations. There is also some nudity; teachers should screen the film before using it with classes.

306.8 Marriage and family

Black Girl. *University of California Extension Media Center,* 1982. (Part of The Planning Ahead Series.) 30 min. Color. $470 (16mm); $355 (video); $39 (rental, 16mm); $32 (rental, video). ▶ EA,JH

This excellently written, directed, and acted film provides a sensitive look at the social and interpersonal issues facing a black matriarchal family and examines their attitudes toward succeeding in a white world. The film shows how members of a poor family deal with privacy and property, the need of children to establish and develop independent goals and identities, and how foster children compete for a mother's affection. The language fits the story beautifully and drives home the complex messages being conveyed. The film is emotional but does not overwhelm the viewers.

Masculinity. *Clearvue, Inc.,* 1982. 4 color filmstrips, 73 frames (average); 4 cassettes, 12 min. (average). $72 (set); $21 (ea.). o.n. P355. Teacher's guide. ▶ JH

The thesis of this filmstrip set is that traditional images of masculinity in the United States during the mid-1970s were incorrect for the times; however, viewers are left in the dark regarding just what is correct. The set explores the cultural foundation of gender differences and identifies historical roots and society's imposition of the traditional masculine role on a young husband. The set can elicit powerful class discussion because it touches the self-identities of both males and females. Purposeful teacher preparation (including complete visual preview) is essential.

My Family and Me. *Encyclopaedia Britannica Educational Corp.,* 1982. 4 color filmstrips, 57 frames (average) ea.; 4 cassettes, 6 min. ea. $108. Teacher's guide. ▶ **EI,EA**

My Family and Me is designed to encourage children's understanding and discussion of family situations. The pictures are colorful and appealing and the narration includes the voices of children as they talk about their families. The families are varied: city and suburban, in houses and apartments, multi-generational and of various races. Family forms are also varied: nuclear families, divorced and widowed parents, adopted children, and so forth. Best of all, while most of the situations presented are ideal, loving, sharing and mutually caring, the filmstrips also show divorce, death, and family disputes.

330 Economics

333.79 Energy and energy resources
See also 371.42 Careers; 539 Fission and fusion; 551.46 Oceanography; 621 Applied physics.

Energy Series. *Marshfilm Enterprises, Inc.,* 1983. 4 color filmstrips, 58–74 frames ea.; 4 cassettes, 17–20 min. ea. $106. Teacher's guide. ▶ **EP,EI,EA,JH**

This series deals with past, present, and future energy use. The filmstrips are produced in a cartoon format with attractive, brilliant colors and detailed artwork. The content is factual, although a distinct bias against nuclear fission is projected. The personification of the sun, wind, and so forth is catchy but may tend to distort the younger student's perception of reality. These four filmstrips build well on each other and, if properly supplemented, can provide a good overview of the energy situation.

The Energy Series. *Moody Institute of Science,* 1982. 4 color filmstrips, 53–64 frames ea.; 4 cassettes, 10 min. (average) ea. $95. Teacher's guides. ▶ **JH**

Each of the four filmstrips addresses one large topic: energy and the rise of civilization; energy and the American life-style; energy conservation; and fuels for the future. The presentation is upbeat and informative, never sermonizing, as the conservation and life-style segments might have been in less capable hands. The "future fuels" segment is comprehensive and balanced. The teacher's guides have some feasible student research activities but little background information, and some data are slightly dated.

Social Problems and Services

362.292–.293   Alcoholism; drug addiction; smoking
See also 613 Personal health.

Alcohol Abuse and Teens: The Turning Point. *AIMS Media, Inc.,* 1986. 29 min. Color. $495 (16mm); $395 (video); $75 (rental).   ▶ **EA,JH**

This program portrays two teenagers who become involved with alcohol due to parental as well as peer pressure and shows how easy it can be for teens to become alcoholic. The program ends with the death of one teen in an alcohol-related driving accident. The messages are clear and concise, and viewers will come away with increased knowledge and awareness of the devastating effects of uncontrolled alcohol use among teens. Very realistic and highly recommended.

Deciso 3003. *Churchill Films.* 1982. (Part of The Say NO Series.) 6 min. Color. $150 (16mm); $150 (video). Teacher's guide.   ▶ **EA,JH**

This film deals with peer pressure by presenting futuristic teenagers faced with decisions that concern drugs and sexual activity. The film could be used effectively to trigger discussions among junior-high students. It portrays realistic situations, delineates the decision-making process concisely and accurately, and is accompanied by a good discussion guide. The animation is only fair, but the music is good. The visual images of the future are dated.

Magic Bill. *MTI Teleprograms Inc.,* 1984. 7 min. Color. $165 (16mm); $115 (video); $50 (rental). o.n. WQ20. Discussion guide.   ▶ **EA,JH**

This film involves a young and ebullient pitchman—Magic Bill—selling alcohol and drugs from the trunk of a car to a group of receptive teenagers. He gives each drug's street name and glowingly extols its "benefits." As each spiel is concluded, it is shot down by Bruce Weitz, of television's "Hill Street Blues", who plays the role of adversary. Weitz scoffingly derides all claims, identifies each drug by its generic name, and details the inevitable serious consequences. As the debate continues, the once enraptured teenagers drift away. Unfortunately, too much is packed into too little time, the dialogue is paced too quickly, and the obviously contrived situation may repel some viewers. Overall, however, the film achieves its purpose.

Parents with Alcoholism: Kids with Hope. *Human Relations Media*, 1985. 2 color filmstrips; 75–77 frames ea.; 2 cassettes, 15 min. ea. Also available in ½-inch video. $108 (strip); $140 (video). ▶ **EI,EA,JH**

This program initially presents illustrative examples of children growing up with one or more alcoholic parent. The problems each child faces are clearly and realistically presented. Perhaps the greatest asset of the presentation is the glimmer of hope it offers and the alternatives it details. The program also shows that these children do not cause the problem and are not alone in their experience. These filmstrips should not only benefit those living with this problem, but they should also sensitize others to the problems faced by families of alcoholics.

Saying No to Alcohol and Drugs. *FilmFair Communications*, 1986. 12 min. Color. $275 (16mm); $275 (video); $30 (rental). ▶ **EA,JH**

This film dramatizes realistic situations that illustrate the realities of peer pressure and shows ways of dealing with them. Several coping strategies are portrayed, each appropriate to ward off the pressure being applied. This film, combined with classroom discussion, will make a worthy addition to the battery of resources available to help our young people resist drugs. Its recommended tactics to resist peer pressure and its clear statement of the dangers of substance abuse make it worth viewing.

Why Say No to Drugs? *Encyclopaedia Britannica Educational Corp.*, 1986. 16 min. Color. $360 (16mm); $290 (video); $36 (rental). Discussion guide. ▶ **EA,JH**

This well produced film features sixth graders who honestly and maturely describe their feelings and impressions concerning the mixed messages about drugs that frequently bombard young people. It gives an overview of accurate, impressive scientific information about how cigarettes, alcohol, and other drugs, especially marijuana, affect human beings. The concept of decision making is also explored, as is the peer pressure that makes it difficult for teens to say "no." Dramatizations show situations where smoking, drinking, or marijuana use is encouraged and illustrate some successful techniques for saying "no." Concise, cohesive, and nonpreachy.

You've Come a Long Way, Rene. *Barr Films*, 1983. 22 min. Color. $485 (16mm); $485 (video); inquire for rental. Teacher's guide. ▶ **JH**

To smoke or not to smoke, that is Rene's dilemma. She is a runner, and cigarettes have no place in her life until her pushy friend Carol tells her how immature she is because she won't light up. Overall, the film has good acting and a good script and can be useful in health or social studies classes or for a discussion of peer pressure.

362.7   Problems of and services to young people

See also 155.4–.5 Child and adolescent psychology; 306.8 Marriage and family; 649.65 Sex education.

Child Abuse and Neglect: The Hidden Hurt. *Guidance Associates, Inc.*, 1986. 4 color filmstrips, 50–82 frames ea.; 4 cassettes, 8–11 min. ea. Also available in video. $179 (strip); $199 (¾-inch video); $179 (½-inch video). Teacher's guide. ▶ EA,JH

This program's stated purpose is to help break the cycle of child abuse by educating the public about its causes and solutions. It is accurate and informative as well as realistic and understanding. It is appropriate for children and abusing adults as well as concerned outsiders who may be aware of or suspect an abusive situation. The technical quality and instructional value are excellent.

The Latchkey Series. *Marshfilm Enterprises, Inc.*, 1985. 4 color filmstrips, 50 frames ea.; 4 cassettes, 15 min. ea. $111 (series). Teacher's guide. ▶ K,EP,EI,EA

This filmstrip set appropriately and interestingly explains survival and success skills to children who may sometimes be left unsupervised. Safety is the overriding issue. There is skillful repetition of some basic rules ("Don't play with matches"), concepts (the meaning of an emergency), and basic emergency techniques (antichoking methods). There are good parenting parallels, too. Although the four filmstrips are sequential, they overlap enough for viewing in any order. Highly recommended for all children.

Meeting Strangers: Red Light, Green Light. *BFA Educational Media*, 1984. 19 min. Color. $395 (16mm); $250 (video); $56 (rental). ▶ K,EP,EI,EA

The theme of this children's film is that people display different safety signals: those who are dangerous to children give "red" signals, just like a red traffic light, and those who are safe give "green" signals. The film stresses that children never have to say "yes" to a strange adult, that it is permissible to say "no." This program is an excellent tool for teaching children to discriminate between dangerous and safe adults. Strangers are depicted as being almost anyone from the street, not stereotypes. The film's strongest point is its emphasis that most strangers are nice people, a refreshing contrast to the current tendency to teach children to fear all strangers.

On Your Own. *Walt Disney Educational Media Co.*, 1985. 14 min. Color. $389 (16mm); $292 (video); inquire for rental. Teacher's guide. ▶ EI,EA

This excellent production addresses the need for children to care for themselves after school. It is an important and useful film for children of about eight years of age but not younger. In a fantasy television program, Sara Miller tells viewers how to get home safely, take care of house keys, check in with parents, avoid risks with strangers, prepare snacks for nourishment, obey rules for fire safety, and, most importantly, deal with the fear of being alone. Advice is concrete, matter-of-fact, and level-headed, with no sensationalism.

Teenage Parenting: A Hard Lesson to Learn. *Marshfilm Enterprises, Inc.*, 1987. 1 filmstrip ea., 51–53 frames ea.; 1 cassette ea., 13 min. ea. Color. $34.50 ea. Teacher's guide. ▶ EA,JH

Teenage Pregnancy: Too Much, Too Soon.

Teenage Parenting presents the difficulties of teenage parenting and single motherhood. A mother, pictured with her ten-year-old son and twelve-year-old daughter, relates the story of her teenage pregnancies, marriage, subsequent divorce, and single parenthood. The filmstrip is of generally high technical quality, with attractive color photographs, and can be useful; however, the dialogue is too rapid and the overall program may be too ambitious. Although the stated objective is to facilitate learning about the difficulties of teenage parenting, the scenario distracts the viewer into compelling side issues. *Teenage Pregnancy* presents the subject from the perspective of a black preteen girl whose older sister became pregnant, married, left high school, and had a son. One of the program's strengths is realism. The filmstrip does an excellent job of contrasting the younger sister's preconceptions and initially idealized views of relationships and child rearing with the less pleasant reality as experienced and portrayed by her sibling. The script strongly conveys the message that teenagers are too young for parenthood and that "people look down on you" if you are pregnant and unmarried. The reflective questions posed by the young narrator are an effective technique to engage the viewer.

What'cha Gonna Do? *Perennial Education, Inc.*, 1985. 11 min. Color. $225 (16mm); $225 (video). Teacher's guide. ▶ K,EP

Narrated by two older children, this film is a series of vignettes about what young children should do if they become lost or are alone and strangers approach them, talk to them, or invite them into their houses. The program can be stopped by a teacher before the solution to a situation is given so that a class can discuss possible solutions. Probably most useful for schools in an urban setting.

363.7 Environmental problems and protection

See also 574.5 Ecology of organisms; 639.9 Wildlife conservation.

Air Pollution: A First Film, revised. *Phoenix Films & Video, Inc.*, 1984. 12 min. Color. $255 (16mm); $175 (video); $38 (rental). ▶ JH

This short but excellent introduction to air pollution can serve as a first-rate vehicle for extended class discussion. It covers the sources of air pollution and gives a simple view of the relevant atmospheric chemistry and meteorology. The harmful effects of air pollution are carefully and colorfully documented, as are general strategies for reducing air pollution. Highly recommended.

Biology at War: The Mystery of the Yellow Rain. *Films Inc.*, 1984. (Prod.: BBC; from the Horizon Series.) 50 min. Color. $298 (¾-inch video); $198 (½-inch video); $90 (rental). ▶ JH

This film uses excellent photography of Laos and Thailand to provide much information about life in these countries, as well as to discuss the possibility that yellow rain is a form of biological warfare. After introducing U.S. Senate testimony and that of victims, the film shifts its attention to the role of bees in producing a possibly toxic substance that may be confused with biological warfare chemicals. The pollen explanation is well demonstrated as it occurs in the jungle, but then the film falters. The individuals who maintained that yellow rain is a biological weapon, and the Russians and Kampucheans, who are accused of using biological agents, are not interviewed concerning either explanation. The film's loss of evenhandedness tarnishes the conclusions it draws for the viewer.

Man Makes a Desert, revised. *BFA Educational Media*, 1985. 10 min. Color. $200 (16mm); $125 (video); $28 (rental, 16mm only). Teacher's guide. ▶ EI,EA

This film shows how a rich grassland became a desert and discusses how the land can be reclaimed by scientists applying the latest technical and scientific knowledge. The damage done by plowing and overgrazing is illustrated, as are the changes in the fauna as the grassland becomes desert. The photography is excellent, and the presentation allows the viewer to see the progressive destruction. Entertaining as well as informative.

"Walter Cronkite's Universe": Disappearance of the Great Rain Forest. *Arthur Mokin Productions, Inc.*, 1983. 12 min. Color. $150 (video); $35 (one-day rental). Teacher's guide. ▶ **EA,JH**

The subject of this film is the Amazon Basin rain forest, which is being cut or converted to other uses at an alarming rate. This rain forest contains plant and animal species (many not yet identified) that constitute the world's largest "pharmaceutical factory." The minimum-sized patch that would be necessary to protect the rain forest's high diversity of plants and animals is a subject of a study by scientist Tom Lovejoy. The film also examines the importance of the Amazon rain forest to the North American climate and how its destruction will affect this climate. The clear assessment of the problems that affect the survival of this critical ecosystem makes this film a splendid resource for use with many audiences.

Science
Education

See also 507 Science: study and teaching.

371.42 Careers

Being an Astronaut. *Guidance Associates,* 1986. (Prod.: Children's Television Workshop.) 29 min. Color. $139 (¾-inch video); $119 (½-inch video). ▶ **EI,EA,JH**

This appealing video depicts astronauts as "real" people and is a timely attempt to rekindle interest in and provide information about our space program. Viewers quickly learn that astronauts are very much like their own friends and family and have a wide variety of outside interests, backgrounds, and abilities. The complex nature of the shuttle program is clearly demonstrated. Younger students will need to have some of the concepts explained in more detail if the program is used as part of a science unit.

The Body. *WETA,* 1984. (Part of the Spaces Series.) 30 min. ea. Color. $70 (video ea.). Teacher's guide. ▶ **EA,JH**

Communications.

Ecology.

Energy.

Space.

The Body examines the work of three scientists, each from a minority group, and then presents a brief biographical sketch that explains why each chose a career in science. The importance of completing basic courses in mathematics and science is reinforced throughout. The importance and usefulness of this film for stimulating junior-high students, especially minority students, cannot be overstated. Designed to acquaint and excite young people about possible careers in the field, *Communications* uses a variety of production techniques to provide an interesting, fast-paced, informative message. Three job opportunities are featured: telecommunications engineer, assistant director at a television station, and physicist working with communication satellites. The film features personable, articulate women and minorities in these technical roles. *Ecology*, a well-paced film, glides smoothly through the introduction of a number of topics, including the work of ecologists. Viewers are exposed to the concept of an ecosystem by way of a conversation between two teenagers about a sow bug. Such intriguing organisms as social termites and plants that chemically resist predation are also discussed. Most importantly, however, viewers experience two ecologists speaking informally about the work they love and how and why they became ecologists. *Energy* focuses on several aspects of America's energy situation and shows how members of minority groups are involved in solving our energy problems. The bulk of the film is devoted to informative profiles of three people: a geological engineer, a scientist working on photovoltaic cells, and a high-school girl who is presenting a science fair project on eutectic salts. The film's best use will probably be to provide early guidance toward possible careers for fifth- through eighth-grade students. In *Space*, interviews with an astronaut, a life scientist working on space adaptation syndrome, and a student involved in a space experiment (all of whom are minorities) are particularly designed to inspire minority children. To grab the youngsters' attention, the film often uses questionable child-oriented interludes; moreover, the long explanation of biofeedback training for motion sickness may cause some children to lose interest. However, the film rarely uses technical terms and can be recommended for young children who need inspiration for careers in science and technology.

Careers in Math and Science: A Different View. *Walt Disney Educational Media Co.*, 1986. 10 min. Color. $469 (16mm); $352 (video); $60 (3-day rental). Also available in filmstrip. ▶ **EA,JH**

Students frequently limit their career choices by not taking enough mathematics and science courses in high school or by not studying these subjects seriously in middle school or junior high. This film forewarns students of this possibility by showing three scenarios of adults, especially women, in which knowledge of math or science is essential for success in particular careers. Two episodes are related to mathematics: fashion merchandising and computer-aided design; the third, genetic engineering, is linked to biology and chemistry. Highly recommended for use in guidance classes with students in junior and senior high school.

The Hero Who Couldn't Read. *MTI Teleprograms Inc.*, 1984. 30 min. Color. $495 (16mm); $395 (video); $75 (rental). o.n. 4543M. Teacher's guide. ▶ **EA,JH**

This film sketches the problems of Freddie Ellis, a black high-school basketball star who can't read. His friends help cover up his illiteracy, but their action also inhibits his intellectual development. Colleges want to recruit him despite his academic handicap. Then Freddie meets Kareem Abdul-Jabbar, who urges him to complete his education. The film can inspire youngsters of all ages as well as teachers, parents, counselors, and psychologists.

An Industrial Chemist. *Hawkhill Associates, Inc.*, 1986. (From the People in Science Today Series.) 12 min. Color. $68 (video); $29 (rental/copy plan). Teacher's guide. Also available in filmstrip, 90 frames; 1 cassette, 12 min. $42. ▶ **EA,JH**

Spenser Silver, the 3M Company chemist who invented the adhesive used in Post-it Notes, discusses not only how the notes were developed but also general aspects of chemistry in an industrial laboratory and the characteristics of the successful industrial chemist. The presentation mentions that pressure-sensitive adhesives are polymers, but the focus is on the broader picture of the process by which an idea is transformed into a successful product. Curiosity, freedom to develop ideas, and the ability to communicate ideas to others are stressed as important to the successful industrial scientist.

The Math/Science Encounter. *Barr Films*, 1984. 24 min. Color. $540 (16mm); $540 (video). Teacher's guide. ▶ **EA,JH**

In this well-done film an enthusiastic soccer player but unmotivated student is removed from the team because of a failing math grade. His disgruntlement at being tutored by the class brain turns into admiration for and fascination with the wonders of math and science and how they can be translated into easy-to-do projects, such as shooting off a homemade rocket. Realistic in situation and dialogue, the film is extremely appealing as a motivator for student interest in math and science and is a good introduction to the ways in which math and science can be used in everyday life.

The Story of Natural Resources. *Hawkhill Associates, Inc.*, 1985. (From the Time, Space, & Spirit Series.) 1 color filmstrip ea., 80 frames ea.; 1 cassette ea., 14–17 min. $39 ea. Teacher's guide. Also available in video. ▶ **JH**

How Scientists Think and Work.

Although *The Story of Natural Resources* presents an overly optimistic view of our control over nature, it does an excellent job of showing how people play an important part in the conservation and use of natural resources. *How Scientists Think and Work* dispels the notion that all scientists use only one scientific method. It shows scientists as human beings with different religious beliefs and life-styles. These filmstrips make good use of the historical approach to bring difficult topics to life.

372   Elementary education

Ask the Teacher. *Journal Films, Inc.*, 1984. (From the Mr. Microchip Series.) 26 min. Color. $300 (video); $30 (3-day rental). ▶ **EA,JH**

Does That Compute?

In *Does That Compute?*, Mr. Microchip presents the point that both computers and people can perceive—see and feel—but only people can understand; a robot demonstrates that it cannot interpret all that it senses in the same way as a human. Two children use a microphone and oscilloscope to make voice patterns on the screen. *Ask the Teacher* explains how the computer functions as a teaching machine. Mr. Microchip and one of his students program a few lines using the Pilot language to show that people are needed to program a lesson. The other student then tries the lesson as Mr. Microchip points out that one cannot vocally interrupt and interact with the machine as with a human teacher. He explains how computers are "taught" one step at a time with a small vocabulary, as are humans, but that a computer's vocabulary may be 150 words whereas a 10-year-old's is 15,000 words. Each session rapidly surveys a considerable amount of information. Teachers will need to review or explain specialized vocabulary and develop the topics presented.

Journey to Tomorrow: Excellence. *Walt Disney Educational Media Co.*, 1983. 20 min. Color. $445 (16mm); inquire for rental. Teacher's guide. ▶ **EA,JH**

This film combines animation and live footage to motivate young students to high achievement. The theme is developed in a logical sequence that begins with the many ways in which excellence can be defined. Using several examples, *Journey* emphasizes that the attainment of excellence requires goal setting, determination, and persistence. Individual examples of excellence include efforts in the arts, athletics, and science. The film's technical aspects are excellent, and its treatment of the topic is realistic.

Library Report. *Barr Films,* 1984. 24 min. Color. $535 (16mm); $535 (video); inquire for rental. Teacher's guide. ▶ **EA,JH**

Set in a future where everything is computerized, this film depicts a young teen, Beverly, who decides to have Kingpin, the family robot, write a four-page library report that she has been assigned. Kingpin tells her that he can only advise her how to proceed because research and writing require creative thinking, which he cannot do. Step by step, Kingpin shows Beverly how to select a topic, how to find and use the necessary library books, and how to take notes. Beverly conducts an interview, does her outline, prepares her final report on the word processor, and compiles her bibliography. Young students will relate to Beverly's dilemma and the film's humor and futuristic angle. The film will help teach students the basics of doing research, but it gives only an introduction to using library resources.

School Library Adventures of the Lollipop Dragon. *Society for Visual Education, Inc.,* 1982. 4 color filmstrips, 55 frames (average) ea.; 4 cassettes, 12 min. (average) ea. $130. Teacher's guide. ▶ **EP,EI**

The purpose of this filmstrip set is to encourage students to use and enjoy library/media centers. The first filmstrip is a general introduction to libraries. The second acquaints students with the types of materials in a library/media center, the function of the librarian/media specialist, and proper behavior in the facility. The third outlines the parts of a book and presents the concepts of alphabetization, arrangement of materials, Dewey Decimal classification, and card catalog. The last filmstrip introduces audio-visual software and hardware and includes a special section on microcomputers. Although the producer suggests that the set be presented in sequence, each filmstrip may also be shown individually. Recommended as a foundation for learning library skills.

Mathematics
and Physical
Sciences

See also 371.42 Careers.

501–502 Science: theory and techniques

The Challenge of the Unknown. *J.C. Crimmins & Co.*, 1984. (Prod.: Phillips Petroleum Co. and the American Association for the Advancement of Science; a 7-part series.) 20 min. ea. Color. Free loan (½-inch and ¾-inch video). Teacher's guide. ▶ **EA,JH**

Challenge is a series of seven films about problem-solving in mathematics, science, and technology. The films are intended for a wide range of math and science students, from elementary to high school (particularly those who need an appreciation of the practical applications of math). Each film is self-contained and addresses one phase of the problem-solving process: understanding the situation, obtaining information, evaluating the problem, understanding outcomes and setting goals, using estimation, and evaluating solutions. The humorous sequences will appeal to adolescents, and the many action scenes will attract attention and maintain interest.

Inferring in Science. *Agency for Instructional Technology*, 1983. (Part of the Whatabout Series.) 15 min. Color. $125 (video); $25 (rental). Teacher's guide. ▶ **EA,JH**

This brief film is one in a series of lessons intended to demonstrate the nature of scientific inquiry by showing how the scientific method is applied to real problems. A production of the University of Arizona, the series makes effective use of the university's scientists and facilities, in this case to demonstrate how scientists gather, interpret, and test data. The specific illustration is the work of a dendroclimatologist who extracts a growth-ring core from a living tree and then studies the pattern of ring widths in the laboratory. By inference, the scientist can reconstruct a lengthy record of growing-season weather. There is considerable question-and-answer dialogue between the interviewer and the scientist. A lively, well-conceived, and engaging program that should appeal to its intended audience.

Jiminy Cricket, P.S. (Problem-Solver). Walt Disney Educational Media Co., 1983. 10 min. Color. $245 (16mm). ▶ EA,JH

This brief film is highly entertaining and technically superb. The theme is how to solve a problem, in this case where Goofy should take his vacation. The solution stresses the scientific method—for example, identify the problem, "brainstorm" possible solutions, research and test the solutions, and evaluate the results. Students are shown that the use of libraries, experts, and other resources are vital to efficient problem-solving. The film will be of particular value in preparing students for science fairs or similar activities.

Observation Games. National Geographic Society, 1986. (From the Look, Listen, Explore Series.) 2 color filmstrips ea., 55 frames ea.; 2 cassettes ea., 10–12 min. ea. $61.95 ea. Teacher's guide. ▶ K,EP,EI

What Do You Think?

The first filmstrip in Observation Games presents groups of four diverse objects that have a common element and then asks the viewing children to supply the word in a rhyme that tells what the common element is. This filmstrip is well designed, the pictures are interesting, and the interactive aspect is handled well. The second filmstrip, not as appealing as the first, is designed to sharpen visual skills by having young children identify an object from a close-up of just a tiny part of the subject, followed by a picture showing more of the subject, and finally a riddle to help the viewer identify the subject. Part one of What Do You Think? encourages children to look and listen as they learn about some of the cycles that occur in nature. After viewing a series of changes, children are asked to answer questions and select the correct missing stage in a sequence. Part two is basically an informational piece about common and unusual careers that children might be interested in pursuing. Both parts ask the student to answer questions, solve riddles, identify sounds and shapes, find patterns, and follow directions.

Observing in Science. Agency for Instructional Technology, 1983. (Part of the Whatabout Series.) 15 min. Color. $125 (video); $25 (rental). Teacher's guide. ▶ EI,EA,JH

This well-done film introduces the skill of observation. In the opening scene, a young girl finds an overturned garbage can and suspects that the culprit is a neighbor's dog. Using photographs taken at night, the girl observes that the culprit is another type of animal. The film then discusses pollination of tropical plants by bats and the ultrasound and light-amplification equipment that were used to observe them. Finally, the film notes that to be a good observer you must have a keen eye, an inquiring mind, patience to stay with a project, and enthusiasm. Some good nature photography, but the audibility of the narration occasionally changes so that some of the words are lost. Teachers will need to introduce some of the film's concepts and define a number of terms so that students will get the full message.

Questioning in Science. Agency for Instructional Technology, 1983. (Part of the Whatabout Series.) 15 min. Color. $125 (video); $25 (rental). Teacher's guide. ▶ EA,JH

This worthy film begins by discussing the kinds of questions that should be asked when embarking on a family bike trip. Turning to food crops, the film states that a lot of land that could be used for raising food does not have enough fresh water to support crops. The film examines the saltbush, a plant not palatable for humans but one that can be eaten by chickens after processing. The solution then is to use the vast amount of salt water available to grow salt-tolerant plants that can be converted into animal protein, which people can then eat. The segment on food processing should have been shortened, and some discussion of the way plants are processed would have been helpful. In sum, the information is accurate, the technical quality is good, and the repetition of examples effectively stresses the importance of asking good questions.

507   Science: study and teaching
See also 170 Ethics; **Science Education** section.

Alike and Different. *National Geographic Society,* 1986. (From the Look, Listen, Explore Series.) 2 color filmstrips, 55 frames ea.; 2 cassettes, 10–12 min. ea. $61.95. Teacher's guide. ▶ **K,EP**

The first of two segments encourages children to compare how four animals— a duck, deer, wolf, and crocodile—are alike and different in their styles of moving and eating, and in the number and names of their offspring. This segment promotes interest and active listening by involving children in "animal games" that encourage them to observe the animals around them and explore the ways in which they are alike and different. Part two shows children how to identify parts of a plant. Active listening and participation are promoted through "plant games" (counting petals on various flowers, for example), and children are encouraged to observe other plants and note how they are alike and different. Overall, the good photography and interactive feature offer a useful and effective teaching tool for young children.

Developing a Science Fair Project. *Library Filmstrip Center,* 1981. 1 color filmstrip, 51 frames; 1 cassette, 20 min. $39. ▶ **EA,JH**

This filmstrip clearly outlines the steps a student should take to prepare a successful science project. It emphasizes that the learning process is in itself a measure of success and that there are no losers in science fairs. The film also points out that a modest project that is well done is better than an unfinished project that was too ambitious. There is special emphasis on safety and the careful use of hazardous chemicals. Clear enough for use with fifth or sixth graders.

OWL/TV. *Bullfrog Films,* 1985. (Prod.: National Audubon Society and the Young Naturalist Foundation; a 10-part series.) 29 min. ea. Color. $285 (¾-inch video ea.); $275 (½-inch video ea.); $2,350 (¾-inch video, series); $2,200 (½-inch video, series). Teacher's guide. Duplication rights available. ▶ **EI,EA**

OWL/TV programs provide children with a fast-paced, usually interesting, sometimes amusing, often creative, and always varied look at nature, scientific phenomena, and our environment. Although some information is presented, the overall purpose is clearly to spark discussions, activities, and additional investigations. Supplementary materials include a teacher's guide and *OWL* magazine for children. Both publications are filled with experiments and activities that can be done with readily available materials. The programs are generally led by children of the same age as the intended audience. A delightful balance of realism and fantasy add to the appeal of these stimulating presentations.

What You Can See and Hear. *National Geographic Society,* 1985. (From the Look, Listen, Explore Series.) 2 color filmstrips, 55 frames ea.; 2 cassettes, 10–12 min. ea. $61.95. Teacher's guide. ▶ **K**

The first segment introduces young children to animal sights and sounds. Slides showing forest animals are accompanied by activities such as listening for the sounds of a woodpecker and looking for a cardinal sitting on a snow-covered branch. The second filmstrip depicts the sights and sounds of a bustling urban scene. Riddles provide hints to questions that can be answered from the pictures. The quality of this set is mixed: while the photography is good and the interactive techniques are excellent, some of the sounds are poorly recorded and some of the activities present confusing messages.

Where Do Lost Balloons Go? *Coronet Films & Video,* 1986. (From The Wonder World of Science Series.) 11 min. ea. Color. $320 (16mm ea.); $225 (video ea.); $75 (rental ea.). ▶ **EI,EA**

Why Doesn't Grass Grow on the Moon?

Through a skillful blend of live and animated sequences, *Where Do Lost Balloons Go?* leads children from daily observations to scientific principles that explain what happens to a helium-filled balloon when it is released out of doors. The film moves, through a series of questions, from what a child already knows to new information. It demonstrates careful attention by the producers to the logical processes of inquiry as well as to clear presentation of information. *Why Doesn't Grass Grow on the Moon?* is an exceptionally good science film—not only does it present scientific information of interest to the intended audience, but it does so in a manner that places new facts in the context of observations that most children have either made or can easily understand. From these observations, the film leads the viewer through a logical derivation of the principles and concepts that explain why grass does not grow on the moon. These principles are then reinforced through an exploration of what would need to be done to make grass grow on the moon. The film is an exemplary model of how science concepts and processes can be appropriately combined into a presentation for children.

510   Mathematics

Beginning Mathematics: Box Introduces Division. *Society for Visual Education, Inc.,* 1984. 3 color filmstrips ea., 55 frames (average ea.); 3 cassettes ea., 9 min. (average ea.). $119 ea. Teacher's guide and worksheets. Optional microcomputer disc. ▶ **EI**

Beginning Mathematics: Box Introduces Multiplication.

These two filmstrip sets use a character, Box, to adequately introduce division and multiplication, although additional information will be required to reinforce the lessons. In *Division,* Box points out the relationship of division to subtraction, the elements of a division sentence and how to write it from left to right, the relation of division to multiplication through fact families, and how to divide simple numbers with the aid of arrays. In *Multiplication,* Box shows students the relationship of multiplication to addition, the elements of a multiplication sentence and how to write it either from left to right or vertically, by the commutative property of multiplication, how to multiply simple numbers with the aid of arrays, and the different meanings of the factors in multiplication.

Beginning Mathematics: Box Introduces Fractions. *Society for Visual Education, Inc.,* 1987. 3 color filmstrips, 37 frames ea.; 3 cassettes, 8 min. ea. $38.50 (ea.); $134 (set). 18 skill sheets and software available. ▶ **EI,EA**

These filmstrips provide a thorough introduction to the concept of fractional parts of objects. Graphics rather than photographs keep the presentation from being dated, especially since the focus is on an animated box and a young black girl. In part one, plans are made for a party, and the first objects cut into fractional parts are cakes. In part two, party toys and favors are purchased, which can be grouped easily into sets and regions with fractional parts that can be identified. Part three compares fractions and reviews the naming of various fractions. The instruction in this program is clear and concise, and the examples provided are good illustrations of the information presented.

Beginning Mathematics: Box Introduces Numbers. *Society for Visual Education, Inc.,* 1984. 3 color filmstrips, 55 frames (average); 3 cassettes, 9 min. (average). $119. Teacher's guide and worksheets. Optional microcomputer disc. ▶ **K,EP**

This filmstrip set introduces preschool or early primary students to the basic mathematical concepts that underlie arithmetic. Together with its ancillary materials, the set is an organized and accurate program that creative teachers will find useful. The set's technical quality is excellent, and the illustrations should hold student interest.

Decimals: Place Value in Decimals. *Agency for Instructional Technology,* 1986. (From the Math Works Series.) 15 min. ea. Color. $125 (video ea.). Inquire for rental. Teacher's guide available. ▶ **EA,JH**

Mental Computation: Using Mental Computation for Addition.

In *Decimals,* several stories illustrate the importance of reading decimals correctly. A cartoon section reinforces the theme. The student worksheet in the teacher's guide stresses understanding of decimals with color-in grids. Within the context of a magic show, *Mental Computation* offers two methods for mentally calculating the results of addition problems: the ancient left-right method and the plus-minus method. Although some students may find some of the explanations too quick, they should get a good start in understanding the techniques, which can then be reinforced by the worksheet in the teacher's guide. Recommended, although a number of the examples could be improved.

Figure Out Series. *Agency for Instructional Technology,* 1982. 15 min. ea. Color. $110 ea. (video); inquire for rental. Teacher's guide. ▶ **EA**

This review covers the first four of 15 programs in math for grades five and six; topics are place value, reading numbers, estimating to tens and hundreds, and estimating to thousands. Each unit features a story about the adventures of a young girl and her friend Mac the computer. The units have excellent electronic graphics, casting, acting, and overall video production. Although at times the learning segments move too fast, there is sufficient reinforcement to make the topics understandable, and the mix of math with story is good. A teacher's guide—with pre- and post-viewing activities and questions but no answers—enhances this already fine series.

Math for Every Season. *National Geographic Society,* 1985. (From the Look, Listen, Explore Series.) 2 color filmstrips, 55 frames ea.; 2 cassettes, 10–12 min. ea. $61.95. Teacher's guide. ▶ **K,EP**

Both filmstrips follow the seasonal changes of an organism and encourage student participation (mainly counting) during viewing. The information presented is accurate, and the presentation is of good quality. The first filmstrip examines the growth cycle of pumpkins, the second deals with birds. The teacher's guide contains background information and classroom activities to strengthen skills in counting, classifying, comparing, and identifying number combinations.

Mathematics for Primary Software Films Series. *AIMS Media, Inc.,* 1986. 4 programs, 7–9 min. ea. Color. $99.95 (video ea.; program master disc, film data disc, program guide); $199.80 (series). User's manual. ▶ **EP,EI**

The video portion of this package defines and demonstrates mathematics by using visual representation groups (sets of objects), empty sets, equivalent sets, mathematical sentences, arrays (rectangular arrangements), pairs, and remainders. The *Software-Film User's Manual* (for the teacher) has a good step-by-step guide for getting started, editing command keystrokes, and administration options such as editing questions, modifying variables, and printing reports on student performance on the computer-based portion of the package. The four concept discs present addition, subtraction, multiplication, and division. The quality of the video is good, and the software would be useful for a class familiar with computers.

Mathscore One. *Films Inc.,* 1983. (A 10-part series.) 20 min. ea. Color. $200 (video ea.); $2,000 (series); $50 (rental ea.). ▶ **EI,EA,JH**

Four of the ten parts in this series were reviewed. The material is well chosen and interesting. In the part on fractions, the narrators use dots, paper folding, sets of tiles of different colors, and groups of girls and boys to illustrate fractions and their equivalencies. In the part on bar graphs, they use stacks of fruit pies to develop the concepts, and then the narrators emphasize the necessity for labeling. The part on coordinate systems starts with a number-letter grid and proceeds to the concept of ordered pairs. Each part has some suitable humor. One possible drawback is that the narrators' British accents may distract American students. Useful as supplementary material or as an introduction or review of the various topics.

Mathscore Two. *Films Inc.,* 1983. (A 10-part series.) 20 min. ea. Color. $200 (video ea.); $2,000 (series); $50 (rental ea.). ▶ **EA,JH**

The format for the series includes a short, humorous skit that involves a math problem, an introduction that explains the resolution of the problem and gives several examples of the concept being considered, a quick verbal quiz, answers to the quiz, expanded commentary on the concept, and a flashy closing scene. The style is clear; the pace is quick but not too fast. Each topic is illustrated with numerous concrete examples, including a number line and blocks for counting where appropriate. The visual aids are excellent and memorable. The topics covered include addition and subtraction, fractions, angles, decimals, bar graphs, area, symmetry, sequences, line graphs, and mass and volume. Coverage includes information beyond the basics and encourages thought and understanding through concrete examples. The series should reinforce and supplement classroom material, as it assumes a basic knowledge of the mathematical manipulations while showing how they work.

Problem Solving with Math Skills I. *Encyclopaedia Britannica Educational Corp.,* 1984. 6 color filmstrips, 60 frames (average); 6 cassettes, 12 min. ea. $168. Teacher's guide. ▶ **EP,EI,EA,JH**

This filmstrip set covers the concepts and strategies that are involved in solving various problems in math. Each part concentrates on one procedure or concept and thus is suitable as introduction, reinforcement, or review. The set's varying methods of attack should keep students' interest as well as enlarge their experience in the methods of approach. The first filmstrip addresses the common problem children have in deciding which operation to use in story problems. Methods, such as visual comparison and counting, are excellently presented. The storyline in the last part involves students who use problem solving to help their teacher. Overall, the accuracy of the information and technical quality are excellent, and the set is interesting and well organized. Although intended for fourth- to sixth-grade students, first- and second-grade students can understand the set, and it will also be useful for slow learners in junior high.

Problem Solving with Math Skills II. *Encyclopaedia Britannica Educational Corp.,* 1984. 6 color filmstrips, 60 frames (average); 6 cassettes, 12 min. ea. $168. Teacher's guide. ▶ **JH**

This filmstrip provides junior-high students with relevant applications of math topics such as ratio, percent, and area. It represents a means for them to understand the utility of math in practical situations and offers a few tips on how they may use math in their future careers. The filmstrip's visual content is quite strong; it is clear, organized, and understandable. However, the section on graphs might be a little too advanced for the audience because of its economic references and vocabulary.

Symmetry: A First Film. *Phoenix Films & Video, Inc.,* 1983. 14 min. Color. $280 (16mm); $30 (one-day rental). ▶ **EA,JH**

This attractive film brings art and mathematics together to introduce some aspects of symmetry. A variety of clear, delightful, color illustrations (paper cutting, ink blots, forms from nature and the arts, and human activities) are accompanied by a pleasing narration. The intuitive presentation completely avoids mathematical terminology as it covers balance, symmetry with respect to one or more lines ("mirror" and "radial" symmetry), rhythm, and asymmetry. Overall, the animation and the technical quality are excellent, but the film's scope is only fair and there are some confusing repetitions and examples.

Understanding Charts and Graphs. *Society for Visual Education, Inc.,* 1987. 3 color filmstrips, 57–69 frames ea.; 3 cassettes, 9–12:25 min. ea. $38.50 (ea.); $134 (set). 24 skill sheets and software available. Teacher's guide. ▶ **EI,EA**

In this excellent program, two fantasy figures show students how to use charts and graphs to organize and display information. The material is presented in a logical progression, from demonstrating a need for a chart or graph to organizing a random collection of facts and showing how to interpret such information and use it in problem-solving. Worksheets and computer software provide related activities that can offer individualized instruction and hands-on experience with the material.

520 Astronomy

Exploring Our Solar System. *Society for Visual Education, Inc.*, 1982. 4 color filmstrips, 55 frames (average) ea.; 4 cassettes, 13 min. (average) ea. $130. Teacher's guide. ▶ EI,EA

Exploring Our Solar System is a four-part teaching program with comprehensive lesson plans for the teacher and study sheets and tests for students. The four parts are entitled "Introduction to the Solar System," "Our Planet Earth," "The Inner Planet," and "The Outer Planet." Artwork is used along with photographs from NASA to give vivid pictures of the solar system. The information is current. The set could be the core of a unit on the solar system in grade four, and might be useful for older students as an introduction or review.

The Heavens on Tape. *Astronomical Society of the Pacific*, 1986. 2 cassettes, 25 min. ea. $14.95 plus $2.00 postage and handling. Transcripts and maps available. ▶ EA,JH

These two cassettes, together with their scripts and maps, constitute an excellent tool to use while viewing the night skies. The listener is carefully led from one constellation to another and to the brighter unassociated stars until all of the prominent features are covered. The narration is clear and leisurely so that the observer has ample time to follow and understand. The script enables one to study the program either before or after viewing to ensure familiarity with the sky. The maps, which relate closely to the scripts, are exceptionally easy to follow. However, the tapes and the sky itself will be enough without the viewer bringing a flashlight to read the script.

Is Anyone Out There? The Quest for Extraterrestrial Life. *Knowledge Unlimited*, 1984. 1 color filmstrip, 39 frames. $13 ($8 for optional cassette). Teacher's guide. ▶ EI,EA,JH

This competent and balanced presentation of the scientific and philosophical aspects of the debate on extraterrestrial life gives teachers a much-needed resource. The filmstrip clearly distinguishes among speculation, belief, and argument, carefully using modifiers such as "many," "most," and "some" to identify scientists and others who hold various positions on this question. It nicely explains why a probable majority of scientists now believe that extraterrestrial life exists despite only the most indirect evidence. The optional cassette tape has two sides—a general discussion suitable for grade school students and an advanced discussion that is also suitable for adult audiences.

Meteorites: Everyman's Space Probe. *Enjoy Communicating, Inc.*, 1987. 1 color filmstrip, 65 frames; 1 cassette, 18 min. $32.50. Teacher's guide. ▶ EA,JH

In this fact-filled educational package, the information is accurate, the narration excellent (no distracting background music), and the visuals sharp and clear. After a historical introduction to the phenomenon of meteorites, the filmstrip describes what they are and where they come from. The chemistry and mineralogy of meteorites help explain why they are important to our understanding of the universe. The teacher's guide is too short and contains errors; a more extensive teacher's guide would greatly increase the usefulness of this material.

The Planet That Got Knocked on Its Side. *Coronet Films & Video*, 1987. (Prod.: "NOVA") 60 min. Color. $250 (video); $125 (rental). ▶ EA,JH

This is an accurate and engaging account of how today's technology has been harnessed to explore Uranus. It is exciting to see the unique ways in which data from Uranus are secured through combinations of computers and cameras. The animation is especially helpful in showing how data are linked to make a model. The film would be especially useful for stimulating students' thinking about how our knowledge is expanded through the use of new technology.

The Solar System and Beyond. *National Geographic Society*, 1985. 4 color filmstrips, 55 frames ea.; 4 cassettes, 15 min. ea. $109.95. Teacher's guide. ▶ **EA,JH**

This filmstrip set describes the sun, earth and moon, the nine planets, the asteroids, comets, and meteorites, and the stars and galaxies. Each filmstrip is so well done that the teacher's guide is almost superfluous. The sound, color, and narration are superb. The choice of photographs, drawings, paintings, and schematics is excellent. Students younger than grade five could certainly enjoy this filmstrip set, and older students with no previous introduction to astronomy could benefit from it.

The Story of the Expanding Universe. *Hawkhill Associates, Inc.*, 1985. (From the Time, Space, & Spirit Series.) 1 color filmstrip, 80 frames; 1 cassette, 17 min. $39. Teacher's guide. Also available in video. ▶ **EA,JH**

This fast-paced, generally accurate filmstrip surveys the universe from the inside moving outward. It is colorful, generally well narrated, and comprehensive. The pace is good, and the music is generally not intrusive, except at the beginning. Like all filmstrips that survey a broad topic, this one tends to be encyclopedic, is extremely dense with new terms and topics, and contains a few minor lapses.

The Sun Dagger. *Bullfrog Films*, 1982. 28 min. Color. $450 (16mm); $225 (video); $50 (rental); 59 min. Color. $850 (16mm); $450 (video); $95 (rental). ▶ **EA,JH**

Both the one-hour and half-hour version of *Sun Dagger* visually depict the interplay of the sun, moon, and rocks at Fajada Butte in the Chaco Canyon of New Mexico. The time-lapse photography is used most effectively to illustrate precisely how the sun, stone slabs, and etched spirals are used to record the summer and winter solstices as well as the spring and fall equinoxes. The astronomical observations represented by the Sun Dagger are placed very effectively in the cultural and historical context of the Indians of the American Southwest. Both versions of the film are excellent, but the longer one is the more provocative film.

The Universe: Frontiers of Discovery, Part 1—The Solar System. *National Geographic Society*, 1984. 5 color filmstrips, 61–73 frames ea.; 5 cassettes, 20 min. (average). $129.50; $188.50 (Parts 1 and 2). Teacher's guides. ▶ **EA,JH**

The Universe: Frontiers of Discovery, Part 2—Deep Space and the Mysteries of the Cosmos. 3 color filmstrips; 72–75 frames ea.; 3 cassettes, 20 min. (average). $79.50.

Part 1 of this handsome, accurate, up-to-date filmstrip set covers the sun, our moon, the inner and outer planets, and asteroids, meteoroids, and comets. The illustrations and the narration are clear, well organized, and complete without being overwhelming. Each filmstrip ends by suggesting that there are still many unanswered questions; unfortunately, the set does not give specific ideas for discussion or student activities. Part 2 covers stars, galaxies, the universe, and the possibilities of life elsewhere. The exceptionally clear text describes theories, speculations, and our tentative understanding of a far more mysterious realm—deep space. The narration leaves much room for wonder, and although quite poetic at times, it presents many facts in an orderly and clear fashion. Great care is taken in developing such complex ideas as the life cycles of stars, the red shift and dynamics of the universe, and the nature of life and our search for it in other places.

530–540 Physics and chemistry
See also 371.42 Careers; 621 Applied physics.

Basic Primary Science: Learning About the Physical Sciences. *Society for Visual Education, Inc.,* 1984. 4 color filmstrips, 53 frames (average); 4 cassettes, 9 min. (average). $149. Teacher's guide and worksheets. ▶ **EP,EI**

Matter, molecules, energy and motion, light and color, and waves and patterns are addressed in this filmstrip set. It is cumulative in its approach, introducing new concepts with each new filmstrip while reinforcing others previously explored. The set's strength is its information, although the realistic and colorful pictures add to viewers' interest. The information is accurate and precise but not too sophisticated for young children. This set is good as long as it is used only supplementally. Its concepts can be confusing if not thoroughly and carefully explained by teachers.

The Behavior of Matter. *Encyclopaedia Britannica Educational Corp.,* 1982. 15 min. Color. $290 (16mm); $29 (rental); inquire for video prices. Teacher's guide. ▶ **EA,JH**

This film begins with comments on the use of models in science and then uses the atomic-molecular model to discuss solids, liquids, gases, and physical and chemical changes. Animated dots representing molecules are shown moving in appropriate ways for solids, liquids, and gases. The dots are juxtaposed with pictures of real solids and liquids plus clouds of vapors. The dots are not used effectively to support a solid's crystalline structure that breaks down when heated, and the animated model of chemical change through addition did not mesh very well with the examples of combustion or decomposition. Other than this, the film is clear and accurate. The animation techniques are of high quality, and the narration is well written and flows smoothly.

Buoyancy. *Coronet Films & Video,* 1985. 15 min. Color. $345 (16mm); $240 (video); $45 (rental). Teacher's guide. ▶ **EA,JH**

This film explains a topic of general interest in a clever and intriguing manner. Questions are proposed and experiments conducted to find the answers. From the colorful experiments, the concepts of density, specific gravity, and Archimedes principle are reached. A one-page teacher's guide furnishes valuable suggestions for introducing the film and for discussion afterwards.

Heat and Energy Transfer. *Coronet Films & Video,* 1985. (From the Physical Science Series.) 13 min. Color. $310 (16mm); $220 (video); $50 (rental). ▶ **EA,JH**

This film focuses on the two ways in which objects can acquire heat: by transformation of other kinds of energy and by transfer of heat between and within substances. In explaining how energy is transformed into heat, the film covers friction (mechanical), resistance (electrical), flame (chemical), the sun (nuclear), and geological mechanisms (claimed to be nuclear). Includes a very good explanation of why good electrical conductors are also good heat conductors. The script is generally accurate, but the scenes used to illustrate it sometimes miss the mark.

Inclined Planes. *Coronet Films and Video,* 1984. (Part of the Simple Machines Series, 2nd edition.) 12 min. ea. Color. $300 (16mm ea.); $205 (video ea.); $40 (rental ea.). ▶ **EA,JH**

Levers.

Pulleys.

Wheels and Axles.

Working Together.

These five films use animated cartoons featuring prehistoric man (the main character) and funny prehistoric animals and situations for humor and interest. *Inclined Planes* demonstrates that less force is needed to push a boulder up a slope than to lift it. The variation of force in relation to the angle of inclination is clearly shown; the wedge, chisel, hatchet, slicing knife, spiraling road, and threads of a screw are all dealt with as examples of inclined planes. In *Levers,* the discussion proceeds logically and clearly from simple seesaws to scissors, pliers, grass clippers, wheelbarrows, and nutcrackers. The film covers a lot of ground, posing many "what if" questions and discussing tradeoffs among force, speed, and distance in each type of lever discussed. *Pulleys* shows how to change a push to a pull, how to increase or decrease the length or force of a pull, what the advantages of counterweights and tradeoffs between distance and force are, and how to use multiple pulleys to advantage. Elevators, cranes, and similar devices are briefly discussed. *Wheels and Axles* uses no mathematics; rather, using illustrations and statements devoid of jargon, it develops a qualitative feel for applied force and distances turned or rolled by wheels of different sizes. Students may need assistance to understand how force varies with a wheel's diameter, but overall, the film adequately presents physical properties of simple wheels and axles. *Working Together* illustrates the principles of simple machines. Work, input, output, and mechanical advantage are precisely defined and demonstrated, with visuals that are clear, colorful, and uncluttered. The use of humor significantly increases the effectiveness of these films as teaching tools.

Introducing Simple Machines. *Society for Visual Education, Inc.,* 1983. 6 color filmstrips, 43 frames (average); 6 cassettes, 10 min. (average). $180. Teacher's guide. ▶ **EA,JH**

This filmstrip set amply illustrates the operation of several simple machines—lever, inclined plane, wheel and axle, pulley, and wedge—and shows how complex tools are made from combinations of simple ones. Several of the filmstrips in this attractive set start with the machine's invention and then move to modern applications. The same examples are used throughout, providing continuity (or boredom). Useful in either a physical or general science course.

Introduction to Basic Physical Science. *Educational Dimensions Group,* 1982. 4 color filmstrips, 80 frames ea.; 4 cassettes, 20 min. ea. $146. o.n. 1256CB. Teacher's guide. ▶ **EA,JH**

This four-part filmstrip set introduces students to the physical sciences. The four parts cover matter, oxidation and the chemistry of water, light energy and color, force, motion and simple machines, and wave motion and sound energy. Although three of the filmstrips develop the science concepts logically, it is unclear why the chemistry of water follows a discussion of matter and oxidation in part one. Simple demonstrations in the filmstrips can be repeated in the classroom. These materials are an excellent supplement to any textbook and provide a concise review for students who need additional help.

Light. *Barr Films*, 1986. 11 min. Color. $275 (16mm); $275 (video). Teacher's guide. ▶ **EP,EI**

Sound. 12 min. $295 (16mm); $295 (video).

This delightful film on light has just enough fantasy and whimsy to attract and keep the attention of its young audience. *Light* clearly presents a few concepts about light, including reflection, refraction, and making a rainbow with a prism. The teacher's guide gives descriptions of concepts in well-planned rhymes. The activities are easy to do, and the script is not encumbered by too many or extraneous concepts or material. *Sound* presents some sound concepts in a whimsical manner that will hold the interest of the intended young audience. Sound waves, the speed of sound, echoes, and vibrations are all briefly introduced. The activities are easy to do in the classroom, and the film may well be requested for repeated showings.

Mass and Density: Investigating Matter. *AIMS Media*, 1986. 20 min. Color. $450 (16mm); $335 (video); $60 (rental). Study guide. ▶ **EA,JH**

Detective Will Slater, a crime lab sleuth, has been investigating mass, density, volume, weight, gravitational attraction, and buoyancy. The local junior high teacher calls on Slater to provide the information and evidence needed for the youngsters in his class to learn about these concepts. The film uses excellent graphics and examples, in a step-by-step process to show the relationships among mass, volume, and density. The film presents simple demonstrations and experiments that can be easily duplicated in the classroom to illustrate conservation of mass, density, and buoyancy. This very useful program can easily be stopped after each sequence, allowing the teacher to reinforce the material shown and evaluate student comprehension.

Physical Science: Energy at Work. *Churchill Films*, 1984. (Part of the Physical Science Series.) 13 min. Color. $285 (16mm); $285 (video); inquire for rental. Teacher's guide. ▶ **EA,JH**

Physical Science: Heat Energy. 15 min. $325 (16mm); $325 (video).

Beginning with an attention-grabbing opener—the operation of a Rube Goldberg device by two young students—*Energy at Work* is enlivened by its young actors and its notable lack of adults in white coats. Without referring to it by name, this accurate and technically excellent film conveys the idea of energy conservation. Transformations of energy from one form to another are illustrated with examples chosen from daily experience. The concept of efficiency and the fact that not all of energy output is useful are mentioned. *Heat Energy* begins by describing heat energy as the kinetic energy of molecules, using about 30 children to represent molecules. Temperature and its measurement are carefully distinguished from heat with the aid of demonstrations that students can easily reproduce. Examples of heat energy use in society appear regularly, and this competent film concludes with descriptions of the three means of heat transfer—conduction, convection, and radiation. The excellent teacher's guide provides a couple of projects and some discussion questions to motivate thinking about heat energy. In addition to being scientifically accurate, the film has entertaining touches that will hold students' attention throughout.

Physical Science: Mechanical Energy. *Churchill Films,* 1984. (Part of the Physical Science Series.) 15 min. Color. $325 (16mm); $325 (video); inquire for rental. Teacher's guide. ▶ **EA**

This film develops the concept of mechanical energy and relates it to molecules moving together and exerting forces, using the clearly narrated and animated example of the internal combustion engine. While the film deals with work, its exact relationship to force and distance is not mentioned. Levers and the wheel are used to illustrate mechanical advantage as the multiplication of force; unfortunately, the concept of conservation of work is omitted. Overall, the excellent use of attractive visuals, imaginative scale models, and "human animation" (children modeling the behavior of molecules in thawing ice cream) make this a good film for grade-school students.

Potential and Kinetic Energy. *Films for the Humanities, Inc.,* 1987. (From the Concepts in Physics Series.) 10 min. Color. $179 (¾-inch video); $129 (½-inch video). ▶ **EA,JH**

This film illustrates the relationships between the mass and speed of an object (kinetic energy) and the work it can do, and the mass and the distance that an object can fall (gravitational potential energy) and the work it can do. Two different experimental setups illustrate these relationships in a clear, non-mathematical manner. (Some teachers will wish for measurements in order to discuss the demonstrations quantitatively.) A third demonstration illustrates the conversion of kinetic energy into potential energy and back again. In some places, the film is confusing, switching from potential to kinetic energy without notice. Terms are used without first being defined, and "weight" is used when "mass" would be more appropriate.

Solid, Liquid, Gas. *National Geographic Society,* 1986. 16 min. Color. $350 (16mm); $245 (video). Teacher's guide. ▶ **EP,EI**

This film introduces matter in its three states. Many common examples of each state are clearly illustrated, and many simple experiments are demonstrated by early elementary school children. The film is short, direct, and holds young students' interest throughout. It emphasizes and reviews key points carefully. An excellent addition to any classroom's resources.

Solids, Liquids, and Gases. *National Geographic Society,* 1982. 1 color filmstrip, 52 frames; 1 cassette, 15 min. $24.50. o.n. 04544. Teacher's guide. ▶ **EI,EA**

The identification of and the distinguishing characteristics of the three states of matter are the focus of this filmstrip. Each state is described, and the properties that make each different from the other two states are illustrated. The properties of mass, volume, and shape are used to emphasize the similarities among all materials in any given state. Temperature variation is identified as the cause of change from one state to another for any specific substance. Each concept is illustrated in several ways by showing the interactions of children with various substances. The presentation does not attempt to explain the three states of matter in terms of molecular motion.

3-2-1 Contact: Forces and Motion. *Guidance Associates,* 1985. (Part of the Children's Television Workshop Series; a 5-part series.) 60 min. Color. $895 (16mm); $209 (¾-inch video); $179 (½-inch video). Teacher's guide. Also available in filmstrip. ▶ **EI,EA,JH**

This film introduces the difficult concepts of gravity, force, motion, and buoyancy by using real-life examples that are familiar to children. Graphics, simple demonstrations, and animated segments are interspersed with interviews and live-action sequences to provide a fast-moving but accurate explanation of the phenomenon presented. (One segment that attempts to define weight will be difficult for elementary students to understand.) The examples range from a roller coaster ride, which is used to explain centrifugal force, to the exciting finale of a chain reaction of 100,000 dominoes. Teachers can easily select segments out of sequence to support their lesson plans.

Using Simple Machines. *Walt Disney Educational Media Co.,* 1986. 15 min. Color. $389 (16mm); $292 (video); $60 (3-day rental). Teacher's guide. Also available in filmstrip. ▶ **EI,EA**

Accompanied by a soft rock beat, this excellent short film explains simple machines. Using a lever as the primary example, the film gives an appropriate definition of force and mechanical advantage and shows how to calculate the latter. The mechanical advantages of inclined planes, pulleys, and wedges are shown. The film illustrates each description of a simple machine with a quickly flashed example—for example, images of a wheelbarrow, scissors, pliers, and car jack follow the lever demonstration. The personable young actors are appealing, and the Rube Goldberg–type machine they construct to end the film is delightful.

537–538 Electricity and magnetism

Electric Currents and Circuits. *Coronet Films & Video,* 1985. (From the Physical Science Series.) 16 min. ea. Color. $385 (16mm); $255 (video); $50 (rental ea.). ▶ **EA,JH**

Electricity and Magnetism.

Static and Current Electricity. $365 (16mm); $250 (video).

The straightforward narration in the well-paced *Electric Currents and Circuits* logically explains the fundamentals of electric current and circuits. Illustrations and examples are used effectively to explain, in easy-to-understand terms, the principles of voltage, current, and resistance as well as the differences between series and parallel circuits. Examples used range from large power-distribution circuits to microcircuits in computers. *Currents and Circuits* concludes by showing how electricity is used to produce light, heat, sound, and motion, emphasizing the importance of electrical energy to the operation of our society. An excellent film for any science class just beginning a unit on electricity. The fast-paced *Electricity and Magnetism* follows a well-organized progression of ideas that holds the viewer's attention and explains the fundamental relationships between electricity and magnetism without the clutter of irrelevant details. Illustrations and examples are used effectively to present the concepts understandably. The film continually emphasizes the relationships among current, magnetism, and motion. It builds on these relationships to illustrate the operational principles of motors, generators, solenoids, transformers, and electromagnets. Many practical applications are given. An excellent film for any upper-elementary, junior-high, or introductory high-school science class in electricity and magnetism. The use of a clothes dryer to demonstrate static electricity brings the subject of *Static and Current Electricity* down to earth for students, even though the film then animates the dryer and puts it in orbit to illustrate how a charge is maintained on electrically isolated objects. The film makes good use of animation and physical demonstrations. It compares static electricity with current (dynamic) electricity, and it puts all these concepts into familiar contexts, using an electrostatic copier and the charge storage capacitor of a photographic flash as examples. Only in the description of arc welding does the film falter, explaining it as a series of lightning discharges.

Learning About Electricity. *AIMS Media*, 1986. 16 min. Color. $380 (16mm); $285 (video); $50 (rental). ▶ **EA,JH**

Using simple demonstrations and examples, this film conveys the importance of electricity in everyday life. It shows children using common household materials to produce static electricity. The vocabulary is well chosen, and new words and scientific terms are defined when used for the first time. There is excellent use of graphics to explain circuits. Throughout, the film emphasizes safety and cautions children about the dangers of electricity.

Magnets! Magnets! *Barr Films*, 1986. 12 min. Color. $295 (16mm); $295 (video). Discussion guide. ▶ **K,EP**

The bright, clean, close-up photography and simple narration invite young children to experiment with the safe and fascinating physical force of magnetism. Educators and educational film makers should be encouraged to stimulate a sense of wonder, so this film is recommended with some minor criticism. First, in showing the objects that are susceptible to magnetic attraction, the film gives the impression that all metals are alike in this respect. Secondly, the film ends abruptly without a summing up of concepts presented.

Physical Science: Electrical Energy. *Churchill Films*, 1984. (Part of the Physical Science Series.) 13 min. Color. $295 (16mm); $295 (video); inquire for rental. Teacher's guide. ▶ **EA,JH**

The objectives of this film, as outlined in the guide, are mostly met. Students will understand that electricity is a form of energy present in electrons and protons within atoms and be able to describe how static electricity is formed. In describing the concept of electric current, an animation of a flow of electrons in a conductor connected to the poles of a battery is used. A simple demonstration alternator is shown and its operation is illuminated by animation. When shown to fifth and sixth graders, the film stimulated many to want to build their own versions of the copper-zinc acid battery or the steam-driven generator.

539 Fission and fusion

Atomic Energy: Inside the Atom, 2nd edition. *Encyclopaedia Britannica Educational Corp.*, 1982. 14 min. Color. $290 (16mm); $29 (rental); inquire for video prices. o.n. 3726. Teacher's guide. ▶ **JH**

This film explores the processes by which energy is released from atomic nuclei. Radioactivity, fission, and fusion are depicted through animation with illustrative applications, but the major emphasis is on fission. The treatment of radioactivity is basic and does not distinguish among the different decay processes. Nevertheless, the animation, which is quite good, and the demonstrations of chain reactions make the film worth viewing.

Fusion: The Ultimate Energy Answer? *Knowledge Unlimited,* 1983. 1 color filmstrip, 26 frames. $13 ($8 for optional cassette). Teacher's guide. ▶ EI,EA,JH

This filmstrip tells the story of nuclear fusion—why it is needed, what it is, the present state of development of the three current lines of research, and future prospects. The narrative is available at two levels—one for the lower grades and one for high-school and nonscience college students. The filmstrip is well narrated, well paced, and fairly complete; however, the story is already so well known that the filmstrip may not appeal to the informed student.

541 Chemical interactions

Chemistry: Elements, Compounds and Mixtures, 2nd edition. *Coronet Films & Video,* 1983. (Part of the Chemistry Series.) 20 min. Color. $453 (16mm); $274 (video); inquire for rental. Teacher's guide. ▶ EA,JH

This film draws the distinctions among elements, compounds, and mixtures through images that raise awareness of the forms of matter found in the world. It also depicts some physical and chemical means of identifying and separating elements and compounds, such as spectroscopy, melting points, boiling points, electrolysis, and sedimentation. High marks for content and accuracy of information, although the visuals do not always carry forward the narrative.

Learning About Chemicals. *National Geographic Society,* 1984. 2 color filmstrips, 55–58 frames ea.; 2 cassettes, 17 min. ea. $59.95. Teacher's guides. ▶ EA,JH

This filmstrip set stresses the idea that chemicals and chemical processes are all around us in our everyday life. The photography is excellent, but the narration is flat. The set's major flaw is one of approach. The script flows in an expository manner that would encourage students to memorize the content rather than to understand the meaning of the concepts. Many of the set's examples can be brought into the classroom and discussed and demonstrated by the teacher in a more inductive manner. Teachers should use this set as a review rather than as a substitute for hands-on activities by students.

Physical Science: Chemical Energy. *Churchill Films,* 1984. (Part of the Physical Science Series.) 16 min. Color. $355 (16mm); $355 (video); inquire for rental. Teacher's guide. ▶ EA,JH

A good, introductory film on the energy that is locked in chemical bonds. Chemical change is illustrated as being different from physical change, with examples including heating, combustion, ore reduction, and cake baking. Oxidation is discussed as the process whereby a substance combines with oxygen to produce a new material. The value of this film lies in its choice of familiar scenes captured in slow motion or time-lapse photography to show chemical energy processes in a new way, with clear explanations in chemical terms.

550 Earth sciences

See also 371.42 Careers.

551.2–.3 Volcanoes; earthquakes; erosion; glaciers

An Animated Atlas of the World. *Walt Disney Educational Media Co.,* 1986. 7 min. Color. $215 (16mm); $161 (½-inch video); $60 (rental). Teacher's guide. ▶ EA,JH

In this delightful, fast-moving, information-packed film, an animated giant, Atlas, spins the earth, rides a "hydrologic cycle," drains the ocean, forms Pangea, recreates modern earth, and pulls the earth in half. As he performs all these dramatic antics, Atlas explains weather, earthquakes, mountain formation, and continental drift and illustrates how the processes at work on the early earth continue to operate today. The humor underlines the content and lightens the film.

The Earth: Changes in Its Surface. *Coronet Films & Video,* 1982. (Part of The Earth Science Series.) 13 min. Color. $303 (16mm); $212 (video). Teacher's guide. ▶ EA,JH

This film shows the many ways in which the earth's surface is affected by both internal and external forces, including specific treatments of folds and faults, earthquakes, igneous processes, weathering, and the effects of wind and water. The examples of each process are well chosen and provide a good "real-world" picture of geologic phenomena for students. The film gives a good introduction to the earth sciences; its only drawback is that the terminology used is a mixture of familiar and difficult words.

The Earth: Its Structure, revised edition. *Coronet Films & Video,* 1982. (Part of The Earth Science Series.) 9 min. Color. $216 (16mm); $151 (video). Teacher's guide. ▶ JH

This film illustrates how geologists piece together data from volcanic eruptions, seismographic records of earthquakes, and observations of surface features to produce a model of the earth's internal structure. Despite the film's brevity, only the description of the use of seismographs is inadequate. Animation illustrates the model of the core, mantle, and crust, and excellent photography highlights examples of igneous, sedimentary, and metamorphic rock. The discussion of the formation of each rock type is complete and adequately illustrated except for the crustal plates and their movements.

Earth Science: Volcano Mt. St. Helens—Fiery Laboratory. *Science Screen Report, Inc.* 1982. (Vol. 11, issue 7.) 13 min. Color. $200 (16mm); $200 (video). Teacher's guide. ▶ EA,JH

This newsreel-format film contains a descriptive introduction to volcanoes, a Mt. St. Helens eruption sequence, effects of the eruption, and what was learned. Much clear and concise information is offered at each stage of the presentation. Concepts such as plate tectonics, magma formation, blast waves, debris flow, eruption prediction, and alteration of ecosystems are described. The material is timely and will remain so for at least a few years. Several still satellite photographs are used with the very good moving sequences, but some of the drawings and maps are only fair.

Earthquakes and Volcanoes. *January Productions*, 1984. (Part of A First Film-strip About, Set III Series.) 1 color filmstrip, 53 frames; 1 cassette, 14 min. $22. Teacher's guide. ▶ EA,JH

This filmstrip is suitable for use as a review rather than as an introduction or a self-contained lesson. Teachers will want to precede it by showing photographs of volcanic scenery and telling the stories of some major earthquakes. Students will benefit from the filmstrip's overview of early myths and current ideas about the causes of earthquakes; types of eruptions; the earth's interior; magma, lava, and other volcanic material; hot springs and geysers; faults and tectonic plates; and seismology. Most of the material is clearly presented through paintings and diagrams; the approach is factual and straightforward.

How We Know About the Ice Ages, revised. *BFA Educational Media*, 1985. 16 min. Color. $275 (16mm); $160 (video); $38 (rental, 16mm only). ▶ EI,EA,JH

How We Know About the Ice Ages uses excellent photography, artwork, and narration to introduce the topic, and it gives both the historical perspective and much of the scientific teachings about glaciation. The film starts with Yosemite National Park's spectacular alpine glaciation and proceeds to ex-amples of continental glaciation in other parts of North America. Geologic terms are introduced by overlaying the word on the picture, an excellent method for students. Highly recommended.

The Story of the Changing Earth. *Hawkhill Associates, Inc.*, 1985. (From the Time, Space, & Spirit Series.) 1 color filmstrip, 80 frames; 1 cassette, 15 min. $39. Teacher's guide. Also available in video. ▶ EA,JH

This fast-paced filmstrip begins with the history of geography and shows how this science led to the science of geology. The history of the earth is presented by means of a 24-hour-day analogy. The program discusses the evolution of the earth and its landforms, touching on plate tectonics and its relation to mountain building as well as glaciation and the possibility of a coming ice age. The filmstrip is free of error; however, it consistently uses the term "float" to describe continental movement, leaving the impression that the continents are waterborne. Little emphasis is placed on process-oriented activities.

Weathering and Erosion. *National Geographic Society*, 1983. 1 color filmstrip, 55 frames; 1 cassette, 17 min. $29.95. o.n. 04634. Teacher's guide. ▶ JH

This filmstrip has attractive photographs and drawings, and the high-quality narrative gives accurate but limited information on weathering and erosion. Topics covered include chemical and physical weathering, soil production, and water, wind, and glacier transport of material erosion. Uplifting and volcanic eruption are depicted as countering actions, and the illustrated results of combined processes are shown, including caves, river and ocean shoreline structure, and wind-eroded rock. The filmstrip stresses what students can detect by merely looking about; this is an attractive motivation. The filmstrip will provide a general awareness of these processes and may motivate viewers to learn more.

551.46 Oceanography
See also 574.92 Marine biology and ecology.

Introducing Oceanography, revised edition. *Society for Visual Education, Inc.,*

1983. 6 color filmstrips, 45 frames (average); 6 cassettes, 13 min. (average). $180. Teacher's guide and worksheets. ▶ EA,JH

This filmstrip set is a visual textbook intended to introduce students to oceanography. The set uses color animation throughout, and explanatory diagrams are carefully detailed. Major definitions are clearly displayed. Teachers can use the collateral materials as the basis for an entire unit on oceanography. The information is accurate and clearly presented, and the collateral materials are of great value to general science teachers who are unfamiliar with oceanography.

Oceanography: The Science of the Sea. *Encyclopaedia Britannica Educational Corp.,* 1984. 6 color filmstrips, 75 frames (average); 6 cassettes, 16 min. ea. $168. Teacher's guide. ▶ EA,JH

In this excellent introduction to the science of oceanography, the photography is outstanding and provides a fine visual accompaniment to the clear, easily understood narration. The greatest value of the set lies in the range of topics covered: introduction to oceanography, chemical and physical oceanography, biological oceanography, plate tectonics and the origin of the ocean bases, ocean sediments and earth history, and the ocean's resources. The information given is accurate. Recommended primarily for earth science in the secondary school years.

The Oceans: Exploring Earth's Last Frontier. *National Geographic Society,* 1986. 3 color filmstrips, 55 frames ea.; 3 cassettes, 16 min. ea. $84.95. Teacher's guides. ▶ EI,EA,JH

These three filmstrips and accompanying cassettes and instructor's guides make an excellent teaching aid to introduce young students to the world's ocean systems. The information is accurate if occasionally oversimplified. English and metric are used; in some places only English units are given. The intermittent use of music detracts from the beautiful color photographs, especially those of the deep sea organisms. Overall, however, a good addition to a teaching collection for grades three through nine.

Riches from the Sea. *National Geographic Society,* 1984. 23 min. Color. $440 (16mm); $340 (video); $30 (3-day rental). ▶ K,EP,EI,EA,JH

This film explores the riches that we obtain from the sea, with particular emphasis on the continental shelf and on extraction of such nontraditional wealth from the sea as offshore petroleum, minerals, or tidal energy to generate electric power. Important legal questions about ownership of the oceans' resources and the need for protection of the esthetic value of the oceans are raised in this well-done film. Accurate information; excellent technical quality.

551.5–.6 Meteorology; climatology; atmosphere

Climate, Weather & People. *Hawkhill Associates, Inc.,* 1985. (Part of the Time, Space & Spirit Series.) 1 color filmstrip, 160 frames; 1 cassette, 29 min. $86. Teacher's guide. Also available in video. ▶ JH

Compelling presentations using carefully chosen photographs and artwork successfully trace the history and technology of the sciences of climate and weather and describe the effects of weather on people. There is no emphasis on any specific technical area, but the flow through history and technology is smooth and some questions are posed for students to consider. The teacher's guide is adequate. This filmstrip is also appropriate for senior high school students; a simplified version is available for younger audiences (see *The Story of Climate, Weather & People*, reviewed below).

Cloud Formation. *BFA Educational Media,* 1986. 15 min. Color. $325 (16mm); $210 (video); $45 (rental, 16mm only). o.n. 72056. ▶ **EA,JH**

The title of this film is somewhat misleading since direct reference is made only to cumulonimbus clouds; other clouds are shown without reference to their names. The general pattern of this film is to use photography, time-lapse and otherwise, to illustrate what happens in the atmosphere. The concept is then illustrated in the laboratory with simple experiments. Excellent visuals illustrate the influence of topography in cloud formation and conditions on the windward and leeward sides of mountain ranges.

The Earth: Its Atmosphere, revised edition. Coronet Films & Video, 1982. (Part of The Earth Science Series.) 9 min. Color. $216 (16mm); $151 (video). Teacher's guide. ▶ **EA,JH**

This fast-paced, lively film is an excellent way to begin a class on weather and climate. In only nine minutes, no one topic can be covered in detail or depth, but the film presents a valuable overview that holds and stimulates interest. The narration is clear, crisp, and engaging, and the content is up to date and scientifically sound—albeit with necessary simplifications. The film also has high-quality photography and particularly dramatic footage of a tornado.

The Earth's Climate. *National Geographic Society,* 1984. 2 color filmstrips, 66–71 frames ea.; 2 cassettes, 20 min. ea. $59.95. Teacher's guide. ▶ **EA,JH**

As a general introduction to a broad topic, this set is excellent. The first part provides a basic introduction to the major climatic regions on Earth and the basic reasons why these regions have their particular climate. The second part traces Earth's climatic history and discusses various reasons for changes that have occurred. The production quality is excellent, and the photographs and illustrations are clear and lively. The information is logically presented and, considering the fast pace of filmstrips in general, this set is not hurried.

Introduction to Weather. *National Geographic Society,* 1982. 3 color filmstrips, 49–51 frames ea.; 3 cassettes, 16 min. ea. $67.50. o.n. 04534. Teacher's guide. ▶ **EI,EA,JH**

This very well organized filmstrip set covers its subject completely. The graphic presentations of fronts and air movement on a global scale are especially good. The filmstrip titled "Observing Changes" gives a fascinating presentation of weather folklore along with a discussion of ways in which individuals can look for weather signs to guide their activities on a short-range basis. The photography and graphics are excellent.

Learning About Air and Water. *National Geographic Society,* 1982. 2 color filmstrips, 51–53 frames ea.; 2 cassettes, 18 min. ea. $47.50. o.n. 04527. Teacher's guide. ▶ **EI,EA**

Part one of this set introduces the phenomena, characteristics, and composition of the atmosphere. Part two deals with streams, ponds, oceans, aquifers, evaporation, condensation, freezing, melting, precipitation, the water cycle, and pollution. Both parts emphasize the importance of air and water to all life, human uses of these resources in industry, agriculture, and recreation, and individual and social responsibility for managing and protecting these resources. Both parts also skillfully use a wide variety of experience to carry the main ideas and lead into the more abstract sections of the content. The photography is interesting, timely, and often beautiful. If there is a fault, it may be that too many concepts and too much vocabulary are presented.

The Story of Climate, Weather & People. *Hawkhill Associates, Inc.,* 1985. (From the Time, Space & Spirit Series.) 1 color filmstrip, 80 frames; 1 cassette, 15 min. $39. Teacher's guide. Also available in video. ▶ **EA,JH**

The visual material is good and the narration is pleasant but understandably fast paced due to the comprehensive coverage of the topics. As with most filmstrips, this one tends to be content-oriented and heavily loaded with new terms and concepts. The program traces the history of climatology, tying its development to the other sciences and to improved technology. The major causes of weather are discussed, and the complexity of weather forecasting is noted. The program concludes with a discussion of long-term weather changes (climate) and the possibilities of a future ice age and of a runaway greenhouse effect.

Tropical Circulation. *Churchill Films,* 1984. 11 min. Color. $230 (16mm); $230 (video); inquire for rental. Teacher's guide. ▶ **EA,JH**

This short film introduces tropical atmospheric circulation. The graphic animation is clear and uses few technical terms to develop hydrologic cycle concepts. Overall, a marvelous film with sufficient material to form the basis for extended discussion and concept development in an introductory, intermediate-level earth-science class.

Understanding Weather and Climate. *Society for Visual Education, Inc.,* 1983. 6 color filmstrips, 45 frames (average); 6 cassettes, 9 min. (average). $180. Teacher's guide. ▶ **EA,JH**

This attractively packaged filmstrip set provides a comprehensive introduction to the vocabulary and concepts of weather and climate. Care has been taken in choosing photographs that will not quickly date the set. The materials are extremely dense in terms of vocabulary and concepts. The first filmstrip alone has well over a dozen new terms and concepts. As a broad introduction or review, this set is excellent, but as a complete unit, it is paced too rapidly.

Weather: A Film for Beginners. *FilmFair Communications,* 1986. 13 min. Color. $320 (16mm); $320 (video); $30 (rental). Teacher's guide. ▶ **EP,EI**

This high-quality, single-concept program explains and illustrates the concept of weather within a limited scope. Elementary school students are shown doing simple, appropriate investigations that are connected directly and effectively to visual sequences of the same phenomena on a global scale—differential heating, evaporation, air currents and wind, condensation, cloud formation, precipitation, and runoff. The film achieves its objectives effectively because it holds the narration tightly to the concept and introduces no extraneous or distracting ideas. Picture selection and photographic quality are superb, and the illustrations are precise, accurate, and stimulating.

552 Rocks

Dust to Rock and Back Again. *Sunburst Communications, Inc.*, 1985. 2 color filmstrips, 72 frames ea.; 2 cassettes, 15 min. ea. $109. Teacher's guide. ▶ EA,JH

These filmstrips make a fair attempt to present the plate tectonic theory of the earth's formation, organization, and operation and to describe the origin of the types of rocks that make up the earth's crust. The coverage is adequate, general, and introductory. The illustrations and artwork are disappointing, however; they would have added considerably to the program if they had been designed with more care. Although oversimplified, this program would be an interesting and useful teaching tool for an introductory earth science course.

Rocks and Minerals. *National Geographic Society*, 1983. 1 color filmstrip, 55 frames; 1 cassette, 17 min. $29.95. o.n. 04630. Teacher's guide. ▶ EA,JH

This attractive filmstrip explains that rocks are composed of minerals, describes some important properties of minerals, and discusses the three major rock types—igneous, sedimentary, and metamorphic. Weathering, erosion, and deposition are dealt with in connection with sedimentary rocks. The filmstrip is accurate, but the concepts mentioned are somewhat oversimplified even for the intended audience. The filmstrip is an introduction for elementary-school students, but it will need elaboration by the teacher.

Paleontology and Physical Anthropology

Animals of Prehistoric Times. *Society for Visual Education, Inc.*, 1987. 4 color filmstrips, 50 frames ea.; 4 cassettes, 12 min. ea. $35 (ea.); $98 (set). ▶ **EI,EA**

This filmstrip set discusses sea life and amphibians, dinosaurs, the flyers, and the mammals, with artists' renditions of selected examples of prehistoric animals, often in natural-looking settings. The major physical and physiologic characteristics of each group are presented; scientific names are shown and sizes are given in meters. The geologic era when each group predominated is clearly shown. Important current questions are discussed, including whether dinosaurs were homeothermic and possible causes of dinosaur extinction. Theories of the origin of flight are handled especially well. The colorful artwork will hold student interest, although old clichés of dinosaurs fleeing volcanic eruptions are included.

Celestial Earth. *Barr Films*, 1982. 10 min. Color. $220 (16mm); $220 (video); inquire for rental. Teacher's guide. ▶ **EI,EA,JH**

Using models, artwork, and photographs, this short film depicts the earth's geologic and natural history at the rate of 600 million years every minute, doing the whole 4.6 billion years in only 10 minutes. The facts are accurately and clearly presented. The first 3.5 billion years of earth are shown from space, and the film depicts atmospheric and crustal evolution. The scene then shifts to the surface to show the evolution of life; a 0.4 second sequence shows a cave painting, then a large rocket launch to illustrate the entire 4 million years of humankind. The film's weakness is the poor quality of its special effects.

Digging Dinosaurs. *Centre Productions, Inc.*, 1986. 12 min. Color. $89 (video); $30 (rental). ▶ **EI,EA,JH**

This short film nicely delineates the many steps necessary to bring a fossil from discovery to museum study. How the dinosaur fossil hunter locates, excavates, protects, transports, cleans, identifies, and assembles the fossil with other skeletal parts of the dinosaur to make a museum display is carefully explored.

The Dinosaur and the Cosmic Collision. *Coronet Films & Video*, 1987. (Prod.:

WGBH; from the KnowZone Series.) 30 min. Color. $550 (16mm); $250 (video); $75 (rental). ▶ **EP,EI,EA,JH**

This film is about the dinosaurs that dominated the earth for 150 million years and then suddenly, 65 million years ago, became extinct along with many other species of animals. The program begins with a look at the fossil evidence used to re-create the age of dinosaurs and how errors in interpretation have been made and then discovered. The program explores how speculation stimulated the development of the asteroid collision hypothesis to account for the iridium layer deposited at the precise time of the dinosaurs' extinction as well as a periodic recurrence of mass extinctions. This film beautifully illustrates scientific facts and the processes scientists use to form explanations from facts.

Dinosaurs: From A to Extinction. *Educational Dimensions Group*, 1986. 4 color filmstrips, 60 frames ea.; 4 cassettes, 12–15 min. ea. $154. Teacher's guide. ▶ **EA,JH**

This attractive, mostly accurate set of filmstrips and sound tapes covers dinosaur history and extinction and use of fossil parts. The excellent full-color frames contain numerous still shots of dinosaurs, which will be extremely interesting to upper-elementary and middle-school students. A great deal of effort has been expended to present materials current in terms of scientific accuracy, and the illustrations are clear and correct. The one weakness is that the program leads students to the conclusion that there is one correct explanation for dinosaur extinction when, in fact, there are many possibilities.

Dinosaurs: The Terrible Lizards, revised. *AIMS Media*, 1986. 10 min. Color. $250 (16mm); $190 (video); $50 (rental). ▶ **EA,JH**

Realistic dimensional models of 11 well-known dinosaurs and their habitats are highlighted in this presentation. There is an informative map of dinosaur fossil finds, and some good animation illustrates the age of dinosaurs with respect to other reptiles, fishes, amphibians, mammals, birds, and humans. The program concludes with a wide-ranging discussion of the several most popular theories of dinosaur extinction. The material is presented vividly and will go a long way toward exciting youngsters to learn more about these interesting reptiles.

Geologic Time. *Encyclopedia Britannica Educational Corp.*, 1986. 24 min. Color. $515 (16mm); $410 (video); $51.50 (rental). Teacher's guide. ▶ **EA,JH**

Modern methods used to determine ages of fossils, rocks, and human artifacts are the focus of this excellent film. Several techniques are explained clearly by the scientists who make the measurements—an excellent touch. Dendrochronology and radiometric techniques using carbon, rubidium, and potassium isotopes are featured. A well-photographed trek into the Grand Canyon introduces superposition, unconformities, faunal succession, and index fossils. A unique animated history of the Canyon area is particularly impressive. Few similar programs are available that cover this topic so well.

Prehistoric Animals. *January Productions*, 1984. (Part of A First Filmstrip About, Set III Series.) 1 color filmstrip, 52 frames; 1 cassette, 14 min. $22. Teacher's guide. ▶ **EI,EA,JH**

This stolid presentation of orthodox paleontology presents those orthodox ideas well. Horse and bird evolution, for example, are not quite so tidy at the species or genus levels as the filmstrip depicts. The filmstrip does not take into account modern evolutionary controversies, and perhaps it should not. Overall, the graphics are excellent but need to be supplemented by photographs of fossils and other information.

Prehistoric Life, revised edition. *Society for Visual Education, Inc.*, 1983. 6 color filmstrips, 43 frames (average); 6 cassettes, 8 min. (average). $180. Teacher's guide. ▶ JH

This set depicts the major developments of evolution. The first filmstrip deals with the origin of the earth and of life. It also introduces the concept of a geologic clock, which becomes the continuing thread of the set. The first four parts are an overview of life during the Archeozoic, Proterozoic, Paleozoic, Mesozoic, and Cenozoic eras. Numerous organisms are shown, many through photographs of original fossil materials. Part three covers the extinction of dinosaurs and does an excellent job of presenting the current theories of their disappearance. Part five presents evolutionary theory, and part six describes how fossils came about, are found, and then are dated and studied. Overall, the set offers a good exposure to many prehistoric organisms and a good discussion of the origin of the earth and evolutionary theory.

Rocks That Reveal the Past, revised. *BFA Educational Media*, 1985. 12 min. Color. $210 (16mm); $130 (video); $29 (rental, 16mm only). ▶ EA,JH

Rocks is a good, brief introduction to fossils that every beginning earth science student will appreciate. The color, techniques, and examples are good. However, sedimentary rocks could have been explained in more detail, which would have helped to complete the general topic. Dating of fossils by their relative positions in the same sedimentary rock is only mentioned, with nothing said about radiogenic methods for absolute dating.

64,000,000 Years Ago. *Barr Films*, 1982. (Prod.: National Film Board of Canada.) 11 min. Color. $245 (16mm); $24.50 (rental). Teacher's guide. ▶ EA,JH

This is an action-packed, "slice of life" film about the end of the Cretaceous period, shortly before the extinction of dinosaur giants such as *Tyrannosaurus*. The animation is delightful even though the theme is a bit trite. The film depicts some generally less well-known aspects of dinosaur behavior—for example, that they probably did guard their eggs and that some were gregarious. It also contains its share of melodrama. The central message implied by the film, that mammals were prevented from spreading and proliferating by the dinosaurs, is misleading. For anyone interested in a visually effective experience rather than information, this film is ideal.

Life Sciences

Cell Division: Mitosis and Cytokinesis. *Carolina Biological Supply Co.*, 1983. 1 color filmstrip, 68 frames; 1 cassette, 10 min. $32.50. Teacher's guide. Also available in slides. ▶ **EA,JH**

In this elementary introduction to mitosis and cytokinesis, no attempt is made to go into the minute detail or the broad implications of either process. The photographs are made from truly outstanding slide preparations and are uniformly excellent. However, the narration is much too fast, giving students scarcely any time to to ask for assistance. The teacher's guide is essentially a script and misses the opportunity to indicate supplements that could extend the usefulness of the filmstrip. In particular, a generalized cell cycle would be useful. Overall, the information is accurate, the scope only fair, and the technical quality excellent.

How Far from the Apes? A New Debate on the Ancestry of Man. *Knowledge Unlimited*, 1984. 1 color filmstrip, 30 frames. $13 ($8 for optional cassette). Teacher's guide. ▶ **EA,JH**

This filmstrip is useful for courses on human and primate evolution and for showing the evidence for including apes in the human pedigree. It examines an important topic but tries to cover too much—an overview of evolutionary theory combined with human-ape genetic relationships would have sufficed. The excellent, accurate narration is on two levels, general and advanced; however, the visuals are only adequate.

Journey into Microspace: A Photographic Odyssey. *Human Relations Media*, 1982. 1 color filmstrip, 80 frames; 1 cassette, 15 min. $69. Teacher's guide. ▶ **EA,JH**

Journey into Microspace introduces the concepts of microscopy, especially comparing the scanning electron microscope with the more familiar light microscope. The interesting photomicrographs are of common subjects with which students should identify even while experiencing a sense of surprise. Subject selection, oriented to the life sciences, is very good. The introductory part of the teacher's guide is excellent and will provide students with information that will enable them to appreciate the microscopic realm.

Living or Nonliving? *National Geographic Society,* 1986. 16 min. Color. $350 (16mm); $245 (video). ▶ **EP,EI,EA,JH**

Living or Nonliving presents an engaging dialogue between a desert-wise Indian school bus driver and his diminutive passengers. When the bus breaks down—"dies"—the comparison between the bus and living desert organisms is elaborated. The bus eats and burns gasoline, moves, and makes noise. Examples of living things responding to the environment, growing, reproducing, and dying demonstrate what nonliving things, such as the bus, lack.

574.5 Ecology of organisms

See also 371.42 Careers; 580 Botanical sciences.

Adapting to Changes in Nature. *Journal Films, Inc.,* 1985. 11 min. Color. $225 (16mm); $25 (3-day rental). Teacher's guide. ▶ **K,EP,EI,EA**

This excellent film introduces the topic of how animals and plants unconsciously adapt to changes in nature. The photography is outstanding, and sequences are nicely linked so that the story line is cohesive and provides a basic understanding of the subject even without follow-up. Using this film as an overview, a teacher should be able to generate a lively class on adaptation.

Autumn. *National Geographic Society,* 1984. (Part of The Four Seasons Series.) 15 min. Color. $350 (16mm ea.); $290 (video ea.); $20 (rental ea.). Teacher's guide. ▶ **EP,EI,EA**

Spring. 16 min. ▶ **EI**

Summer. 16 min. ▶ **EI**

Winter. 13 min. ▶ **EP,EI,EA**

Autumn shows major changes that occur in autumn and how they affect plants and animals. Falling leaves are shown and discussed, and the difference between deciduous and evergreen trees is considered briefly. More detail is given in sequences that depict how animals respond to the changing season, and the discussion of fall harvest provides an insight into rural life for urban students. The film also examines migration, food gathering, and hibernation. Although part of a series, this film can be used independently with equal effectiveness. *Spring,* part of a series photographed at a farm in the north temperate zone, portrays the farm and its plants and animals, both wild and domestic, as they enter springtime. This excellent, low-key film gives ample opportunity for involvement, without the anthropomorphism so often associated with such films. Recommended as both a pre- and post-field trip tool since much of what is included should be seen by students at a nature center, park, woods, or farm. *Summer* continues the series (above) and portrays the farm and the surrounding plants and animals as spring ends and summer begins. Birth and tending of farm animals are illustrated in a logical sequence that forms a backdrop for the discussion of wild plants and animals. A brief time-lapse sequence depicts the carefully explained metamorphosis of the monarch butterfly. After establishing the concept of seasonal change, *Winter* describes the winter environment in the temperate region of North America. Particular emphasis is placed on how the climatic change affects animals and, to a limited degree, humans. Hibernation and migration are discussed as means of winter survival, and many interesting examples of animals that remain active during winter are included.

Biological Clocks. *National Geographic Society*, 1984. 2 color filmstrips, 69–70 frames ea.; 2 cassettes, 17–19 min. ea. $59.95. Teacher's guide. ▶ EI,EA,JH

A sense of timing is a fundamental property of life, and the pervasiveness and diversity of this cyclic time sense are catchingly demonstrated in this filmstrip set. Plant and animal species from the common to the curious are used to demonstrate circadian, tidal, lunar, and seasonal behavioral rhythms. The set also depicts experimental designs that test innate versus environmental influences on these behaviors. One is left with a sense of mystery as to how innate rhythms are controlled at the molecular level. Excellent photographs and fine narration, with background sounds that bring the colorful photographs to life, will hold viewers' attention.

Looking at Living Things. *National Geographic Society*, 1986. 2 color filmstrips, 50–55 frames ea.; 2 cassettes, 15 min. ea. $61.95. Teacher's guide. ▶ K,EP,EI

This filmstrip set accurately describes six basic characteristics of living things: the fundamental need for food, water, and air; independent movement; response to environment; and reproduction, growth, and adaptation. The photography is visually appealing, with familiar and unusual examples from the plant and animal kingdoms used to illustrate key concepts.

Seasonal Stories. *Society for Visual Education*, 1985. 4 color filmstrips, 45 frames (average); 4 cassettes, 9 min. (average). $35 (ea.); $154 (series). Teacher's guide. ▶ K,EP

These four filmstrips cover the seasons by presenting examples of an organism or an area. *Fall: The Story of a Butterfly* describes the life cycle and migration of the monarch butterfly and its protective coloration that the viceroy butterfly copies. *Winter: Story of a Sugar Maple* presents the making of maple syrup and the role of sap in the annual tree cycle. *Spring: The Story of a Bee* describes pollen gathering by bees and the role of bees in pollination. *The Story of a Beach* covers fragmentation of rock into sand, plants that grow in beach areas, and summer reproduction and growth activities of living organisms.

Up Close & Natural. *Agency for Instructional Technology*, 1986. (Prod.: New Hampshire Public Television.) 15 programs, 15 min. ea. Color. $125 (video ea.); $1,499 (series). Teacher's guide. ▶ K,EP,EI

These units provide much factual information on natural history for young elementary school students. Among the 15 programs are *Insects, Mammals, Animals Without Backbones, Winter at Squam Lake, Marsh and Swamp*, and *Outside Your Door*. The photography is well done, and there is nothing to fault in the facts given or the manner of delivery. The narrator, acting as an onscreen teacher, questions her audience directly, and the dialogue is appropriate for the intended students. A solid and worthy series on natural history for young students.

574.5263 Ecology of aquatic environments
See also 551.46 Oceanography; 574.92 Marine biology and ecology.

Ecology of a Bay. *Enjoy Communicating, Inc.*, 1982. 1 color filmstrip, 77 frames; 1 cassette, 11 min. $26. Teacher's guide. ▶ EI,EA,JH

This filmstrip explores the many uses of the Chesapeake Bay. Natural habitats and plant and animal populations are surveyed extensively, and stresses such as salinity and turbidity due to erosion are described. The photography is clear and attractive, and the narration is good, although certain segments seem hurried. The filmstrip would be particularly useful as an introduction or as a culminating activity to a study of the ecology of bays and estuaries.

The Ecology of a Stream. *Carolina Biological Supply Co.*, 1983. 1 color filmstrip, 73 frames; 1 cassette, 12 min. $32.50. Teacher's guide. Also available in slides. ▶ **EA,JH**

Stream does an excellent job of introducing young students to the complex ecosystem of moving waters, but it should be used in conjunction with a fieldtrip to a suitable habitat where students can collect samples and make simple observations. For greater student appreciation of the subject, a creative presentation in the classroom of live and preserved specimens should be considered as well. This presentation is best suited to eighth to tenth graders, but it could also be used with younger students in gifted and talented programs. Teachers should be wary of occasional oversimplifications in the script.

The Margins of the Land. *Time-Life Video*, 1984. (Prod.: BBC; from The Living Planet Series.) 55 min. Color. $900 (16mm); $300 (video); $100 (rental). ▶ **EA,JH**

An excellent example of effective teaching and high entertainment, with technically superb filming and editing. Devoted to the natural history of intertidal zones, the film follows David Attenborough as he travels to some of the most fascinating and inaccessible habitats on Earth. Each stop illustrates a phenomenon, such as adaptations of animals to inhospitable environments, the action of erosion, and the zonation of life in response to a graded change in environmental stresses. By avoiding technical jargon and using examples to illustrate and explain difficult concepts, the film reaches the widest possible audience.

Shores: The Edge of Things. *Clearvue, Inc.*, 1982. 6 color filmstrips, 61 frames (average); 6 cassettes, 12 min. (average). $21 (ea.); $103 (set). o.n. P-004. Teacher's guide. ▶ **EA,JH**

This filmstrip set considers the forces that create shores, beaches, and marshes as well as their makeup, inhabitants, and the changes that occur to the biotic and abiotic components. The relationship between the scientific material presented and its effects on humans is continually repeated. The narration is dynamic and enthusiastic and offers motivation through the questions that are posed. In addition, the use of sound effects adds realism. There has been a conscious and successful effort to provide geological, ecological, and meteorological information in an interesting and meaningful way. A pleasant and instructive experience.

A Small Body of Still Water. *New Dimension Films*, 1984. 16 min. Color. $320 (16mm); $250 (video). ▶ **EI,EA,JH**

This interesting film about life in a pond has excellent photography of protozoans, algae, mosquitoes, damsel flies, tadpoles, and frogs. The microscopic organisms are aways in focus, and movements of both locomotion and internal structures are well demonstrated. The film's primary emphasis is ecological, mainly the relationships between organisms, with particular attention to trophic or food levels. The sequence on metamorphosis of the tadpole to the adult frog is particularly fascinating and well presented. The photography will fascinate young children, but the film's terminology makes it of greater value for older students and general audiences.

574.5264–.5267 Ecology of land environments
See also 362.7 Environmental problems and protection.

Alaska's Islands in the Bering Sea. *Enjoy Communicating, Inc.,* 1986. 1 color filmstrip, 71 frames; 1 cassette, 11 min. $32.50. Teacher's guide. ▶ EA,JH

This filmstrip presents a very nice set of photographs of the Aleutians and other west Alaskan islands and some of the flora, fauna, and people of the islands, giving a good representation of the bleak landscape. It successfully acquaints the viewer with this remote and historic area, stimulates interest in the flora and fauna, and shows the life-styles of the people of this isolated region. Some incongruities between the printed and recorded matter.

Antarctica. *Enjoy Communicating, Inc.,* 1982. 2 color filmstrips, 67 frames ea.; 2 cassettes, 11 min. ea. $52. Teacher's guide. ▶ EI,EA,JH

Part one of this set is an informative and well-presented account of the large animals on and near Antarctica; part two is a mixture of ecology, paleontology, and current events, including an examination of political matters relevant to the area. The section on ecology is well done and filled with facts that will catch viewers' imagination. The discussion of the several species of penguins is especially well done. The discussion of the Antarctica treaty shows how nations have been able to agree on the uses of this continent. The photography and sound are excellent, the information is accurate, and the discussion is general enough to remain timely.

Canyon Creatures. *Marty Stouffer Productions Ltd.,* 1984. (Part of the Wild America Series.) 26 min. Color. $350 (16mm); $250 (video); $50 (rental). ▶ EA,JH

Stouffer narrates this low-key program on the canyon areas of Zion, Bryce, Canyonlands, Arches, Glen Canyon, Monument Valley, and the Grand Canyon. He describes the effects of climate and man's presence on canyon topography and adaptations of animals to the topography. With the example of a cougar stalking and catching a mule deer, the narration turns to the 1920s when most predators were eliminated, resulting in the overpopulation and starvation of tens of thousands of deer within a decade. The program teaches that all wildlife is interdependent.

The Living Mosaic: The Tamaulipan Biotic Province. *Adams & Adams Films,* 1983. 27 min. Color. $440 (16mm); $45 (rental). ▶ EA,JH

The Living Mosaic is an excellent example of nature photography at its best. The sound effects are excellent, as are the optical techniques (especially the incredible sunsets at the end of the film), and the editing could not be better. This film is literally appropriate for any age group, beginning with the fifth grade. The viewer may not come away with a great deal of new knowledge, but the sheer esthetics of the film allow for 27 minutes of total enjoyment.

Rain Forest. *National Geographic Society,* 1983. 59 min. Color. $595 (16mm); $545 (video); $43 (rental). Teacher's guide. ▶ EA,JH

This excellent film focuses on the animal and plant life of Costa Rica's tropical rain forest. Some of the best footage is of insects, but viewers will also enjoy the coverage of frogs, snakes, lizards, and mammals. If the film lacks anything, it is the description of trees and plant life in the forests. Controversial subjects such as soil nutrient depletion and the regeneration of natural forests are only briefly discussed.

Skydive to Autana. *Films Inc.,* 1986. (Prod.: BBC/RKO.) 50 min. Color. $298 (¾-inch video); $198 (½-inch video); $90 (rental). ▶ **EA,JH**

In this natural history adventure and expedition film, 12 explorer-scientists parachute onto the mountainous plateau atop Autana, 1,000 meters above the forest floor of a Venezuelan jungle. The film discusses how isolation affects speciation in plants and animals on mountain tops, using the concept that chains of mountain tops are similar to island chains. Orchids, pitcher plants, bromeliads, dragonflies, amphibians, lizards, and birds are clearly photographed and used to demostrate the effects of isolation on speciation, race development, adaptation, and niche development. This film will hold the interest of students and could be successfully used with life science, biology, earth science, and general science classes, especially at junior and senior high levels.

Soil & Water: A Living World. *Barr Films,* 1984. 16 min. Color. $355 (16mm); $355 (video). Teacher's guide. ▶ **EI,EA,JH**

In this film, four young campers and their counselor go on an expedition to learn about the organisms that inhabit topsoil and pond water. They see worms, snails, insects, ducks, frogs, and the microscopic creatures in soil and water, and they learn about the role of these animals in recycling organic matter. The film allows viewers to observe clearly not only the structure but also the movement of microorganisms. The photography is excellent and captures nature in all its freshness. The accuracy of the information and the teacher's guide are excellent. The film teaches a difficult topic so entertainingly that it is a delight.

Worlds Apart. *Time-Life Video,* 1984. (Prod.: BBC; part of The Living Planet Series.) 55 min. Color. $900 (16mm); $300 (video); $100 (rental). ▶ **EA,JH**

Worlds Apart covers aspects of plant and animal island biogeography and includes examples from the islands of Aldabra, Komodo, Hawaii, Easter Island, and New Zealand. The means by which plants and animals get to remote islands are examined, and special adaptations needed for travel by land and water are illustrated. The effects of isolation on living forms are covered in depth, and there is an interesting discussion on the evolution of the large sizes of species. Examples of the extensive speciation of honeycreepers and *Drosophila* in Hawaii are shown.

574.92   Marine biology and ecology

See also 551.46 Oceanography; 574.5263 Ecology of aquatic environments.

Coral Reefs and Coral Reef Fishes. *Enjoy Communicating, Inc.,* 1986. 2 filmstrips, 60–65 frames ea.; 2 cassettes, 9–10 min. ea. Color. $65. ▶ **JH**

These filmstrips provide a visual field trip to the coral reefs of the world. Strictly a survey of the reef and its inhabitants, they only briefly touch on human effects on this ecosystem. A serious weakness is the omission of a script and supplementary information to help teachers plan and conduct more in-depth activities. On the technical side, the frames must be advanced manually, and the signal tone is almost inaudible, so it is easy to fall behind. Recommended with only these minor reservations.

The Islands: Watery Outposts of Australia. *Centre Productions, Inc.*, 1986. (From the Animal Wonder Down Under Series.) 25 min. Color. $299 (¾-inch video); $279 (½-inch video); $50 (rental). ▶ **EA,JH**

This beautifully photographed film provides an overview of species inhabiting the islands and their associated waters off the coast of Australia. Most of the film is devoted to those animals that either live in the sea or use food from the sea. The splendor and diversity of the fauna of coral reefs are illustrated with fine underwater footage. The diverse cycle of activity over a 24-hour period is graphically pictured and described.

Wonders of the Sea. *Society for Visual Education, Inc.*, 1987. 4 color filmstrips, 42 frames ea.; 4 cassettes, 7 min. ea. $35 (ea.); $159 (set). 24 skill sheets available. Teacher's guide. ▶ **JH**

This well-conceived filmstrip set stimulates interest in marine biology by focusing on some of the ocean's more awesome inhabitants—sharks, whales, cephalopods, and lower life forms (anemones, sponges, and corals). Each filmstrip clearly and simply describes some basic characteristics of marine organisms, such as their physical attributes, feeding habits, propulsion mechanisms, reproductive activity, and defense adaptations. Each segment also does a good job of dispelling some popular myths about sea creatures, such as the hostility of sharks. The narrative is lively and scientifically sound.

580 Botanical sciences

See also **Agriculture** section.

Flowers at Work, 3rd edition. *Encyclopedia Britannica Educational Corp.*, 1982. 16 min. Color. $315 (16mm); $31.50 (rental); inquire for video prices. o.n. 3735. Teacher's guide. ▶ **EA,JH**

This film is sharp, clear, has excellent color, and provides clear, simple explanations and labeling. It nicely covers reproduction and fruit and seed production in a manner that most viewers can easily relate to, yet the film is not condescending. The time-lapse sequences are excellent. Flower parts are shown in natural settings and in laboratory dissection; the use of models, animation and exotic flowers is kept to a minimum. Self- versus cross-pollination, bud grafting, tissue culture, and cloning are adequately explained in detailed sequences.

The Forest Seasons: An Introduction to Ecology. *Oak Woods Media, Inc.*, 1981. 6 color filmstrips, 50 frames (average); 6 cassettes, 10 min. (average). $27.50 (ea.); $159 (set). Teacher's guide. ▶ **EA,JH**

The first of these generally excellent filmstrips introduces the deciduous forest; the next four present the dynamic nature of the forest through the year. By the end of the fifth filmstrip, such concepts as vertical structure of the forest, food chains, trophic levels, succession, insect life history, migration, hibernation, winter survival, forest hydrology, leaf color change, and tree identification have been introduced. The last filmstrip, "The Woodland Photographer," adds little to the set, which, overall, would have benefited from the addition of graphics to summarize concepts such as trophic levels, succession, and forest hydrology.

Growth of Flowers, 2nd edition. *Coronet Films & Video*, 1984. 11 min. Color. $265 (16mm); $185 (video); $50 (rental). Teacher's guide. ► EP,EI,EA,JH

Time-lapse scenes illustrate the patterns of movement of garden flowers. Pollination by common pollinators (bees and butterflies) and fruit set and seed production illustrate reproductive cycles. Flowering plants are followed through their growing season and dormant period. The film could be used for classroom discussion or laboratory exercises dealing with movement, growth, dormancy, and the internal and external factors affecting these processes. A fascinating introduction to the changes associated with flowering; use would be especially effective if correlated with seasonal changes.

How Green Plants Make and Use Food, revised. *Coronet Films & Video*, 1986. 12 min. Color. $280 (16mm); $200 (video); $40 (rental). ► EI,EA,JH

A good general introduction to green plants and the interdependence of life forms through food chains. Time-lapse photography demonstrates that green plants require water, minerals, air, and light for growth and development. Also presented are microscopic views of xylem cells, stomates, and chloroplasts, and the point is clearly made that plants respire as well as photosynthesize. The use of sugars as raw materials to produce proteins for growth and starch for energy storage is depicted, as is the use of energy by plants to sustain metabolic activities. Useful in middle school earth science classes.

Plants in Action. *Educational Media International*, 1983. 10 min. Color. $210 (16mm); $165 (video); $20 (3-day rental). ► EI,EA,JH

The photography in this film is extremely well done, and the poetic scenes of nature, as the background music keeps time with the swaying plants, are beautiful. The film can serve as an excellent introduction to the more obvious types of plant movements: nongrowth turgor movements, phototropic movement, geotropic response, and thigmotropism. Although none of this is new, its simple presentation will excite both school children and members of the local garden club. A discussion of the biochemistry and biophysics of plant movement would be helpful before viewing the film.

Plants That Grow from Leaves, Stems, and Roots, revised. *Coronet Films & Video*, 1983. 14 min. Color. $335 (16mm); $235 (video); inquire for rental. Teacher's guide. ► JH

The first part of this film describes and illustrates sexual reproduction in plants; the rest of the film illustrates vegetative reproduction and describes how plants that reproduce asexually will look exactly like the single parent from which they are derived, whereas plants that originate from seeds might not look like either parent. Vegetative reproduction is shown to occur naturally in leaves, stems, and roots. Introduced terms are clearly illustrated. A nicely illustrated overview of an important topic that should prove interesting to middle-school and junior-high students.

Plants: What Happens in the Winter. *National Geographic Society*, 1983. 1 color filmstrip, 50 frames; 1 cassette, 15 min. $29.95. o.n. 04615. Teacher's guide. ► K,EP,EI

This filmstrip will stimulate kindergarten through fourth-grade students to observe nature. The major theme concerns what happens to plants in winter, and this theme is developed in a fall-to-spring format. Good use is made of minor deviations from the theme, such as scenes of animals exhibiting winter-related behavior. The filmstrip contains many details and presents its central theme well. Its best use will be as an introduction to other class-related activities such as field trips and discussions.

Seed Dispersal. *Moody Institute of Science,* 1982. 15 min. Color. $300 (16mm); $255 (video); $27 (rental). Teacher's guide. ▶ EI,EA,JH

This well-executed documentary details seed dispersal among flowering plants. Time-lapse photography allows viewers to witness pinegrass "planting itself," oxalis forcibly ejecting seed, and how the mangrove's specialized seed germinates on the tree and falls root down in the mud to gradually extend the forest shoreline into the sea. The function of flowers and fruit in dispersal are explained, as are the roles of animals and humans in purposeful seed dispersal. Most appealing is the selection of unusual types of seed dispersal.

Seeds and How They Travel. *National Geographic Society,* 1983. 1 color filmstrip, 51 frames; 1 cassette, 14 min. $29.95. o.n. 04655. Teacher's guide. ▶ K,EP

When used in support of classwork and fieldtrips, *Seeds and How They Travel* will be valuable for introducing young students to the world around them. Color photographs illustrate the many types of seeds, and photographs and drawings present the common methods by which seeds travel and begin to grow at new locations. One small deficit is the comparative lack of pictures for seed movement in water, but seed movements by wind, animals, and people are well covered.

Seeds Scatter. *Churchill Films,* 1984. 14 min. Color. $290 (16mm); $290 (video); inquire for rental. Teacher's guide. ▶ EI,EA

Using excellent photography, *Seeds Scatter* illustrates several ways in which plants disperse seeds, including wind, water, and the fur and intestinal tracts of animals. The activities and discussion questions suggested are too complicated, the vocabulary level of the narration is too high, and the use of time-lapse photography is possibly too sophisticated for primary grades. The best level for the film is for third to sixth graders, but these students may feel that the narrative talks down to them. In sum, a good film with an inappropriate narrative for the ages for which it is best suited.

What Do Plants Do: A First Film, revised. *BFA Educational Media,* 1985. 12 min. Color. $255 (16mm); $175 (video); $30 (rental, 16mm only). ▶ EP,EI,EA,JH

The characteristics, parts, functions, and uses of plants are illustrated in this film. The photography is excellent, and the use of time-lapse photography to show processes typically not observed adds a significant dimension to the film. A good short survey that contains little in-depth information.

What Do Seeds Do: A First Film, revised. *BFA Educational Media,* 1985. 12 min. Color. $255 (16mm); $175 (video); $30 (rental, 16mm only). Teacher's guide. ▶ EI

This introductory film describes and illustrates the parts, function, and variety of seeds and how seeds fit into plant ecology. Facts and ideas are introduced simply, and care is taken to illustrate everything. Photographs of living plants are used extensively, and diagrams help to illustrate details not easily seen on living specimens. Excellent follow-up activities accompany the package. Busy elementary school teachers will find this an excellent starting place for the study of seeds.

Zoological Sciences

Best Friends. *Films Inc.*, 1984. 10 5-min. episodes. Color. $990 (16mm); $399 (¾-inch video); $246 (½-inch video). ▶ **K,EP**

This series introduces young children to the care and appreciation of animals; each segment is devoted to one animal. Each film is fully animated with basic use of color and illustration. The films show that animals are not toys but living things that require care.

591 Zoology

See also 639 Wildlife conservation.

591.1–.4 Animal physiology and anatomy

Animals Breathe in Many Ways, revised. *Phoenix Films & Video, Inc.*, 1983. 12 min. Color. $240 (16mm); $150 (video); $30 (rental). ▶ **EP,EI,EA**

Teachers who want their students to learn about or review the ways in which all types of animals breathe will find this film valuable. Although the content might be too advanced for students in the earliest grades, the film uses an unsophisticated vocabulary that should not be difficult for average and above-average students. The film's brevity, simple graphics, and clear and concise narrative will help make it comprehensible to young students; however, some words are given too broad an interpretation, and the background music is barely acceptable.

Animals Hear in Many Ways, revised. *Phoenix Films & Video, Inc.*, 1983. 12 min. Color. $240 (16mm); $150 (video); $30 (rental). ▶ **EA,JH**

After the basics of sound production and propagation are covered, a significant amount of this film is devoted to the sound receptors (ears) of several different animals. This technique will hold children's interest because of their natural desire to watch animals. The film is strong in biology but a little weak in physics. The photography is good, the well-chosen demonstrations appropriately interpret the situation, but the animation is weak.

Locomotion. *Carolina Biological Supply Co.*, 1986. (Prod.: Cabisco Video/BBC; from the Biovideo Series.) 30 min. Color. $169 (16mm); $149 (video); $50 (rental). Teacher's guide. ▶ **EI,EA,JH**

This well-organized program is an excellent survey of methods of locomotion in protozoa and higher animals. In phylogenetic order, it addresses four groups: protozoans, invertebrates, fish and reptiles, and birds and animals. It draws from over 80 species to illustrate pseudopodia, flagella, cilia, circular and longitudinal muscles in association with hydrostatic skeletons, and flexor and extensor muscles in exoskeletons and endoskeletons. It includes many features of movement that are difficult to observe in the wild.

What's an Animal: A First Film. *Phoenix Films & Video, Inc.*, 1984. 17 min. Color. $375 (16mm); $250 (video); $53 (rental). ▶ **EP,EI**

This film begins with a general discussion of the characteristics of animals and illustrates how they can be grouped by common body features. Ignoring technical language, the film describes animal groups as "one-celled," "hollow-bodied," "spiny skinned," "joint-footed," and so on. Although this approach is advantageous because it does not present too much information before students are ready, it does limit the potential audience. The photography is superb, and sequences are logically presented and shown at a comfortable pace.

591.5   Animal ecology and behavior

Adventures in Animal Land. *Random House Media*, 1983. 6 color filmstrips, 64–71 frames ea.; 6 cassettes, 11–16 min. ea. $141. Teacher's guide. ▶ **K,EP,EI**

This filmstrip set is interesting and informative. The material is presented in the storybook form of adventures of cartoon characters visiting from outer space. They experience six different idealized ecosystems—plains, mountains, jungle, desert, woodlands, and farm—and encounter the animals typically found there. It would be best to present each program alone and on separate days with many comments by the teacher. A useful supplement to a science education program.

Animal Babies. *Encyclopaedia Britannica Educational Corp.*, 1983. 10 min. Color. $225 (16mm); $225 (video); $22.50 (rental). Teacher's guide. ▶ **K,EP,EI, EA**

This excellent introduction to the natural history of 13 species of animals depicts, in their natural habitats, crocodiles and sea turtles, robins and swans, and whales, seals, beavers, red foxes, coyotes, cougars, bears, mountain goats, and pikas. The narration skillfully compares and contrasts the self-sufficiency and survival adaptations of these animals as babies. The film also emphasizes those skills that each young animal has to learn in order to survive. The information, scope, and technical quality are excellent.

Animal Games. *National Geographic Society*, 1985. (From the Look, Listen, Explore Series.) 2 color filmstrips, 55 frames ea.; 2 cassettes, 10–12 min. ea. $61.95. Teacher's guide. ▶ **K,EP**

"Mystery Animals" teaches young children to recognize the whole animal from its parts and to compare the eyes, ears, and noses of different kinds of animals. The ecological context for each animal is shown, and an explanation of the adaptive significance of the characteristic being discussed is given. "Animal Riddles" also has a strong ecological approach and emphasizes a multisensory format. Riddles, reinforced by animals sounds, pose questions to the audience. The strength of this program lies in its effective narration and interactive approaches. Overall, the strong ecological and multisensory emphasis is very effective in this useful addition to biology and natural history classes for the early primary grades.

Are They Really Dumb? Intelligence and Language Among Animals. *Knowledge Unlimited*, 1984. 1 color filmstrip, 118 frames. $13 ($8 for optional cassette). Teacher's guide. ▶ JH

This filmstrip uniquely portrays the theory of intelligence and language among animals. The pictures are well synchronized with the narration, and the background music and narration provide an unusually mesmerizing program that encourages attention and retention. It supports the concept that apes can communicate with humans through sign language and sounds. Care has been taken in the choice of photographs.

Baby Animals in Rhyme and Song. *Society for Visual Education, Inc.*, 1984. 4 color filmstrips, 45–51 frames ea.; 4 cassettes, 7 min. ea. $125. Teacher's guide. ▶ K

This filmstrip set introduces preschool children to baby animals in zoos, forests, on farms, and as pets. The parts can be used separately or together. The important features of the animals are highlighted with refreshing accuracy— no misconceptions distort the impression of the animals' basic behaviors. The catchy rhymes sung to familiar melodies and first-class illustrations capture and hold a young child's attention and give this set its charm and appeal. Highly recommended for its clarity of presentation, opportunity for audience participation, expansion possibilities, and appropriate approach to the intended audience.

The Human-Animal Bond: New Findings About an Old Friendship. *Knowledge Unlimited*, 1984. 1 color filmstrip, 36 frames. $13 ($8 for optional cassette). Teacher's guide. ▶ EA

This filmstrip focuses on the bond between humans and animals, successfully combining vivid pictures and descriptive words. It can be used in science as well as social studies classes; however, it does not give any specific experiments or documented facts to prove the science concepts presented. The vocabulary and concepts are suitable for a wide range of ages.

Instincts in Animals, revised. *Journal Films, Inc.*, 1985. 11 min. Color. $225 (16mm); $25 (3-day rental). Teacher's guide. ▶ EP,EI,EA

The basic theme of this unit is that certain behaviors necessary for survival are apparently natural, instinctive impulses. The animal examples selected are a good cross section and include insects, fish, birds, and mammals. The vocabulary is very well developed, and the concepts introduced are reinforced. Photography varies from very good to fair. A good production from which even adults can profit.

Tracking Wildlife. *Marty Stouffer Productions Ltd.*, 1986. (From the Wild America Series.) 30 min. Color. $250 (16mm); $150 (video); $50 (rental). ▶ EA,JH

This film uses spectacular photography to dramatize briefly some of the techniques used to track wildlife. While some of the encounters with animals are obviously staged, the action proceeds so naturally that viewers will be left with the impression that tracking always leads to actually spotting the animal being tracked. In all other respects, the film is accurate and informative, covering not only identification of animals by their tracks but also the use of scrapes and scat as clues to animal life.

591.52 Animal adaptations to specific environments

See also 595.4–.7 Insects; spiders; 597 Fishes; amphibians; reptiles; 599.2 Marsupials; 639.9 Wildlife conservation.

Animal Predators and the Balance of Nature. *Journal Films, Inc.*, 1985. 11 min. Color. $225 (16mm); $25 (3-day rental). Teacher's guide. ▶ **K,EP,EI,EA**

This excellent film addresses two basic questions: what is a predator, and what is the balance of nature. Through a nice blend of striking photography, simple examples, and quality narration, the answers clearly emerge. The sequence showing a praying mantis eating another insect "to help control the insect population . . . to help us" is a neat summary of the whole concept of predation and the food chain. Viewers will come away with a basic understanding that in the balance of nature all creatures, including humans, have a role.

Animals in Spring & Summer, 2nd edition. *Encyclopaedia Britannica Educational Corp.*, 1983. 11 min. Color. $280 (16mm); $225 (video); $28 (rental). Teacher's guide. ▶ **EI,EA**

The growth and changing activities of animals, especially the young, from the beginning of spring and through the summer, are the subjects of this film. Using excellent photography with a subdued but useful narration, the film shows the progression of events. The film will help students relate animal activities to seasonal changes and to events in animal development. The accuracy of information and technical quality are excellent.

Backyard Wildlife. *Marty Stouffer Productions Ltd.*, 1983. 26 min. Color. $350 (16mm); $250 (video); $50 (rental). ▶ **EP,EI,EA,JH**

This film portrays some wild animals that have survived human progress and are now actually thriving within many urban areas. Raccoons, deer, birds, and other animals are shown to have adapted to a habitat increasingly shared with humans. The film brings a small part of nature closer to home and offers a few tips on attracting wildlife to the viewer's own backyard. Overall, a highly satisfying natural science film that will appeal to young viewers.

Dogtown Community. *Centre Productions, Inc.*, 1982. 2 color filmstrips, 73 frames (average); 2 cassettes, 10 min. ea. $50. o.n. CE397. Teacher's guide. ▶ **EI,EA,JH**

Dogtown Community is an exceptional filmstrip presentation. The narration is animated, clearly enunciated, and accurate, and the photographs are beautiful and intriguing. In addition to prairie dogs, gold eagles, burrowing owls, and pronghorns are depicted. Although a broad spectrum of information is included, ecological terms and concepts are emphasized. Even young viewers will be able to follow the explanations and examples; certainly, the liveliness of the presentation should hold their interest.

Fauna of Australia. *Centre Productions, Inc.*, 1986. (From the Animal Wonder Down Under Series.) 25 min. Color. $299 (¾-inch video); $279 (½-inch video); $50 (rental). ▶ **EI,EA,JH**

Australia and its nearby islands are examined through satellite photographs, then close-up to study particular ecosystems. Animals associated with each ecosystem are illustrated, and the program shows why they find a particular ecosystem optimal. The impact of humans on each ecosystem and the impact on the associated fauna are also briefly examined. Eight different ecosystems are covered; no single aspect in much detail.

The Henderson Avenue Bug Patrol. *Media Projects, Inc.*, 1984. 15 min. Color. $325 (16mm); $325 (video); $35 (rental). Teacher's guide. ▶ EA,JH

In this film a group of neighborhood children are passing the time playing video games. After they run out of money, they try to discover what Mr. Bruce, the local naturalist, is buying in the store. He offers to take them on a search for new neighbors. As he stops frequently to point out bees, ants, wood lice, and small vertebrates, the children realize that the "new" neighbors have been there all along, and they begin to explore on their own. The cartoon renditions that introduce each new species make their points effectively and maintain interest. This good awareness film should have a long half-life in most upper-elementary classes.

Masterbuilders. *Beacon Films*, 1983. 15 min. Color. $350 (16mm); $350 (video); inquire for rental. ▶ EA,JH

This film shows the nests of a variety of weaver finches found on the East African plains and ends with a step-by-step observation of one male black-headed weaver finch as he builds his nest. The photography throughout is excellent, although the soft impressionistic lighting is a bit distracting at times. The emphasis is primarily on the mechanics of building, and the nest-building sequences are truly spectacular. The main problem with this film is an absence of biological focus. This underlying weakness—plus a tendency to anthropo-morphism in the narrative—limits the usefulness of the film.

Mountain Monarchs. *Marty Stouffer Productions Ltd.*, 1982. (Part of the Wild America Series.) 27 min. Color. $550 (16mm); $450 (video); $50 (rental). ▶ EP,EI,EA,JH

This film examines the special adaptations that allow animals to live in a severe mountain environment and features excellent photography of several predator and prey species. Much of the film is devoted to three closely related sheep—the Dall and stone sheep and the Rocky Mountain and desert bighorns. This excellent film is clearly designed as television entertainment; however, as a classroom tool, it is useful for illustrating mountain ecosystems, especially the larger animals, and predator-prey relationships.

Mzima: Portrait of a Spring. *Benchmark Films, Inc.*, 1983. 30 min. Color. $595 (16mm); $595 (video); $60 (rental). Teacher's guide. ▶ EA,JH

Mzima shows how a unique association of environmental factors has produced an oasis spring in the midst of an arid African landscape. The spring, called Mzima, is a heterotrophic community dominated by the resident hippopota-mus population. The feeding behavior of these huge herbivores results in an impressive import of terrestrial primary productivity into the spring ecosystem. Glimpses of various animals exploiting this abundant resource are given, and good illustrations of various adaptations by a number of animals are shown.

Nature's Builders. *Educational Media International*, 1984. 8 min. Color. $175 (16mm); $140 (video); $15 (3-day rental). ▶ K,EP,EI

This film presents three different animals that build complex structures, pointing out to the viewer that these creatures were never taught this skill. Swallows are shown gathering mud balls and shaping them into nests. A spider builds a web to snare its prey, then wraps its victim in silk to be eaten later. Finally, a caterpillar is shown building a cocoon to protect itself during metamorphosis. The photography, especially the close-ups, are well done. Useful in early elementary-school science lessons for illustrating complex, instinctive animal behavior, metamorphosis, and protective coloration.

Pinkfoot. *Beacon Films*, 1983. 19 min. Color. $440 (16mm); $440 (video); inquire for rental. ▶ **EP,EI,EA,JH**

Pinkfoot focuses on the spring migration of pink-footed geese as they fly from their wintering grounds in Britain to their breeding grounds in Iceland. The scenery photography is beautiful, and there are excellent close-ups of the animals. The film shows behaviors related to mating and courtship, territoriality, incubation, hatching, care of the young, and molting. An enjoyable and useful film for introducing viewers to the behavior and ecology of the species.

Sleeping and Resting. *National Geographic Society*, 1983. 1 color filmstrip, 54 frames; 1 cassette, 15 min. $29.95. o.n. 04691. Teacher's guide. ▶ **EA,JH**

The major theme of *Sleeping and Resting* is the great variability in sleeping patterns throughout the animal world. The variability is clearly demonstrated with numerous examples of animals sleeping at different times during the day, for different durations, and in a variety of locations and positions. The filmstrip also includes a brief discussion of human sleep and introduces the concepts of dreams and brainwave activity. The quality of the photographs is superb.

Social Animals. *National Geographic Society*, 1986. 3 color filmstrips, 55 frames ea.; 3 cassettes, 16 min. ea. $84.95. Teacher's guides. ▶ **EA,JH**

Each segment can stand alone in this set that describes the organization and structure of three different classes of animal societies. The first segment deals with social insect species, primarily ants, termites, wasps, and bees. The second segment presents social structures of birds, including the effect of climate, food supply, predators, and access to nesting areas on social behavior. The third segment deals with social mammals using zebras, elephants, baboons, lions, and Cape hunting dogs as the principal representatives. The photography is visually appealing and appropriate.

592–595 Invertebrates

Fastest Claw in the West. *Films Inc.*, 1986. (Prod.: BBC.) 25 min. Color. $198 (¾-inch video); $129 (½-inch video); $50 (rental). ▶ **EI,EA,JH**

Living up to its intriguing title, this film looks at the life of the predacious mantis shrimp, named for its mantid-like second thoracic limb. From real-life opening sequences that resemble a science fiction movie to an equally otherworld ending, the film moves quickly from the shrimp's social behavior—courtship, mating, and intraspecific conflicts—to interspecific competition and predation. A poetic exploration with imaginative filming, outstanding close-up action photography, an excellent script well narrated by David Attenborough, and well-chosen background music.

The Octopus. *Barr Films,* 1986. (From the Animal Families Series.) 11 min. Color. $275 (16mm); $275 (video). ▶ **K,EP,EI,EA**

In an aquarium setting, the octopus's unique features are introduced: the eight feet (tentacles with suction cups) that enable the octopus to climb and capture prey; the siphons that force water over the gills and move the octopus through the water; the vertebrate-like eyes; and a beak-like mouth that can crush and eat lobsters and crabs. After briefly introducing the octopus's marine habitat, the film returns to the aquarium to cover this mollusk's reproductive habits. This film has outstanding photography and an accurate script that treats its subject as science for young people.

The Portuguese Man-of-War. *Carolina Biological Supply Co.,* 1986. 9 min. Color. $134.95 (¾-inch video); $119.95 (½-inch video); $45 (rental). ▶ **EA,JH**

Esthetically and technically pleasing photography shows the life cycle, morphology, and feeding activities of the Portuguese man-of-war, along with several other aquatic species. The film would have been improved with animated sequences of the life cycle and the taxonomic position of the various organisms discussed; supplemental handouts will be necessary to make these points. Although interesting and informative, the film does not provide in-depth information about this fascinating animal and its associates.

595.4–.7 Insects; spiders

Amazing Ants. *Coronet Films & Video,* 1983. 11 min. Color. $261 (16mm); $183 (video), inquire for rental. Teacher's guide. ▶ **EI,EA,JH**

The social and physical structure of an ant colony is beautifully illustrated in this film, although the real focus is the variety of foods consumed by ants. The film explains why ants are called social insects and shows the relationships of worker ants with larvae and cocoons. The dangers that ants face when gathering food provide an unusual look at these insects as well as some real drama. The narration contains little scientific terminology, the technical quality and the accuracy of information are excellent, and the close-up photography makes one feel like a member of the colony.

Cabbage White. *Journal Films, Inc.,* 1986. (From the A Place to Live Series.) 15 min. ea. Color. $275 (16mm ea.); $275 (video ea.). Program guides available. ▶ **EA,JH**

Flies!

Hunters and Trappers.

Cabbage White focuses on the life cycle, biology, and psychology of the moths that, as caterpillars, plague gardeners. The film discusses sensory organs and capacities of moths, camouflage and palatability, and anatomical specializations for mating and clinging to leaves and twigs. *Hunters and Trappers* is about spiders and their two different adaptations of securing prey; some are active hunters, and some use their webs to trap. Differences in size, web form, and egg laying and hatching are shown for several species. *Flies!* is about hover flies, blow flies, horse flies, dung flies, and crane flies. Mating behaviors are discussed, as are life cycles. Several anatomical and sensory specializations are illustrated, such as hair cells used for touch, taste, and smell. The film makes clear that not all flies are pests; some are important plant pollinators.

The Gypsy Moth: A Dilemma. *Encyclopaedia Britannica Educational Corp.*, 1982. 14 min. Color. $290 (16mm); $29 (rental); inquire for video prices. o.n. 3713. Teacher's guide. ▶ **EA,JH**

Impressive footage of the life cycle of the gypsy moth nicely interweaves that life cycle, and the problems it creates, with the habits of humans. The gypsy moth, introduced into the northeastern United States 100 years ago, has no natural enemies; thus, the dilemma. Should we wait for natural enemies to adapt and prey on the insect or should we use synthetic chemicals to attempt to halt its spread? The film focuses directly on an ecological problem and illustrates some entomological principles in nontechnical terms.

An Inordinate Fondness for Beetles. *Carolina Biological Supply Co.*, 1986. (Prod.: Oxford Scientific Films Ltd.) 60 min. Color. $295.95 (¾-inch video); $269.95 (½-inch video); $50 (rental). ▶ **EA,JH**

This attractive, nontechnical program emphasizes the diversity of beetles and the fact that there are more species of beetles than any other animal group. Different methods of beetle defense are depicted. The excellent photography incorporates time-lapse sequences on the metamorphosis of ladybird beetles and destruction of crops by grain weevils and Colorado beetles, and slow-motion footage of beetles in flight, a tiger beetle larva tossing pebbles out of its burrow, and a frog eating an adult tiger beetle. The British narration is articulate; the sequences on predation by the tiger beetle larva and the dung beetle are particularly good.

Insects Are Amazing. *National Geographic Society*, 1987. 2 color filmstrips, 55 frames ea.; 2 cassettes, 14 min. ea. $62.95. Teacher's guide. ▶ **K,EP,EI**

"What Is an Insect?" presents the basic characteristics and life history of insects and illustrates how they use their specialized body parts to communicate, feed, and find mates. "Helpful and Harmful Insects" shows some of the ways in which insects interact with people and other organisms. A nice balance is achieved in showing how insects help people in activities such as plant pollination and the production of honey and how they harm people by feeding on crops, stinging, and spreading disease.

Ladybug, Ladybug. *Carolina Biological Supply Co.*, 1986. (From the Natural History Series.) 10 min. Color. $134.95 (¾-inch video); $119.95 (½-inch video); $45 (rental). ▶ **EP,EI,EA,JH**

This program explains the medieval origin of the ladybug's name and why this beetle is one of the insects most beneficial to man. The excellent photography incorporates time-lapse sequences showing development from egg to adult and slow-motion footage of ladybugs in flight. The ladybug, well equipped for evading predators, is shown escaping from a sheet-web spider, a tiger beetle larva, and an adult tiger beetle. The more serious threat to this insect is the widespread use of chemical insecticides. The narration is nontechnical but a bit stilted.

Small World: Insects and Spiders. *Society for Visual Education, Inc.*, 1987. 4 color filmstrips, 55 frames ea.; 4 cassettes, 9 min. ea. $35 (ea.); $159 (set). 24 skill sheets available ($27.50). Teacher's guide. ▶ **EP,EI**

After a general introduction that distinguishes spiders from insects, the three remaining strips cover caterpillars, butterflies, and moths; bees and wasps; and spiders. Important biological concepts—life cycles, anatomical similarities within groups, interdependence, social organization, and specialized adaptations such as camouflage—are discussed. The photography throughout is excellent. When coupled with field and laboratory activities, these materials can broaden understanding and appreciation of terrestrial arthropods.

Spiders in Perspective: Their Webs, Ways and Worth. *Educational Images Ltd.*, 1984. 2 color filmstrips, 68–76 frames ea.; 2 cassettes, 14–15 min. ea. $69.95. Teacher's guide. ▶ **EA,JH**

Part one discusses arachnophobia, spider classification, predatory techniques, the visual and sensory systems of spiders, silk production and uses, webs, and eight common spider families. Part two covers predators of spiders and protective mechanisms spiders have evolved. Kleptoparasitism, spider courtship and mating, indirect internal fertilization, egg production, care of the young, and the abundance of spiders and their impact on insects and humans are also reviewed. The narration is good, but the photographs vary in quality from excellent to only fair. The supplemental information is valuable.

Weave and Spin. *Carolina Biological Supply Co.*, 1986. (From the Natural History Series.) 12 min. Color. $134.95 (¾-inch video); $119.95 (½-inch video); $45 (rental). ▶ **EA,JH**

A study in the evolution of behavior and the influence of natural selection, this excellent film traces the possible evolution of the orb web from simpler, accidental insect traps and webs for encasing spider egg masses. A beautiful sequence demonstrates the construction of a classic orb web.

597 Fishes; amphibians; reptiles

Amphibians, revised. *Coronet Films & Video*, 1985. (From the Vertebrates Series.) 14 min. Color. $365 (16mm); $250 (video); $60 (rental). o.n. 4450. Teacher's guide. ▶ **EA,JH**

Reptiles, revised. o.n. 4457.

Snakes, 2nd edition. 1986. 15 min. $345 (16mm); $240 (video); $40 (rental).

Amphibians relates the use and uptake of oxygen to the habitat and structural adaptations seen in these creatures. It also shows feeding, mating, and egg-laying behavior, with excellent underwater views of eggs, egg masses, embryos, larvae, and adults. Also shown are structural and behavioral adaptations developed for temperature changes in the habitat. The dialog is clear and concise but not technical, and *Amphibians* provides excellent shots of habitat and close-ups and action shots of the animals. Students viewing *Reptiles* will receive a good visual overview of the diversity of reptiles and the biological characteristics that have allowed them to flourish in various environments. The film demonstrates thermoregulation of cold-blooded vertebrates and emphasizes the significance of the reptilian egg and other aspects of reproduction that made reptiles the first true land animals. The usefulness and nonpoisonous nature of most snakes is stressed, comparisons are made with other vertebrates, and the differences between amphibians and reptiles are well covered. After a brief and general introduction to the more than 2,200 species of snakes in the world, *Snakes* examines the wide variety of habitats in which snakes can be found. A fairly detailed presentation of the 19 venomous species found in the United States is followed by a brief discussion of snake reproduction, both egg laying and live birth. The film also covers predation of snakes and their economic value in helping to control rodents. Snakes are clearly depicted as magnificent creatures in their own right.

Fascinating Fishes. *Marty Stouffer Productions, Ltd.*, 1984. (Part of the Wild America Series.) 26 min. Color. $350 (16mm); $250 (video); $50 (rental). ▶ EA,JH

This film about freshwater fishes—primarily how they feed and reproduce—deals with primitive fishes, such as the lamprey eel and the alligator gar, and higher fishes such as the tiny darters and the migrating salmon. The paddlefish sequence is by far the best in the film, and the efforts to save this fish in the few habitats in which it still thrives are described in detail. The narration, although somewhat simplistic, is accurate and adequate. Wildlife conservation is stressed throughout.

Fish, revised. *Coronet Films & Video*, 1985. (From the Vertebrates Series.) 14 min. Color. $365 (16mm); $250 (video); $60 (rental). o.n. 4456. ▶ EI,EA,JH

This film makes good use of various examples to illustrate the diversity of shapes, sizes, and other adaptations found among fish, especially the bony fish. The characteristics shared by all fish are covered in depth, and there is a very useful explanation of gill structure and function. An introduction to how fish are classified is given, and variations in their patterns of reproduction and protective coloration are stressed. The film includes a brief but interesting section on fishing and fish hatcheries and the importance of fish as a food source.

Frogs and Toads—Watch Them Sing! *International Film Bureau Inc.*, 1986. 11 min. Color. $295 (16mm); $195 (video); $20 (rental). Teacher's guide. ▶ K,EP,EI,EA

This interesting film has excellent footage of several frogs and toads singing. The pictures are close-ups, and the sound is excellent. Some general information on life histories of these amphibians is also given, along with footage of mating, egg laying, and tadpole development. The film could be used repeatedly with children to develop skills in listening, observing, creative thinking, and writing, as well as to provide scientific information.

Remarkable Reptiles. *Marty Stouffer Productions Ltd.*, 1986. (From the Wild America Series.) 30 min. Color. $250 (16mm); $150 (video); $50 (rental). ▶ K,EP,EI,EA,JH

This program provides a remarkable glimpse into the mysterious world of some of America's reptiles. Scenes of writhing masses of red-sided garter snakes during mating and rare looks into snake dens are enhanced with appropriate music and factual commentary. There is also a good slow-motion examination of a rattlesnake striking a mouse. The survival technique of tail shedding in lizards is photographed well, as is the color change and molting of the anole. Overall, the photography and the commentary are excellent.

Reptiles. *January Productions*, 1984. (Part of A First Filmstrip About, Set III Series.) 1 color filmstrip, 56 frames; 1 cassette, 15 min. $22. Teacher's guide. ▶ EI,EA,JH

The refreshing format of this filmstrip is distinguished by its use of graphics only—simple, colorful drawings and diagrams that highlight major points. Even though some of the drawings lack sophistication, their simple appeal will capture young audiences. All the major features of reptiles are simply and clearly explained in a way that photographs could never achieve. Unfortunately, the supplementary materials are minimal, containing few discussion questions and no references.

Snappers. *Wombat Productions*, 1985. 18 min. Color. $360 (16mm); $180 (video); $36 (rental). Teacher's guide. ▶ **EA,JH**

This clear and beautifully photographed presentation introduces viewers to the natural history of the snapping turtle. Spectacular underwater sequences depict the mating behavior and development of these large predators. The film shows clearly that their continued survival depends on the preservation of their habitat, although the distinctly Canadian perspective may confuse younger students through "south of the border" references.

598 Birds

The Barn Owl. *Encyclopaedia Britannica Educational Corp.*, 1984. 20 min. Color. $400 (16mm); $320 (video); $40 (rental). Teacher's guide. ▶ **EI,EA,JH**

The film follows a barn owl pair through nest selection, courtship, incubation, and care of young and fledglings and promotes the timely message of the preservation of the barn owl. The photography is well done and gives a thrilling view of some seldom-seen events in the life of the barn owl: capture of prey, hatching of young, and paternal care and feeding of young. While obviously a European production intended for European audiences, the facts and statistics quoted are also applicable in North America.

Birds. *January Productions*, 1984. (Part of A First Filmstrip About, Set III Series.) 1 color filmstrip, 55 frames; 1 cassette, 15 min. $22. Teacher's guide. ▶ **K,EP,EI**

With an excellent mixture of color graphics and pictures, this filmstrip covers birds, from their evolutionary beginnings as relatives of reptiles to their present-day situation where some are in danger of extinction. The colorful photographs range widely, from turkeys and pheasants to kiwis and terns. Topics such as migration, flight, food gathering, and feathers and claws are handled well, both visually and orally. The labeled diagrams and pictures are clear and easy to understand and are reinforced by the narrative.

Birds, revised. *Coronet Films & Video*, 1985. (From the Vertebrates Series.) 14 min. Color. $365 (16mm); $250 (video); $60 (rental). o.n. 4458. Teacher's guide. ▶ **EA,JH**

This short, technically superior film has clear sound tracks, excellent shots of habitat, and close-ups and action shots of representative members of the species. It shows similarities and differences among birds and includes song, beaks, feet, feathers, and care of young. The film also illustrates adaptations to specific habitats using excellent close-up views, showing all the information needed to relate the key items used in avian taxonomy. The dialog is clear and concise but not technical.

Birds: A First Film. *Phoenix Films & Video, Inc.*, 1982. 12 min. Color. $240 (16mm); $150 (video); $38 (one-day rental, 16mm only). ▶ **EP,EI**

This delightful film explains the characteristics of birds. It describes flight, feathers, and behavior reasonably well but does not menton internal anatomy. It does an excellent job of depicting the great variety of birds as well as a number of their adaptations. A fine prelude to a classroom project that involves attracting birds to a feeder or even for a birding trip to a zoo or museum.

Birds, Birds, Everywhere! *Society for Visual Education, Inc.*, 1987. 3 color filmstrips, 40 frames ea.; 3 cassettes, 9 min. ea. $35 (ea.); $124 (set). 18 skills sheets available. Teacher's guide. ▶ **EP,EI**

This program introduces the world of birds, identifying many species and describing their habits, habitats, and calls. The filmstrips emphasize three major topics: diversity and habitat, structure and function, and life cycle. The information is accurate, but a few explanations appear somewhat Lamarkian. Accurate artwork is used throughout, the narration is well paced, and the background music and bird calls enhance the program. The content correlates with commonly used elementary science textbooks.

Birds of North America. *Society for Visual Education*, 1986. 4 color filmstrips, 43 frames (average); 4 cassettes, 8 min. (average). $35 (ea.); $99 (series). Teacher's guide. ▶ **EI,EA**

These filmstrips cover ornithological aspects of common land birds, water birds, birds of prey, and water fowl. They include good photographs of the various birds in their natural habitats as well as paintings by Roger Tory Peterson, Robert Bateman, and Maynard Reese. The narration is closely tied to the visual presentation and includes some information on the danger of DDT to bird survival, the balance of nature's food chain, and the role of humans in birds' survival.

Bluebirds . . . Bring Them Back. *Berlet Films*, 1985. 20 min. Color. $345 (16mm); $230 (video); $35 (rental). ▶ **EI,EA,JH**

Using superior photography and narration, this program shows truly outstanding in-the-box shots of the Eastern bluebird. Feeding the young, removal of fecal sacs, and hatching of the eggs are clearly illustrated. The film also examines the dangers of predators, the lack of available nesting cavities, and the competition with other species for nesting sites. The film ends with children constructing bluebird boxes and with bluebird trails being established in different parts of the country.

Kakapo: The Night Parrot. *New Dimension Films*, 1984. 30 min. Color. $535 (16mm); $385 (video). ▶ **EA,JH**

The story of a rare and unusual nocturnal parrot of New Zealand, told as a fairy tale, shows how this large, flightless, and endangered bird has managed to survive on remote Stuart Island. The music, moonlight, and remarkable filming and editing create a mood of mystery and sense of the past. A fairy-tale format may not be the most effective way to disseminate facts and the overall level of difficulty of the script is uneven, but the story and photography are exceptional.

Meet the Grebes. *Berlet Films*, 1986. 20 min. Color. $345 (16mm); $230 (video); $35 (rental). ▶ **EA,JH**

This film examines the six species of grebes found in North America, emphasizing the behavior of western and eared grebes. The film documents their elaborate courtship and unusual nesting and parental behavior in considerably more detail than is found in most nature films. Also included are some shots of a biologist studying nesting behavior from a blind and a closing plea to save the grebes by curbing water pollution and habitat destruction.

Silver Gull. *Centre Productions, Inc.*, 1986. (From the Animal Wonder Down Under Series.) 25 min. Color. $299 (¾-inch video); $279 (½-inch video); $50 (rental). ▶ **EA,JH**

This film provides a detailed introduction to the natural history of a species of bird that not only is highly successful in its natural surroundings but also has achieved one of the best adaptations to the human environment of any bird. Silver gulls demonstrate an extraordinary utilization of a wide range of foods, including natural items as well as man-made sources. The film shows some fine footage of the large colonies of the ground-nesting birds. Problems the gulls experience with lizards and snakes preying on their eggs are illustrated. Overall, a fascinating account of a species that inhabits two worlds— the wild and the civilized.

Trumpeter Blues: A Swan Story. *Trailwood Films*, 1987. 24 min. Color. $400 (16mm); $370 (¾-inch video); $350 (½-inch video); $40 (16mm rental). ▶ **EI,EA,JH**

This outstanding film reviews why the original U.S.–Canadian trumpeter swan population of thousands was reduced to the present 600 birds distributed in two flocks. Habitat ecology is well covered in a description of their yearly cycle, but past efforts by scientists to improve their survival are only briefly mentioned. Transplantation experiments are shown not to have worked well, and only one possible cause of their decline—the ingestion of lead shot is mentioned. The photography is exceptional, the sound and narration are excellent, and the organization is orderly and coherent. A top-caliber natural-history film.

Two Little Owls. *Berlet Films*, 1984. 20 min. Color. $345 (16mm); $230 (video); $35 (rental). ▶ **EA,JH**

Two Little Owls follows the growth and development of two great horned owls, from soon after hatching to several weeks after fledging. The film also briefly illustrates several techniques of field study, such as bird banding, analysis of regurgitated pellets, and the treatment of an injured owl. It does not contain any discussion of basic ecological or ethological principles, limiting its usefulness for grades above junior high. The photography is well above average, and the content should hold the interest of the film's intended audience.

599 Mammals

Mammals, revised. *Coronet Films & Video*, 1986. (From the Vertebrates Series.) 14 min. Color. $365 (16mm); $250 (video); $60 (rental). o.n. 4459. ▶ **EA,JH**

This film focuses on the adaptive characteristics by which mammals have become the most successful group of vertebrates. A good selection of examples is shown, from egg-laying mammals to marsupials and placentals. Variations in the key characteristics among different mammals are well illustrated, and adaptations for maintaining body temperature under all conditions including hibernation are discussed in detail. The film is able to cover material on variations in dentition and diets and differences in parental care and the development of the young. Typical marine mammals are also introduced, and the distinctions between their characteristics and those of fish are presented.

599.2   Marsupials

Egg-Laying Mammals: The Echidna and Platypus. *Educational Media International*, 1984. 15 min. Color. $310 (16mm); $250 (video); $30 (3-day rental). ▶ **EA,JH**

This interesting film describes the life of the only three members of egg-laying mammals known as monotremes. These three species, the duckbill platypus and two echidnas (spiny anteaters), are found only in Australia and New Guinea. All three species are shown in their natural habitats with fascinating footage of the young breaking out of the egg and being suckled by the parent. The photography is excellent.

The Little Marsupials. *Centre Productions, Inc.*, 1986. (From the Animal Wonder Down Under Series.) 25 min. ea. Color. $299 (¾-inch video ea.); $279 (½-inch video ea.); $50 (rental ea.). ▶ **EI,EA,JH**

The Remarkable Bandicoots.

The World of the Koala.

The Little Marsupials examines seven different small marsupials that occupy a wide range of ecosystems in Australia. It also examines the spiny anteater, a more primitive mammal that is neither placental nor marsupial. The program presents many interesting scenes in the daily lives of these animals, their adaptations for survival, and their diets. The photography and narration are excellent, making this film both pleasurable and interesting. *The Remarkable Bandicoots* examines the several species of bandicoot, Australian marsupials about the size of squirrels, omnivorous and nocturnal. They are common on the island of Tasmania but seem to be declining in number in Australia itself. However, this may in fact not be the case because these animals are small, very shy, elusive, and nocturnal and are just not seen very often. Excellent photograpy and narration. *The World of the Koala* succinctly describes the physical features of the koala, some of its behavior patterns, and its life cycle. Also featured are the unique ecosystems of the Australian eucalyptus forests and some of the unusual inhabitants found there. Since the koala is the only warm-blooded vertebrate that feeds entirely on eucalyptus leaves, its destiny and history are tied to the forests. At present, people and fire are the koala's two main threats. The film's photography is quite good, but the narration is sometimes trivial.

599.323   Beavers

The Beaver Family, 2nd edition. *Encyclopaedia Britannica Educational Corp.*, 1982. 14 min. Color. $290 (16mm); $29 (rental); inquire for video prices. Teacher's guide. ▶ **K,EP,EI,EA,JH**

This well-produced film chronicles a year in the life of a beaver family in the Rocky Mountains. In addition to the contrast of beaver activities with seasonal changes, beaver behavior with respect to colony maintenance, defense, and parental care is detailed. The narration avoids complex terminology and is skillfully done. The superb optical techniques include underwater footage trailing a swimming beaver and shots inside of a beaver lodge. Conservation, ecology, and behavior are all treated lightly but beautifully.

599.5   Cetaceans

Dolphins. *National Geographic Society,* 1983. 15 min. Color. $280 (16mm); $250 (video); $20 (rental). Teacher's guide. ▶ **EA,JH**

This short film provides a good introduction to selected aspects of the biology of dolphins. Experiments illustrate the ability of dolphins to find objects through the use of echolocation, and the anatomical and physiological bases for diving are described. Very young viewers may be somewhat bothered by the scenes of killer whales hunting a group of sea lions and singling out a baby, but the natural aspects of the predator-prey relationship are handled well, and the actual violence is not shown. A brief sequence captures the underwater birth of a dolphin. Some beautiful footage of dolphins in the open ocean and spectacular scenes of "porpoising" are also shown.

Dolphins: Our Friends from the Sea. *AIMS Media, Inc.,* 1986. 13 min. Color. $290 (16mm); $215 (video); $35 (rental). Study guide. ▶ **K,EP,EI,EA**

This attractive film of dolphins in a marineland environment shows how they are captured and trained. The anatomy, physiology, and activities of the dolphin are described in a very good animated sequence. The capture, training, and care of dolphins is well portrayed and treated with great sensitivity. Unfortunately, toward the end, the narration takes on an unnecessary, anthropomorphic tone.

Manatees: A Living Resource. *Educational Images Ltd.,* 1984. (Prod.: Buchan Publications.) 1 color filmstrip, 96 frames; 1 cassette, 21 min. $49.95. Teacher's guide. ▶ **EP,EI,EA**

This filmstrip describes the biology, habitat, relationships, and ecology of manatees. The photography is well done, and the narration is appropriate for elementary school children. The filmstrip shows that many of these rare marine mammals have been killed or severely injured by boat propellers, and there are some gory photographs of injured manatees that may not be appropriate for children. Although it explains that manatees are endangered both through direct killing and by the destruction of their habitat, the filmstrip shows many efforts by scientists, citizen's groups, and government agencies in Florida to save this remarkable creature.

The Mysterious Manatee. *The Pet Project,* 1983. 14 min. Color. $255 (16mm); $255 (video); $49 (3-day rental). Teacher's guide. ▶ **EA,JH**

Capturing interest with mysterious music and underwater footage, the film shows and describes the manatee's habitat, behavior, and anatomy; it also deals with some ecological relationships and environmental problems. Viewers' interest is maintained with almost continual footage of live manatees. Overall, the information is accurate, and the technical quality is good. Well worth showing to classes studying marine mammals, ecology, or conservation.

599.725 Hoofed mammals

Bighorn. *Marty Stouffer Productions Ltd.*, 1982. (Part of the Wild America Series.) 26 min. Color. $450 (16mm); $350 (video); $45 (rental). ▶ EA,JH

Bighorn provides a basic introduction to the life history of the Rocky Mountain bighorn sheep. The film also emphasizes the environmental and ecological aspects of the conservation of the bighorn's habitat. All viewers should enjoy the fine, often spectacular, photography. The sequences of the rams battling during the fall rutting season are excellent and make good use of slow-motion photography. At times, however, the narration seems too cute for all but the youngest audiences, and the soundtrack is too often melodramatic.

Born to Run. *Marty Stouffer Productions, Ltd.*, 1983. 26 min. Color. $350 (16mm); $250 (video); $50 (rental). ▶ EA,JH

This educational and entertaining film about the American pronghorn is well done and enjoyable to watch. The life of the pronghorn is traced from birth to death, showing many of this animal's struggles for survival and some of the adaptations that have helped it. The photography is excellent, especially the slow-motion shots of the pronghorns running.

Gazelle. *Encyclopaedia Britannica Educational Corp.*, 1984. (From the Silent Safari Series.) 12 min. ea. Color. $260 (16mm ea.); $210 (video ea.); $26 (rental ea.). Teacher's guide. ▶ K,EP,EI,EA,JH

Impala.

Rhinoceros.

Gazelle provides glimpses of several daily activities of the Thomson gazelle: grazing, territorial marking, male sparring, mother-fawn relationships, and predator interaction. As the film progresses, the sequences become longer and tend to center on herd behavior and predator-prey relationships. The film, presented without narration, is accompanied by an excellent set of background notes so teachers can prepare their classes for the viewing and add comments before, during, or after the show. *Impala* provides intimate glimpses of several daily activities of the impala: grazing and browsing, resting, grooming, male displays and jousting, some male-female relationships, and predator interaction. The longest sequences deal with herd behavior. The film is presented without narration, which expands its audience range. The excellent set of background notes in the teacher's guide can be used for preparatory instruction and for commentary before, during, or after viewing *Impala*. The notes can be tailored to the level and background of the class. *Rhinoceros*, which gives an excellent, close-up view of the rhinoceros in its habitat, completely lacks narration; instead, it is filled with the sounds of nature. This change is refreshing because it forces viewers to look closely to determine what is going on. There is a wealth of detail, and each viewing permits the audience to discover more information. The written guide supplied with *Rhinoceros* is scarcely needed.

The Majestic Wapiti. *Beacon Films*, 1984. (From the North American Species Series.) 16 min. Color. $360 (16mm); $330 (video); inquire for rental. Teacher's guide. ▶ EP,EI,EA,JH

Although the title suggests that it is primarily concerned with the wapiti, or elk, this film devotes considerable time to other North American ungulates, including moose, caribou, mule deer, and white-tailed deer. The photography of the animals and their scenic surroundings is beautiful, but the scientific content is not as fully developed as it might have been. The film does explore several aspects of the ecology and behavior of elk, and teachers can use it as a simple introduction to problems in ecology and conservation.

The Pig. *Barr Films,* 1986. (From the Animal Families Series.) 11 min. Color. $275 (16mm); $275 (video). ▶ **K,EP,EI,EA**

Young viewers will be delighted to meet the domestic pig on a modern hog farm. The film covers some basic pig anatomy, such as the split hooves and the snout adapted for rooting in the ground. Young pigs are featured while they nurse and as they play, displaying their curiosity and the development of social dominance. With outstanding photography, crisp editing, an excellent script, and well-paced narration, this short film is just right to hold the full attention of its intended audience.

The Remarkable Mountain Goat. *Berlet Films,* 1984. 20 min. Color. $345 (16mm); $230 (video); $35 (rental). ▶ **EA,JH**

This film briefly summarizes the life cycle of the mountain goat (*Oreamnos americanus*), using a single annual cycle as a framework. Most life stages are shown, and the close interaction between these animals and their high-altitude habitat is emphasized. The problems created by human-goat interactions are also addressed. The photography is good, and the usual dramatic symphonic music provides the acoustic background. The script is biologically correct, although elementary. The film avoids sentimentality as well as most temptations to anthropomorphize.

Trail of the Buffalo. *Encyclopaedia Britannica Educational Corp.,* 1983. 9 min. $215 (16mm); $215 (video); $21.50 (rental). Teacher's guide. ▶ **K,EP,EI,EA,JH**

This film presents significant events of a year in the life of a small herd of buffalo. The action follows newborn buffalo and their almost immediate struggle to walk, run, nurse, play, graze, and grow with the seasons. There are excellent sequences of bulls contending for mates and interesting close-ups of foraging and feeding behavior (especially in winter). A worthwhile addition to the natural history materials in school libraries.

Wildebeest. *Encyclopaedia Britannica Educational Corp.,* 1984. (Part of the Silent Safari Series.) 20 min. Color. $360 (16mm); $290 (video); $36 (rental). Teacher's guide. ▶ **EI,EA,JH**

This film, in an interesting departure from the typical nature documentary, does not have narration. Excellently filmed sequences depict the wildebeest during migration and feeding. One good sequence shows the birth of a calf. The predator-prey relationships are demonstrated as well, with a kill made by a cheetah. A long episode involves a lioness and cubs stalking, chasing, and catching a wildebeest calf. For the sake of younger viewers, the calf escapes and the cubs are merely practicing. The film gives a very good demonstration of how play trains juveniles for adult behavior.

The Year of the Wildebeest. *Benchmark Films Inc.,* 1984. 30 min. Color. $595 (16mm); $60 (rental). ▶ **EP,EI,EA,JH**

This film portrays the annual migration of the wildebeest of East Africa. It chronicles the attrition of the wildebeest at all stages of its life cycle. The problems of parasites, predation, and starvation are presented with care, and reasonable attention is given to the environment that the animals migrate through. Animated maps clarify the direction and extent of the wildebeest migration from the Serengeti Plain to the Olduvai Gorge. A remarkable presentation of a year in the life of these creatures that gives thoughtful attention to their place in nature and their prospects for survival.

599.74   Carnivores

Bears of the Ice. *National Geographic Society,* 1982. 23 min. Color. $400 (16mm); $360 (video); $30 (rental). Teacher's guide. ▶ EA,JH

This excellent, generally optimistic film examines the life of the polar bear, how its living habits affect a human community, and how the human community affects the bears. The efforts of the local officials to protect both the bears and the people are closely examined. Some events pictured (such as the shooting of a wounded bear) may be too graphic for children in kindergarten through fourth grade. For students who wish to know what a park ranger or wildlife biologist does, this film provides a clear, balanced image of their daily duties.

A Cougar and Her Cubs. *Encyclopaedia Britannica Educational Corp.,* 1983. 11 min. Color. $225 (16mm); $225 (video); $22.50 (rental). Teacher's guide. ▶ EP,EI,EA

This film depicts a cougar and her cubs throughout the seasons of the year. It stresses the relationship between the cougar and its prey in its natural habitat, but except for a few instances the film does not show how young cougars learn survival skills. The photography is excellent and the information is accurate.

Fishers in the Family, Parts 1 & 2. *Marty Stouffer Productions Ltd.,* 1984. (Part of the Wild America Series.) 26 min. Color. $350 (16mm); $250 (video); $50 (rental ea.). ▶ EI,EA,JH

North Woods Lynx. 1986. 30 min. $250 (16mm); $150 (video).

Wild Cats. 1983. 26 min. $350 (16mm); $250 (video).

The storyline in *Fishers in the Family* is simple: two orphaned fishers are raised in Stouffer's house, and then reintroduced to and released in the wild. Included are the standard scenes of young animals playing with each other and with humans, explorations of the outdoors, encounters with other animals, chasing and catching food, and finally their successful reintroduction into the wilderness. Many scenes appear contrived, and some of the animals exhibit behavior that indicates frequent association with humans, but the compelling story and the quality of the photography will hold the interest of upper elementary and junior high students. *North Woods Lynx* has high-quality photography and an instructive narration. Since the lynx is surviving fairly well in the extreme northern United States and especially in Canada, hunting and habitat extermination by man are only briefly discussed. The snowshoe hare is the lynx's major food source, and the ten-year cycle of increasing and decreasing hare population and its resulting effect on the lynx population are explored in detail. The prey-predator relationship is so well described and the necessity for the relationship is so sympathetically orchestrated that even the youngest viewer will appreciate why an appealing snowshoe hare must be eaten. *Wild Cats* is a beautifully photographed film on the various wild cats of America. The opening scenes are devoted to the cougar, then the film shifts to short scenes on the lynx, jaguar, jaguarundi, margay, ocelot, and bobcat. The film covers the role of play in learning, styles of caring for the young, general feeding habits, and some of the quirks of each species. Throughout, the point is made that humans have driven these predators to extinction and that our lack of knowledge of these cats has resulted in undue pressure on their survival. A good film for a general audience that has little scientific background.

The Great White Bears. *Enjoy Communicating, Inc.,* 1984. 1 color filmstrip, 71 frames; 1 cassette, 12 min. $29.95. Teacher's guide. ▶ **EI,EA,JH**

This informative and entertaining filmstrip presents the ecology of the polar bear. It also examines the conflict between humans and bears, using the bear population around Churchill, Canada. Methods of study and management are presented along with the closely regulated hunting activities of the local Inuit residents. The filmstrip concludes with a discussion of the new threats of oil prospecting and habitat pollution to the bears.

Land of the Tiger. *National Geographic Society,* 1985. 59 min. Color. $575 (16mm); $400 (video). ▶ **K,EP,EI,EA,JH**

A tiger stalking through a jungle to the tune of screaming animals taking flight establishes tigers as the jungle's primary predators and aptly leads into the story of this magnificent animal and the land it inhabits. The tiger's patience, cunning, stealth, and parenting habits are well illustrated in scenes that allow the viewer to follow the tigers throughout a year. The film was shot in two national parks in India, each offering different habitats. Through this superlative film, nature is portrayed as a dynamic interaction of the animal with its environment.

Lions of the African Night. *National Geographic Society,* 1987. 60 min. Color. $450 (16mm); $280 (video); $54 (rental). Study guide. ▶ **EA,JH**

This film offers the unusual opportunity to witness the nocturnal activity of the South African bushveldt. Focusing primarily on the night-hunting of lions, it also documents the nocturnal activity of various insects, amphibians, and other mammals. The movie is technically excellent, with fascinating closeups of animal behavior—hippos feeding at night, lions digging a warthog out of his hole, a centipede carrying her babies on her body, and foam frogs spawning as well as lions on kills and at play.

The Real Mr. Ratty. *Films Inc.,* 1984. (Prod.: BBC; from the Wildlife on One Series.) 30 min. Color. $495 (16mm); $198 (¾-inch video); $129 (½-inch video); $55 (rental). ▶ **EA,JH**

A thoroughly entertaining and educational documentary about the common European water vole. The vole's riverine environment and extensive tunneling in river banks are described. Outstanding photography reveals other animals common to the environment, including the vole's principal predators, blue herons and barn owls. The vole's short life span is outlined, and the film notes a behavior unique to these rodents—the young drive out their parents and take over their territory; the parents then die during the ensuing winter.

The Serengeti Lion. *Lucerne Media, Inc.,* 1986. (From the Let Them Live Series.) 20 min. Color. $405 (16mm); $205 (video). ▶ **EA,JH**

The focus of this film is the work of scientist George Schaller in the Serengeti National Park in the 1960s, where he studied the effect of lion predation. The film portrays Schaller's strong belief that it is crucial to know animals' biological and ecological characteristics, especially of predators, if we are to take significant steps to preserve a place for them in the world. Many misconceptions about lions are dispelled. The film also has excellent footage of how, when game isn't plentiful, the female lion may let her cubs starve while she feeds herself. Lions are shown to be cooperative in their hunting, but when it comes to actual feeding, it is every lion for itself. Highly recommended for classes studying ecosystems and predator-prey relations.

The Tiny Carnivores. *Centre Productions, Inc.*, 1986. (From the Animal Wonder Down Under Series.) 25 min. Color. $299 (¾-inch video); $279 (½-inch video); $50 (rental). ▶ **EA,JH**

A good film for introducing the basic biology of small carnivores using some of the fascinating animals of Australia. Most of the examples are taken from the marsupials, although there are some good illustrations of hopping mice and several species of lizards. The human role in extinction of species could be developed nicely after showing the material on the Tasmanian tiger. The film's value would be enhanced by maps and spellings of unfamiliar animal names, but it does provide excellent opportunities for teachers to build on concepts introduced.

Wolves and Coyotes of the Rockies. *Beacon Films*, 1983. (Part of the North American Species Series.) 15 min. Color. $360 (16mm); $360 (video); inquire for rental. ▶ **EP,EI,EA,JH**

The most interesting sequences in this handsomely produced film are on the hunting techniques of wolves and coyotes. The social and competitive interactions of wolves around a kill are also well developed. Because little of the film concerns itself with coyotes, the title is deceptive. The photography is a definite plus, but the information content is thin.

599.8 Primates

Baboon. *Encyclopaedia Britannica Educational Corp.*, 1984. (Part of the Silent Safari Series). 20 min. Color. $360 (16mm); $290 (video); $36 (rental). Teacher's guide. ▶ **K,EP,EI,EA,JH**

This beautiful film depicts a day in the life of a baboon troop in the northern Tanzanian Ngorongoro conservation area. Sleeping, traveling, foraging, and grooming are depicted, as are both affiliative and agonistic encounters, such as infant care, play, and aggression between males. Of special interest are the baboons' reactions to water buffalo, a lioness, a thunderstorm, and human observers. Although very brief, the sequences are wonderfully descriptive and instructive. The film lacks narration and analysis; only background music and some baboon vocalization and other animal sounds are included.

The Monkey. *Barr Films*, 1986. (From the Animal Families Series.) 11 min. Color. $275 (16mm); $275 (video). ▶ **K,EP,EI,EA**

This film features only the short-tailed, rather heavily built macaque. It explores several facets of the life of the macaque that relate to monkeys in general: the use of fingers and thumbs to manipulate food and to groom one another;

the foot with its opposable toe (in effect giving the primate four hands); feeding habits and climbing ability; social organizaiton; a degree of intelligence that enables simple problem solving; and parental care. The film illustrates the macaques' food and habitats and follows their seasonal movements. The color photography is outstanding.

Medicine

See also 371.42 Careers.

Does It Hurt? Preparing a Child for the Hospital. *Filmakers Library, Inc.*, 1983. 18 min. Color. $225 (¾-inch video); $40 (rental). ▶ **EP,EI,EA**

This charmingly natural film chronicles a boy's experience with a tonsillectomy from the time that he wakes up with another sore throat through complete recovery several days after surgery, and it shows actual patients and family members. Importantly, it takes John (and his family) through his surgery and hospitalization, recovery, and return home to show him fully restored a few days later. The realistic dialogue is especially effective.

Having a Sibling Go to the Hospital. *MTI Teleprograms, Inc.*, 1982. (Part of The Children's Medical Series.) 10 min. Color. $150 (video); $35 (one-week rental). ▶ **K,EP,EI**

This film is designed to help children and families deal with feelings such as hostility, fear, envy, and loneliness that an illness raises. It uses Muppet-like figures to represent the girl who is going to the hospital for a tonsillectomy and the boy who is to be taken care of by his grandmother while his sister is there. The film is very valuable for children, but it would be useful also for parents or others who care for children because the adult in the film responds well to the concerns raised by the puppets.

Living in the Future: Health. *The Media Guild*, 1983. (Part of the Living in the Future Series.) 15 min. Color. $310 (16mm); $220 (video); $25 (rental). ▶ **EA,JH**

This film is a pleasant introduction to the idea of using computers for a medical history interview. By pressing an electronic pad to record their responses, students answer questions that appear on a small television-style monitor (CRT). The excellent graphics, particularly near the beginning, are attention grabbers. Unfortunately, the British accents and idioms may create some difficulty for younger American children. The end of the film shows how a microchip can help to operate a prosthesis for a disabled child, but there is no transition from the medical-history segment. In addition, the film's ending is abrupt, and there is no overview. While this film will stimulate questions about automation in our lives, it does not convey much information.

My CAT Scan. *American Journal of Nursing Co.*, 1986. 10 min. Color. $200 (video); $40 (rental). ▶ **EP,EI,EA,JH**

This gem of a teaching film combines scientific accuracy, educational skills, and sensitivity to children's feelings. It is addressed to children who are facing computerized axial tomography, the CAT scan. The narrator is a small boy who describes his experience as an adventure in which a special kind of x-ray "took pictures" inside his body. His recollections and grasp of facts are clear and comforting to any audience. The few technical terms are clearly defined, and the film deals frankly with the natural fears that arise before a diagnostic test.

Preparing Children for the Hospital Experience. *American Journal of Nursing Co.*, 1986. 28 min. Color. $250 (video); $60 (rental). Study guide. ▶ **EI,EA,JH**

The rationale behind this film narrated by a clinical nurse specialist is that preparation of young patients for the hospital experience will save time for a busy nurse. This film and related study guide are a treasury of anticipatory guidance and hands-on pre-hospital and in-hospital preparation of children and their families, combining scholarship with practical pointers. There are sections on teaching methods and suggested readings for professionals, families, and the children themselves.

Slim Goodbody's Health Series. *Society for Visual Education, Inc.*, 1982. 4 color filmstrips, 45 frames (average) ea.; 4 cassettes, 8 min. (average) ea. $112. Teacher's guide. ▶ **K,EP**

This series of four filmstrips is an excellent springboard for discussions about health and visits to a doctor, a dentist, and a hospital. The set is generally well done and lively, although the "How to Have a Healthy Day" strip contains too many messages for most young viewers. The material is generally interesting, accurate, and sufficiently short to retain children's attention. Most children probably equate a visit to the doctor with receiving immunizations; unfortunately, the topic is missing from the germane filmstrip.

The Story of Disease & Health. *Hawkhill Associates, Inc.*, 1985. (From the Time, Space, & Spirit Series.) 1 color filmstrip, 80 frames; 1 cassette, 14–17 min. $39. Teacher's guide. Also available in video. ▶ **JH**

The Story of Disease & Health does a marvelous job of tracing the history of health and disease, simultaneously showing the effects of excessive eating, smoking, and driving after drinking. It mentions AIDS and Legionnaires' disease, making it an excellent aid for discussion of these topics with students. The filmstrip makes a seemingly uninteresting topic come alive via the historical approach.

A Visit with Health E. Elf. *Marshfilm, Inc.*, 1986. 4 color filmstrips, 50 frames ea.; 4 cassettes, 11–14 min. ea. $34.50 (ea.); $116.80 (set). Teacher's guide. Entire set with hand puppet, $126. ▶ **EP,EI**

This package portrays visits by Health E. Elf and his human friends to the dentist, doctor, hospital, and optometrist. Typical procedures are explained in easy-to-understand langauge, and the set is intelligent but not overly technical.

Production, film quality, and accuracy are excellent. The package should be used not alone, but as a part of a larger health science unit.

611–612 Human anatomy and physiology
See also 617 Surgery; dentistry; 618.4 Childbirth; pregnancy; 649.65 Sex education.

Bellybuttons Are Navels. *Multi-Focus, Inc.*, 1985. 12 min. Color. $250 (16mm); $40 (rental). ▶ K,EP

This film teaches the correct names for the various parts of the body. A grandmother babysitting her grandchildren (a boy of three and a girl of four) reads them a bedtime story of two similar children taking a bath. The storybook children identify and compare their own body parts, starting with the eyes, nose, mouth, arms, and fingers, and proceeding to the nipples and bellybutton (or navel). They conclude with the vulva, clitoris, vagina, penis, scrotum, buttocks, anus, legs and feet. All this is done matter-of-factly, without embarrassment.

Biomedicine Rebuilds the Human Anatomy. *Science Screen Report*, 1986. (Prod.: Allegro Productions, Inc.) 12 min. Color. $225 (16mm); $125 (¾-inch video); $100 (½-inch video); $50 (rental). Teacher's guide. ▶ JH

This film highlights advances in biomedical engineering that were in development or in use with patients in 1986. The design, manufacture, and operation of implantable cardiac pacemakers and artificial hearts are the most thoroughly discussed. Some animation illustrates functioning of organs or operation of devices, but the film moves quickly and teachers must supply details. One unfortunate statement, "the heart contracts in response to nerve impulses," is wrong, since nerves affect only the rate and force of the spontaneously beating heart. Otherwise, the film is a useful general introduction to biomedical engineering products.

The Body Systems Series. *Marshfilm Enterprises Inc.*, 1987. 32 min. Color. $99.95 (video). Teacher's guide. ▶ EI

The digestive, circulatory, respiratory, and skeletomuscular systems are covered in this presentation of four filmstrips that have been transferred to videotape. Students are asked questions and instructed to perform simple activities; this participatory approach is especially strong in the unit on bones and muscles. The original filmstrip format of still pictures makes it difficult to illustrate the dynamic processes of blood circulation and muscle contraction. In fact, the still illustrations peresent little more than what is found in most elementary textbooks. However, the tape is accurate and would be helpful to teachers looking for another way to introduce material on body systems.

Bones and Muscles: A Team. *Barr Films*, 1987. 18 min. Color. $425 (16mm); $425 (video). ▶ EA,JH

Glands and Your Body. 17 min. $410 (16mm); $410 (video).

In *Bones and Muscles*, animation illustrating the structure and function of the musculoskeletal system is set within a simple, well-acted plot of a teacher explaining bones, joints, and muscles to a group of junior-high students practicing for a ballet. The interaction of story line and teaching works and will hold students' interest. The information level is adequate and the technical quality is excellent. Animation is also used in *Glands and Your Body* to explain the location and function of the major human glands (except for the testis and ovary). The animation sequences are set within the simple and well-acted plot of a teacher explaining the glands to a group of junior-high students practicing a play. The animation is lively, but some of the concepts used to illustrate glandular function may lead to confusion. This film could serve as a general introduction to the glands, but careful and thorough teacher preparation will be needed.

Eyes—Seeing the Light. *Coronet Films & Video*, 1982. 15 min. Color. $370 (16mm); $259 (video). o.n. 80526. ▶ **EA,JH**

This accurate introduction to the anatomy and physiology of the human eye also emphasizes its care and protection. The thoroughness of coverage and level of concepts are certainly challenging enough for eighth and ninth graders, but quite a few segments use actors rather than animation, are very slow, and have poor acting and overly simplistic speeches. The narration is slow enough for note taking, and the cartoon-like illustration of how the parts of the eye function is excellent. There are good explanations of the conversion of light energy to an electrical signal, the role of the nervous system, and the formation of the image on the retina. The second part of the film has good coverage of near- and farsightedness, followed by a somewhat lengthy discussion of eye accidents, eye care, eyestrain, and signs of eye disease. Overall, clear, thorough, but rather dull in spots.

The Five Senses. *Clearvue, Inc.*, 1982. 5 color filmstrips, 33 frames (average); 5 cassettes, 10 min. (average). $21 (ea.), $88 (set). o.n. P287. Teacher's guide. ▶ **EP,EI**

This is a series of five short filmstrips, each devoted to one of the major senses: seeing, hearing, smelling, tasting, and touching. The first several frames tell about the nature of the stimulus involved and why it is important. Then the sense receptor is described, and its function is discussed. The captions are read by a narrator who tells the children to read along with him. Scientific terms are kept to a minimum. Each filmstrip concludes with several frames of self-testing review.

Growth and Change. *Films for the Humanities and Sciences, Inc.*, 1985. (From the Human Biology Series.) 26 min. ea. Color. $495 (16mm ea.); $199 (¾-inch video ea.); $149 (½-inch video ea.). ▶ **EA,JH**

Landscapes and Interiors.

Growth and Change can be used on several levels, depending on the maturity of the audience. The photography is spectacular. There is just enough content to make the film worthwhile for more than its esthetics, although the film-makers do appear to strive for visual impact. The discussion of bone growth and the differentiation of cells is particularly interesting. The circus performers who illustrate certain key points will catch the attention of younger viewers but may distract a more serious audience. *Landscapes and Interiors* explores the channels and surfaces of the human body. As such, it is an excellent way to introduce the mechanics of living animals. It does not pretend to be thorough, but it does achieve more visually esthetic goals. Nudity is tastefully handled, perhaps even too reticently at times. Viewers will probably be most intrigued by the internal shots of body passageways, joints, and functioning parts.

Human Growth II Series. *Marshfilm Enterprises, Inc.*, 1984. 4 color filmstrips, 50–57 frames ea.; 4 cassettes, 14–17 min. ea. $106. Teacher's guides. ▶ EI,EA,JH

This four-part filmstrip deals with the physical and sexual development of adolescents in separate sections for girls and boys. The set also includes a section on reproduction called "A Baby Is Born." Some of the set's strong points include its mixture of animation and photography, detailed information, technical quality, racial balance, and attempt to move away from traditional sex-role sterotypes. For older students, the set's lack of discussion questions, the total exclusion of birth control information, and the avoidance of nonreproductive sexuality are a deficit.

I Am Joe's Ear. *Pyramid Film & Video*, 1986. 25 min. Color. $450 (16mm); $395 (video); $65 (rental). ▶ EA,JH

This film attempts to make us more aware of our daily exposure to noise pollution and how it can damage our hearing. There are good illustrations of the functions of the outer, middle, and inner ear and of how sound is received and transmitted to the brain. Techniques to protect against hearing loss and hearing tests to diagnose problems are emphasized.

Inside Your Body. *National Geographic Society*, 1984. 4 color filmstrips, 46–52 frames ea.; 4 cassettes, 15 min. ea. $105.95. Teacher's guides. ▶ EI

This excellent introduction to the human body is rich with examples and illustrations that will appeal to 8- to 10-year-old students. Although the set does not overwhelm students with technical information, it does introduce a wealth of topics. The first filmstrip gives an overview and points out the many functions that the body performs. The next filmstrip discusses muscles, bones, and movement, and the third covers the respiratory, digestive, and circulatory systems. The last filmstrip discusses the brain and is interesting and informative. Overall, each filmstrip contains so much information that it is best to view them in sections.

Listen! Hear! *National Geographic Society*, 1982. (Part of The Human Senses Series.) 15 min. Color. $255 (16mm); $220 (video); $18 (3-day rental, 16mm only). o.n. 06088 (16mm); o.n. 06089 (video). Teacher's guide. ▶ JH

Listen! Hear! provides a good explanation of the anatomical and functional characteristics of the human auditory system. The examples are very good and appropriate for young students, and the photography is excellent. The teacher's guide has an excellent list of activities that will help young people increase their understanding of sound and ear anatomy and function.

Muscles and Joints: Moving Parts. *Films for the Humanities and Sciences, Inc.*, 1985. (From the Living Body Series.) 26 min. ea. Color. $495 (16mm ea.); $199 (¾-inch video ea.); $149 (½-inch video ea.). Teacher's guide. ▶ JH

Muscles and Joints: Muscle Power.

Moving Parts makes excellent use of graphics to demonstrate the relationships among muscle, ligament, bone, and joints and how the brain, inner ear, and various feedback mechanisms are involved in muscular coordination. Arthritic changes and some excellent views from within a knee joint are shown. This highly polished film cleverly uses a skilled water skier to illustrate the elements and mechanisms of human movement. *Moving Parts* is well executed technically and is comparable in quality and coverage to public television shows. Using a movie featuring a dangerous martial arts expert, *Muscle Power* teaches viewers how voluntary and involuntary muscles work. It is unconventional but humorous, enjoyable, comprehensive, and effective. Technical terms are generally not used. Mechanisms of contraction are simply portrayed with excellent graphics, and computer animation demonstrates intestinal peristalsis. *Muscle Power* has well-executed segments showing the beating of isolated heart cells as seen under a microscope, peristalsis viewed from within a living intestine, the emptying of a bladder, and vascular smooth muscle controlling the flow of blood through small vessels. A significant film of high technical quality that succeeds in every regard.

3-2-1 Contact: Your Body Systems at Work. *Guidance Associates,* 1986. (Prod.: The Children's Television Workshop.) 65 min. Color. $197 (video). Teacher's guide. ▶ EA,JH

The segments on genetics and reproduction, digestion, and the nervous system are excellent, while the discussions of the circulatory, respiratory, and muscular-skeletal systems are good. The coverage of kidney function is brief and poorly presented but does not detract from the overall excellent quality of the material. The lesson on genetics and reproduction includes fascinating film clips of the developing fetus and DNA replication. The terrific section on digestion includes the examination and dissection of the intestinal tract of a pig. Many of the techniques used to present the material are original and entertaining, and the overall technical quality of the film is good.

Your Body: Series II. *Focus Media, Inc.,* 1982. 4 color filmstrips, 86–100 frames ea., 4 cassettes, 13–17 min. ca. $140. o.n. S010E. Teacher's guide. ▶ EI,EA

This excellent filmstrip set covers the human circulatory and digestive systems. It provides accurate, detailed scientific facts in an interesting and useful way. The photography and illustrations are accurate and clear, and the set is highly recommended.

613 Personal health

See also 362.292–.293 Alcoholism; drug addiction; smoking.

Be Healthy! Be Happy! revised edition. *Perennial Education, Inc.,* 1983. 11 min. Color. $225 (16mm); $225 (video); $25 (rental). Teacher's guide. ▶ EP,EI

This excellent animated film presents five animal characters as prototypes of poor health habits. Dirty Duck is not acceptable because of unkempt hair, filthy clothes, and a dirty body. Picky Puss finds fault with all aspects of a wholesome meal and becomes obese by eating junk food. Musty Mole dislikes any physical activity and contact with fresh air and becomes weak, out of shape, and irritable. Sneezy Weasel constantly spreads a cloud of germs to all of her friends. Noddy Nightowl delays going to bed by puttering around with late-night television, games, and eating. The narrator is a child who speaks in rhymes and summarizes good health habits.

Boy Stuff. *Churchill Films,* 1987. 16 min. Color. $350 (16mm); $245 (video); inquire for rental. Teacher's guide. ▶ EA,JH

Girl Stuff. 1982. 21 min. $395 (16mm); $245 (video).

Girl to Woman, 2nd edition. 1984. 17 min. $340 (16mm); $340 (video).

Boy Stuff explains several hygiene problems that plague boys during preadolescence, adolescence, and early manhood. Amusing artwork and a light touch make this an engaging presentation of down-to-earth hygiene. The program covers fungus infections of the feet and genital area, unpleasant odors of body and clothing, dandruff, breast swelling, head lice, acne, and hygienic care of the penis. There are reassuring explanations of the obvious physical changes that occur in puberty and the even more unsettling changes in emotions, such as feelings toward girls and new embarrassments like surprise erections. This lighthearted approach to these troublesome topics gives wholesome and practical advice. In *Girl Stuff*, a pleasant and friendly voice interviews and discusses with three teenage girls of different ethnic origins certain aspects of feminine hygiene related to puberty. Most of the content centers around vaginal odor and menstruation. The anxiety that accompanies the onset of pubertal changes, the physiology and anatomy of the processes involved, and various commercial products are all completely illustrated. Deodorants, douches, and sanitary napkins and tampons are illustrated and explained. The symptoms of vaginal irritation and onset of menstruation are presented in an accurate, informative, and nonfrightening manner. The accuracy of the information and the photography are excellent. A group of teenaged girls appears throughout *Girl to Woman* in various situations that illustrate the points to be made. Some of these points are that growth rates differ for each person; your present size and shape are "normal" for you; and if you are dissatisfied with your body now, just wait a few years, it will improve. Acne, menstruation, the male reproductive system, and the process of fertilization are also described; intercourse is mentioned but not shown. The film ends with the statement that physical maturity does not indicate psychological maturity and readiness for parenthood and that it takes several years to get used to one's adult body and status. The film's tone is positive and upbeat, and its accuracy of information and clarity of purpose are excellent.

Breathing Easy. *MTI Teleprograms Inc.*, 1984. 30 min. Color. $495 (16mm); $300 (video); $75 (rental). o.n. 4630M. ▶ **EA,JH**

This film presents information about some of the hazards and deleterious side effects of smoking, such as bad breath, stained teeth, and chronic coughing. Using the format of a typical morning television program, the film introduces facts about smoking in a novel fashion. While many of the facts presented are highly technical, the general information concerning the health hazards of smoking is clear. The film employs personal interviews with television personalities who do not smoke.

Growing Up Female. *Journal Films, Inc.*, 1983. (Part of the Female Health Series.) 12 min. Color. $255 (16mm); $255 (video); $30 (three-day rental). Teacher's guide. ▶ **EA,JH**

This brief film cleverly dramatizes the physical changes and some psychological changes that accompany puberty. It uses a pajama party of three premenstrual girls as the source of questions and comments about puberty, and a sensitive older sister and animated illustrations provide the answers. Illustrations of the genitalia and reproductive organs, the functions of hormones in physical and emotional changes, the menstrual and reproductive cycles, as well as brief mention of intercourse, contraception, and masturbation are provided.

Marijuana and Human Physiology. *AIMS Media, Inc.*, 1986. 21 min. ea. Color. $475 (16mm ea.); $350 (video); $50 (rental). ▶ **EA,JH**

Tobacco and Human Physiology. $355 (video); $75 (rental).

Marijuana and Human Physiology teaches students that marijuana is a toxic, mind-altering drug; demonstrates the serious medical problems it causes; reveals that marijuana is a major cause of accidents at work and on the highway; describes the harmful psychological effects of marijuana through the testimonials of recoverying drug addicts; provides viewers with the facts so that they will reject marijuana; and supplies information needed in drug abuse rehabilitation and prevention programs. The information in this exemplary, well-produced program is current, accurate, and presented well, using anatomical drawings, x-rays, and tissue specimens. The dangers of smoking are presented well in this excellent production, *Tobacco and Human Physiology*. The graphics and illustrations support the material and are appealing and interesting. Topics covered include nicotine, smokeless tobacco, and the effects of smoking on the lungs, cardiovascular system, and the reproductive system. Highly recommended.

Noise: How Much Can We Take. *Educational Dimensions Group,* 1983. 2 color filmstrips, 76 frames ea.; 2 cassettes, 12 min. ea. $73. o.n. 1258BT. Teacher's guide. ▶ **EA,JH**

Approximately half of the first filmstrip documents our noisy environment with well-chosen, technically attractive photographs that range from forest and library background noise to NASA blastoffs. The kinds of sounds, but fortunately not the relative volumes, appear as accompaniment for the related narration. This filmstrip also provides a brief introduction to the nature of sound and to the anatomy and physiology of the ear. The second filmstrip raises questions about pleasurable sound—rock concerts or high-volume symphonic music, party noisemakers, firecrackers, and so forth. The presentation will make students aware of noise where they may never have noticed it before as well as showing them the problem of the loud noises of 20th-century living.

Not Without Sight. *Phoenix Films & Video, Inc.,* 1983. 20 min. Color. $325 (16mm); $195 (video); $30 (rental). ▶ **EI,EA,JH**

Produced for the American Foundation for the Blind, this film promotes public understanding of severe visual impairment—understanding in the sense of informed knowledge and in the sense of acceptance of those who have visual disabilities. It begins by pointing out that half of the general population has some degree of visual malfunction. Then it depicts the major types of visual impairment—macular degeneration, cataract, glaucoma, retinitis pigmentosa, and diabetic retinopathy—and presents simulations of vision with such impairments. Representative individuals are portrayed as having normal lives.

Smokeless Tobacco: It Can Snuff You Out. *Alfred Higgins Productions, Inc.,* 1986. 13 min. Color. $295 (16mm); $265 (video); $30 (rental). ▶ **EA,JH**

Smokeless Tobacco addresses the "newly discovered" addiction to smokeless tobacco through a variety of formats: narration; interviews with medical experts; personal comments from users, their peers, and victims of mouth cancers; and graphic pictures of medical consequences. The transition from one format to another is not always smooth, and the use of so many formats doesn't help an audience settle down with the message from any one source. The film uses the sort of "horror pictures" that prevention experts have avoided in recent years but which children and adolescents still find riveting.

Smoking and You. *Learning Tree Filmstrips,* 1983. (Part of the Health Decisions: Drugs, Alcohol & Smoking Series.) 3 color filmstrips, 50 frames (average); 3 cassettes, 8–10 min. ea. $68. Teacher's guide. ▶ **EA,JH**

The health effects of smoking are outlined for young adolescents who are frequently under peer or adult pressure to begin smoking. The set emphasizes that to smoke or not to smoke is a personal decision that individuals make. The set lists negative aspects of smoking while pointing out that there are no positive aspects to smoking. The set will have a much greater effect on those who have not begun to smoke than on those who are already smoking.

William Shatner's Mysteries of . . . "Getting Sick and Getting Well." *Lucerne Media, Inc.,* 1986. 10 min. Color. $220 (16mm); $105 (video). ▶ **K,EP**

This program employs animated three-dimensional figures to convey the importance of maintaining cleanliness. It is a reminder to kindergartners and first graders to wash their hands and certain foods, such as apples. Charming but sinister bacteria characters are shown doing battle with (antibody) "soldiers" within the body of a little boy who failed to wash an apple he ate. There are a number of biological inaccuracies in the script and visuals, but given the age of the intended audience, these do not present enough of a problem to not recommend the program.

615 Poisons and poisoning

Poisoning from Common Household Products. *Enjoy Communicating, Inc.,* 1984. 1 color filmstrip, 72 frames; 1 cassette, 13 min. $29.50. Teacher's guide. Also available in video. ▶ **EI,EA,JH**

This filmstrip is a useful supplement to a presentation on poisons. It explains what poisons are, mentions the routes of entry into the home, and gives a room-by-room survey of possible poisonous household items. Numerous ways adults can protect themselves and their children from accidental poisoning are discussed. The value of poison control centers in treating poison cases is stressed.

Poisonous Plants in the House and Garden. *Enjoy Communicating, Inc.,* 1983. 1 color filmstrip, 73 frames; 1 cassette, 13 min. $30. Teacher's guide. Also available in video. ▶ **EA,JH**

This filmstrip is supposedly designed to introduce children to common plants in homes and in gardens that may be poisonous. Unfortunately, it vacillates between addressing children and addressing parents or teachers. Nonetheless, the filmstrip is very useful because it shows why philodendron, dieffenbachia, yew, holly berries, nightshade, pokeweed, pyracantha, and Jerusalem cherries are the plants most often reported as poisoning children under five years of age. The filmstrip emphasizes not ingesting any plants not identified as edible by knowledgeable sources. It also strongly recommends calling the local Poison Control Center or family physician when poisoning is first suspected.

616 Specific health problems

Allergy? Aller-Choo! *Coronet Films & Video,* 1982. (Part of The Health Wise Series.) 15 min. Color. $319 (16mm); $275 (video). Teacher's guide. ▶ **K,EP,EI**

This attractive film combines puppetry, role-playing, and real-life glimpses of allergic children at home, in clinics, or in school. The film glides comfortably into the subject of allergy, a topic that affects and puzzles a high proportion of children. The film's detective approach to diagnosis will appeal to children and can pave the way for the tests and care that children need and need to understand.

Asthma. *MTI Teleprograms, Inc.*, 1982. (Part of The Children's Medical Series.) 10 min. Color. $150 (video); $35 (one-week rental). ▶ **EP,EI**

Asthma portrays a conversation between an asthmatic child (puppet) and his or her parent (puppeteer). Despite the film's brevity, it provides insight into the fear, anger, frustration, and isolation felt by an asthmatic child. The parent shows empathy toward the child without demonstrating pity or over-protectiveness. Throughout, the parent helps the child first express and then deal positively with his or her feelings.

Bacteria: Invisible Friends and Foes. *Human Relations Media*, 1983. 3 color filmstrips, 62–79 frames ea.; 3 cassettes, 20 min. ea. $140. o.n. 772-00-CS. Teacher's guide. Also available in slides. ▶ **JH**

This welcome addition to introductory bacteriology reviews the evolution of bacteria from primordial mud to bacterial genetic engineering. Part two, which discusses several medical aspects of bacteria, includes some misplaced emphasis on the use of antibiotics. Part three is an interesting examination of how bacteria affect the environment, particularly the worldwide ecosystem. The set's technical quality and microphotographs are excellent, and the information is accurate.

Cancer. *Time-Life Video*, 1983. (Part of the Getting Well Series.) 26 min. Color. $500 (16mm); $300 (video); $100 (rental). ▶ **EA,JH**

Viewers are provided with a needed review of the psychological and emotional factors of cancer. Narrated by Angie Dickinson, the film takes viewers through a series of self-help sessions led by Norman Cousins, and biofeedback is demonstrated as a method of combating illness and depression. Support groups are shown in action, aiding those who have or who are close to persons with cancer. The film is extremely well done technically, and the topic is not stressed nearly enough in our society.

Consequences: Spinal Cord Injury. *University of Washington Press*, 1986. 9 min. Color. $150 (16mm); $120 (¾-inch video); $110 (½-inch video). ▶ **EA,JH**

Consequences is an excellent risk-awareness film for young people. The action is fast paced, with exhilarating footage of sports such as hang gliding, diving, surfing, and automobile racing. Each sequence is dramatically interrupted by a cut-away to a young person in a wheelchair describing his or her accident. This film skillfully warns of risk without preaching and without admonishing complete abstinence from high-speed sports.

Contact Lenses and a Look at the Future of Seeing. *Knowledge Unlimited*, 1983. 1 color filmstrip, 25 frames. $13 ($8 for optional cassette). Teacher's guide. ▶ **JH**

Topics in this interesting general survey of contact lenses and vision include the anatomy of the eye, eyeglasses, eye surgery, and some common eye diseases. Although brief, the presentation is informative. The material is offered in anecdotal fashion at general and advanced levels, with a few more scientific terms and concepts introduced at the latter level.

First Aid: Newest Techniques, Series A. *Sunburst Communications,* 1985. 8 color filmstrips, 39–50 frames ea.; 8 cassettes, 6 min. ea. $299. Teacher's guides. ▶ **JH**

This series outlines basic first-aid techniques and is intended to clarify students' personal values and attitudes about helping others, to enhance their ability to set priorities, and to encourage development of judgment skills. The filmstrips cover artificial respiration, bleeding, poisoning, shock, burns, fractures, and rescue and transfer. Each subject is introduced in the context of a dramatized situation. Prevention is dealt with unevenly. A worthy, well-produced series with only minor flaws.

Head Lice. *Clearvue, Inc.,* 1982. 1 color filmstrip, 37 frames; 1 cassette, 7 min. $25. o.n. CL573. Teacher's guide. ▶ **EI,EA,JH**

This short filmstrip on head lice is remarkably lucid, straightforward, and utilitarian. The narration provides clear statements about the nature, detection, and treatment of this irritating parasitic insect. The vocabulary can be understood by third graders but is also suitable for well-educated adults. The head louse is a cosmopolitan problem that affects all ages and social classes, and this film handles the subject frankly and simply. A pleasing blend of photographs and cartoon illustrations conveys the basic points of handling infestation. The filmstrip recommends insecticides that are suitable for human body contact. Should be included in any good general hygiene program from the early elementary grades upward.

Health: Communicable Diseases, 2nd edition. *AIMS Media,* 1984. (Part of the Primary Health Series.) 10 min. Color. $220 (16mm); $165 (video); $30 (rental). ▶ **EP,EI,EA**

A pitiable E.T.-like germ opens this film by threatening viewers with communicable illness. The film illustrates how children can allay this menace by practicing good hygiene, washing their hands, and not sharing glasses, toothbrushes, or towels. Viruses and bacteria are not defined, potential fomites are not discriminated, and perhaps too little emphasis is placed on hand washing. Simple homilies on preventing contagious disease are given at least twice. One might object to the "war-against-germs" theme and the rapid-fire dietary advice; nevertheless, this film is on target most of the time.

Hemophilia. *MTI Teleprograms, Inc.,* 1982. (Part of The Children's Medical Series.) 10 min. Color. $150 (video); $35 (one-week rental). ▶ **EP,EI,EA**

A brother and sister, represented by two puppets, and their "mother" discuss the frustration and anger experienced by the child with hemophilia. The impact on other family members and their responses are also aired. The dialogue is excellent and shows a superb understanding of children and their feelings. A patient and the family, however, would need preparation before viewing the film because it assumes that viewers have basic knowledge about hemophilia. An excellent vehicle for fostering group discussion.

How to Catch a Cold: New Edition. *Walt Disney Educational Media Co.,* 1986. 10 min. Color. $269 (16mm); $202 (½-inch video). $50 (3-day rental). Teacher's guide. Also available in filmstrip. ▶ **K,EP,EI,EA**

This short film teams cartoon characters and a young boy to teach children how colds are caught and how they can be avoided. The cartoon graphics depict in a humorous way information that is difficult for children to visualize, such as the spread of germs through the air. The importance of maintaining good general health habits is emphasized, and children are cautioned to take medicine only under a parent's direction. Overall, an informative, factual, and appealing catalyst for discussion.

Seizures. *MTI Teleprograms, Inc.*, 1982. (Part of The Children's Medical Series.) 10 min. Color. $150 (video); $35 (one-week rental). ▶ **EI,EA,JH**

Seizures is a thoughtful, lively film of a discussion between two children (puppets) and an adult (ventriloquist). It addresses the major concerns of children who have seizures: fears of hurting themselves or others, accusations of being crazy, anxiety about wetting their pants in school, the importance of ongoing medical treatment, their hopes of a cure through future research, and their uncertainties about vocational opportunities.

VD: Attack Plan. *Walt Disney Educational Media Co.*, 1982. 16 min. Color. $360 (16mm). ▶ **EA,JH**

This is an entertaining film about a grim subject. What the film does, it does well; unfortunately, what it doesn't do might be even more important. It provides basic facts about gonorrhea and syphilis in an unoffensive but forthright manner without preaching, pleading, or prurience. It combines a simple story line with clever animation to create an effective teaching instrument; the only technical defect is a tendency toward long-windedness by the narrator. However, there is very little here to motivate behavior modification, which, at present, is the only prevention method that works. Moreover, the film deals only with gonorrhea and syphilis. No mention is made of the sexually transmitted diseases that are most in need of educational tools: herpes and nongonococcal urethritis.

Vocal Nodules. *MTI Teleprograms, Inc.*, 1982. (Part of The Children's Medical Series.) 10 min. Color. $150 (video); $35 (one-week rental). ▶ **K,EP,EI**

Children with vocal nodules will be happy with this film because it highlights and dispels worries about this ailment. The film relies on an engaging dialogue between an empathetic adult and two appealing puppets, one of whom expresses the concerns that may develop in a child with vocal nodules. Youngsters are reassured that their voices will not permanently disappear and that if they inadvertently raise their voices occasionally, they will not suffer serious consequences. The film excels in its attention to the psychological consequences of the ailment.

617 Surgery; dentistry

Plastic Surgery. *MTI Teleprograms, Inc.*, 1982. (Part of The Children's Medical Series.) 10 min. Color. $150 (video); $35 (one-week rental). ▶ **K,EP,EI,EA,JH**

This short film is directed toward any child who needs to enter the hospital for plastic surgery, in this case, the removal of a facial lesion. In the film, two puppets discuss with the puppeteer their feelings about the lesion and its removal. The dialogue is designed to alleviate children's fears about this procedure and help them deal positively with it. The film is both informative and entertaining, and the color and sound are excellent.

Preventive Dental Care. *Journal Films, Inc.,* 1983. (Part of The Dental Health Series.) 14 min. Color. $295 (16mm); $295 (video); $30 (3-day rental). Teacher's guide. ▶ **EA,JH**

This film combines excellent microscopic cinematography with clear animation that focuses on flossing technique and why to do it. The instruction in this technique is thorough and detailed, and the intraoral photography is superior. The film also includes instruction on brushing and oral irrigation.

The Tooth and Gum Revue. *Barr Films,* 1986. 18 min. Color. $425 (16mm); $425 (video). Study guide. ▶ **EP**

Puppets discuss (in short songs) the role of diet and bacterial plaque in tooth and gum disease. Flossing and brushing techniques are illustrated and explained. Children are encouraged to work with their parents in dental care since their young motor skills aren't yet up to flossing. The vocabulary and repetition are appropriate for the target audience. This film could be used with large groups or individually with professional, individual oral hygiene instruction.

618.4   Childbirth; pregnancy

See also 611–612 Human anatomy and physiology.

The Miracle of Life. *Time-Life Video,* 1983. (Part of the "NOVA" Series.) 57 min. Color. $850 (16mm); $250 (video); $85 (rental). ▶ **EA,JH**

This beautiful and interesting film about human reproduction is appropriate for anyone above sixth grade. Many potentially difficult subjects are handled with good taste, but parental guidance is suggested for the very young. The photography is terrific. Unfortunately, the film is flawed by small errors, but despite these problems, it is well worth viewing.

Pregnant Teens: Taking Care. *Perennial Education, Inc.,* 1983. 22 min. Color. $450 (16mm); $450 (video); $45 (rental). Teacher's guide. ▶ **EA,JH**

This clearly narrated account of teen-agers' reactions to their pregnancies focuses on the need for prenatal care. Developed by the March of Dimes, the film's objective is to help prevent birth defects. Although it mainly depicts a middle-class setting, the film can be useful in working with a wide range of teens, preteens, adults, and health professionals and will be most effective if used by a discussion leader and accompanied by active group participation.

Engineering

621 Applied physics

See also 371.42 Careers; 530–540 Physics and chemistry.

The Amazin' Laser. *Educational Dimensions Group,* 1982. 2 color filmstrips, 65–71 frames ea.; 2 cassettes, 15 min. ea. $73. o.n. 1254. Teacher's guide. ▶ **EA,JH**

This filmstrip set first develops the definitions of light, amplification, stimulated emission, and radiation and details the various types of lasing materials. The second part shows uses of lasers in research, industry, medicine, and communications. The presentation is accurate, concise, and well organized, but the visual portion relies heavily on what appear to be corporation publicity stills.

Journey to Tomorrow: Communication. *Walt Disney Educational Media Co.,* 1983. 20 min. Color. $445 (16mm); inquire for rental. Teacher's guide. ▶ **EI,EA,JH**

The film traces the role of technology in the development of communication. Donald Duck is transported through time to witness the assumed beginning of language in 34,000 B.C.; the development of Gutenberg's press, the telegraph, and radio; and the advent of video libraries, cable TV, satellites, and computers. The film mentions application of communication technology to business, the home, health care, entertainment, and government and stresses the continuing importance of message content. The film's visuals are good, but the loud soundtrack message is delivered by the quacking Duck, whose body language has always been superior to his verbal clarity.

The Laser Beam, 2nd edition. *Handel Film Corp.,* 1982. 20 min. Color. $360 (16mm); $360 (video); $36 (rental). ▶ **EA,JH**

Laser Beam is a high-quality film that leads viewers through brief explanations of the laser, light, and coherence, the advantages of laser light, and the different types of lasers. The film shows many uses of lasers: in surgery, industry, communication, measurement, the military, and to generate fusion energy. The photography, animation, color, and narration are all very good.

Living in the Future: World. *The Media Guild,* 1983. (Part of the Living in the Future Series.) 15 min. Color. $310 (16mm); $220 (video); $25 (rental). ▶ EA,JH

Using vivid color, attention-getting music, and impressive photography, this film covers a digital communications system, but without going into any detail as to how the components work or interface. The film's message is that through modern communications, people can understand each other's problems and minimize or prevent natural and man-made catastrophes. However, because of the vivid scenes of emaciated children—one child is covered with flies—teachers should discuss this subject matter with young students before presenting it to them.

Robots: The Computer at Work. *Educational Media International,* 1985. 22 min. Color. $450 (16mm); $395 (video); $40 (rental). ▶ EA,JH

This film contrasts new computer-based control systems with early mechanical control devices and answers some basic questions about robots. Nearly half the film deals with research on techniques to make robots behave more like humans. The segment on hand-like manipulator arms and walking robots is excellent. However, the presentation of basic ideas may not excite students enough for them to benefit from the film. Most of the footage is from Japan.

Windsong. *Centre Productions, Inc.,* 1984. 20 min. Color. $385 (16mm); $275 (video); $40 (rental). ▶ EA,JH

Windsong traces windmill technology from its origins in Holland to its development and adaptation to conditions in the New World, where it proved to be a particularly important and interesting influence on settlement of the American West. Though *Windsong* does a commendable job of explaining the rise and seemingly sudden decline of windmills during an era of cheap electrical energy from other sources, the case for a bright future as an alternative energy source is weak. A useful film for classroom use in science or American history courses.

629.1 Aerospace engineering
See also 371.42 Careers.

***Gossamer Albatross*—Flight of Imagination.** *Coronet Films & Video,* 1985. 14 min. Color. $320 (16mm); $225 (video); $45 (rental). ▶ K,EP,EI,EA,JH

Gossamer Albatross is the story of fantasy made real—the dream come true of flying by our own power. It chronicles the *Albatross* airplane from its development through its celebrated flight across the English Channel, presenting the technology of featherweight materials that have the strength of steel. Unfortunately, the difficulties, advancements, and final glory are all presented in a boring, disconnected, and technically poor manner. In addition, the program lacks a study guide and bibliography and is plagued with poor sound. However, in the absence of another film on the *Albatross,* even this one is worth seeing.

Orbital Shapes and Paths. *Journal Films, Inc.,* 1984. (From the Space Science Series.) 10 min. ea. Color. $185 (16mm ea.); $185 (video ea.); $20 (3-day rental ea.). Teacher's guide. ▶ JH

Rendezvous.

Through animation, *Orbital Shapes and Paths* illustrates equatorial orbits and ground tracks for inclined orbits, showing satellite coverage of the earth. While communication from geostationary orbit is treated, the film lacks examples of ground coverage for different applications. The animation is simple and clearly illustrates the narrative. Targeted for junior- and senior-high students, this film will not present much of a challenge, but it is well done and clearly presents the simple relationships among orbital parameters. *Rendezvous* presents the problem of rendezvous and docking of spacecraft as a paradox: to catch up to another object in orbit, one needs to slow down (decrease orbital velocity) to fall into a lower orbit with a shorter rotational period. Without being quantitative, the film nevertheless relates orbital velocity with radius and period and shows circularization of orbits and plane changes. Vectors are introduced to illustrate plane changes. *Rendezvous* is enhanced by numerous beautiful sequences of two vehicles actually docking and is aided by good use of animation. Correct, challenging, and interesting, it is recommended for seventh- to eighth-grade science and math classes.

The Space Race. *Walt Disney Educational Media Co.,* 1985. 4 color filmstrips, 76–93 frames ea.; 4 cassettes, 10–12 min. ea. $129. Teacher's guide. ▶ **EA,JH**

This four-part program covers highlights of the United States and Soviet space programs, from their beginnings through the 1985 *Challenger* mission. The main historical events of the space race are presented, providing an excellent springboard for studying the historical, technical, political, or sociological aspects of the space race. The four parts would be best used in separate but sequential study sessions. The program has excellent narration and a good blend of historical pictures and modern NASA color photographs.

Space Research and You: Your Home and Environment. *National Audio Visual Contor,* 1982. (Part of the Space Research and You Series.) 15 min. ea. Color. $145 (16mm ea.); $70 (video ea.). Teacher's guide. ▶ **EA,JH**

Space Research and You: Your Transportation.

Your Home and Environment shows the many benefits for earth's environment that have accrued from NASA's exploration of space. The film discusses how Landsat photographs have been used in discovering new resources, in land-use studies, and in the detection of large-scale pollution; then it shows how they are being used to alleviate some of our pollution problems. As a diversion from other studies and as educational entertainment, *Your Home and Environment* is useful; it should stimulate discussion and provoke ideas. NASA produced the polished and well-photographed film *Space Research and You: Your Transporation* to show the public how their research benefits transportation on this side of outer space. The major point is that NASA innovations are transferred to American companies so that air, land, and sea transportation become safer and more efficient. *Your Transportation* does not offer an economic analysis of these spin-offs, nor does it question whether the public or American corporations are the main beneficiaries of space program products. It is a public relations film that is designed to enhance NASA's image, superficial but nonetheless quite interesting.

Space Science: Space Shuttle—Yesterday, Today and Tomorrow. *Science Screen Report, Inc.,* 1984. 13 min. Color. $250 (16mm); $250 (video). ▶ **EA**

This film, a brief composite of some visually appealing footage from various shuttle missions, asks viewers to imagine that they are crew members on a space shuttle trip. Astronauts are shown launching a satellite from the payload bay, getting suited up for work outside the shuttle, and repairing the Solar Maximum Mission satellite. Excellent animation and superb computer graphics illustrate concepts for a future space station. Re-entry is illustrated by rarely seen footage of the high-temperature glow surrounding the shuttle as seen from inside the cockpit. Although marred by a number of misleading statements and visuals that sometimes do not match the narration, the film is a good discussion starter for the elementary grades.

Agriculture

See also 580 Botanical sciences; 641 Nutrition.

Food: A Basic Need. *Encyclopaedia Britannica Education Corp.*, 1982. 4 color filmstrips, 64 frames (average) ea.; 4 cassettes, 8 min. ea. $108. Teacher's guide. ▶ **EI,EA**

The first part of this filmstrip set is an excellent, very informative introduction to the basic concepts and history of the role of food in meeting community and individual needs. It is also very effective in showing the ways various communities acquire, preserve, and transport food. The second part classifies plant foods and demonstrates how they are grown, processed, and marketed in contemporary society. Part three very effectively takes an approach similar to part two but with animal products. The final part takes a very creative perspective in looking at food in other cultures and encouraging students to try a wide variety of food products.

Get Ready, Get Set, Grow! *Bullfrog Films*, 1987. (Prod.: Brooklyn Botanic Garden.) 15 min. Color. $325 (16mm); $250 (video); $35 (rental). Two activities booklets. ▶ **EP,EI,EA,JH**

This presentation features children participating in the Brooklyn Botanic Garden's yearly project of growing plants in a vegetable garden. This program, narrated by a child, shows the children as they prepare the soil, plant seeds, weed and mulch, harvest, and eat their produce. Time-lapse photography of root growth is done very well. The narration is well timed and uses familiar analogies meaningful to children. The two booklets that accompany the program are excellent; one is a child's calendar guide to gardening, and the other suggests activities for parents and teachers to involve children in gardening.

Our Food. *International Film Bureau Inc.*, 1983. 19 min. Color. $300 (16mm); $285 (video); $25 (rental). ▶ **EP,EI,EA**

This film traces typical foods in the Western diet from source through various processing techniques to the consumer. Visits to various sites show viewers how grain, dairy products, poultry and eggs, meat and fish, and fruits and vegetables are produced. Where appropriate, early methods as well as modern techniques of food production are described.

Where Does Food Come From? *Alfred Higgins Productions, Inc.*, 1986. 17 min. Color. $380 (16mm); $340 (video); $38 (rental). Teacher's guide. ▶ EI,EA

This delightful production introduces many aspects of food production and processing to young children. The child actors are somewhat amateurish, but their brief presentations do not detract from the important lessons of the film. The photography and script provide viewers with a behind-the-scenes look at animals and crops on farms and at machinery and packaging in food-processing plants. Animated characters of milk, carrots, apples, bread, beef, and spaghetti are followed from the farm to the market in a series of travelogues that relate to the scientific, social, and nutritional aspects of the food we eat.

639.9 Wildlife conservation

Another Africa: Wildlife and People in Conflict. *Centre Productions, Inc.*, 1986. 25 min. Color. $500 (16mm); $300 (¾-inch video); $275 (½-inch video); $50 (rental). ▶ EA,JH

This exceptional educational film explores the cultural, social, and ecological implications of the growing conflict between people and wildlife in East Africa. In addition to fine narration and outstanding nature photography, the film effectively uses interviews with a safari guide, a native Masai, and a farmer to elucidate various concerns. A clear and objective explanation of one of the great conservation dilemmas of the developing world.

Cricket, Tiglet & Friends. *Bullfrog Films*, 1985. 9 min. Color. $200 (16mm); $95 (video); $25 (rental). Teacher's guide. ▶ EI,EA

This film is about work that is done at the Owl Rehabilitation Research Foundation in Ontario, Canada. The film begins with researcher Kay McKeever and a young friend examining a burrowing owl that has come to believe that McKeever is its mother. Because of this misconception the owl will have to remain in captivity throughout its life. The youngster is then shown other owls and how to avoid imprinting them so that they may be returned to the wild. The photography is superb, and the dialogue contains an excellent message.

Discover Wildlife in Your World. *National Wildlife Federation*, 1986. 1 color filmstrip, 80 frames, or 80 color slides; 1 cassette, 10 min. $24.95 (strips); $26.95 (slides). Teacher's guide. ▶ EI,EA

This filmstrip explores wildlife in various rural, suburban, and urban settings and suggests ways to improve the wildlife habitat where students live. Most of the photographs are well chosen, and the narration is clear and well paced. However, the script is weakened in places by oversimplification, and it would be more effective if the emphasis had been restricted to only one of the themes. The value of the program will be directly proportional to the knowledge of the teacher who shows it.

The Dream Forest. *Centre Productions, Inc.*, 1985. 24 min. Color. $475 (16mm); $275 (video); $50 (rental). Study guide. ▶ K,EP

The Dream Forest, about a young girl and a raccoon, attempts to provide grade-school children with a "more mystical concept of animals," including a sense of awe for the mystery of life itself. This film is loaded with beautiful wilderness scenes, and the script is warm and sentimental. Young people will enjoy the fantasy, and talented teachers will be able to turn it into a good lesson.

Harp Seals on the Pack Ice. *Enjoy Communicating, Inc.*, 1982. 1 color filmstrip, 55 frames; 1 cassette, 9 min. $26. Teacher's guide. ▶ **EI,EA,JH**

Part of this filmstrip deals with the migration and whelping of harp seals, but the main focus is the controversy between commercial hunters and conservationists. This controversy is well defined, and both sides of the issue are clearly and fairly stated. The technical quality of the presentation is adequate, although a few photographs do not coincide with the narration. Closeups of the pups are the most artistic and appealing photographs, but to add sparkle to the presentation, additional color and/or underwater photographs could have been used.

Legacy for a Loon. *Berlet Films*, 1983. 20 min. Color. $340 (16mm); $170 (video); $34 (rental). Teacher's guide. ▶ **EA,JH**

The quality of photography here is far better than in most educational films. The first half of the film traces the life cycle of the loon on a New Hampshire lake, beginning with courtship and mating and moving on to nesting and parental behavior. The second half deals with the present threat to the loon, mainly from increased use of its habitat for recreational purposes. The main purpose is to increase the awareness and sensitivity of students to environmental issues that concern threatened species; the film does this well.

Project Puffin. *Learning Corporation of America*, 1982. 13 min. $275 (16mm); $30 (rental). Teacher's guide. ▶ **EI,EA,JH**

This delightfully entertaining and highly educational film is about the Atlantic puffin and the present efforts to preserve this species. The photography is excellent, as is the narrative about the planned actions that are leading to the reestablishment of nesting colonies. Unlike many films about the environment, this film is a success story. It explores the general structures and functions of puffins, food gathering and eating, locomotion, life cycle, protective behavior features, habitat, and predator-prey relationships. Excellent story and film work.

Sound of the Lake Country. *Centre Productions, Inc.*, 1986. 11 min. Color. $225 (¾-inch video); $150 (½-inch video); $30 (rental). ▶ **EA,JH**

This brief program describes a specific local environmental problem, its causes, and some possible solutions. The problem is a recent dramatic decline in the breeding population of the common loon in Wisconsin. The film shows the efforts of the state wildlife department to count the loons on the lake and illustrates the probable causes of the population decline. The program could be used as a case study to stimulate a general discussion of the social and economic forces affecting many environmental issues. It is technically well done, clearly organized, and appears factually accurate.

Vanishing From the Earth. *National Geographic Society*, 1986. 3 color filmstrips, 53 frames ea.; 3 cassettes, 17–18 min. ea. $84.95. Teacher's guides. ▶ **EA,JH**

Part one of this excellent series explores the causes of extinction and the accelerated rate of extinctions in recent years due to habitat destruction, overhunting, and pollution. Part two presents the consequences of extinction, the interdependence of species in natural communities, and the potential value of species in the future. The third part suggests how endangered species might be saved through habitat protection, biological gardens, conservation, and reintroduction. The photography is superb and visually stimulating in this clear and well-ordered presentation.

Watching Wildlife. *Marty Stouffer Productions Ltd.*, 1982. (Part of the Wild America Series.) 27 min. Color. $550 (16mm); $450 (video); $50 (rental). ▶ EA,JH

The aim of this film is to create the desire and impart some knowledge about where, when, and how to watch animals. The narrator points out the need for a library search to understand the animal to be watched before entering the field. The film has a logical and carefully developed story line that presents a wide range of animals inhabiting various environments. The excellent photography provides a panoramic view of different environments, with numerous closeups of the animals that will intrigue viewers.

Will They Survive. *Centre Productions, Inc.*, 1982. 2 color filmstrips, 100 frames (average); 2 cassettes, 12 min. ea. $50. o.n. CE398. Teacher's guide. ▶ EI,EA,JH

This filmstrip set deals with a select group of endangered and threatened species of animals. Problems and some attempts at solutions are illustrated; in some of the examples the management efforts show real success and promise. The stress on habitat destruction and real conflict between man's interests and the well-being of certain species is quite appropriate, although the set does not really stress the significance of species loss. The subtle and indirect arguments may be difficult for elementary students.

Home Economics
and
Family Living

Clothing: A Basic Need. *Encyclopaedia Britannica Educational Corp.*, 1982. 4 color filmstrips, 63 frames (average) ea.; 4 cassettes, 8 min. ea. $108. Teacher's guide. ▶ **EP,EI**

Each filmstrip focuses on a specific topic related to clothing, including reasons for wearing clothes, sources and production of cloth, making clothes, and clothing from different cultures. The information is accurate, the concepts are appropriate for elementary pupils, and major concepts are reinforced. Children will be able to relate to many of the examples in the photographs but may have difficulty with some of the vocabulary. Could be used for either social studies or science instruction in the elementary grades.

641 Nutrition
See also 611–612 Human anatomy and physiology; **Agriculture** section.

Basic Nutrition: Let's Make a Meal. *Journal Films, Inc.*, 1983. (Part of the Nutrition Series.) 17 min. Color. $350 (16mm); $350 (video); $35 (3-day rental). Teacher's guide. ▶ **EA,JH**

Using an upbeat, TV game show format, this film moves rapidly through a number of major nutritional areas. The four food groups are covered, and nutrients are classified into carbohydrates, fats, proteins, minerals, and vitamins. The film mentions the importance of water and fiber, and foods are presented as a combination of nutrients with variety a key factor in obtaining all the needed nutrients. Some diseases related to nutritional intake are discussed. The film will catch and hold the attention of young audiences and is an excellent springboard for further discussion.

Food for Thought: Fruits and Vegetables. *Beacon Films*, 1982. (Part of the Food for Thought Series.) 9 min. Color. $220 (16mm); $220 (video); inquire for rental. Teacher's guide. ▶ **EI,EA,JH**

This film depicts a trip to a huge vegetable farm that sparks the interest of two teenagers as they discover the many steps involved in processing fruits and vegetables. Well photographed, it accurately presents many nutritional sources found in fruits and vegetables. Recommended to promote general awareness of fruit and vegetable food group sources and the steps needed to process these foods from the field to the supermarket.

Food: Keep It Safe to Eat. *Alfred Higgins Productions, Inc.*, 1982. 20 min. Color. $395 (16mm); inquire for rental. Teacher's guide. ▶ EA,JH

This film describes in understandable language the causes, consequences, and prevention of food-borne disease. It accomplishes this very well through a combination of comic acting and straightforward narrative. Entertaining as well as educational, the message is clear and lasting. The photography, scope, and information are all excellent.

A Food-Chooser's Guide to the Well-Fed Cell, 3rd edition. *Coronet Films & Video*, 1982. 22 min. Color. $425 (16mm); $297 (video). ▶ EA,JH

This animated film's upbeat treatment approaches nutrition in a witty and exciting way without neglecting or detracting from basic nutritional knowledge. An easily remembered mnemonic (4420) describes the daily portions of the major food groups that growing children should consume. Metabolic and biochemical information is integrated with descriptions of body growth and development. The focus on food substitutions in making informed choices helps viewers to translate knowledge into behavior while permitting individual and cultural variation.

Learning About Nutrition. *Encyclopaedia Britannica Educational Corp.*, 1982. 4 color filmstrips, 54 frames (average) ea.; 4 cassettes, 6 min. ea. $108. Teacher's guide. ▶ EP,EI

This four-part filmstrip set creates an awareness of the link between food intake and health while encouraging wise food choices. The first part acquaints viewers with the many reasons for eating, part two encourages children to select a balanced diet from a variety of foods found in the four basic food groups, part three looks carefully at the differences in the nutrient quality of snacks, and the last part accurately shows serving sizes and food groups needed to promote health. Technically, there is no such thing as a "junk food," only junk diets that reflect poor food intake for an entire day. Many ethnic groups are represented, and excellent examples of nutritious food patterns for many cultures are given. Overall, the set combines accurate cartoon symbols with photography and would be most valuable for reinforcing nutrition concepts.

Nutrition: Building Better Health. *Encyclopaedia Britannica Educational Corp.*, 1982. 4 color filmstrips, 56 frames (average) ea.; 4 cassettes, 12 min. ea. $108. Teacher's guide. ▶ EA,JH

These filmstrips emphasize the role of nutrition in good health, explain basic nutrition principles, and provide general guidelines for choosing an adequate diet. Although each filmstrip is self-contained and could be used alone, they will be most effective when used together. Some of the information is understandably repetitious, but the filmstrips are generally accurate and well done, with attractive and colorful art. A few questionable statements will need correction by the teacher.

Nutrition for Better Health. *Encyclopaedia Britannica Educational Corp.*, 1985. 15 min. $295 (16mm); $295 (video); $29.50 (rental). ▶ EA,JH

Four main nutrients are highlighted, enhanced by good graphics and color. Calories are presented with discussions on energy, fat, and carbohydrates. The tissue-building properties of protein are explained. Vitamins are treated as part of food, not as necessary supplements, and the importance of minerals for good health is included. The film promotes a balanced diet for good health, pointing out the dietary problems that most Americans have.

Nutrition: Try It, You'll Like It. *AIMS Media, Inc.*, 1981. 11 min. Color. $220 (16mm); $25 (3-day rental). o.n. 9693. ▶ **K,EP,EI**

This elementary film has a simple message about poor human nutrition. Using a zoo setting and excellent photography of animals, it asks: If the animals at the zoo receive carefully selected foods, should humans settle for anything less? Vivid examples of how television influences food choices are portrayed. Examples of human populations that have few nutritional disorders and their low animal-fat diets and high-activity life-styles point to the poor choices made by most Americans in their diets. A seven-point National Dietary Guideline is given. The film would be a good introduction to an elementary unit on animal or human nutrition. Because none of the points in the film is discussed in depth, numerous questions will undoubtedly follow its use.

Nutrition: Who Cares? You Should! *Guidance Associates*, 1982. 4 color filmstrips, 57–62 frames ea.; 4 cassettes, 9–10 min. ea. $115. Teacher's guide. ▶ **EI,EA**

Protein, carbohydrate, fat, vitamins, minerals and water, and how the body uses them are described along with their food sources. The filmstrips emphasize the importance of variety in food choice and include sources of nonmeat protein and foods from different ethnic groups. The set also stresses that food choice should be based on whether food is tasty, nutritious, and economical and not on advertising claims. The organization and pace of the filmstrips are lively and smooth, and the music and clever cartoon graphics maintain interest throughout.

The Price of Hunger. *Barr Films*, 1982. 21 min. Color. $420 (16mm); $420 (video). o.n. A318. Teacher's guide. ▶ **EA,JH**

This film presents the current reality of malnutrition in developing countries, focusing on political and economic causes. Two major causes of world malnutrition—failure to breastfeed and early weaning—are given relatively little attention. Although the visual and intellectual messages are very disturbing, the film includes a positive, practical approach to the problem—the development of appropriate agricultural technology.

3-2-1 Contact: Food and Fuel. *Guidance Associates*, 1985. (Part of the Children's Television Workshop Series; a 5-part program.) 35 min. Color. $795 (16mm); $209 (¾-inch video); $179 (½-inch video). Teacher's guide. Also available in filmstrip. ▶ **EI,EA,JH**

This film is a suitable introduction to the concept of food as fuel, but it does not cover specific nutrients. At the Bronx Zoo, Lisa sees animals fed, and a food chain featuring a hippo is explained. In part two, Marc tours a pig farm. However, the idyllic visit does not cover either the slaughter and odor of pigs or the existence of corporate farms. In part three, a nutritionist teaches Lisa about the value of bread and how to bake a loaf. In part four, Marc prepares a pizza, and Trini supplements this dish for a lumberjack who expends calories chopping wood. An animated segment shows the flow of energy from the sun to cow's milk to feet pedaling a bicycle. In part five, a farmer shows Lisa how to make gasohol from cornmeal to run a tractor. Impressive visual effects enhance this informative program.

649.65 Sex education

> See also 362.7 Problems of and services to young people; 618.4 Childbirth; pregnancy.

Better Safe Than Sorry. *FilmFair Communications,* 1986. 16 min. Color. $380 (16mm); $380 (video); $40 (rental). ▶ **EA,JH**

This film opens with a correct and adequate definition for its young audience of child abuse and its other current names. Young actors play roles in an exceptionally clear and understandable manner. In addition to the more common examples, two unique situations are depicted: an aunt molesting her young nephew and a stepfather molesting a handicapped, deaf girl. In both instances the film stresses that help seldom comes from the victim's parents. In all the dramatized instances, appropriate and effective courses of action are presented, with special emphasis on prevention.

Child Sexual Abuse: What Your Children Should Know. *Indiana University,* 1984. 5-part series, 30–90 min. ea. Color. $360–$770 (16mm ea.); $150–$340 (video ea.); $25–45 (rental ea.). ▶ **K,EP,EI,EA,JH**

Each of the five units in this highly recommended package delivers essentially the same message but to different age groups. In each, students respond to penetrating, insightful questions about sexual abuse as posed by a knowledgeable expert. The discussions are then followed by dramatizations of situations that could lead to or could have resulted from actual or potential sexual abuse. The abuse prevention educator then explains, elaborates, draws conclusions, and gives advice regarding the dramatized situations.

Feeling Yes, Feeling No Series (Programs 1–3 for Children). *Perennial Education, Inc.,* 1985. 14 min. ea. Color. $305 (16mm ea.); $305 (video ea.); $900 (series, 16mm or video); $30 (rental ea.); $90 (rental series). Teacher's guide. ▶ **EP,EI,EA,JH**

This timely series teaches children the right to control their own bodies and the need to act decisively. The first segment offers an excellent introduction to the concept of "yes" feelings and "no" feelings, gives examples, and emphasizes the importance of saying no. The second unit clearly defines sexual assault and teaches children how to assess an encounter with a stranger. The third section focuses on intrafamilial sexual assault. The material is presented in a classroom setting with three teachers playing the roles in the accurate illustrations. Superb!

Now I Can Tell You My Secret. *Walt Disney Educational Media Co.,* 1984. 15 min. Color. $373 (16mm); inquire for rental. Discussion guide. ▶ **K,EP,EI**

This film is designed to make five- to ten-year-olds aware of sexual abuse and to teach them how to protect themselves. It covers the topics of what constitutes a good touch, a bad touch, and a confusing touch, assures children that abuse is not uncommon and that no one is immune to it by virtue of gender or neighborhood, examines the confusing and harmful emotional sequelae generally associated with sexual abuse, points out children's fears in revealing the abuse and the importance of "telling the secret," and tells children what they can do to minimize the risks of being abused or halting it once it has happened. Unfortunately, the film gives minimal attention to incest and lacks guidelines for direct preventive action by parents.

Touch. *MTI Teleprograms Inc.*, 1984. 32 min. Color. $495 (16mm); $395 (video); $80 (rental). o.n. MX01. Teacher's guide. ▶ **K,EP,EI,EA**

Terms, concepts, emotional reactions, and techniques for responding to sexual abuse are pleasantly presented through examples and stories. Preventive strategies are emphasized, but children are provided with many ways to deal with sexual abuse after it has occurred. The ideas and information are given as direct questions to the children in the audience, as skits, and through interviews with children. The film is especially effective in explaining the dangers of "bad" or "confusing" touch, while at the same time preserving the positive aspects of "good" touch. This serious and frightening topic is presented in an upbeat and positive manner.

The Touching Problem. *MTI Teleprograms, Inc.*, 1982. 18 min. Color. $350 (16mm); $315 (video); $60 (one-week rental). ▶ **EI,EA**

This film presents accurate information about the incidence of child abuse and what parents should do if they suspect abuse of their child. The film also describes well how children can be delicately taught to know what their private parts are and how to say no to an adult. The discussion centers around a scene that is staged by actors (child, mother, abuser) who portray what is probably a typical incident of sexual abuse. The film could be effectively shown to groups of children who are at least eight years of age if a discussion were led by an experienced adult.

What Tadoo. *MTI Teleprograms Inc.*, 1984. 18 min. Color. $350 (16mm); $315 (video); $60 (rental). o.n. 4647M. Teacher's guide. ▶ **K,EP**

What Tadoo is a superb film for young children about sexual abuse. After viewing it, children will not only know the necessary facts but will be equipped with specific tools to protect themselves. Fear and uncertainty will be replaced with knowledge and a sense of self-confidence and control. Common tricks and lures are depicted; practice sessions encourage children to try out and refine their new skills. The content of the film is presented through a delightful combination of real life and fantasy, as a boy is instructed by magic puppets about real-life problems and hypothetical situations. Excellent discussion guide.

Yes You Can Say No. *AIMS Media, Inc.*, 1986. 19 min. Color. $420 (16mm); $315 (video); $75 (rental). Discussion guide. ▶ **EP,EI,EA,JH**

This program is a dramatization of a day in the life of a ten-year-old boy whose uncle has made sexual advances to him. With the help of two school friends and the encouragement of his teacher, the boy learns to adopt certain assertive and protective behaviors. Ultimately he rejects the advances of his uncle and reports the problem to his parents. The actor is straightforward and honest, the message is clear, and the presentation as a whole is appropriate.

Indexes

Book Authors

Book Titles & Subjects

Book Series Titles

A-V Titles & Subjects

A-V Materials Distributors

Adams & Adams Films
706 Wayside Drive
Austin, TX 78703

512-477-8846

Agency for Instructional
   Technology
Box A
Bloomington, IN 47402

812-339-2203; 800-457-4509

AIMS Media, Inc.
6901 Woodley Avenue
Van Nuys, CA 91406

818-376-6406; 800-367-2467

American Journal of Nursing Co.
Educational Services Division
555 W. 57th Street
New York, NY 10019

212-582-8820; 800-621-7018

Astronomical Society of the Pacific
1290 24th Avenue
San Francisco, CA 94122

415-661-8660

Barr Films
12801 Schabarum Avenue
Irwindale, CA 91706-7878

818-338-7878

Beacon Films
930 Pitner Avenue
Evanston, IL 60202

312-328-6700; 800-323-5448

Benchmark Films, Inc.
145 Scarborough Road
Briarcliff Manor, NY 10510

914-762-3838

Bergwall Productions, Inc.
106 Charles Lindbergh Boulevard
Uniondale, NY 11553

516-222-1111

Berlet Films
1646 W. Kimmel Road
Jackson, MI 49201

517-784-6969

BFA Educational Media
468 Park Avenue South
New York, NY 10016

212-684-5910

Bullfrog Films, Inc.
Oley, PA 19547

215-779-8226

Carolina Biological Supply Co.
2700 York Road
Burlington, NC 27215

919-584-0381; 800-334-5551

Center for Humanities Inc.
Box 1000
90 South Bedford Road
Communications Park
Mt. Kisco, NY 10549

914-666-4100; 800-431-1242

Centre Productions, Inc.*
1800 30th Street
Suite 207
Boulder, CO 80301
(*now distributed by Barr Films)

Churchill Films
662 N. Robertson Boulevard
Los Angeles, CA 90069

213-657-5110; 800-334-7830

Clearvue, Inc.
5711 N. Milwaukee Avenue
Chicago, IL 60646

312-775-9433

Coronet Films & Video
108 Wilmot Road
Deerfield, IL 60015

312-940-1260; 800-621-2131

J. C. Crimmins & Co.*
165 Duane Street
Suite 9D
New York, NY 10013
(*now distributed by Karol Media,
201-628-9111)

Walt Disney Educational Media
Co.*
500 S. Buena Vista Street
Burbank, CA 91521
(*now distributed by Coronet
Films & Video)

Documentary Educational
Resources, Inc.
101 Morse Street
Watertown, MA 02172

617-926-0491

Educational Dimensions Group
Box 126
Stamford, CT 06904

203-327-4612; 800-243-9020

Educational Images Ltd.
P. O. Box 3456
West Side Station
Elmira, NY 14905

607-732-1090

Educational Media International*
175 Margaret Place
P. O. Box 1288
Elmhurst, IL 60126
(*now distributed by AIMS Media,
Inc.)

Encyclopaedia Britannica
Educational Corp.
425 N. Michigan Avenue
Chicago, IL 60611

312-321-7105; 312-321-6800

Enjoy Communicating, Inc.
P. O. Box 1637
Falls Church, VA 22041

703-256-8586

Family Communications
Marketing Department
4802 Fifth Avenue
Pittsburgh, PA 15213

412-687-2990

Filmakers Library, Inc.
124 E. 40th Street
New York, NY 10016

212-808-4980

FilmFair Communications
10900 Ventura Boulevard
Box 1728
Studio City, CA 91604

818-985-0244

Films for the Humanities and
Sciences, Inc.
Box 2053
Princeton, NJ 08540

609-452-1128

Films Inc.
5547 N. Ravenswood Avenue
Chicago, IL 60640-1199

800-323-4222

Focus Media, Inc.
135 Nassau Boulevard
Garden City, NY 11530

516-794-8900

Guidance Associates, Inc.
Communications Park
Box 3000
Mt. Kisco, NY 10549

914-666-4100

Handel Film Corp.
8730 Sunset Boulevard
West Hollywood, CA 90069

213-657-8990

Hawkhill Associates, Inc.
125 E. Gilman Street
Madison, WI 53703

608-251-3934

Hayden Book Co., Inc.
10 Mulholland Drive
Hasbrouck Heights, NJ 07604

201-393-6000

Alfred Higgins Productions, Inc.
9100 Sunset Boulevard
Los Angeles, CA 90069

213-272-6500

Human Relations Media
175 Tompkins Avenue
Pleasantville, NY 10570

914-769-6900

Indiana University
Audio-Visual Center
Bloomington, IN 47405

812-335-8087

International Film Bureau Inc.
332 S. Michigan Avenue
Chicago, IL 60604

312-427-4545

January Productions
249 Goffle Road
Hawthorne, NJ 07506

201-423-4666

Journal Films, Inc.
930 Pitner Avenue
Evanston, IL 60202

312-328-6700; 800-323-5448

Knowledge Unlimited
1409 Greenway Cross
Madison, WI 53701

608-271-2771; 800-356-2303

Learning Corporation of America
130 East 59th Street, 10th floor
New York, NY 10022

212-755-8600; 800-323-6301

Learning Tree Filmstrips
7108 S. Alton Way
P. O. Box 3009
Englewood, CO 80155

303-740-9777

Library Filmstrip Center
205 E. Locust Street
Bloomington, IN 60701-3005

309-827-5455

Lucerne Media, Inc.
37 Ground Pine Road
Morris Plains, NJ 07950

201-538-1401

Marshfilm Enterprises, Inc.
P. O. Box 8082
Shawnee Mission, KS 66208

816-523-1059

Media Guild
11722 Sorrento Valley Road
Suite E
San Diego, CA 92121

619-755-9191

Media Projects, Inc.
5216 Homer Street
Dallas, TX 75206

214-826-3863

Arthur Mokin Productions, Inc.
P. O. Box 1866
Santa Rosa, CA 95402-1866

707-542-4868

Moody Institute of Science
Educational Film Division
12000 E. Washington Boulevard
Whittier, CA 90606

213-698-8256

MTI Film & Video*
108 Wilmot Road
Deerfield, IL 60015
(*formerly MTI Teleprograms, Inc.)

312-940-1260; 800-621-2131

Multi-Focus, Inc.
1525 Franklin Street
San Francisco, CA 94109

800-821-0514

National AudioVisual Center
National Archives & Records
  Service
General Services Administration
Washington, DC 20409

202-763-1850

National Geographic Society
Educational Services
17th & M Streets, NW
Washington, DC 20036

202-857-7103

National Wildlife Federation
8925 Leesburg Pike
Vienna, VA 22180

703-790-4000

New Dimensions Films
85895 Lorane Highway
Eugene, OR 97405

503-484-7125

New Front Films Programming
  Services
1409 Willow Street
Minneapolis, MN 55403

612-872-0805

Oak Woods Media, Inc.
P. O. Box 527
Oshtemo, MI 49077-0527

616-375-5621

Perennial Education, Inc.
930 Pitner Avenue
Evanston, IL 60202

312-328-6700; 800-323-9084

Pet Project
121 N. W. Crystal Street
Crystal River, FL 32629

904-795-6144

Phoenix Films & Video, Inc.
468 Park Avenue South
New York, NY 10016

212-684-5910

Pyramid Film & Video
Box 1048
Santa Monica, CA 90406

213-828-7577

Random House Media
School Division
201 E. 50th Street
New York, NY 10022

212-572-2484

Science Screen Report, Inc.
2875 S. Congress Avenue
Delray Beach, FL 33444

305-265-1700

Society for Visual Education, Inc.
1345 Diversey Parkway
Chicago, IL 60614

312-525-1500

Marty Stouffer Productions Ltd.*
300 S. Spring Street
Aspen, CO 81611
(*no longer distributed)

Sunburst Communication, Inc.
Pleasantville, NY 10570

914-769-5030

Time-Life Video
Time & Life Building
1271 Avenue of the Americas
New York, NY 10020

212-484-5930

Trailwood Films
P. O. Box 1421
Huron, SD 57350

605-353-1153

University of California Extension
  Media Center
2176 Shattuck Avenue
Berkeley, CA 94704

415-642-0618; 415-642-0460

University of Washington Press
Box 50096
Seattle, WA 98145

206-543-4050

WETA
Dept. of Educational Activities
Box 2626
Washington, DC 20013

202-998-2600

Wombat Productions
250 W. 57th Street
Suite 916
New York, NY 10019

212-315-2502

DATE DUE
